Collective Intentionality and the Study of Religion

Expanding Philosophy of Religion

Series Editors:

J. Aaron Simmons, Furman University, USA
Kevin Schilbrack, Appalachian State University, USA

A series dedicated to a global, diverse, cross-cultural, and comparative philosophy of religion, Expanding Philosophy of Religion encourages underrepresented voices and perspectives and looks beyond its traditional concerns rooted in classical theism, propositional belief, and privileged identities.

Titles in the series include:

Philosophical Hermeneutics and the Priority of Questions in Religions,
by Nathan Eric Dickman
Philosophies of Religion, by Timothy Knepper
Collective Intentionality and the Study of Religion, by Andrea Rota
Diversifying Philosophy of Religion, edited by Nathan R. B. Loewen
and Agnieszka Rostalska

Collective Intentionality and the Study of Religion

Social Ontology and Empirical Research

Andrea Rota

BLOOMSBURY ACADEMIC
LONDON • NEW YORK • OXFORD • NEW DELHI • SYDNEY

BLOOMSBURY ACADEMIC
Bloomsbury Publishing Plc
50 Bedford Square, London, WC1B 3DP, UK
1385 Broadway, New York, NY 10018, USA
29 Earlsfort Terrace, Dublin 2, Ireland

BLOOMSBURY, BLOOMSBURY ACADEMIC and the Diana logo are trademarks of Bloomsbury Publishing Plc

First published in Great Britain 2023
This paperback edition published in 2024

Copyright © Andrea Rota, 2023

Andrea Rota has asserted his right under the Copyright, Designs and Patents Act, 1988, to be identified as Author of this work.

For legal purposes the Acknowledgements on p. x constitute an extension of this copyright page.

Cover design by Louise Dugdale
Cover image: Improvisation 26 (Rowing), 1912. Found in the collection of Städtische Galerie im Lenbachhaus, Munich. Artist Kandinsky, Wassily Vasilyevich (1866–1944). (Photo by Fine Art Images/Heritage Images via Getty Images).

This work is published open access subject to a Creative Commons Attribution-NonCommercial-NoDerivatives 4.0 International licence (CC BY-NC-ND 4.0, https://creativecommons.org/licenses/by-nc-nd/4.0/). You may re-use, distribute, and reproduce this work in any medium for non-commercial purposes, provided you give attribution to the copyright holder and the publisher and provide a link to the Creative Commons licence.

Bloomsbury Publishing Plc does not have any control over, or responsibility for, any third-party websites referred to or in this book. All internet addresses given in this book were correct at the time of going to press. The author and publisher regret any inconvenience caused if addresses have changed or sites have ceased to exist, but can accept no responsibility for any such changes.

A catalogue record for this book is available from the British Library.

A catalog record for this book is available from the Library of Congress.

Library of Congress Control Number: 2023939367.

ISBN: HB: 978-1-3503-0374-4
PB: 978-1-3503-0378-2
ePDF: 978-1-3503-0375-1
eBook: 978-1-3503-0376-8

Series: Expanding Philosophy of Religion

Typeset by RefineCatch Limited, Bungay, Suffolk

To find out more about our authors and books visit www.bloomsbury.com and sign up for our newsletters.

A la mè sciura

Contents

List of Illustrations	viii
Preface	ix
Acknowledgements	x
1 General Introduction	1

Part I

2 Introduction to the Theoretical Framework	17
3 John Searle—Collective Intentionality in Individual Minds	29
4 Raimo Tuomela—Non Mihi, Non Tibi, Sed Nobis	41
5 Margaret Gilbert—Plural Subjects and Joint Commitment	57
6 Collective Intentionality and Empirical Research	71

Part II

7 Empirical Orientation—The Jehovah's Witnesses	85
8 Collective Action—Advertising the King and the Kingdom	91
9 Collective Beliefs—The Domestication of New Media	127
10 Collective Emotions—The Collective Excitement of Conventions	153
11 Collective Aesthetic Experiences—The Feeling of the Bible	187
12 Conclusion	219

Primary Sources	229
Notes	231
References	235
Index	257

Illustrations

Figures

8.1	Question Formulation in the 2005, 2010, and 2015 Editions of *Our Kingdom Ministry* (N=352)	115
9.1	Number of Articles on Television per Year (1945–2015)	136
9.2	Media Use Frequency (N=183)	139
10.1	Most Important Aspects of the Assemblies (N=183)	164
11.1	Frequency of Religious Media Use (N=183)	205
11.2	Average Religious Use of Media (in minutes over eight days; N=10)	207

Table

7.1	Overview of the Interviewed Jehovah's Witnesses	89

Preface

At the origin of this study are a book and a phone call. The book is John Searle's (1996) *The Construction of Social Reality*. Jens Schlieter recommended that I read it in the summer of 2013, when I was preparing a paper for the biennial Conference of the German Society for the Study of Religion (DVRW). Drawing on an article by Ansgar Jödicke (2010), I wanted to discuss the theoretical premises that allow scholars to identify a "religious community." While my paper centered around the adjective "religious," Searle's social ontology drew my attention to the challenges of grasping the *collective* dimension of religion encapsulated in the noun "community." In particular, his reference to the idea of "collective intentionality"—a concept completely new to me at the time—prompted me to further probe this matter. In the following years, I discovered the works of philosophers such as Raimo Tuomela, Margaret Gilbert, and Michael Bratman and became immensely fascinated with the way these authors think. I also grew increasingly convinced that the study of religion could benefit from their insights. The theoretical endeavor of this book is to suggest how to make their philosophical reflections fruitful for empirical research on religion.

The phone call occurred a year earlier. From my lonely postdoc apartment in Bayreuth, I called Oliver Krüger at the University of Fribourg. My contract in Germany was about to end, and I wanted to pitch him a few rough ideas I had for a research project. On the phone, they amounted to little more than "something or other, media, and religious communities." Back in Switzerland, a three-month writing grant from the University of Fribourg allowed me to further develop these first intuitions. Thanks to Oliver's support and expertise, that "something or other" became the SNSF-research project *Die Dynamik von Mediennutzung und den Formen religiöser Vergemeinschaftung*, which I had the pleasure of carrying out with Oliver, Fabian Huber, and Evelyne Felder from 2014 to 2018. The bulk of the empirical data discussed in this study comes from the fieldwork that we conducted as a part of our inquiry among Jehovah's Witnesses in Switzerland and Germany.

From 2016 onward, theoretical reflection and empirical research slowly merged. However, most of the first manuscript's chapters were written between spring 2018 and summer 2019. That manuscript was submitted to the Faculty of Humanities at the University of Bern in October 2019 and was accepted in April 2020 as a habilitation thesis in the science of religion. The need to adapt the original manuscript to a book format has required me to drastically abridge most sections and to simplify the presentation of some rather complex topics. However, I am confident that these changes have in fact improved the overall clarity of my argument and contributed to a more pleasant reading experience.

Acknowledgements

For their help and guidance, I want to express my gratitude to my teachers, mentors, and advisors (in chronological order): Giuseppe Fossati, Richard Friedli, Ansgar Jödicke, Oliver Krüger, Christoph Bochinger, Jens Schlieter, and Karénina Kollmar-Paulenz. For their comments and suggestions, I am also grateful to the further members of my habilitation committee in Bern, Claus Beisbart and Crispin Thurlow.

This study owes a huge debt to friends and colleagues at the Universities of Bern and Fribourg, who may recognize their names in the numerous thought experiments that serve to illustrate this or that philosophical idea. These *clins d'oeil* are meant as signs of my esteem and thankfulness (and as a way to lighten the writing process with a few inside jokes). Special thanks go to Fabian Huber and Evelyne Felder, who have been precious traveling companions.

The empirical research upon which this study relies would not have been possible without the help of the Public Information Department of the Watch Tower Society's branch office in Selters (Germany) and the cooperation of the many Jehovah's Witnesses who opened the doors of their homes and Kingdom Halls to me and my colleagues. I am thankful to them. Preliminary versions of several ideas contained in this work have been presented at conferences and workshops in Switzerland and abroad. I thank profusely all those who have provided valuable comments and input on those occasions. I also thank the editors of *ONLINE—Heidelberg Journal of Religions on the Internet* for allowing me to use, in Chapter 9, some sections previously published in the article "Religion, Media, and Commitment. Jehovah's Witnesses as a 'Plural Subject'" (Rota 2019).

I owe a heartfelt thank-you to Nicole Edwards and Emma S. for proofreading my English in large portions of the original thesis, and to Graeme Currie for his editorial work on the book manuscript. I am also very thankful to the "Expanding Philosophy of Religion" series editors, Kevin Schilbrack and J. Aaron Simmons, and to Colleen Coalter at Bloomsbury Academic, for their assistance and commitment all along the publishing process.

I am especially grateful to my parents, Monique and Renzo, my late grandmother, Lidia, and my family and friends who have supported and encouraged me every step of the way. I am devoutly thankful to my wife, Sandra, *che sa tutti i perché*.

The open access version of this publication was funded by the Swiss National Science Foundation.

1

General Introduction

1.1 The Religious "We" in the Age of the Ego

Throughout the twentieth century, one of the most discussed social phenomena has been the perceived loosening of the social ties that bind people to one another and the progressive disappearance of collective forms of social life. As Robert Putnam (2000) phrased it in a famous study, people are increasingly "bowling alone." Likewise, the dwindling of collective religious practices is a well-established trend in numerous Western countries, while individual religious beliefs do not seem to fade as quickly (see, e.g., Campiche and Dubach 1992; Davie 1994). Although the loss of community is an old *topos*, a growing number of scholars concur in regarding the 1960s and 1970s as a watershed moment in the social and religious history of the West, marked by the rise of a new form of individualism. According to Ronald Inglehart (1977), in those decades several Western countries experienced a "silent revolution," during which individual priorities shifted away from the search for material security to the quest for personal self-fulfillment. Similarly, Charles Taylor (2007) speaks of the beginning of a new "Age of Authenticity," in which each individual is called on to find and express his or her true self in a continuous pursuit of personal happiness, including in the domain of religion. Stolz and his colleagues (2014) have dubbed this context, in which the individual is able, as never before, to make an incredible number of autonomous decisions, an "*Ich-Gesellschaft*" (a "me-society").

The present study is not an investigation into such macro-sociological trends, and it is not my intention to challenge these analyses. Rather, I regard them as a foil against which to develop a specific conceptual reflection. My aim is to redress what I consider to be a certain imbalance that they may have introduced into the study of religion. I believe that the "discovery" of the "Age of the Ego" (Stolz et al. 2015) has redirected the attention of most scholars toward the individual, which has become not only the main object of empirical research but also the focal point of the theoretical reflection on contemporary religion. Consequently, much less effort has been put into the systematic analysis of collective forms of religion. To put it bluntly, we have many resources to analyze individual religious trajectories and preferences but, with some notable exceptions, we have few instruments to conceptualize the actions, beliefs, emotions, and aesthetic experiences of religious collectivities, that is, of collective religious agents.[1]

This imbalance also follows from a methodological—or ontological—skepticism about religious groups as intentional agents. However, this idea is not so bizarre. Indeed, in political discussions at both the national and the international level, the issue of religious communities as the subjects of collective rights has gained increasing relevance in recent years (Jödicke 2010). Moreover, despite—or perhaps because of—the increasing interest in the individual, unreflective references to religious groups holding certain beliefs, carrying out certain rituals, or experiencing certain emotions abound in academic publications. The fact of the matter is that the appeal to such collective agents usually provides vivid descriptions of social reality and oftentimes has considerable explanatory power. Nevertheless, much of this potential remains untapped in the absence of an appropriate framework that would allow us to speak about religious groups without dissolving their collective character into the sum of their members' attitudes or, conversely, reifying it as a dubious metaphysical reality. In this study, I will argue that recent philosophical inquiries into the phenomenon of "collective intentionality" can provide fruitful resources for thinking about the nature of religious groups, that is, for analyzing religion in the "we"-form.

To start pondering how religion in the "we"-form (think, for instance, of "*we* pray") may differ from religion in the I-form ("I pray"), we can first rely on a simple intuition: there is a difference between doing something individually and doing it *together* with other people—say, between, on the one hand, me wanting to eat ice cream and you wanting to eat ice cream, and, on the other hand, us wanting to eat ice cream together. Even so, clarifying this distinction is not as easy as it may first seem. To begin with, the adverb "together" appears to embrace various social situations that one might consider distinct. For instance, if I am dancing a tango with my wife, and, at the same time, you, by sheer coincidence, are dancing tango with your partner in the same ballroom, there is a sense in which an external observer may say that you, I, and our respective partners are all dancing a tango together. Nevertheless, the sense in which one may say you and I are dancing the tango together differs from the sense in which I am dancing the tango together with my wife. On an intuitive level, the difference may appear trivial. However, its detailed investigation, as I will show, may prove both challenging and exciting, and hold valuable insights for the social sciences.

Similar issues arise with the pronoun "we." When each person in my building individually decides to oppose the construction of a new garage on the front lawn, I can truthfully say of me and my neighbors that "we oppose the construction of the garage." However, if the same sentence is pronounced, say, by the president of our residents' committee at the closing of our monthly meeting, that "we" seems to entail something more for us residents than the first one does. What, for instance, if I am one of *us* but, in this case, I do not personally oppose the construction project?

To figure out what the differences in these situations are and what exactly they entail for the people involved (and why) is one of the tasks of the philosophical investigation into the topic of collective intentionality. In this study, I will argue that similar problems often emerge in the analysis of religious practices, beliefs, emotions, and aesthetic experiences. Consider another hypothetical situation. In a place of worship, people arrive one by one for a religious service. At the sound of a gong, each of them begins to perform a series of codified and repetitive gestures. Everyone there knows that the others are performing a certain ritual, and each person is known by the others to be performing such a ritual. When a second gong sounds, the movements stop and the place of worship slowly empties. Did the people gathered in the place of worship simply perform the same ritual gestures "in the company" of others or is there a deeper relationship between the movements of each individual and the collectivity performing the ritual? This question may be the object of speculations but social scientists may also want to know how to determine *empirically* which is the case.

These vignettes provide a first glimpse into the interrelated epistemic problems that I want to address in this study. The first issue concerns the distinction between various forms of sociality in order to identify what is proper to religious collectivities in contrast to mere aggregates of religious people. As I have indicated, I am convinced that the concept of collective intentionality provides the necessary resources for this task. However, the philosophical debate on this subject is highly complex and scholars disagree about the precise nature of collective intentions. For this reason, the first part of this study provides a systematic and comparative discussion of various approaches to collective intentionality. This discussion will lay the theoretical groundwork for my subsequent analysis.

The second issue concerns the practical utility of these philosophical deliberations for empirical analyses. Thus, in the second part of this book, I turn to a concrete case study, namely that of the Jehovah's Witnesses. In doing so, my aim is to develop a way to make the insights from philosophical debates fruitful for the analysis of various data collected through the standard methods of the social sciences: observations, interviews, and surveys. In this regard, I follow the old saying according to which the proof of the pudding is in the eating. By this, I mean that the value of my approach will be demonstrated by its capacity to illuminate how Jehovah's Witnesses constitute a religious collectivity, a "we," by means of their collective actions, beliefs, emotions, and aesthetic experiences—and to clarify what all this entails for them as individuals and as a group. Succinctly put, the question is not why one becomes a Jehovah's Witness, but what constitutes the Jehovah's Witnesses as a religious group as opposed to a collection of individuals who happen to be Jehovah's Witnesses. Still, the overall goal of this study is not so much to examine the case of the Jehovah's Witnesses for its own sake but rather to use it in order to push the envelope in the study of religion and foster the theoretical understanding of forms of religious life that do not rely primarily on the fulfillment of the "me" but find their expression through the pronoun "we."

In the remainder of this introduction, I will provide a closer look at these twin issues—the conceptualization of collective religious agents and the transposition of such a conceptualization into an empirical framework—and at my approach to them. In the second section below, I will call attention to some problematic aspects of the classical and contemporary analyses of religious collectivities. As a corrective, I will introduce the idea of collective intentionality and sketch the origins and development of this philosophical field. In the third section, I will present my case study and further clarify the scope and goal of my empirical analysis. Finally, in the fourth section, I will show how my research is firmly anchored in the field of the academic study of religion and detail the plan of the book.

1.2 Conceptualizing Religious Collectivity

1.2.1 Religious collectivities as a sociological topic

In the sociological discussion on religious collectivities, the concept of "community" often serves as an explicit or implicit ideal reference and thus constitutes a good starting point for our discussion (see Lüddeckens and Walthert 2018; Rota and Krüger 2019). Against the backdrop of accelerating industrialization and urbanization, the concept of *Gemeinschaft*—and its dynamic reinterpretation as a process of *Vergemeinschaftung*, or "communalization"—provided the early sociologists with a foil for reflecting on the evolving forms of collective life in a societal context (*Gesellschaft*; *Vergesellschaftung*).

Despite their different theoretical frameworks, the likes of Ferdinand Tönnies, Max Weber, and Émile Durkheim endeavored to explain the progressive transformation of human coexistence from an idealized time in which human interactions were devoid of utilitarian considerations and based on personal contacts toward a social condition characterized by the rise of impersonal, calculated exchanges (see Lüddeckens and Walthert 2010: 21–23). Because of the close entanglement of religion and the social form of the community in their works, the process of *Vergesellschaftung*—driven by its core dynamics of rationalization and differentiation—became a fundamental element in the constitution of the secularization paradigm, which predicted the progressive fading of religion within modern societies (Tschannen 1991).

After the Second World War, the crisis of the traditional churches convinced sociologists across Europe that even rational social forms of religious organization were not immune to the corrosive effects of a rising modernity (see Schlamelcher 2018). It is within this context that Thomas Luckmann published his influential essay *The Invisible Religion* (1967). In it, Luckmann scolds the so-called church sociologists for their unilateral focus on the faith of traditional churches and insists on the possibility—and even the necessity—of dissociating religious life from both the traditional form of the community and the modern institutional organizations of the churches. According to Luckmann, in contemporary society, religion becomes a "private affair" and a matter of subjective choices that individuals can make within a pluralized field of religious suppliers. In the wake of this critique, much research has focused on how individuals construct their religiosity through their "peregrinations" across the religious field (Hervieu-Léger 1999; Bochinger, Engelbrecht, and Gebhardt 2009) and on non-institutional forms of spirituality (Heelas and Woodhead 2005; Knoblauch 2009; Hero 2010).

For several decades, most of the scholars working on religious collectives were concerned with so-called new religious movements. In this domain, sociologists operated mostly from a macro-sociological perspective and aimed at classifying the various religious groups according to Weber's distinction between churches and sects (see Beckford 1973). As social tensions surrounding these groups grew (Beckford 1985; Introvigne and Melton 1996), scholars also addressed the question of how the choice to join such a movement was compatible with the individual freedom of rational agents (Barker 1984).

Since the 1990s, however, a number of sociologists have argued that the increasing individualization of Western societies creates, almost in dialectical fashion, the conditions for new forms of community. In their opinion, the transition from modernity toward a new "reflexive" (Beck 1986) or "liquid" (Bauman 2000) late modernity confronts each person with an ambivalent situation. On the one hand, the individual experiences a newfound sense of freedom and autonomy; on the other, the acceleration of social change threatens his or her sense of security (see Soeffner 2010). The creation of new "tribes" (Maffesoli 1996) constitutes a way to alleviate the negative effects of these transformations and to find a place of safety (Hitzler and Pfadenhauer 1998; Bauman 2001).

Nevertheless, these contemporary forms of sociality differ from traditional communities, in particular because of their voluntary, transient, and noncommittal character, hence the label, "post-traditional communities" (Hitzler 1998; Hitzler, Honer, and Pfadenhauer 2008). As new social forms, they find their expression in events— such as the Catholic World Youth Days (Hepp and Krönert 2009) and the Burning Man festival (Gauthier 2014)—during which like-minded individuals gather more or less anonymously for short periods of intense, shared emotional experience and part ways thereafter without establishing any lasting relationships with one another (Gebhardt 2010).

These fleeting assemblies are not the only places in which sociologists are looking for collective forms of religion in contemporary societies. During the last 30 years, scholars have also paid increasing attention to more established forms of voluntary religious organizations, namely parishes and other congregations, which many would regard as "[T]he Maginot line in defending religion's core functions against the onslaught of larger, more impersonal, and more secular forces in increasingly complex societies" (Demerath and Farnsley 2007: 193). This new wave of so-called congregation studies originated in the USA (e.g., Ammerman 1997; Warner and Winter 1998) and has only recently reached Europe (Monnot and Stolz 2018a). Two main lines of inquiry drive these studies (see Ammerman 2018: vii–xii). The first is an ecological perspective, through which scholars study how congregations change and adapt to local context, for instance, in diasporas (e.g., Baumann 2009). The second perspective regards a congregation as an organizational unit (DiMaggio and Powell 1991; Wind and Lewis 1994; Demerath et al. 1998).

The latter approach insists on the congregation as the focus of collective religious life (Monnot 2013: 32). In an influential book assessing how religious collectivities contribute to structuring the religious field and how they impact public life, Chaves (2004: 9) argues that the frequent and regular production of *collective* religious events is the *raison d'être* of most congregations. However, congregation studies seem to have little to say about what is actually "collective" in these events besides the fact that the participants "gather physically for the ritual" (Monnot and Stolz 2018b: 17). Certainly, their analyses demonstrate how the participants in each congregation tend to share certain social traits, such as class or ethnicity, and how these factors affect, for instance, the style of worship (e.g., Chaves 2004: 134–143). However, they do not really clarify the sense in which the people in a congregation "believe together" (see Monnot 2013: 15).

In sum, a large part of the ongoing research into contemporary religion in the West is concerned with individualized forms of religion. Religious collectivities appear to be marginal in the study of religion. Congregations are mostly conceived of within an organizational perspective and discussed in macro-sociological terms that frame them as producers of religious goods in competition over social power and individual "customers"—religious organizations are thus still a proxy to speak about individuals and their preferences. New forms of community, by contrast, are mainly addressed through the perspective of an idyllic past characterized as "warm," "soothing," and "intimate" (Gebhardt 1999) but which appears to have been lost forever and which may, at best, be revived through fleeting personal experiences. Accordingly, such analysis offers important insights into the way that people and scholars alike envision "community" but is less useful for grasping the idea of a religious collective as a social reality beyond the imagination of more or less isolated individuals. Instead, the analysis that I am pushing for is one that would elucidate the mode of existence of religious collectives on the basis of the collective intentions that they involve. Let me clarify this point in the next section.

1.2.2 A framework for collective intentionality

The topic of collective intentionality constitutes a central issue in the broader philosophical investigation of the ontology of the social world. At the core of this field of research, there is the question of how humans construct the social reality in which they live. One of the central tenets of this inquiry is that,

> Every social institution, relation, practice, or interaction rests upon the capacity of groups of individuals to engage in various forms of collective intentional behavior. A fundamental understanding of the social requires an understanding of the nature of collective agency and of how the various aspects of the social world are grounded in it. (Ludwig 2016: 2)

In the present study, I will stop short of discussing the ramifications of a full-blown social ontology for the study of religion—although I have not resisted the temptation to sketch some ideas elsewhere (see Rota 2016). Instead, my goal is to reflect on how the framework of collective intentionality can help us clarify a certain sense in which people "do" religion *together* and thus constitute a religious collective of a particular type. To grasp intuitively how this issue is related to the problem of social ontology, we can turn to our everyday use of language.

In our conversations, we often ascribe intentions and attitudes to (religious) groups, but what does it mean when we say that a religious community opposes certain rights, say, regarding abortion; that an assembly is ecstatic; or that a church has revised its beliefs? Does it mean that each and every member opposes abortion rights, that the majority of the congregation is in awe, or that a few church leaders have introduced a new doctrine? Or none of the above? In the end, do these statements refer to a concrete social reality, or are they merely figures of speech?

On the one hand, an instrumentalist point of view (see Tollefsen 2004) would suggest that our language is in fact metaphorical and that our ascriptions are, strictly speaking, false. This standpoint would deny that there is anything genuinely "collective" about a group of individuals sharing a goal or a belief. Conversely, a strictly anti-reductionist approach to group agency and group thinking would postulate a form of collective consciousness that transcends the sum of the individuals. As Schweikard and Schmid (2013) note, these two somewhat caricaturized positions constitute "the Scylla and the Charybdis of the analysis of collective intentionality," between which a number of philosophers have endeavored to find a safe route.

Certainly, the discussion of this issue has had a long career in the history of ideas and, indeed, scholars working on collective intentionality acknowledge overlaps between certain aspects of their work and the insights of authors such as Rousseau, Hume, Durkheim, and Simmel—though the same scholars are also quick to point out the differences (e.g., Searle 2006). One of the main appeals of a collective intentionality framework for the study of religious (and other social) collectives is that it offers a number of novel and highly systematized instruments to analyze how human agents are able to join forces toward the realization of a collective project and come together to act, believe, and feel *as a group*. This capacity is regarded as being rooted in the fundamental intentionality of human minds.

What is the intentionality of human minds? As the philosopher John R. Searle puts it, "'Intentionality' is a fancy philosopher's term for that capacity of the mind by which it is directed at, or about, objects and states of affairs in the world, typically independent of itself" (Searle 2010: 25). For instance, my *belief* that it is raining, my *fear* of my neighbor's dog, and my *desire* to eat chocolate are all intentional states of my mind. Despite the possible linguistic confusion (in English), my *intention* to do something, say, to exercise more, is simply one type of intentional state among others (see Searle 1983: 1). Accordingly, collective *intentionality* can be minimally defined as "the power of minds to be *jointly* directed at objects, matters of fact, states of affairs, goals, or values" (Schweikard and Schmid 2013, my emphasis). What lies behind this idea, however, is a matter of debate. Indeed, as Searle (2010: 49) notes, "[W]hen it comes to 'collective intentionality,' there is no commonly used notion corresponding to this expression."

In the first half of the twentieth century, a number of German phenomenologists and existentialist philosophers, such as Max Scheler, Martin Heidegger, Gerda Walther, and Dietrich von Hildebrand were already pondering the question of the collective dimension of intentionality (see Schmid 2012). Their reflections, however, have found only a limited reception in the current philosophical debate on this topic, which, with some notable exceptions (Schmid 2005), is confined to the so-called analytic tradition. The work of the American philosopher Wilfrid Sellars in the late 1960s and early 1970s is sometimes mentioned as the starting point of the current discussions. However, it was only during the 1980s that the field of collective intentionality was progressively established as a specific field of philosophical inquiry.

The use of "collective intentionality" as an umbrella term to designate a certain phenomenon (or set of phenomena) and its philosophical investigation is probably due to Searle. Searle first presented his views on collective intentionality in 1990 in an influential article entitled "Collective Intentions and Actions." Together with the works of Margaret Gilbert, Raimo Tuomela, and Michael Bratman, this article belongs to the "first wave" of analytic investigations into this subject. Margaret Gilbert's dissertation *On Social Facts* (1978), revised, expanded, and published with the same title a decade later (Gilbert 1989), was possibly the first monographic work in this domain. In 1984, Raimo Tuomela published his book *A Theory of Social Action*, which was aimed at extending the purposive-causal theory of individual action that he had previously developed to multi-agent cases. Finally, in the early 1990s, Michael Bratman published a number of articles—later collected under the title *Faces of Intention* (1999a)—in which he demonstrated the relevance of his planning theory of action for explaining basic forms of shared action.

Since the turn of the millennium, the philosophical research on collective intentionality has become increasingly institutionalized and diversified, thanks to new scholars joining the debate. The volume *Kollektive Intentionalität* (Schmid and Schweikard 2009) presents an anthology of classic and recent articles, while the recently published *Routledge Handbook of Collective Intentionality* (Jankovic and Ludwig 2018) provides a structured overview of the current discussions in this dynamic field.

Despite these ongoing developments, in this study I will focus on three of the major authors mentioned above: Searle, Tuomela, and Gilbert, and touch upon the work of the fourth, Bratman. I have good reasons for doing so, the main one being that most of the contributions published by other scholars in the last three decades directly or indirectly deal with a number of crucial questions put forward by these authors; likewise, most philosophical disagreements can be traced back to differences in these authors' positions. The shorter treatment of Bratman's framework is dictated by pragmatic reasons related to my goal of devising a theoretical framework allowing for a practical implementation of fundamental philosophical insights. For reasons that I will detail in the next chapter, I consider Bratman's approach to collective intentionality less suited to this goal than those of his colleagues. Nevertheless, an overview of his core ideas will provide an important foil to situate those ideas that I regard as most useful for the social sciences.

In the field of philosophy, the main approaches to collective intentionality have been reviewed, discussed, and criticized in a number of edited volumes (e.g., Tsohatzidis 2007 on Searle; Vargas and Yaffe 2014 on Bratman; Preyer and Peter 2017 on Tuomela). However, these analyses already presuppose an extensive knowledge of the relevant theories. Similarly, the few existing overviews of key positions are tailored for readers who are already acquainted with the problem of collective intentionality or at least with some aspects of it (Tollefsen 2004; Schweikard 2011; Schweikard and Schmid 2013). Thus, my aim in the first part of this study is to explain and compare the positions that have fundamentally shaped the debate on this subject in a way that may be useful for scholars of religion who study collective practices and beliefs. My presentation of the positions held by each author has a similar structure and is oriented toward this goal by drawing attention to the ontological and methodological premises of each approach, its conceptualization of collective intentionality, and the corollaries of such a conceptualization with respect to the empirically observable constituents and consequences of collective intentions.

The reception of philosophical approaches to collective intentionality in the social sciences remains limited, and it is generally confined to Searle's views, within the broader context of his social ontology (see, e.g., D'Andrade 2006; Bessy 2011; Binder 2013; Couldry and Hepp 2017). In the study of religion, a small number of scholars also regard Searle's theory as an interesting resource to advance the debate over the mode of existence of religion and religious symbols (Stausberg 2010; Schilbrack 2014; Rota 2016; Jensen 2017; Schlieter 2017) and to investigate the relationship between cognitive and cultural dimensions of religion (Jensen 2003, 2014, 2016a, b). References to other major philosophers in the field of collective intentionality are extremely rare and generally succinct. I believe that this is somewhat unfortunate, because closer scrutiny of the different philosophical standpoints on collective intentionality can reveal new and interesting insights for the study of religious collectivities. The first part of this book will provide such a comparative assessment.

Some scholars of religion may regard my systematic treatment of this subject as too far removed from the discipline's core concerns. I have to disagree with them. Since the institutionalization of the academic study of religion in the late nineteenth century, this discipline has benefited from (theoretical) imports from various disciplines—from anthropology to sociology, linguistics, and the cognitive sciences, to name only a few—so what I am attempting here is not new. Unfortunately, however, scholars of religion have often regarded philosophy—and particularly analytical philosophy—with a measure of suspicion. This may be due to the narrow scope of classical philosophy of religion, which for the greater part still focuses on questions pertaining to the existence of (the Judeo-Christian) God and the truth value and referentiality of religious statements (see Schilbrack 2014). Thus, this study can be read both as an invitation to scholars of religion to acknowledge the heuristic potential of philosophical approaches, and to philosophers of religion to expand the scope of their inquiries in a way that takes into account their relevance for empirical research.

1.3 Approaching Empirical Research

When developing their theories, philosophers working on the issue of collective intentionality often start by using their mind's eye to sketch a simple situation in which two or more people are doing something together, such as walking down the street, carrying a piano upstairs, painting a house, or preparing an elaborate French sauce. These thought experiments allow them to form conjectures about the behavior of the people involved and what they would think and say in such a situation; from there, the philosophers can then abstract a number of sufficient and necessary conditions that would define what counts as sharing a collective intention to carry out that activity. By contrast, empirical social research—in particular when it uses qualitative methods—often begins with the observation of concrete interactions. While the data collection is always informed by certain preconceptions, the researcher has to register—not conjecture about—how people behave and what they say and then try to figure out "what's going on" in that situation. Whether a philosophical approach will have descriptive and explanatory power in addressing such issues depends on the possibility of building a bridge between the "messy" reality of the empirical field and the theoretical construction extrapolated from paradigmatic cases.

It is such a bridge that I will endeavor to find in the second part of the present work. To do so, I will explore the case of the Jehovah's Witnesses through an array of empirical data. Most of this material has been collected as a part of the research project *Die Dynamik von Mediennutzung und den Formen religiöser Vergemeinschaftung*, based at the University of Fribourg (Krüger, Rota, Huber, Felder 2014–2018). I will detail my methods and sources in Chapter 7. It is more important here to clarify how I intend to approach my case study.

In the 1970s, Jehovah's Witnesses attracted the attention of sociologists of religion working on new religious movements (e.g., Beckford 1975b, 1972; Wilson 1970, 1973). Although the Watch Tower Society—the corporate body of the Jehovah's Witnesses—had existed since the 1880s, these scholars considered that this organization and its members provided an interesting point of comparison for their research. In this context, James Beckford's (1975a) monograph *The Trumpet of Prophecy* undoubtedly constitutes a groundbreaking work and remains a point of reference in the academic study of Jehovah's Witnesses to this day. Beckford provides a historical account of the development and organization of the Watch Tower Society, an overview of its doctrinal positions, and a sociological analysis of Jehovah's Witnesses in Britain.

In the introduction to his book, Beckford notes that the study of the Witnesses and similar groups has been curiously underdeveloped when compared with the study of smaller, sometimes more obscure groups. While this observation was certainly accurate at the time, it has become almost a trope in the research on Jehovah's Witnesses. For instance, in an influential article published in 1997, Stark and Iannaccone complain that "[I]f the Witnesses frequently appear on our doorsteps, they are conspicuously absent from our journals" (Stark and Iannaccone 1997: 133). A few years later, in the introduction to his monograph *Jehovah's Witnesses: Portrait of a Contemporary Religious Movement*, Holden (2002) similarly denounces the "dearth of academic literature on the Witnesses" since its short-lived flourishing three decades earlier.

At each iteration, this kind of statement becomes more rhetorical and less factual, particularly if one cares to look beyond English-language output (see Dericquebourg 2003). Of course, this is not to say that there is nothing left to study, only that, in addition to numerous investigations pertaining to specific religious or social aspects of Jehovah's Witnesses,[2] academic overviews presenting a comprehensive portrait of the Watch Tower Society and its members are by now available in various languages (e.g., Blandre 1987, 1991; Chryssides 2008, 2016; Introvigne 1990, 2015; Noss 2002; Penton 2015).

The present work does not provide such a comprehensive overview. Strictly speaking, I do not consider this book primarily as a study about the Jehovah's Witnesses. Let me clarify this point. Without question, the reader will have the opportunity to find abundant information concerning the Watch Tower Society in Chapters 7 to 11. Furthermore, my work is based on empirical data collected first-hand among Jehovah's Witnesses and provides an original analysis of various aspects of their religious life that will be of particular value to specialists in this denomination. However, taking my cue from an often-quoted passage by Jonathan Z. Smith, I am interested in the case of the Witnesses "insofar as it can serve as exempli gratia of some fundamental issue" in the study of religion (Smith 1982c: xi). *By this, I mean that in my research, the study of*

Jehovah's Witnesses serves to elucidate a certain paradigmatic or theoretical problem. That is, it aims to show how the philosophical resources presented in the first part of my work can help us illuminate, in an empirical research setting, what it means for a group of people to follow (in the broadest sense of the word) a religion *together*, to constitute a "we" with respect to such a religion. For this reason, hopefully, my research will be of interest to scholars of religion beyond the circle of those specifically interested in the Witnesses.

In the following, less-often quoted sentence, Smith underscores that "the student of religion must be able to articulate clearly why 'this' rather than 'that' was chosen as an exemplum" (Smith 1982c: xi). My choice of focusing on Jehovah's Witnesses was not completely premeditated. In an early phase of my research, my sample also included several congregations of Latter-day Saints and a number of churches within the Evangelical Assembly of Vineyard Churches—indeed, I intuitively assumed that these would constitute appropriate cases of religious collectives in a strong sense. To some extent, the decision to limit my inquiry to the Jehovah's Witnesses has been dictated by pragmatic reasons regarding the quantity of material that a single researcher can analyze and present in a self-contained work.

More importantly, however, increased familiarity with these denominations through observations and interviews has convinced me that the Jehovah's Witnesses case was the best one to illustrate the theoretical points that I wanted to make. To borrow a metaphor from Searle (1969: 54), this example, "like a mountainous terrain, [...] exhibits its geographical features starkly." Once the relevant features have been aptly "mapped," it will be easier, in future research projects, to look for them in different settings where they are less apparent. So, to reiterate, I do not ascribe any intrinsic uniqueness to the Jehovah's Witnesses, beyond the fact that they allow me to illuminate my arguments in a particularly clear way.

A further choice concerning the scope of my empirical research was to focus on the production, use, and interpretation of media among Jehovah's Witnesses. This decision was based on both observational evidence and analytical reflections. The publications of the Watch Tower Society, in particular the magazines *The Watchtower* and *Awake!*, are among the principal reasons why the Jehovah's Witnesses are known in the public sphere (second probably only to their house-to-house ministry); they are also important reference sources for Witnesses themselves. Indeed, there is a case to be made that various printed media—and, more recently, an array of digital media—underpin the communicative structures of the Watch Tower Society and play an important role in shaping the Witnesses' interactions with one another and with the world.

Admittedly, I am not the first author to make such a claim. In particular, the French sociologist Arnaud Blanchard (2006, 2008) has suggested regarding the Jehovah's Witnesses as a "community of readers and repeaters." However, his analysis, while insightful, remains theoretically underdeveloped. The search for a more sophisticated bridge between the media landscape of the Witnesses and a theoretical account of their collective actions and attitudes prompted me to pay closer attention to their ritualized use of various media. In turn, this led me to analyze the structure of their biweekly meetings and the communicative interactions that take place during them, as well as other recurring events, such as their conventions and Memorial celebrations. Although many scholars acknowledge that these meetings take up much of Witnesses' time, academic publications rarely elaborate on them.[3]

In my analysis, I will also pay attention to the historical dimension of the above-mentioned focuses. However, the overall goal of my analysis shapes how this dimension is presented and discussed. Other than a short general orientation in Chapter 7, the reader will not find an autonomous chapter with a detailed presentation of the history of the Watch Tower Society. Instead, the relevant historical information will be integrated into the theoretical discussion. Through this deliberate decision, I wanted to avoid relegating the historical analysis to a marginal role and framing it as merely the "context" of my analysis. On the contrary, I aim to underscore how historical and historiographical considerations contribute to my theoretical reflection. I will briefly come back to this point in Chapter 7. However, there is more to the issue of theory in the study of religion, as I will explain below.

1.4 Addressing (the Study of) Religion

The unifying features of the academic study of religion constitute a recurring topic of debate (see, e.g., Lehmann and Jödicke 2016). As I noted above, since its foundation, this discipline has had close relationships with neighboring fields of research and has integrated insights from various sciences. Not all imports, however, will be automatically considered relevant by other scholars of religion. Here, then, lies a particular challenge when trying to introduce a new and, to a large extent, unfamiliar theoretical perspective: it must be possible to link the new approach to ongoing discussions in the discipline in a way that provides, as Luhmann might say, a form of "connecting communication" (*Anschlusskommunikation*). In the present study, I do this in several ways.

In the first part, I begin by providing a general introduction to the topic of collective intentionality and underscore some major distinctions that run through this field of philosophic inquiry, most importantly the divide between reductionist and antireductionist standpoints. Drawing on a summary of Michael Bratman's approach to shared intentions, I formulate what I regard as three core requirements for a heuristically fruitful transposition of a philosophical framework into an empirical setting (Chapter 2). Against this backdrop, I then introduce and discuss the ideas defended, in turn, by Searle, Tuomela, and Gilbert (Chapters 3 to 5). In the last chapter of the first part (Chapter 6), I provide a comparative assessment of their views and move toward a framework allowing for their practical application. To do so, I call attention to the pioneering theoretical reflection carried out in the field of social anthropology, notably by Roy Rappaport, which I use as a stepping stone toward the formulation of a practical strategy for the fieldwork.

The second part continues this connecting effort at both the thematic and theoretical levels. Chapter 7 eases the transition into the empirical part by offering a short orientation on the history of the Jehovah's Witnesses and the data used in my research. The following four chapters address, in turn, a number of topics that should be very familiar to scholars interested in the systematic study of religion—actions, beliefs, emotions, and aesthetic experiences—although, of course, the focus is on their collective dimension. Furthermore, each of these chapters discusses a "competing" theoretical approach that has already been appropriated by the study of religion and that (more or less explicitly) entails a particular understanding of the nature of religious collectivities.

Chapter 8 approaches the topic of collective action by discussing the Witnesses' famous door-to-door ministry and by comparing the idea of rationality put forward by rational choice theorists with a different one that emerges from speech act theory and the framework of collective intentionality. This chapter also provides a detailed discussion of Jehovah's Witnesses' ritual use of printed media and discusses the relationship between the structure of their meetings and the formation of collective agency. These insights are fundamental for understanding the other facets of collective intentionality discussed in this study, and the other chapters build upon them.

Chapter 9 follows the golden thread provided by the topic of media but changes the perspective in order to tackle the subject of collective beliefs. In this chapter, I analyze the Witnesses' domestic use of various media in light of some of the Watch Tower Society's teachings. From a theoretical point of view, this offers me the opportunity to review Heidi Campbell's idea of the Religious-Social Shaping of Technology and to suggest some amendments to it.

Chapter 10 leaves for a moment the smaller settings of the congregation and the home and invites the reader into the large venues in which Jehovah's Witnesses gather for their regional conventions. These annual events assemble several thousands of Witnesses over a period of three days. Against such a backdrop, I will deal with the issue of collective emotions. My sparring partner in this chapter will be no less a figure than Émile Durkheim or, to be more precise, a certain interpretation of Durkheim developed by Anne Rawls and Randall Collins, among others.

Finally, Chapter 11 focuses on an ongoing revolution within the media landscape of Jehovah's Witnesses, namely the Watch Tower Society's progressive move away from the printed page and toward digital media. This change not only concerns the Society's magazine and books but also the book that they seek to interpret and comment upon, the Bible. The increasing use of tablet computers and smartphones to read scripture creates a dynamic environment that will allow me to examine the issue of collective aesthetic experiences and discuss Birgit Meyer's concepts of sensational forms and aesthetic formations.

Despite all these efforts, the inveterate scholar of religion may still complain that the problem of *religion* is not sufficiently addressed in this study. What has all this to do with *religion*? The short answer is the following: I do not see anything inherently religious in the forms of collective intentionality that I will describe in this book, just as I do not think that there are any specific religious emotions or any objects that are intrinsically religious. However, I would argue that not only is collective intentionality a recurrent phenomenon in settings that we may deem religious, but that these settings are often particularly conducive to the construction of collective intentions. I will have more to say on this topic, but for now, I will pull an old trick out of Max Weber's playbook and postpone the discussion of this issue until the concluding chapter of the book (Chapter 12).

Part I

2

Introduction to the Theoretical Framework

2.1 Introduction

The study of collective intentionality is a relatively young field in analytical philosophy. Nonetheless, a number of competing positions and accounts have emerged over the last four decades. It is not the goal of this chapter to provide a summary of these often complex and challenging debates (see Tollefsen 2004; Schweikard 2011; Schweikard and Schmid 2013). Rather, these pages should clarify some core distinctions among philosophical standpoints and help situate the work of the authors whose ideas I will detail in the next three chapters, namely John Searle, Raimo Tuomela, and Margaret Gilbert. These philosophers present three distinct and original approaches to the analysis of collective intentions. However, their accounts share a fundamental premise. All of them consider that collective intentions are a primitive phenomenon that cannot be assimilated to mere personal intentions and their conjunctions (Tuomela 2018). To this crucial extent, they contrast with what are called reductivist approaches, which have precisely this goal: to account for collective intentionality in terms of individual intentions.

Reductivist approaches play an important role in the current philosophical debate on collective intentionality (Alonso 2018). Among the contemporary proponents of such views, the philosopher Michael Bratman is certainly the most influential thinker. Together with the three other authors mentioned above, he belongs to a core group of thinkers sometimes referred to as the "Big Four" in the field of collective intentionality (Chant, Hindriks, and Preyer 2014). This honorary title indicates the status of these philosophers as pioneers in the research on collective intentionality: most, if not all, new approaches to this domain in analytical philosophy draw on or attempt to go beyond the work of one or more of these authors (Jankovic and Ludwig 2018).

The choice to focus in this book on non-reductivist approaches to the study of collective intentionality was mainly dictated by pragmatic reasons related to the development of a framework that would enable researchers to apply the insights of the philosophical discussions to the analysis of empirical data. As I will demonstrate, non-reductivist approaches offer more powerful instruments for the social-scientific study of collective intentions in real-life settings, allow for more compelling analysis and far-reaching conclusions, and are more readily translatable into workable research instruments. I will come back to this point below and in the last chapter of the book's first part. From a strictly philosophical point of view, these advantages come at a cost, particularly with regard to the necessary conceptual apparatus. Without attempting here to offer a robust philosophical defense of non-reductivist approaches against reductivist ones, it is important to get a sense of their major differences and some consequences thereof.

To do so, I will first need to clarify the idea of reductivism, calling attention to the distinction between ontological and conceptual reductivism. The work of major classical sociologists will help me illustrate this point by way of analogy. Against this backdrop, I will offer a summary of Bratman's influential positions. Indeed, from a philosophical point of view, his ideas would deserve a full chapter alongside the other authors. However, since his approach will not find a concrete application in the empirical part of this study, a shorter presentation will suffice. In particular, Bratman's framework will serve as a foil to highlight the relevant specificities of the non-reductivist standpoints. Yet, before approaching these topics and in order to avoid some common misunderstandings, it is worth clarifying what a collective intention, on any account, *is not*.

2.2 What a Collective Intention Is Not

Despite their disagreement on how to frame the concept of collective intentionality, the Big Four in this field of inquiry share a common understanding of what phenomena (usually involving more than one person) do not count as instances of collective intentions. The characterizations that they reject are those that can be described as "summative" or "aggregative" accounts of group behaviors or attitudes (see Tollefsen 2004). According to such accounts (e.g., Quinton 1976), an intention (a belief, a goal, an emotion, etc.) can be ascribed to a collective when all of its members, or at least most of them, hold that attitude. For instance, we could say that a class of students appreciate the teacher if and only if all of the students, or at least most of them, appreciate her. Although this account seems the most intuitive description of a group attitude, there are several reasons to question its adequacy, and many of them will be discussed in the course of this book.

For now, we can note that a major difficulty arises from the fact that individual attitudes and intentions can be kept private. If each student privately appreciates the teacher in their heart, it seems evident that there is not much "collective" going on in the classroom. The fact that the students may be mutually aware of their individual attitudes, that is, each of them knows that the others appreciate the teacher as they do, does not radically change the situation with respect to the construction of a social collective. Weber (1978: 23) had already come to a similar conclusion in a famous thought experiment involving a number of people simultaneously opening their umbrellas to avoid getting soaked by a sudden rainfall. Rather than a collective action, this is rather "homogeneous mass behavior." Even if everyone's intention of avoiding the rain were known to everyone, this would not yet justify any clearly recognizable reference to a social group. Indeed, mutual knowledge can be a necessary condition for the constitution of social collectives in the sense explored in this book, but is not a sufficient one.

In light of the discussion so far, summative accounts of social groups can be regarded as too encompassing to define a social collective in a strong sense. At the same time, however, they can also be considered too restrictive, because they exclude *a priori* certain forms of sociality that can be regarded as clear examples of collective life, such as political parties. Indeed, it is not difficult to imagine a party defending a certain policy for electoral reasons while most of its delegates personally disagree with it. In this case, a summative account fails completely to grasp the social reality at stake, since a certain attitude that can be correctly ascribed to a group is not being personally held by most of its members (Tollefsen 2004).

For similar reasons, it is possible to argue that social-scientific concepts that organize people by sets, types, classes, or categories—e.g., "ethnic minorities," "Catholics," "Westerners," "low-income families"—do not describe social groups predicated on collective intentions. Intuitively, this can be observed by pointing out that it is always possible to find a criterion to unite a collection of people under a certain label without them even being aware of such a description. This does not mean that concepts such as "class" or "ethnicity" as they are used by sociologists and anthropologists are not otherwise heuristically useful. However, to put it bluntly, a concept defining a "they" does not necessarily apprehend a "we"—unless, that is, "they" constitute themselves as a "we" in a specific way. The analytic definition of such a "we" is the task of the philosophy of collective intentionality and the point about which the Big Four disagree.

2.3 Ontological and Conceptual Reductivism

As I have indicated above, a major fault line runs between Bratman and his colleagues. To better understand the form and scope of the philosophical disagreements, it is first important to make a distinction between ontological and conceptual problems. Ontological questions pertain to the nature of reality. For instance, we can ask, "Do group agents *exist*, in any strong sense of the term, as a separate, autonomous entity?" Conceptual questions, instead, deal with our way of making sense of reality. For example, we can ask, "Under what condition can we properly speak of a social collective?" or, "What kind of action counts as a collective one?"

These kinds of questions were already a concern for the classics of sociology. Max Weber acknowledged the fact that, in our everyday communication, we attribute intentionality to families, sports teams, congregations, and so on. However, he insisted that "for sociological purposes there is no such thing as a collective personality which 'acts'" (Weber 1978: 14). The causal condition of action is, in this perspective, always and exclusively an individual psychological force. In this sense, Weber defended an ontological reductivism, in the sense that group agents have no existence beyond the individuals that compose them. But Weber's individualism also extended to the conceptual domain. Indeed, for him an action can be considered social "in so far as, by virtue of the *subjective meaning* attached to it by the *acting individual* (or individuals), it takes account of the behavior of others and is thereby oriented in its course" (Weber 1947: 88, my emphasis). Accordingly, Weberian sociology requires analysis of collectivities on the basis of the attitudes of their individual members and the organization that results from these attitudes.

By contrast, Durkheim's position in regard to ontological matters may at first appear more radical. Famously, the father of French sociology considered social facts as a *sui generis* phenomenon and insisted on the importance of studying them as a "thing" external to individuals (Durkheim 1982: 60). However, in the preface to the second edition of his *Rules of Sociological Method*, Durkheim was pressed to dispel some misunderstandings. Fending off the attacks of his critics, Durkheim categorically distanced himself from any form of "realism and ontological thinking" regarding the nature of collective representations (Durkheim 1982: 34). However, he also noted that a commonsense ontological individualism, according to which society comprises only individuals, does not yet allow us to eliminate the conceptual specificity of *collective* representations. On the contrary, he insisted that, just as the hardness of bronze cannot be found in either copper or tin alone, society "gives rise to new phenomena, different from those which occur in consciousnesses in isolation" (Durkheim 1982: 39).[1] For this reason, even the most accurate understanding of individual psychology could not provide adequate instruments for the study of society (Durkheim 1982: 41). Thus, despite some ambiguity in his formulations, we can say that Durkheim wished to draw a distinction between ontological and conceptual reductivism, accepting the first but rejecting the latter.

If we come back, after this short excursus into the realm of sociology, to the debates among philosophers, we can see that the disputes among them do not revolve around ontological issues. Despite their different stands on social ontology, all of the Big Four espouse a form of ontological reductivism and discard the existence of any collective agent as an autonomous entity metaphysically distinct from the thoughts and interactions of individual humans—although some differences in emphasis must be noted (see Tuomela 2018: 32). John Searle expresses this idea in the most explicit way when he states that any plausible account of collective intentionality must comply with a fundamental ontological constraint: "It must be consistent with the fact that society consists of nothing but individuals. Since society consists entirely of individuals, there cannot be a group mind or group consciousness. All consciousness is in individual minds, in individual brains" (Searle 2002b: 96).

In the absence of an ontologically autonomous intending "collective," all major accounts frame collective intentionality, roughly, as a distinctive way in which the (potential) members of a group come to view themselves in relation to other group members (Tollefsen 2018: 394). One way in which they fundamentally differ, however, is in the formulation of the conceptual requirements that this particular way of perceiving oneself and the others entails. In this respect, in a way that is reminiscent of Durkheim's position, Searle, Tuomela, and Gilbert maintain that any conceptualization of collective intentionality in terms of individual intentions is bound to be inadequate. This is because collective intentions entail on the part of the participants the reference to an irreducible and ineliminable concept of a group, of a "we." For this reason, their respective positions can be labeled as *conceptually non-reductivist*.

From a non-reductivist point of view, collective intentionality is not merely a question of two or more people each intending a joint action, but a matter of them *collectively* intending the joint action. Broadly speaking, for Searle and Tuomela, this requires a special "mode of intentionality," involving attitudes that are to be verbalized using the plural pronoun, "we." In Gilbert's opinion, collective intentionality requires the mobilization of the primitive concept of "joint commitment," which allows for the creation of a unit "of a special kind" that will constitute the "plural subject" of the collective intention. All this may still sound pretty mysterious, and it will be the task of the next chapters to elucidate these ideas.

Bratman's standpoint mainly contrasts with those of his colleagues on the ground of what he calls the "continuity thesis," which states, roughly, that the conceptual, metaphysical, and normative structures of basic collective intentionality—or as he prefers to label it, shared intentionality—must be contiguous with the structures of individual intentionality (Bratman 2014: 8). This means that Bratman explicitly refrains from introducing any new irreducible concept for the analysis of collective agency besides those required by an analysis of individual intentions. Accordingly, his approach is predicated on the complex interlocking of the personal intentions of individual agents. In the following section, I will explore Bratman's ideas more closely.

2.4 Michael Bratman's Conceptual Reductivism

In his essay *Modest Sociality and the Distinctiveness of Intention*, Michael Bratman (b. 1945) offers a thought experiment along the following lines: Imagine that you and I set off from the university building and walk together down the street toward the railway station. Another person unknown to us—a Stranger—is walking in the same direction in physical proximity to us without, however, bumping against you or me. "What distinguishes your and mine [sic] relation to each other," Bratman asks, "from each of our relations to the Stranger"? (Bratman 2009a: 150)

For Bratman, the difference between our walking together and our relationship with the Stranger resides in the distinct intentional structures that occur in each case. In a nutshell, "[Y]ou and I *share an intention* to walk together [...] but you and the Stranger do not" (Bratman 2009a: 152). Our sharing an intention thus plays a causal role in the explanation of our joint activity. Now, when it comes to defining what sharing an intention actually means, Bratman looks for a conceptually and metaphysically conservative approach that is able to characterize the idea of shared intention on the sole basis of the resources available to a theory of *individual* intentionality. Thus, departing from other strategies in the study of collective intentionality, he explicitly avoids introducing new irreducible concepts, such as "we-intentions" (Searle, Tuomela) or "joint commitment" (Gilbert). For this reason, his approach can be characterized as an ontologically *and* conceptually reductionist one.

The concept of individual intentionality that underpins Bratman's work is his Planning Theory of Intention, which he developed in his 1987 book *Intention, Plans, and Practical Reason* (reprinted as 1999c). Bratman assumes that intentions are specific attitudes that entail a certain commitment to action; thus, they provide us with reasons for acting in a certain way and support our rational behavior as planning agents. This means that when a person formulates an intention to do something, that intention serves as the foundation for further rational decisions that will guide her future behavior. For instance, if today at 8 p.m. I formulate the intention to take the train to work tomorrow at 8 a.m., my intention will exert a rational pressure on my future decisions: for example, I will set an alarm clock for 7 a.m. and refrain from going to bed too late this evening, so that I do not miss my train tomorrow.

Coupled with the norms of practical rationality, intentions and plans create expectations that allows us to coordinate, structure, and guide our individual actions over time. For Bratman, shared intentionality helps us "to organize and to unify our intentional agency" but in relation to interpersonal actions, providing a basis to organize our shared activity according to rational constraints (Bratman 1999e: 112). Indeed, in both cases of temporally extended and shared agency, thoughts and actions are manifestly connected in a special manner (Bratman 2010: 8–9). The task at hand, therefore, is to expand the theory of planning action to account for the special ties of shared intentionality.

Bratman understands shared intentionality to be, at its core, a web of interlocking personal intentions (Bratman 1999e: 114). The full description of this web is fairly complex (Bratman 2014: 84). Here, I will limit myself to a brief exposition of its cornerstones. According to Bratman, in order for you and me to share an intention to perform an action *J*, a number of conditions must be satisfied:[2]

1. (a) I intend that we *J* and (b) you intend that we *J*.
2. I intend that we *J* because of 1(a) and 1(b); you intend that we *J* because of 1(a) and 1(b).
3. 1 and 2 are common knowledge between us.

The condition expressed in (1) calls attention to the fact that for us to have the intention that we *J*, we each have to intend that we *J*. This condition, however, does not provide any "cognitive linkage" (Bratman 1999e: 117): you and I could have this intention without either of us being aware of the other's intention.

Thus, (3) introduces a condition of common knowledge that connects the shared intention to each participant's knowledge that the necessary conditions obtain (Bratman 2014: 58). The form of knowledge in question, however, differs from individual knowledge of one's own intentions, to which one usually has direct epistemic access. To assess the intention of the other, each participant will have to rely on ordinary and, thus, fallible "sources of evidence" (Bratman 2014: 58–59). Accordingly, on Bratman's account, shared intentions are characterized by a degree of uncertainty. In this respect, it is worth noting Bratman's reluctance to link shared intentions to language or other forms of symbolic communication, probably because such a connection may force him to accept concepts into his model that are foreign to his analysis of individual intentionality.

Condition (2) includes your intention that we *J* as part of my reason for intending that we *J*, and vice versa, and thus introduces a fundamental interlinkage between the intentions of the participants. In other words, when we share an intention, my intention that we *J* includes the efficacy of your intention that we *J*, and vice versa (Bratman 1999e: 119). This clause is intended to avoid certain forms of coercion. According to Bratman, if I should, for instance, force you to walk with me to the railway station, our activity would indeed be unified, but in a way that "bypasses your relevant intentions" (Bratman 1999e: 118). In this case, he argues, it would not be appropriate to speak of a *shared* intention, since you would lack the necessary personal intention that we walk to the station.

On closer inspection, clause (2) calls attention to another source of potential uncertainty in the structure of shared intentions. If your intention that we *J* is part of my reason that we *J*, and vice versa, how can we independently get to the intention that *we J*? On the one hand, I cannot intend that we act if I consider that this is in part up to you. On the other hand, I cannot "continue to regard the matter as partly up to you, if I have already decided that we really are going to act" (Velleman 1997: 35). Bratman's solution to this dilemma consists, in part, in assuming that ordinary agents are usually predictable in their actions (Bratman 1999b: 155). As he puts it, in the case of shared intentionality, "I can many times reliably predict that if I were to intend that we *J* and make that manifest, then your knowledge of my intention would lead you also to intend that we *J*" (Bratman 2014: 75). In other words, I can consider you a free agent and recognize that you still need to concur to the creation of our shared intention that we *J* while confidently predicting that you will do so. Still, it is almost too easy to imagine real-life situations in which such predictability is anything but certain. For this reason, the successful creation of a shared intention seems to always be plagued by a degree of indeterminacy that, one might argue, can only be dissipated through some form of symbolic communication.

To complete Bratman's basic model, we have to include a further condition. This condition states that each of us has to act not only in accordance with the conditions stated by condition (2) but also to ensure that the subplans that arise from our intentions are compatible with one another, or, as Bratman puts it, that they *mesh*. This means that, if, in accordance with planning theory, we consider our respective intentions that we *J* as part of larger but incomplete individual plans, we can see that each of us will have to fill those plans with related subplans about means, preliminary steps, etc.—for instance, if we share the intention to walk to the railway station, we will have to plan our walk at a time that suits the both of us. Indeed, while we may both intend that we *J*, we can disagree on the means, etc. of our *J*-ing. This can potentially jeopardize our shared intention. This does not mean that our subplans have to be identical, but that they must at least be "co-realizable" (Bratman 2014: 54).

Since our intention that we *J* cannot be realized if our subplans do not mesh, there is a tendency inherent to shared intention to "track and conform to a norm of compatibility across the relevant sub-plans of each," which "helps explain the coordinating role of shared intention" (Bratman 2014: 53). Furthermore, since I consider you a co-participant in my intention that we *J*, I am committed, at least to a certain degree, "[t]o helping you play your role in our joint action" (Bratman 1999d: 103). This is true because, if we each intend that we *J*, "I am under rational pressure in favor of necessary means to that, and in favor of filtering out options incompatible with that," which means not only avoiding actions that would block you from playing your role, but also intervening to avoid scenarios in which you are not able to play your role (Bratman 2014: 56).

Accordingly, Bratman's account also allows for shared intentions in cases in which the parties have different reasons for participating. For instance, I can intend that we go for a walk because I know that you walk fast and I need the exercise, while you intend that we go for a walk because you know that I am a good listener and you will share your concerns with me (see e.g., Bratman 1999e: 122). Despite these divergent reasons, our shared intention maintains its structuring role, for our respective intentions still "favor the coordinated, interlocking, meshing execution of each person's intentions and subplans in favor of the shared activity" (Bratman 2007: 292). However, Bratman (2006: 9) also acknowledges that "such difference in background reasons does have a potential impact both on the stability of such common frameworks and on the depth of their ability, even if stable, to guide shared deliberation and action in hard cases."

The problem of instability arises from the possibility that I may still have my reason for sharing an action when you no longer have yours. This might end our shared action (Bratman 2006: 5). The problem of depth arises when divergences in our background reasons make it more difficult for us to respond to complex challenges to our shared intention—if my background reason to go for a walk was to have a chat, and *not* to exercise, and your reason was the same, it would be easier for me to deal with your unexpected slow pace. Indeed, the only stabilizing force inherent to Bratman's model is the purposive creation of mutual expectations that all individuals will maintain the relevant intentions in accordance with the rules of their practical reason (Bratman 2006: 9–14). These expectations, however, do not entail any further normative dimension.

Bratman (1999f: 132) acknowledges that "the normal etiology of a shared intention does bring with it relevant obligations and entitlements." For instance, it seems intuitively the case that if, while we are going for a walk, I should suddenly run away from you, you would be entitled to an explanation. However, Bratman considers that "this etiology is not essential to shared intention itself" (Bratman 1999f: 132). Conversely, he maintains that mutual obligations, such as those that can arise from an exchange of promises or a binding agreement to *J*, do not guarantee the presence of a shared intention, because "one or both parties may be insincere and have no intention to fulfill the promise" (Bratman 1999f: 134). And if (even) one participant lacks the personal intention "that we *J*," no shared intention can come to be, at least on Bratman's account.

For Bratman, forms of obligation within a group are not a corollary of basic shared intentions but rather a kind of second-order phenomenon that entails familiar forms of moral obligation. This is for instance the case for various complex social activities, such as getting married or voting. The conditions of the emergence of these second-order shared intentions remain however unclear (Bratman 2009b: 45–46; 2014: 47).

Thus, Bratman's model of shared intentionality remains essentially confined to the study of minimal forms of "modest sociality" (Bratman 2014: 8), such as two people walking together toward the railway station.

2.5 Some Limitations of Conceptual Reductivism

The succinct overview provided so far reveals both a point of consensus and a fundamental divide running through the philosophical field of collective intentionality. On the one hand, a consensus emerges from the rejection of the idea that collective intentions can be analyzed in terms of a simple aggregation or sum of individual intentions. On the other hand, a distinction appears between the reductivist (or singularist) standpoint defended by Bratman and the non-reductivist stance of the competing accounts. How ought we to evaluate these different standpoints?

From a philosophical point of view, a comparative assessment may rest on the criteria of simplicity and goodness to fit (see Baker 2016). To support the superiority of his position, Bratman (2014: 35–37 and passim) likes to invoke the principle of Ockham's razor, according to which among competing theories the most parsimonious one must be preferred. Accordingly, he emphasizes that his theory starts with an analysis of individual intentionality (more precisely of individual planning agency) and accounts for shared intentionality without adding anything "fundamentally new—conceptually, metaphysically, or normatively" (Bratman 2014: 8). However, the appeal to such a principle of simplicity is not in itself so simple. Three preliminary points can be raised in this regard.

First, in regard to their *ontological* parsimony, the four approaches to collective intentionality are on the same footing, since none of them introduce any new metaphysical entities. Second, Bratman appears to privilege conceptual parsimony over syntactic simplicity. The latter criterion, however, appears more relevant if we seek to understand how collective intentions shape the actions of human agents and their understanding of the social world. In this respect, it is possible to argue that conceptually irreducible collective intentions may provide a cognitively more economic foundation for collective actions since, among other things, they limit the amount of information about the mental states of other participants needed to plan one's individual action as a group member (see Tuomela 2013: 7). By contrast, Bratman's interlocking web of personal intentions requires one not only to integrate another agent's personal intentions in one's intentional structures, but also to infer on the ground of incomplete information what one can reasonably expect the other agent to do in the future.

Third, the principle of parsimony must be counterbalanced by a principle of explanatory sufficiency: "[I]f three things do not suffice for verifying [an affirmative proposition], one has to posit a fourth, and so on in turn" (Chatton 2002; quoted in Keele and Pelletier 2018). In this regard, Bratman's approach seems to fall short of explaining a number of intuitive aspects of collective intentionality, beginning with the ubiquitous use, in social life, of a unifying "we." Most importantly, a reductivist approach appears unable to grasp the normative dimension that, according to experimental philosophers, most people associate with collective intentions—that is, the idea that if *we* intend to do something together, *I*, as a member of *us*, am subject to special obligations (see Gomez-Lavin and Rachar 2019). Therefore, we may ask whether, when comparing the various theories, Bratman actually applies Ockham's razor on the condition of "other things being equal."

Finally, we can consider the question of parsimony not only from an ontological and epistemic but also from a methodological point of view. When the introduction of new concepts allows for a syntactic simplification of the theory, thus making it easier to manipulate, there may be *pragmatic* reasons for preferring this over a more parsimonious approach. This is particularly true if one intends to apply the theory for the analysis of empirical data. Philosophers usually do not have this problem in mind when they present their reflections and thus do not address it in a direct and systematic way. I will deal extensively with this issue in the conclusion to this book's first part, drawing on the work of Searle, Tuomela, and Gilbert, respectively. However, a short prospectus, on the basis of Bratman's approach, on some central points that will be treated there may provide useful orientation to help navigate the more technical aspects of subsequent chapters.

2.6 Prospectus

Empirical research deals—and is forced to deal—with public phenomena. By "public," I do not mean something taking place in the social sphere as opposed to the private domain of the home. Rather, I use this adjective to underscore the need for empirical research to work with data that is epistemically accessible to an external observer, if not directly at least indirectly through some of its manifestations or practical prerequisites. Intentionality as such has a "first person ontology" (Searle 1992: 16) and while the content of my intention is directly accessible to me, the question whether it is epistemically knowable from a third-person perspective is one of the crucial questions in the philosophy of mind (Nagel 1986; Chalmers 1995). Indeed, we can measure brain waves, elicit the verbalization of someone's thoughts, or track patterns of behavior, and so on, but we cannot directly grasp what someone believes, feels, or intends. How does this problem translate to the field of collective intentionality? What can we observe if we want to study collective intentionality? These questions point to what I will call the problem of public accessibility.

Let us examine Bratman's point of view in light of this issue. Bratman conceptualizes shared intentions in terms of interlocking personal intentions. However, it is important to note that, on his account, shared intentionality is not itself a personal intention. In fact, in his view shared intentionality is not a property of any individual mind (Bratman 1999e: 123), but rather "a public, interlocking web" of personal intentions outside of the individual participants (Bratman 1999b: 143). Thus, it appears that shared intention is by its nature a public phenomenon and thus, at least in principle, also accessible to external investigation. But is this the case also in practice?

This leads us to a second problem, which I shall label the problem of distinctive constitution. In order to be empirically recognizable against the background of other psychological or social phenomena, collective intentionality has to manifest some distinctive features that would enable a researcher to recognize it. Otherwise, it may well be like a chameleon on a tree: potentially "public," but nonetheless invisible. One possible way to discern our object is to look for signs of a change in the (social) world that indicate that a collective intention is being created, where before there was none. In this respect, communicative or symbolic exchanges of some sort seem to be good candidates for empirical research.

From this point of view, Bratman's approach is profoundly ambivalent. On the one hand, his model requires a situation of common knowledge among the parties in a shared intention regarding their interrelated intentions both at the beginning of their shared activity and throughout its execution. On the other hand, when defining the conditions of such a common knowledge, forms of symbolic communication appear to be bracketed out in favor of other "ordinary sources of evidence" (Bratman 2014: 58), such as satisfied expectations. In consequence, the parties' shared activity seems to rest on an uncertain foundation, since the formation of the relevant shared intention is vulnerable to an important degree of indeterminacy. Even more so, shared intentions as Bratman conceptualizes them, appear to lack any distinctive element in their constitution that a researcher could assess on the basis of her observations or through other methods of data collection.

In the absence of a distinctive form of constitution, however, it may be possible to look for distinctive consequences of collective intentions. These would amount to a change in physical or communicative behavior on the part of the people acting on the ground of a collective intention—a change that would set them apart from, for instance, people acting on the ground of plain personal intentions. Of course, for a researcher to observe such a consequence would not necessarily amount to observing the collective intention itself (the same remark also applies to the problem of distinctive constitution); however, such an observation could support a reasonable inference to be triangulated with other relevant data. Since the study of (collective) intentionality covers a large number of mental states (volitions, beliefs, etc.) with a potentially infinite number of propositional contents, it is impossible to imagine a specific behavior as the mark of collective intentionality. For these reasons, it seems more promising to look more generally for changes in the kinds of actions that the collectively intending agents can, cannot, or even ought to perform. This leads us to investigate the normative dimension of collective intentionality.

Again, we see that Bratman's approach does not provide us much to work with. In his view, people sharing an activity do not act completely independently of one another and are not free to do whatever they please. The fact of considering another person as a co-participant in a shared action commits each agent to a certain responsiveness to the actions of the other and to helping him to play his part. However, for Bratman this commitment is grounded in each agent's practical reasoning. Indeed, shared intentions provide the agents with rational reasons for coordinating their actions even when their reasons for participating in the shared action differ. But since a shared intention rests completely on the parties having the appropriate interlocking *personal* intentions, nothing prevents one or more of them from simply changing their mind. In the absence of corresponding personal intentions on the part of one or more agents, the shared intention would simply dissolve. Thus, we could conclude that, on Bratman's model, shared intention affects an agent's behavior; until it no longer does.

In conclusion, the reductivist approach to collective intentionality that Bratman advocates does not provide a clear path toward an application of its core insights to an empirical research project. Do the non-reductivist standpoints put forward by Searle, Tuomela, and Gilbert fare better in this respect? I think they do, albeit in different degrees. So let us now turn to them, starting with the work of John Searle.

3

John Searle—Collective Intentionality in Individual Minds

3.1 Situating Searle's Argument and Method

3.1.1 The central question

Among the philosophers discussed in this book, John Searle (b. 1932) is undoubtedly the most famous and the most influential. He is also the author who is most often credited for calling attention to the problem of collective intentionality. Basically, for Searle, collective intentionality is the capacity of humans (and of some animals) to "share intentional states such as beliefs, desires and intentions" and to "engage in cooperative behavior" (Searle 1996: 23)—though collective intention in planning and acting constitutes the paradigmatic case in his analysis (Searle 2010: 43). Collective intentionality constitutes a key element in Searle's account of the nature of social reality (see Meijers 2003). Indeed, as he argues in his latest work on the making of the social world, it is through collective intentionality that society is created (Searle 2010: 25).

However, Searle's original contribution on the issue of collective intentionality was not explicitly connected to a general account of social ontology. Rather, his starting point was the question of whether his 1983 theory of human intentionality could be applied to the case of collective human behavior. His most detailed answer is spelled out in his 1990 contribution "Collective Intentions and Actions," republished with other essays in 2002. In it, Searle defends the thesis according to which "[T]here really is such a thing as collective intentional behavior that is not the same as the summation of individual intentional behavior" (Searle 2002b: 91). To provide initial support for this intuition, he proposes a thought experiment.

Searle imagines some people in a park who run to a central shelter upon being surprised by a sudden rain shower. In this case, the intention of each person is independent of the intention of the others, each of them thinking, "I am running to the shelter." He then imagines the same people converging to the shelter as part of an outdoor ballet. While an external observer may not be able to distinguish the movements of the dancers from those of the people fleeing the rain, the intentions underlying the two situations are clearly different. In the second case, the intentions of the individuals to execute certain dance steps are derived from the collective intention to perform the choreography (Searle 2002b: 92). But can a group have an intention? According to Searle, this is not possible in any literal sense involving something like a group mind—a conception that he briskly brushes aside as "at best mysterious and at worst incoherent" (Searle 2002b: 93).

To further explore the nature of collective intentionality, Searle (2002b: 92–93) offers another thought experiment. He imagines a football team deploying a particular offensive strategy. In this case, the team intention can be expressed, in part, by a "we-intention," that is, by an expression of intentional behavior in the first-person plural—for example, "We are executing this particular strategy." However, no individual member can execute the strategy independently, and thus no individual player can lay claim to this proposition as the exclusive terrain of his intention. Each player must have the intention to play a specific contribution in the form, say, "I am going to run to the left" or "I am throwing the ball." This observation prompts the question of whether the individual players' intentions to do their part can add up to the collective intention, "We are executing this particular strategy." Searle's main concern is to demonstrate why this *is not* the case.

3.1.2 Ontological considerations: all intentionality is in individual minds

According to Searle, most philosophical accounts of collective intentionality seek precisely to reduce collective intentional behavior to a sum of intentions in the first person singular, that is, "I-intentions," complemented with some form of mutual belief.

> The idea is that if we intend to do something together, then that consists in the fact that I intend to do it the belief that you also intend to do it; and you intend to do it in the belief that I also intend to do it. And each believes that the other has these beliefs, and has these beliefs about these beliefs, and these beliefs about these beliefs about these beliefs ... etc., in a potentially infinite hierarchy of beliefs. "I believe that you believe that I believe that you believe that I believe....," and so on. (Searle 1996: 24)

By contrast, Searle's central thesis is that "[w]e-intentions cannot be analyzed into sets of I-intentions, even I-intentions supplemented with beliefs, including mutual beliefs, about the intentions of other members of a group" (Searle 2002b: 93).

To substantiate this claim, Searle introduces yet another thought experiment. He imagines a class at Harvard Business School in which the students learn and assimilate Adam Smith's theory of the invisible hand. Accordingly, each student concludes that, in order to help humanity, she has to pursue her selfish interest and formulates the following intention: "I intend to do my part toward helping humanity by pursuing my own selfish interest and not cooperating with anybody" (Searle 2002b: 94). Furthermore, there is the mutual belief among the students that all other classmates have formulated a similar intention.

This example is meant to show that even if the classmates have the same (altruistic) goal of helping humanity and each of them believes that the others have individually intended to do their part in achieving this goal, there is no collective intentional behavior at play; the students are not helping humanity *together* in any sense other than they are all separately doing the same thing. What is fundamentally lacking in this case is a cooperative effort in achieving their goal. In fact, Searle's notion of collective intentionality, or we-intention, "implies the notion of *cooperation*" (Searle 2002b: 95; see also Searle 2010: 49). The case of the Harvard students would have been different if the classmates had formed *a pact* to all help humanity together by way of each pursuing her own selfish interest (Searle 2002b: 94), since, as per my reading of Searle's comment, that pact would have provided a basis for cooperation and, thus, proper collective intentional behavior.

Against this backdrop, Searle argues that "[c]ollective intentionality is a biologically primitive phenomenon that cannot be reduced to or eliminated in favor of something else" (Searle 1996: 24). The fact that so many philosophers have thought otherwise, however, is in itself revealing. Searle (1996: 25) conjectures that those who do so may accept a fallacious argument, according to which, "because all intentionality exists in the heads of individual human beings, the form of that intentionality can make reference only to the individuals in whose heads it exists." To think otherwise would, in their view, commit them to accepting the existence of "some Hegelian world spirit [...] or something equally implausible" (Searle 1996: 25). However, when it comes to collective intentionality, the opposition between ontological reductivism and superindividualism constitutes a false dichotomy. Indeed, any valid account of collective intentionality must respect the fact that "all human intentionality exists only in individual human brains" (Searle 2010: 44). Nevertheless, it does not follow that the mental life of an individual can only be expressed in a singular grammatical form (Searle 1996: 25–26; 2010: 47). To solve the conundrum, "We simply have to recognize that there are intentions whose form is: We intend that we perform act A; and such an intention can exist in the mind of each individual agent who is acting as a part of the collective" (Searle 2002b: 96–97).

3.1.3 Methodological considerations: speech acts and intentional states

Searle's solution may not be as simple as it intuitively appears. If we go back to the example of the football team, we will note that a player will have, in his head, the intention "We are executing this particular strategy." As noted, however, he will not be the one carrying out the whole strategy, so he also appears to need an intention in the form, say, "I will throw the ball." What is the relationship between these intentions? This amounts to inquiring about the structure of collective intentionality. For Searle, any adequate answer to this question must be consistent with two constraints: the first, encountered earlier, is "the fact that society consists of nothing but individuals" and "all consciousness is in individual minds, in individual brains" (Searle 2002b: 96); the second is the fact that since collective intentionality is in the minds of individuals, it is subjected to the same constraints as individual intentionality. Thus, to understand the structure of collective intentionality, one has first to understand the structure of individual intentionality, which Searle detailed in his 1983 book *Intentionality*, and, more specifically, the structure of individual intentional action (see below).

From a methodological point of view, Searle's analysis of intentionality is built upon the theory of speech acts that he developed in the 1960s (e.g., Searle 1968, 1969, 1976). Thus, a review of this theory constitutes a necessary stepping stone toward the topics addressed in the next section. (Furthermore, these ideas will also be relevant in the discussion of other authors.) Searle's approach to the study of language continues the work of his mentor J. L. Austin (1911–1960). In his lecture series *How to Do Things with Words* (1962), Austin seeks to break with the longstanding preoccupation of the philosophy of language with the truth value of descriptive statements (Krämer 2001; Sbisà 2007). In this respect, he notes that "[s]ome statements appear to be used for other goals than to describe" (Austin 1962: 2). For instance, "When I say, before the registrar or altar, &c., 'I do,' I am not reporting on a marriage: I am indulging in it" (Austin 1962: 6). In this case, to speak is, in a strong sense, to act. Austin dubs this kind of statements "performative statements," to be distinguished from constative (or descriptive) ones.

Austin notes that performative statements are *per se* neither true nor false (Austin 1962: 5) but can still be infelicitous. For instance, if the person stating, "I hereby declare you man and wife" does not have the authority to do so, the couple at the altar would have gone through a form of marriage, but would not be married. In Austin's "doctrine of the *Infelicities*" (Austin 1962: 14), which details the various ways in which performative statements can "fail," this would be a case of a "misfire," because certain external conditions necessary to make a performative statement felicitous are not met.

The situation is different in the cases of "abuses," the second major class of infelicities. Abuses do not make a performative void, "although it is still unhappy" (Austin 1962: 39). What is at stake here are certain thoughts or feelings that the speaker should have and upon which he should subsequently act (Austin 1962: 15). For instance, if a person promises without the intention of keeping his word, it is not the case that his utterance "I promise that..." misrepresents what it is stated. Indeed, the person *does* make a promise, but his promise is somehow vitiated by his bad faith (Austin 1962: 11).

Reassessing his preliminary distinction, Austin notes that constative statements are also subject to infelicity because, just as performative utterances imply some intentions, feelings or thoughts, constative statements imply some beliefs: "Suppose I did say 'the cat is on the mat' when it is not the case that I believe that the cat is on the mat, what should we say? Clearly it is a case of *insincerity*" (Austin 1962: 50), a particular kind of abuse. This consideration serves as the starting point for sketching out a more systematic and general theory of speech acts that no longer relies on the contrast between performative and constative statements (Austin 1962: 91), a task that will be continued by Searle.

Drawing on Austin's insights, Searle proposes to analyze each speech act in terms of its propositional content, p, and its illocutionary force, F. The illocutionary force determines whether an utterance with a certain propositional content, for instance my saying "You will like it," is a prediction, a promise, an order, a threat, and so on. For Searle, each kind of speech act points to a psychological state that determines the "sincerity" of a given statement. For example, to offer a sincere apology I have to feel regret, and to promise something sincerely I have to intend to keep the promise. But what about an insincere promise—is it still a promise? According to Searle, that is indeed the case, because the insincere promisor still purports to have the right intention and, in the end, what counts is the "expression of intention, whether sincere or insincere" (Searle 1969: 62).

To analyze a promise in terms of an *expression* of intention amounts to saying that the speaker "takes responsibility for having the intention rather than stating that he actually has it" (Searle 1969: 62). In this sense, the speech act of promising *commits* the speaker to a particular intention while allowing for the possibility that he is insincere. This last observation applies to the whole range of possible speech acts. In fact, it implies that "[w]henever there is a psychological state specified in the sincerity condition, the performance of the [speech] act counts as an *expression* of that psychological state" that entails the associated commitment of the speaker (Searle 1969: 65). For instance, to assert "that *p*" counts as an expression (sincere *or* insincere) of the belief "that *p*" and entails a commitment to such a belief.

Still, the felicitous performance of a speech act does not only depend on the presence of appropriate psychological states. A certain relationship between the speech act and the world must also obtain. Searle (1979: 126–131) regards this relationship as the condition of satisfaction of a speech act. For instance, if I (sincerely) order you to leave the room and you stay, my order (while still being an order) will be infelicitous. Similarly, my (sincere) statement that "the cat is on the mat" will be satisfied only if the cat is on the mat.

The "conditions of satisfaction" of a speech act are determined by its propositional content but also by the so-called direction of fit of the speech act. The point of speech acts such as statements is to get their propositional content to match the realities found in the world. For example, when I list all the books on my shelf, what I say is meant to match a certain state of affairs in the world. Thus, my speech act has a word-to-world direction of fit—my felicitous statement *fits* the world. Conversely, when I tell the waiter what I want on my pizza, I want to change the world so that it fits what I say—in this case the direction of fit is world-to-word (Searle 1976: 3–4).

For Searle, the core ideas of this philosophical approach to speech acts also apply, *mutatis mutandis*, to the study of intentions. Just as a speech act has an illocutionary force F and a propositional content p, each intentional state can be analyzed in terms of a psychological mode, S, and a representative (or intentional) content, r. Examples of psychological modes are belief, fear, desire, etc. The representative content expresses what is believed, feared, desired, etc. For instance, I can believe that it is raining or strive to make a good first impression.

The notions of "direction of fit" and "conditions of satisfaction" can also be carried over from the analysis of speech acts to the discussion of intentionality. Each intentional state intrinsically represents the criteria to judge whether it was successful. Believing, for instance, has a mind-to-world direction of fit. This means that my belief that it is raining will be true only if it matches something in the world, namely that it is raining. Conversely, my striving has a world-to-mind direction of fit: It is my responsibility to change the world (in this case, my behavior) in such a way that I will make a good first impression. If I make a poor first impression, my striving will not be satisfied, although I can still say that I have (unsuccessfully) strived to make a good first impression (Searle 1983: 1–10). Armed with this methodology, we can now explore the structure of individual intentional action as a preliminary step toward understanding the structure of collective intentionality.

3.2 The Conceptualization of Collective Intentionality

3.2.1 The structure of individual intentional action

To discuss the structure of individual intentional action, Searle uses the example of a very simple action: raising one's arm. Let us say that I intend to raise my arm and that my arm goes up. For Searle, every action has two constitutive elements: a bodily movement and a mental or intentional component. The bodily movement is a given state of affairs in the world, in our case, my arm actually going up; the intentional component is what Searle calls an "intention in action," and in our case, it is identical to the experience of my arm going up (Searle 1983: 91). What is the link between these two elements? In a nutshell, the two are connected by the fact that the experience of my arm going up has intentionality, that is, it has *conditions of satisfaction*, namely that my arm goes up (Searle 1983: 87). Let us unpack this idea.

Imagine that, without my knowledge, my arm has been anesthetized. As I raise my arm, I have the experience of it going up, but it does not actually move. In this case, I had the intention in action with the content, "Arm goes up," but, since the arm did not move, my intention was unsuccessful. We can say that I have *tried* to raise my arm, but I have failed to do so. We can also imagine the opposite situation: say, through some electrodes in my brain, someone causes my arm to go up. In this case, there is no action at all because, although there is movement, the intentional component is absent (Searle 1983: 88–89, 107–108). The latter example calls attention to another central feature of intentional action, namely its causal self-referentiality. This means that in order for my intention to raise my arm to be satisfied, it is not enough that I raise my arm; I have to raise my arm *because* I intended to raise my arm, that is, my intention in action must function causally in the achievement of the conditions of satisfaction (Searle 1983: 85; 2010: 34).

This conceptual model can also explain the structure of more complex intentions, which include conditions of satisfaction that go beyond one's bodily movement. These intentions cover actions that are constituted *by way of* or caused *by means of* performing a bodily movement (Searle 1983: 99). For instance, a person can vote *by way of* raising her hand. Searle observes that, in this case, raising the hand and voting are not two separate actions; rather, "[T]hey are one action with two levels of description of the two different features of the action" (Searle 2010: 36). In the appropriate circumstances, raising one's hand *constitutes* voting. Similarly, a person can, as a single action, fire a gun *by means of* pulling the trigger; the pulling of the trigger *causes* the gun to fire. Note that the intention in this case is also causally self-referential: if, during a meeting, my stretching my cramped arm is counted as a vote, I did not vote intentionally; nor have I fired the gun intentionally if I accidentally drop it and a bullet shoots out of the chamber (see Searle 2002b: 99).

In sum, on Searle's account, an action "is a causal and Intentional transaction between mind and the world" (Searle 1983: 88). In his view, however, intentionality itself is not enough to account for our capacity to have such transactions. Searle reaches this conclusion after analyzing all the premises that intervene in a person's intention to do something, and noting that each intention is part of a network of other intentional states. Searle (1983: 143) argues that a thorough reconstruction of the threads of that network would eventually lead to finding "a bedrock of mental capacities that do not themselves consist in Intentional states (representations), but nonetheless form the preconditions for the functioning of Intentional states," such as the presupposition that the ground under our next step will also be solid. He refers to this "set of nonrepresentational mental capacities that enable all representing to take place" as "the Background" (Searle 1983: 143). The Background refers to a set of (preintentional) assumptions about "how things are" and "how to do things"; such know-how, however, cannot be properly reframed as "knowing that." Thus, the Background does not consist of representations or constitutive rules, and yet, it provides "necessary but not sufficient conditions for understanding, believing, desiring, intending, etc." (Searle 1983: 158).

3.2.2 Extending the structure to the collective case

How do these ideas apply to the case of the intentional collective action of two or more actors? Once again, following Searle (2002b: 99–100), we can start with a thought experiment. This time, let us imagine Baz and Fred preparing a sauce that requires some ingredients to be poured carefully onto others while energetically whisking the concoction. Baz is doing the pouring, while Fred is doing the whisking. Each of them has a we-intention of the form "We are preparing the sauce." Using the terminology introduced in the previous sections, we can see that this is an intention in action to prepare the sauce, which has the sauce being prepared as its condition of satisfaction. As such, it must also be causally self-referential, meaning, for instance, that if Baz is preparing the sauce alone, the intention in action that "*we* are preparing the sauce" is not satisfied. Yet, Baz can only pour the ingredients, and Fred can only whisk them together. How do they cause the sauce to be prepared? They are, in fact, the only agents, and their intentionality can only cause things that they can do: Baz, for instance, cannot cause Fred's whisking (Searle 2010: 44–45). Furthermore, as we have seen above, their individual I-intentions (that is, "I will whisk"; "I will pour") do not add up to a we-intention.

Searle's solution to this problem consists in analyzing collective intentions as a case of complex individual intentions. In the case of me firing a gun, my intention can be understood as an intention to the non-bodily event B (fire the gun) *by means of* doing the bodily movement A (pulling the trigger). Similarly, in the case of a collective intention, each agent has the intention to achieve the collective goal B *by means of* performing the individual intentional action A. If we go back to our culinary example, Baz's and Fred's intentions in action could be formulated like this:

- **Fred**: intention in action collective B by singular means A (this intention in action causes: ingredients are whisked, which causes: sauce is prepared)
- **Baz**: intention in action collective B by singular means A (this intention in action causes: ingredients are poured, which causes: sauce is prepared)

Baz and Fred each have a single intention with two levels of description. Thus, each agent's performance can be framed as a contribution to the collective performance (Searle 2002b: 101; 2010: 52–53).

As some commentators have noted (e.g., Gilbert 2007: 39–40; Tuomela 2013: 85) in relation to Searle's account, the content of the expression "collective B" remains somewhat opaque. Implicitly, it expresses the fact that each agent believes that he "is not acting alone but as part of a collective and that the goal of achieving B is shared by the other members of the collective" (Searle 2010: 53). In our example, Fred believes that Baz has an intention in action of the same form (although not exactly with the same content) as his; that is, he believes that Baz is collaborating with him to prepare the sauce by means of doing his part. Indeed, Fred does not need to know the content of Baz's singular intention and simply takes for granted that he will do his part to achieve the collective goal, and vice versa (Searle 2010: 54).

Of course, this allows for the case in which Baz or Fred (or both) has a false belief (Searle 2010: 55). Let us imagine that Baz challenges Fred to wear a blindfold while preparing the sauce. Fred accepts and starts whisking. Baz, however, is a prankster and simply looks at Fred without pouring. In this case, we can say that Fred still had the collective intention in action of the form described above; this intention in action was not successful, however, since its condition of satisfaction, that is, that the sauce was actually (collectively) prepared, was not achieved. This possibility is a central feature of Searle's account. Indeed, Searle (2002b: 96) insists that the structure of an individual's intentionality, be it in the singular or collective form, "has to be independent of the fact of whether or not he is getting things right, whether or not he is radically mistaken about what is actually occurring." This means that "all intentionality, whether collective or individual, could be had by a brain in a vat or by a set of brains in vats" (Searle 2002b: 96). This conclusion has left more than one commentator perplexed, and I will return to it below.

3.3 The Constitution and Consequences of Collective Intentionality

3.3.1 The presupposition of the Background

On Searle's account, a collective intention, or we-intention, is something that exists in individual minds and, as shown by the preceding example, a person can have a collective intention independently of any particular states of affairs in the world, as long as she believes that she is engaging in a cooperative behavior with others. Thus, to investigate the formation of collective intention can mean, in this case, to inquire about the requirements for an individual mind to have a collective intention. Searle's answer is rather succinct and points to some "general and pervasive" features of the preintentional Background of intentionality (see above). In particular, Searle (2002b: 103) advances that "the capacity to engage in collective behavior requires something like a sense of 'the other' as an actual or potential agent like oneself in cooperative activities," which is not in itself a product of collective intentionality. In this respect,

"[C]ollective intentionality seems to presuppose some level of sense of community before it can ever function" (Searle 2002b: 103).

Indeed, according to Searle, language itself appears to require "a ground floor form of collective intentionality [...] which makes the use of language possible at all" (Searle 2010: 50; see also Searle 1996: 72–76). Against this backdrop, Searle considers that collective behavior can also be pre-linguistic and does not necessarily rest on conventions. As he puts it, "For example, I see a man pushing a car in the street in an effort to get it started; and I simply start pushing with him. No words are exchanged and there is no convention according to which I push his car. But it is a case of collective behavior. In such case *I* am pushing only as a part of *our* pushing." (Searle 2002b: 91–92).

3.3.2 Language and commitment

All in all, the contours of Searle's take on the formation of collective intentions appear fuzzy. Although he repeatedly refers in his discussion to collective intentionality and collective intentional behavior, it is not clear that he is consistently speaking of one and the same phenomenon. For instance, the use of the term collective intentionality to describe both an intentional state *and* a preintentional capacity is misleading. The fact that the intentional state rests on a preintentional capacity does not entail that the former can be assimilated to the latter nor that the preintentional capacity is a sufficient condition for having the intentional state. Thus, a statement like the following appears fallacious:

> If you assume that [A] collective intentionality results in commitments undertaken through conversation, then you have to presuppose [B] collective intentionality even to begin to have the conversation that results in the commitment. (Searle 2010: 50)

The statement rings true, but it uses the term "collective intentionality" to describe two mental phenomena, [A] and [B], that should arguably remain distinct.

Second, the car-pushing example fits Searle's description of collective intentional behavior only because he adds the clause "*I* am pushing only as a part of *our* pushing." This implies that I am having a we-intention and that I assume that the other person pushing also has one. However, that person might in fact think that I am trying to steal his car. On Searle's account, this would not entail that I lack a we-intention, only that I am having one based on a false belief. However, without the above-mentioned clause, there is no clue in Searle's example that the action in question is an expression of collective intentional behavior. For instance, I could perform the same action on the basis of an individual, *by-means-of* intention in action, such as the I-intention of helping the person by means of pushing the car. This intention can be successful even if the other person stops pushing the car, which does not seem to be the case if we stick to the letter of Searle's example.

In relation to this second point, Gilbert notes that Searle's central examples of collective intentional behavior involve some form of agreement, notably the case of the

Harvard Business School students who make a *pact* to help humanity by each pursuing their selfish interest. In this regard, she observes that agreements always entail some form of communication, even a minimal one, between the parties. Against this backdrop, Gilbert argues that the *primitiveness* of we-intentions cannot mean that the analysis of their formation must be limited to saying that a we-intention is an irreducible psychological state (Gilbert 2007: 39–40).

According to Gilbert, this point is particularly important because it shows how Searle's account leaves out one intuitively central feature of collective intentional actions, namely the fact that they appear to entail duties and obligations (Gilbert 2007: 43). For instance, if we assume in the example above that I am engaged in a *collaborative* action with the other person pushing the car, should he stop pushing, I would feel entitled to an explanation as to why he is no longer doing his part. In his 2010 book on *The Making of the Social World*, Searle appears to address this issue. Discussing his famous 1990 Harvard Business School example, he notes that there is a tremendous difference between the scenario in which the students act alone and the one in which they make a pact to help humanity by being selfish. This is so because

> [I]n the second case there is an obligation assumed by each individual member. In the first case [...] if someone changes his or her mind, that person is free to drop out at any point and go to work for the Peace Corps. But in the second case, there is a solemn promise made by each to all of the others. (Searle 2010: 48)

Searle, however, does not provide any further discussion on the connection between such an obligation and the conceptualization of collective intentionality. For Meijers (2003: 177–178), the reason why Searle seems to have little to say on this point is a direct consequence of his solipsistic notion of we-intentionality, which does not incorporate the idea of sharing one's intentionality or does so only in an underdeveloped way. Let us briefly explore this issue.

3.3.3 Solipsistic we-intentions

Searle considers that in a normal case, a we-intending agent will consider that her intentionality is, in fact, shared with the others who participate in the collective action (Searle 2002b: 97). However, this must not necessarily be the case. As Searle writes,

> I could have all intentionality I do have even if I am radically mistaken, even if the apparent presence and cooperation of the other people is an illusion, even if I am suffering a total hallucination, even if I am a brain in a vat. Collective intentionality in my head can make a purported reference to other members of a collective independently of the question whether or not there actually are such members. (Searle 2002b: 97)

As a consequence, the we-intending agent could be mistaken not only about the state of affairs in the world but also about what she is doing, that is, about the fact that she is performing her part in a collective action.

This possibility has been met with skepticism by various commentators, who note that Searle's account would pick up a number of situations which, intuitively, do not appear to involve any form of collective intentional behavior. Gilbert, for instance, rethinks Searle's example of the people in the park we-intending to perform a choreography. This time, however, each person hallucinates that they are having a we-intention to perform the dance with the others and believe that the others will do the same. In this case, just as in the case of a sum of I-intentions, it seems that something is missing in order to claim, intuitively, that the people involved are doing something *together*, even though they all share we-intentions of a similar form (Gilbert 2007: 43; see also Ludwig 2007).

The missing aspect might be, as suggested by Meijers (2003: 177), a foundation of the relations involved in collective intentionality *in re*, without seeking to reduce such relations to the intrinsic properties of the individuals involved. This would mean that in collective intentional states,

> The existence of other agents is not incidental [...], but is a *condition* for the possibility of collective intentional states. These states are *relational* states that have a foundation in the participating individuals. Having a foundation means that the intentional states are one-sidedly dependent upon *two* or more participants. In case these participants do not exist in the real world, there is simply no collective intentionality. (Meijers 2003: 179)

As I understand it, Tuomela makes a similar point when he states that, despite the similarities between his and Searle's account of collective intentionality, Searle's approach "is not quite right, because it ignores that one participant's part-performance is dependent on the other participants' part-performances" (Tuomela 2000a: 63). These criticisms are relevant beyond the issue of collective intentionality and raise some questions with regard to Searle's overarching social ontology.

Collective Intentionality and Social Ontology

A major premise of John Searle's overall philosophical project is his standpoint that "we live in exactly one world" (Searle 1996: xi). This means that we ought to understand phenomena such as atoms, desires, promises, and money as parts of the same reality, without postulating a realm of the mind that is distinct from the physical world of biology or even a third realm inhabited by cultural and social productions (see Popper 1978). Accordingly, every step of his analysis is bound to be completely naturalistic, and when it comes to the discussion of cognitive, linguistic, or social reality, the appeal to a noumenal world, a categorical imperative, or any supernatural features is excluded on principle. In this regard, the philosopher Georg Meggle (2002: 261) observes that "[o]ne of the many things which explain why Searle is one of the great figures of modern-day philosophy is that he has something like an overall view, something like a vision of how everything may ultimately fit together."

A rough attempt at summarizing this "overall view" may look like this: Searle's philosophy of mind deconstructs the Cartesian mind-body problem as a false dichotomy (Searle 1983: 262–272), inviting us to consider consciousness "as a part of the natural biological order as any other biological features such as photosynthesis, digestion, or mitosis" (Searle 1992: 90), with intentionality as one of its structural features (Searle 2004: 134–145). Along these lines, Searle conceives of human language as a natural extension of the prelinguistic capacities of our mind (Searle 2009). His analysis of speech acts and their condition of satisfaction illuminates the extent to which public, social representations of our intentional states are possible and how our words commit us to certain courses of action (Searle 1964, 1969). In such ways, human minds create systems of rights and duties, which provide them with desire-independent reasons for acting (Searle 2001).

Through collective intentionality, humans can constitute social phenomena "of a higher sort" (Searle 1996: 88) called social institutions. They do so by declaratively imposing a status function onto people and objects, "where the function cannot be achieved solely in virtue of physics and chemistry but requires continued human cooperation in the specific forms of recognition, acceptance, and acknowledgment of a new status to which a function is assigned" (Searle 1996: 40). Institutional facts, such as money or governments, have the following structure: X counts as Y in C, where X indicates a "brute fact"; the locution "counts as Y" expresses a constitutive rule through which a new status is collectively imposed on X; and C circumscribes the context in which such a rule is valid (Searle 1996: 43–51; see also Hindriks 2005; Hindriks 2009; Rota 2016).

Surprisingly, considering the centrality of the concept of collective intentionality in his overall philosophical program, Searle has devoted only a few texts to its analysis and never departed from the account that he spelled out in his 1990 contribution "Collective Intentions and Actions." Despite their succinctness, Searle's views proved to be highly influential and sparked a number of commentaries (e.g., Mathiesen 2002; Meggle 2002; Zaibert 2003). Yet after reviewing his positions, it seems necessary to join the many reviewers who, while underscoring his lucidity in identifying a central question in the analysis of intentional collective behavior, also observe that some aspects of his answer remain ambiguous, if not inadequate. For this reason, for the purpose of an empirical application of a theory of collective intentionality, we cannot satisfy ourselves with this one account, and we need to continue our exploration, turning now to the work of Raimo Tuomela.

4

Raimo Tuomela—Non Mihi, Non Tibi, Sed Nobis

4.1 Situating Tuomela's Argument and Method

4.1.1 The central question

The Finnish philosopher Raimo Tuomela (1940–2020) has been among the most productive authors in the field of collective intentionality. His work on this issue spans more than five decades and includes six single-authored books in addition to an impressive number of journal articles and contributions to edited volumes. During this time, Tuomela extended his "purposive-causal theory" of individual intentional human action (Tuomela 1977) to multi-agent cases, opening the door to an analysis of collective forms of intentionality and the ontology of social institutions (Tuomela 1984). Over the years, Tuomela constantly refined, extended, and developed his account of collective intentionality and constructed a complex network of technical concepts and formal models aimed at its analysis. This chapter offers an introduction to selected core ideas.

Drawing on psychological and evolutionary evidence, Tuomela considers that human beings have an inherent disposition that we may call "sociality," which consists, in the most general sense, in the capacity for doing things *together* (e.g., Tuomela 1995: 185; 2013: 1). However, Tuomela calls attention to the fact that the adverb "together" is open to different interpretations that do not always amount to the performance of a collective social action (Tuomela 1995: 88–89). A collection of people can be said, in a sense, to enjoy an afternoon in the park *together* even if each person is doing his or her thing, simply paying attention not to bump into the others (see Amit 2020). In this case, however, besides the physical co-presence in the park, it is hard to see any form of sociality. Similarly, the action of the people in the park who, surprised by a rain shower, run to a shelter *together* does not amount to a social action, even if the people are aware of each other's intentions to avoid getting wet (see Searle's thought experiment in the previous chapter).

A different scenario arises when the people in the park have the idea to organize a picnic on the grass in the evening. A notice is displayed at the gate stating, "We will organize a picnic tonight!" Those who wants to participate can put their name on a list and indicate what they are going to bring. Accordingly, the person bringing the wine and the person contributing the potato salad will do it as their part of the collective intention to organize the picnic. This last case is what Tuomela calls a proper (or full-blown) joint action (Tuomela 1995: 93). In this case, the collective action can be considered the action of a group—of a "we" sharing a specific intention: a "we-intention."

A central aspect of Tuomela's work consists in providing an analytic account of this final case, considered as paradigmatic, and in detailing how the form of intentionality that it involves differs from the other cases sketched in this example. The concept of "we-intention" constitutes the keystone of his discussion. I will progressively flesh out this concept in the various sections of this chapter.

4.1.2 Ontological considerations: we-intentions as attitude *de nobis*

Tuomela's work on the nature and form of collective intentionality is rooted in a line of philosophical investigation initiated by the American philosopher Wilfrid Sellars (e.g., 1963b, 1974), who is credited as the inventor of the concept of "we-intention." Sellars introduced this concept mainly to solve certain problems pertaining to the intersubjectivity of moral norms (see Tuomela 1984: 31–33). Tuomela, however, is less concerned with such (meta)ethical questions than with the role of collective concepts (such as "we" or "us") in the philosophical underpinning of the social sciences. In his view, since human beings are "social beings, whose accounts of their social life inherently rely on the social group notions involving the core concept of 'us' [...] social scientists and philosophers of social science also need to employ such 'we-concepts' in describing and explaining social life" (Tuomela 1995: ix).

Tuomela's analysis of social groups and collective intentions does not postulate any literal group mind but introduces "a kind of modern counterpart of group-minds" (Tuomela 1995: 231) in the form of conceptually irreducible we-intentions, that is, intentions that do not merely amount to openly shared individual attitudes but rather constitute attitudes *de nobis* in a stronger sense, on the ground that they involve an ineliminable notion of "us" (Tuomela 1995: 45). Nevertheless, we-intentions are *per se* not holistic features of a group, but rather "reflect the idea of a group at the level of the individual" (Tuomela and Miller 1988: 371). Thus, Tuomela's notion of group intentionality is *ontologically* individualistic—it is individuals who have we-intentions—although it remains *conceptually* irreducible to the personal intentions of individuals. This means, in a nutshell, that a group ontologically consists of its members functioning as a coherent unit in their role as group members (Tuomela 2007: 124; 2013: 22).

The early formulations of this position have caused some confusion even among prominent philosophers. In an influential contribution, John Searle considers Tuomela's approach exemplary of what he regards as a typical flaw in the conceptualization of collective intentions, "in that it attempts to reduce collective intentions to individual intentions plus beliefs" (Searle 2002b: 93). Tuomela has rejected this as a faulty interpretation of his work on multiple occasions (e.g., Tuomela 2005) while emphasizing that he regards the notion of we-intentions as a primitive one, which can *in principle* be "mapped directly onto neural states and events" and thus goes "all the way down [...] not only conceptually but also in this factual psychological sense" (Tuomela 2007: 57).

4.1.3 Methodological considerations: conceptual functionalism

To some extent, these misunderstandings may be the consequence of Tuomela's dense prose and complex methodology. How does Tuomela proceed to develop his analytical framework? It is not easy to provide a simple answer to this question. Tuomela's early publications on collective intentionality are rooted in a very sophisticated functionalist program inspired by Wilfrid Sellars' theory of mind (Tuomela 1984: 17–30). However, his presentation of this program and its practical application remain fairly obscure. Concretely, his analysis consists of introducing a number of basic psychological, social, and action-related notions and defending general theses about their relationships (Tuomela 1995: 3). Thus, instead of presenting a systematic methodological summary, I consider it more productive to proceed genealogically and show how successive building blocks were developed and connected to one another, starting with Tuomela's conceptualization of the intentionality of individual action, before moving to collective cases.

4.2 The Conceptualization of We-Intentions

4.2.1 A purposive-causal theory of individual action

Tuomela's account of collective intentionality is rooted in a specific theory of human action, the Purposive-Causal Theory, which he developed in the mid-1970s (Tuomela 1975, 1977). Indeed, the earliest formulations of Tuomela's account of collective intentionality explicitly seek "to extend the single-agent purposive-causal theory to the social case, viz. to the multi-agent case" (Tuomela 1984: 79).

Proceeding in the footsteps of Sellars (1963a), Tuomela pursues a causalist program in the explanation of action (see, e.g., Tuomela 1975: 167; 1982: 55–78). This means, roughly, that he seeks to analyze intentional actions "as movements caused by certain kinds of mental events or states" (Tuomela 1982: 16). Since mental states are not directly accessible to scientific scrutiny, their analysis has to be modeled *in analogy* to language (see de Vries 2016). Thus, concepts such as wanting, intending, and believing should not be regarded as granting any direct access to extralinguistic phenomena, but rather as the building blocks of a *theoretical* framework. As such, they are "functionally construed as dispositional states with a certain propositional structure" (Tuomela 1977: 114) that serve as potential causes of behavior.

As a theoretical construction, intentions are specific mental states that are connected to beliefs and wants, but cannot be reduced to these dispositions (Tuomela 1977: 128–134; 1984: 82). Among other things, a conceptual requirement of intentions is that the agent intending to do X must also believe that she can do X: an agent cannot intend what she believes to be impossible. Furthermore, an intention has a behavior-guiding role insofar as it generates beliefs that specify the external events that would qualify as realizations of said intention (Tuomela 1977: 136). For instance, my intention to ventilate my office by opening the window generates my belief that my opening the window will satisfy my intention. Simply opening the door would not satisfy my intention, although it might achieve the result of my office being ventilated. Intentions also entail a commitment of the agent to action and can be strung together into conduct plans that guide the agent toward her goal (Tuomela 1977: 212). It is for this reason that Tuomela speaks of *purposive* causation.

Conduct plans can be typically described through the form of the practical syllogism consisting of two premises and a conclusion: "The first premise of this pattern of thought is a statement about an agent's intention to achieve a certain end. The second premise is a statement about what he believes to be required of him to do in order to achieve his aim. The conclusion is a statement which, roughly, says that the agent does or proceeds to do what is required of him in the second premise" (Tuomela 1977: 170). For instance, my intentional action of opening the window (conclusion) results from my intention to ventilate my office by opening the window (first premise) and my belief that unless I open the window, I cannot reach my goal (second premise). In other words, my intention to ventilate the office together with my beliefs *purposively* generate and guide my behavior to open the window to the effect that the office is ventilated. A similar description can be given, *mutatis mutandis,* of intentional *social* actions.

4.2.2 We-intentions in the context of a theory of action

Tuomela characterizes social actions as "actions suitably put together from the actions of single agents" (Tuomela 1984: 91). Importantly, not all actions with multiple agents count as social actions, but only those that present "special conjunctions of the participating agents' individual conduct plans" (Tuomela 1984: 86). The core concept of we-intending, to be specified below, serves to clarify the nature of these special conjunctions.

To illustrate Tuomela's approach, we can imagine a simple case involving only two agents acting together. We can think of my colleague Daniela and me together assembling a new Ikea couch for my office (true story!) Let us also assume that only two actions are needed: putting the backrest in place and attaching the legs. For Daniela and me to build the couch together, we both need conduct plans that include the end action to build the couch and the belief that unless we each contribute with individual actions—say, my pushing against the backrest to put it in place and Daniela's twisting the legs to attach them—the total action of building the couch cannot be achieved. Crucially, our respective conduct plans must be grounded in our we-intentions to build the couch together.[1]

There are different ways of framing the concept of we-intention. The first and perhaps more intuitive one is to consider we-intentions as conveying the intentions that individuals have *as members of a collective or group*. In this sense, each individual agent in the collective can express his or her we-intention with respect to the joint action X by means of the locution, "We will do X." In this expression, "will" is used volitionally (and not predictively, in the future tense), and "we" refers to the collective (Tuomela 1984: 121). For instance, should my boss inquire why Daniela and I are carrying two big packages to my office, I would answer, "We will assemble an Ikea couch!"

But what does it entail for *me* to say that *we* will assemble the couch? Or, to put in a more systematic way, what is the relationship between "the concept pair, 'I'–'we'"

(Tuomela 1984: 33), when I am we-intending to do X as a member of "our group" G? Mirroring the case of an individual intentional action, the answer can be expressed, in part, in the form of a practical syllogism. For me to we-intend means (ideally) to follow, in my practical reasoning, the following schema:

(W1) (i) We will do X.
     (ii) I am one of us, *viz.* the group G.
     (iii) I will do my part of X.   (Tuomela and Miller 1988: 368)

Here, premise (i) expresses my we-intention, and premise (ii) my belief regarding my membership to the group G. The conclusion (iii) relates my action to the joint action X of the group in terms of a part of the total action. Thus, according to (W1), part of my reason for performing my part of X is that I, as a member of G, "have the intention expressed by (i)" (Tuomela and Miller 1988: 368). In our example, I would put the backrest in place in part because I we-intend that Daniela and I—"our group," "we"—assemble the couch together (see Tuomela 1995: 115–116).

Conclusion (iii) can also be formulated in more general terms as (iii'): "I will do whatever I regard as necessary for me to do for our doing X" (Tuomela 1984: 33). The possibility of such generalization suggests that we-intentions can also figure in more complex reasoning. In particular, the inferences I make "as a member of our group" can include further reasons for my actions that refer to other members of the group. The schema (W2) below provides an example of such an inference (see also Tuomela 1984: 34):

(W2) (i) We will do X.
     (ii) A is one of us.
     (iii) Our doing X requires that A does his part of X.
     (iv) Unless I do Y (e.g., teach A to do something) A cannot do his part.
     (v) I will do Y.

(Tuomela and Miller 1988: 368)

If we go back to our example, we can say, for instance, that Daniela's we-intending would ground her inferring that she must explain to me how to put the backrest of the couch in place before attaching the legs, since she is the only one who has read the instructions. Both the inferences (W1) and (W2) are normally considered to be satisfied by any we-intention (Tuomela 1984: 121). (On closer inspection, however, the differences between the two schemas prefigure the distinction between the so-called I-mode and we-mode that I will discuss below.)

Tuomela uses this fairly intuitive approach to the notion of we-intentions as a stepping stone toward a more technical account, which I will now present and elucidate. However, instead of simply introducing his formal model of a we-intention, (WI) for short, I will reconstruct it step by step, starting with what we already know. So far, we have seen that, at least to some extent, we can understand a we-intention as the intention that an agent has as a member of a collective. Furthermore, a we-intention can be characterized in terms of practical inferences leading the agent to conclude that he or she will (in a conative sense) play a part in the total social action. Against this backdrop, we can already state the first clause of the model, knowing that A_i can stand for any member of the collective G, composed by $A_1, \ldots, A_n$.

(WI) A member A_i of a collective G *we-intends* to do X if and only if
  (i) A_i intends to do his part of X.

This formulation shows clearly that the agent A_i has in fact two intentions: the we-intention to do X and the individual intention "to do his part of X."

Tuomela recognizes that to think of an individual agent (we-)intending to do a collective action may seem odd (imagine a musician playing the triangle in a philharmonic we-intending to perform Beethoven's fifth symphony). Would it not be more straightforward to say that the content of A_i's we-intention is "to do his part?" Tuomela rejects this suggestion on "holistic" grounds. Following (W1), A_i does not merely act on the intention "I shall do my part of X"; rather "the agent in question here is supposed to share the group G's intention, or its members' joint intention, to do X, and this is in part reflected in his accepting the intention-expressing statement 'We shall do X' as true of himself" (Tuomela and Miller 1988: 376).

In this sense, A_i intending to do his part of X is not sufficient to say that he we-intends to do X: His action counts as his part of X only if he performs it with the purpose of the total action X coming about (Tuomela 1995: 99). If Daniela successfully attached the legs of the couch with the sole purpose of training her dexterity, she would not have done her part with respect to our we-intention to assemble the couch, even though under some description, this might seem the case (see Tuomela 1995: 128). Furthermore—and in accordance with the schema (W2)—her intending to do her part might involve more than attaching the legs of the couch—for instance showing me how to put the backrest in place.

In light of the previous paragraphs, we can see that the expression, "We will do X" stated in the first clause of (W1) is meant to apply "both to a group of persons denoted by 'we' and to a single member [...] of that group" (Tuomela 1995: 116). A_i's we-intention to do (the full action) X, however, fails to satisfy an important core element defining individual intentions. As I have mentioned above, in order to (individually) intend to do X, an agent A_i also has to believe that he can do X. On the contrary, when A_i we-intends to do X, he usually has the opposite belief; that is, that without the participation of (some of) the other group members he will not be able to do X. However, in the same situation, A_i believes that he, together with (some of) the other members of G can do X. Therefore, to we-intend to do X (and, thus, to intend to do his part of X), A_i has to believe that the other agents in the collective also we-intend to do X and, thus, will do their parts to bring about X (Tuomela and Miller 1988: 373).

In more practical terms, this means that unless I believe that Daniela will (at least try to) attach the legs of the couch, I cannot unconditionally intend to put the backrest in place as my part of *our* assembling the couch. Or, the other way around, if I definitely believe that Daniela will not attach the legs, I cannot intend to do my part in *our* assembling the couch (Tuomela and Miller 1988: 374). In light of this discussion, it is now possible to introduce the second clause of Tuomela's model:

(ii) A_i has a belief to the effect that the joint action opportunities for X will obtain, especially that at least a sufficient number of the full-fledged and adequately informed members of G, as required for the performance of X, will (or at least probably will) do their parts of X.

Clause (ii) of the model "relates the agent's plain intention to do his part to his expectations of what the coactors are going to do" (Tuomela and Miller 1988: 377) and constitutes a precondition of (i). In accordance with the discussion in the previous paragraph, absent the belief that others will participate, A_i cannot unconditionally formulate the intention in clause (i).

Let us now consider that, in the case of our Ikea couch, clauses (i) and (ii) are satisfied for my part. That is, I intend to do my part of our we-intention, and I believe Daniela will do hers. But what about Daniela's intentions and beliefs? It seems that if "our group" can say in chorus "We will do X," Daniela must also accept "We will do X" as true for herself. This entails that she intends to do her part of X as her part of X. But to intend so unconditionally, she has to have, as I do, the appropriate belief regarding our joint action opportunities as stated in clause (ii). Thus, Tuomela notes that, in order for two agents to act *together*, each must believe "that the other one will intentionally do his part of the total action" (Tuomela and Miller 1988: 371), that is, they have to share the appropriate mutual beliefs. Mutual beliefs "make we-intentions social" (Tuomela and Miller 1988: 380).

This gives us the complete model (WI):

(WI) A member A_i of a collective G *we-intends* to do X if and only if
  (i) A_i intends to do his part of X.
  (ii) A_i has a belief to the effect that the joint action opportunities for X will obtain, especially that at least a sufficient number of the full-fledged and adequately informed members of G, as required for the performance of X, will (or at least probably will) do their parts of X.
  (iii) A_i believes that there is (or will be) a mutual belief among the participants of G to the effect that the joint action opportunities for X will obtain.

In the paradigmatic case of a we-intention, it is assumed that all participants in the joint action truly have the appropriate mutual beliefs. However, the model requires only A_i subjectively to *believe* that the other participants share the relevant mutual belief. Tuomela explains this less strong requirement by noting that "A_i's relevant action (based on his intention to do his part) after all depends on how he views the world rather than on how the world in fact is" (Tuomela and Miller 1988: 381). Indeed, A_i can be mistaken in his beliefs, including his belief regarding the existence of the other participants. Thus, as long as clauses (i) to (iii) are satisfied for him, a single agent "can in principle have a we-intention" (Tuomela 2005: 341). Tuomela, however, considers this an exceptional case, and further clarifications pertaining to the distinction between so-called I-mode and we-mode we-attitudes make it virtually impossible. This distinction and the social consequences of these modes will be the subject of the next section.

4.3 The Consequences of Collective Intentionality

Branching out from his original theory of collective action, in the 1990s Tuomela started to explore other collective attitudes, or we-attitudes. The expansion of his previous framework also corresponds to the development of new analytical instruments. While these innovations do not really constitute a fresh start, they entail a new terminology that I need to introduce here, starting with the definition of we-attitudes. We-attitudes are collective forms of plain individual attitudes with a propositional content *p* and can have all possible directions of fit: "We-attitudes encompass we-intentions, we-wants, we-beliefs, and in fact almost all kinds of psychological attitudes one cares to name" (Tuomela 1995: 38). Thus, collective intentions of the type captured by the (WI) model constitute particular instances of this broader category, namely *we-mode we-intentions* (see below).

We-attitudes are distinct from plain individual attitudes because they entail a doxastic reference to the other members of the group (Tuomela 1995: 37), that is, they entail certain "social beliefs" (Tuomela 2003b: 94). Tuomela (2007: 66) indicates three stipulations that need to be satisfied for any individual member of a group to have a we-attitude:

a. She must have an attitude with a given propositional content.
b. She must believe that others in the group have the same attitude with that propositional content.
c. She must also believe (or at least be disposed to believe) that there is a mutual belief among members of the group that they hold that attitude with the same propositional content.

For instance, for Sarah, a member of the Flat Earth Society, to accept that "we," the members of the Society, believe that the earth is flat means (a) to hold that belief, (b) to believe that the other members also believe so, and (c) to believe that there is a mutual belief in the Society concerning the flatness of the earth (Tuomela 1995: 37–38).

Against this backdrop, the most important innovation in Tuomela's analysis of we-attitudes consists in the distinction between different *modes* in which a person can have a we-attitude. The two most important modes are the "I-mode" and the "we-mode" (see Tuomela 2003b: 104). I will get to these concepts shortly, but it is worth getting the terminology straight first, because, as Tuomela (2007: 17) himself admits, these labels can be misleading. I-mode and we-mode are both modifiers of "we-attitudes" and correspond to "two kinds of collective intentionality" (Tuomela 2013: 23). This means that it is possible for a subject to have an *I-mode we-attitude* with content *p* or a *we-mode we-attitude* with the same content and direction of fit.

The two modes distinguish two ways of "functioning (that is, thinking and acting) qua a group member" (Tuomela 2003b: 98) and outline different relationships between the individual subjects and their reference group. A way of spelling out this point is to consider the two modes as expressing a subject's *reasons* for having a particular we-attitude. Tuomela (2007: 17) defines an "I-mode reason" as a reason that motivates and (inferentially) *privately commits* a group member to perform a certain action for a *private reason* in accordance to her wants, beliefs, or intentions. Conversely, he defines a "we-mode reason" as a reason that motivates a group member to perform a certain action for a *group reason* and, in a situation of mutual belief, (inferentially) *collectively commits* her to perform her part in a collective action in accordance with what the group in question wants, believes, intends, or requires to be the case *for the group*. Let us examine the characteristics of each mode more closely, starting with the we-mode.

As indicated in the previous paragraph, a central feature of the we-mode is what Tuomela calls for-groupness: "[T]he we-mode conceptually requires thinking (including 'emoting') and acting because of a group reason" (Tuomela 2007: 56). When forming a group or joining an already existing group, the members are assumed to "collectively accept" (see below) a *realm of concern*, that is, a set of topics that are considered of interest in a group context (but not necessarily in a private context), and about which the group has certain attitudes, for instance, beliefs (Tuomela 2007: 15; 2013: 27). To act "as a group member in the *core* sense is to act intentionally within the group's realm of concern" in a way that furthers the satisfaction and maintenance of the group core attitudes, or *ethos*, for the sake of the group and not merely for private interest (Tuomela 2013: 37).

It is important to note that acting for group reasons does not entail a wholehearted identification with—or a private endorsement of—group reasons (Tuomela 2013: 38). As Tuomela (2013: 93) emphasizes, "[S]ince the members of a group agent are themselves intentional agents, we must distinguish reasons for action on the level of the group agent and on the level of its members." In this sense, group reasons are "desire-independent reasons" with normative implications for the subjects holding them (Tuomela 2013: 40).

The idea of we-mode attitudes as "thinking and acting because of group reasons" has important consequences for the structure of Tuomela's argument. In particular, it entails the conceptual—although not ontological—priority of the group over the individual members (Tuomela 2005: 330). Consequently, the individual we-mode we-attitude of a single member no longer appears as a primitive phenomenon, but rather as an "individual slice" of the members' "joint attitude" (Tuomela 2013: 63) that a member has qua "one of us."

The concept of for-groupness constitutes the first of three fundamental characteristics or conditions of the we-mode. Tuomela calls the second one, the Collectivity Condition. This condition can be concisely illustrated with an example. Let us imagine that you and I share the we-intention expressed by the sentence, "We will get to the top of the hill." This sentence can be interpreted in at least two ways. In the first case, each of us separately has the goal to get to the top of the hill (and we know about each other's goal). According to this interpretation, as soon as you reach the top of the hill, your intention will be satisfied, even though I am still at the bottom of the slope. This, as we will see, corresponds to an I-mode we-intention.

A we-mode interpretation of the same sentence, however, entails that if I am still at the bottom of the slope, your goal would not be satisfied, because, even though you are at the top of the hill, "we" are not. In short, the Collectivity Condition expresses the idea that, within a collective g, a we-mode collective goal is satisfied for a member of g (as a member of g), "if and only if it is satisfied for every other member of g (qua a member of g)" (Tuomela 2007: 48). Although cases of collective goals or intentions provide the clearest examples, this condition can be generalized to any attitude (Tuomela 2007: 49). The Collectivity Condition has an interesting corollary that calls attention to specific situations in which a few members of the group or even a single member can satisfy the condition. This may be the case when the joint action of a group involves a task-relative division of labor between active and more passive group members or, as Tuomela (1984: 145–146) calls them, operative and nonoperative members. To grasp this distinction intuitively, we can think of a hockey team scoring a goal. The team includes the players on the bench, the trainer, the technical staff, etc., but the concrete act of scoring the goal was carried out by one or more players on the ice, that is, its operative members (Tuomela 1989: 472).

The third defining trait of the we-mode is the presence of a collective commitment among the group members. For Tuomela (2007: 27), the term commitment primarily means "being bound to something in a way that gives a sufficient reason for action related to the object of commitment." The collective nature of the commitment in the case of we-mode attitudes is grounded in the joint attitude of which the individual we-mode attitude is a slice. Let us consider the previous case of our we-mode we-intention to get to the hilltop and imagine that for some reason I have a problem that hinders my ascent, say, my backpack is too heavy. Our we-mode we-attitude would give you a reason for helping me out (for instance, by encouraging me or by carrying my backpack). As Tuomela puts it, with respect to such cases:

> That we really must be collectively committed can be seen by looking at what a group's successful action amounts to from the members' point of view: we must be collectively committed in a coordinated way for being able to see to it that X really comes about as planned; and this requires that we not only do our parts properly but also that we may help or even pressure others, if needed for X's successful coming about. (Tuomela 2013: 76)

The reasoning at play here is, indeed, a form of the inference (W2) discussed above (see Tuomela 2005: 342).

This kind of inference also allows we-mode-thinking members of the group to rebuke other we-mode-thinking members who deviated from the group's *ethos* (Tuomela 2007: 37). Furthermore, a similar criticism can be leveled against a group member who unexpectedly defects from the group. As Tuomela (2013: 43) puts it, a we-mode-thinking member of a group "cannot unilaterally rescind her collective commitment without the other's permission. This is because, so to speak, she has given up part of her authority to act to the group and needs the other's permission to get it back." In sum, the collective commitment requirement condenses the specific normative dimension of the we-mode and draws attention to the forms of "ought" and "may" that it entails. Like the previous condition, the collective commitment also extends to all sorts of attitudes.

This detailed discussion of the we-mode provides the backdrop for a shorter discussion of I-mode we-attitudes. To think and act in the I-mode, basically means "to think and act as a private person" (Tuomela 2013: 37), that is, to be privately committed to satisfying a certain attitude only for oneself and qua a private person (Tuomela 2013: 70). A we-attitude can be in the I-mode as long as the stipulations characterizing a we-attitude given at the start of this section are satisfied. For instance, the runners taking part in an organized sporting event can each have the I-mode we-attitude to finish the race and win it, believe that the other participants have the same attitude, and believe that this is mutually believed among the participants (Tuomela 1984: 37; 2013: 33).

Indeed, members acting or thinking in the I-mode can be highly committed to the group's *ethos*. These persons, however, would not be "full-fledged 'arms and legs in the collective body' in question," because their intentions rest on their *private* commitment (Tuomela 2007: 36). More generally, the I-mode "cannot satisfy any of the three constitutive criteria of the we-mode: group reason, the collectivity condition, and the collective commitment" (Tuomela 2013: 71). For instance, the "I-mode runner" will not feel bound to help another participant to finish the race—unless that participant happens to be a teammate with whom he shares the we-mode we-attitude that "we," that is, our team, will win the race. Accordingly, when compared to the we-mode, the I-mode does not provide the same kind of "glue" between the members (Tuomela 2007: 36).

4.4 The Constitution of Collective Intentionality

The distinctive nature of we-mode we-attitudes deserves closer scrutiny with regard to their constitution. How does an individual agent form the intention fully to act as a group member? How does a joint intention—that is, a we-mode we-intention—provide the "conceptual and metaphysical bridge between the group's intention and the personal we-mode we-intentions of its members" (Tuomela 2013: 63)? How do the specific commitments of we-mode joint intentions arise? The answers to these questions need to take into account the dynamic evolution of Tuomela's approach to the construction of group reasons. In this section, I will review three interconnected takes on this issue: the role of agreements, the Collective Acceptance Theory, and the Bulletin Board View as an example of an authority system.

4.4.1 Joint intentions through agreement

In his book *The Importance of Us*, Tuomela (1995: 127) introduces the idea of (we-mode) joint intentions as resulting from "a process involving the making of an explicit or implicit agreement." Tuomela (1995: 74) emphasizes that, in practice, any form of agreement-making "requires a 'communicative' change in the world—a relevant sign indicating agreement." This is necessary because all participants are "autonomous agents" who need some kind of communication or signaling to "make up their minds depending on what the others are thinking and doing" (Tuomela 2005: 335). Once the agreement is concluded, however, it entails a number of consequences for the participants, who now "1) are committed to performing their parts in the joint action, 2) are responsible to each other for performing their parts [...], and 3) are committed to furthering X [the object of the agreement] if they believe their extra contributions [...] are needed" (Tuomela 1995: 127).

This normative dimension of joint intentions has various sources. On the one hand, the notion of intention entails the idea of a commitment to action. Thus, "[J]oint intentions, *qua* intentions, must be taken to be commitments to realize their contents" (Tuomela 1995: 75). On the other hand, according to Tuomela (2000b: 60), the "entailment of an obligation can be regarded as a conceptual truth about the notion of agreement." At least in our culture, "Agreement making entails a publicly existing 'quasi-moral' obligation to participate in joint action" (Tuomela 2000b: 60). In fact, Tuomela, while insisting on the constitutive role of this obligation for we-mode we-intentions, remains quite vague with respect to its underlying nature, and remains open to different philosophical explanations (see Tuomela 1995: 421 n9 ; 2005: 337).

4.4.2 The Collective Acceptance Thesis

The discussion of the role of agreements in the formation of we-mode we-intentions constitutes an important stepping stone toward the development of Tuomela's Collective Acceptance Thesis. Collective acceptance can be considered the generative principle underlying the formation of joint intentions by collective agreement (Tuomela 2013: 124): it is through collective acceptance that the attitudes of the individual in a collective are amalgamated into "a group attitude collectively binding the group members" (Tuomela 2013: 125).

At its most basic level, collective acceptance amounts to upholding a content p as true for the group. To understand this idea, it is important to clarify first the notion of acceptance. We can start with a single agent, let us call her Marion, who accepts a content p, such as, "The sun shines" or "I shall read a book today." For Marion to accept p means that she accepts that p is true in the sense of a correspondence theory of truth (for instance, "The sun shines" is true if and only if the sun shines) or in the sense of the "correct assertability" of p (for instance, "The sun shines" can be correctly asserted as a true proposition in a given pragmatic context). Having accepted p, Marion can "use p as premise in her theoretical and practical reasoning and to act on the entailed truth (or correct assertability) of p" (Tuomela 2007: 125).

To do so, however, Marion must also think and act "in the right way" with respect to p, that is, she must consider the direction of fit of the sentence with content p. For instance, taken at face value the sentence "The sun is shining" has a word-to-world direction of fit. Since Marion accepts this sentence, she will have to deny, if asked, that it is overcast. The second example has instead a world-to-word direction of fit. In this case, Marion is responsible for the satisfaction of the sentence "I shall read a book today." In her practical reasoning, thus, she will for instance avoid going out for a day-long bike ride. We can then conclude that, because of her acceptance of p, Marion "is committed 'in the right way' to p (to its truth or correct assertability)" (Tuomela 2007: 125).

The idea of collective acceptance extends this analysis of individual acceptance in terms of correct assertability, premisibility, and commitment to a group context. For a group to collectively accept a content p means that the participants have collectively committed themselves (in the we-mode) to considering p as correctly assertable by the group members and to employing it, with the right direction of fit, as a premise "in their relevant inferences and as grounds for action when functioning as group-members" (Tuomela and Balzer 1999: 178).

Since the content p is accepted by the group and for the group, its correct assertability or truth will be "group-relative" (Tuomela 2007: 127). This observation has important corollaries. First, in the relevant group contexts, the members are both entitled and committed to the "right" use of p as a premise in their reasoning independently of its "objective" truth (Tuomela and Balzer 1999: 178). Thus, for a member of the Flat Earth Society, the notion that the earth is flat will constitute a valid premise for her further reasoning (say, for her explanation of sunsets).

Second, the correct assertability of a certain content and its premisibility is limited to group contexts and therefore applies only to the group members "when they act as group members as opposed to privately" (Tuomela 2003a: 128). In this sense, a "flat-earther" is entitled and in some cases ought to use the flatness of our planet as a premise in her reasoning and acting, while as a private person she can plan her trip overseas using a globe. To generalize this point, it is not possible for someone to rationally accept s and not-s. However, "[O]ne can to some extent rationally accept s *qua a member* of [group] G and accept not-s *as a private person*" (Tuomela 2003a: 128–129).

Leaving the broadest implications of this thesis for the last section of this chapter, we can now return to the central question of how we-mode we-attitudes emerge and how we-mode-functioning groups are created. In this respect, Tuomela (2013: 125) notes that "rational collective acceptance must involve a 'procedural' element where the members must fit together their 'we-mode proposal' for creating the group's intention (or their collective intention)." Tuomela first referred to this procedural element as an "authority system" and later refined his view by introducing what he calls the Bulletin Board View. The discussion of these two notions concludes this section.

4.4.3 Authority systems and the "Bulletin Board View"

Several accounts aimed at analyzing the constitution of social groups—some of which I will discuss in the second part of this book—are predicated on individuals sharing personal feelings of belonging. For Tuomela, however, the existence of such feelings (or similar concepts) does not provide a sufficient base for the constitution of proper social groups. What is missing in these cases is "a mechanism or procedure representing the process of the group members' [...] going from the multitude of 'I's' to a 'we'" (Tuomela 1995: 176–177). Through this procedure, they "give up their wills (involving rights to act) with respect to some relevant items in favor of a group will" (Tuomela 1995: 12). Tuomela names such a collective's group-will-formation system an authority system, or *a-system* for short.

To illustrate how an authority system works, Tuomela uses the image of a bulletin board stating a number of particular goals for the group and inviting the members to sign up. Tuomela interprets the act of putting one's signature on the board as a "communicative signaling of acceptance to participate" (Tuomela 2000b: 59). Assuming that a sufficient number of participants add their names, the signature collection would produce "an adequate categorical agreement and agreement-based joint intention" to pursue the joint goal mentioned on the board (Tuomela 2000b: 59). To append one's signature on the board has a double effect. On the one hand, it gives each participant "a group reason for participating in the agreed-upon action." On the other hand, "[I]t also gives a reason for each participant normatively to expect that the other participants indeed will participate" (Tuomela 2013: 132). This means that "a participant has the right to expect that the others will perform their parts and is also obliged to respect their analogous rights" (Tuomela 2013: 132).

Thus, Tuomela's Bulletin Board View underscores the generative power of an authority system: if a social group does not yet exist prior to the procedure, it emerges as its outcome; if it does exist, "those members who actually do sign up will form a subgroup of it" (Tuomela 2013: 132). But another interpretation is also possible: each time the group members put their signatures on the board they dynamically reconstitute or reaffirm the existence of the group around the newly stated (or restated) joint goal.

The Bulletin Board View draws attention to a number of requirements for an authority system to work properly (Tuomela 2007: 88–89; 2013: 132–133). First, the topic of the proposed joint action must be brought to the participants' attention in one way or another. The choice of the topic can originate from the initiative of a single person (or decision-making body) or be the result of discussion and negotiation. Second, the set of potential and actual participants has to be publicly indicated. The set may comprise all members of the group or a subset thereof. If the group does not preexist, it should be made clear which persons may join the prospective group. Third, the information about the intention to participate must be publicly available, at least within the group. The public nature of this information allows the participants to acquire mutual knowledge about each other's participatory intentions: they will know who intends to contribute to the joint goal and that others also know who those persons are. In sum, the Bulletin Board View "emphasizes the epistemic publicity (the public availability of relevant information) of full-blown joint intention" (Tuomela 2005: 336).

Tuomela (2005: 338–339) notes several advantages of the Bulletin Board View with respect to other generative concepts of collective intentionality. The most important is certainly the following: According to the Bulletin Board View, the formation of a joint intention, one that satisfies all the criteria of the we-mode, does not require a prior joint intention among the participants (thus avoiding circularity). As Tuomela (2013: 136) underscores, "We-mode collective acceptance [...] does not require that the process leading to collective acceptance satisfy those criteria [of the we-mode]." Indeed, "[M]ere personal intentions are enough for entering one's signature on the board" (Tuomela 2005: 339). Thus, according to Tuomela's account, collective intentionality (in the we-mode) is a conceptually irreducible phenomenon that can arise, in appropriate conditions, on the ground of plain intentionality.

4.5 Collective Intentionality and Social Ontology

In his work, Tuomela mostly focuses on the role of we-intentions in the constitution of social actions and social groups. However, he clearly considers collective intentionality, and notably we-mode we-attitudes, as the key ingredient in the creation and maintenance of social institutions. Tuomela touches upon broader questions of social ontology in particular in relation to his Collective Acceptance Thesis (see above). In this respect, it is worth noting the performative dimension conceptually entailed in the notion of collective acceptance, which confers to a sentence *s* a collective-social character. As Tuomela puts it,

> A sentence *s* is *collective-social* in a primary sense in a group *G* if and only if (a) it is true for group *G* that the members of group *G* collectively accept *s*, and that (b) they collectively accept *s* if and only if *s* is correctly assertable (or true). (Tuomela and Balzer 1999: 181)

Collective acceptance allows for the production of new social facts to the extent that, if a group collectively accept *s*, say, "Squirrel furs are money," then squirrel furs are money, at least within the group (e.g., Tuomela 2002: 126). Conversely, to count as money, squirrel furs must be accepted as such within the group. This "reflexive" implication (Tuomela 2002: 194–200) brands the content or proposition *s* with the "mark of the social" (Tuomela and Balzer 1999: 189).

Tuomela also outlines a path to extend his model beyond the scale of face-to-face interaction to larger groups. His strategy emphasizes the role of operative members carrying out the group joint intentions and actions. In the case of large groups such as an international corporation, "[T]he nonoperative members can in a central way take part in the group's intentions simply by functioning as group members who accept the operatives' joint intentions" (Tuomela 2013: 89). For instance, the employees in a local store, as members of the company, can accept the joint decision of the board of directors to push a new technology on the international market by selling the latest company's products to their customers. A precise knowledge of the company's commercial strategy on their part is not necessary. Tuomela's reflections in this domain remain a rough sketch. However, they suggest the possibility of accounting for anonymous social groups relying, for instance, on a centralized and remotely accessible "bulletin board," thus dispensing with the need for pairwise communication (Tuomela 2013: 135).

Indeed, the importance of publicly available information for the constitution of we-mode we-intentions in a group context of any size makes Tuomela's account an ideal candidate for a social-scientific analysis of collective intentionality. Before turning to the empirical data, however, there is another approach to collective intentionality that is worth discussing in some detail, namely the one put forward by Margaret Gilbert.

5

Margaret Gilbert—Plural Subjects and Joint Commitment

5.1 Situating Gilbert's Argument and Method

5.1.1 The central question

The work of Margaret Gilbert (b. 1942) on collective intentionality is rooted in the analysis of the building blocks of human sociality. Throughout her work, Gilbert develops and refines a framework to tackle the following question: "What precisely is a social group?" (Gilbert 1989: 1). Her shortest answer is that a social group is a *plural subject*. Defending a holistic conception of sociality, plural subject theory is intended to capture those phenomena which, in our everyday parlance, we address or imply when we express a collective standpoint, such as when we speak of *our* goal, *our* belief, or *our* effort (Gilbert 1996b). As Gilbert argues, plural subjects are an omnipresent feature of human life. Not only "paradigmatic social groups" such as families, guilds, or armies are plural subjects; a large portion of our everyday reality can be understood in terms of plural subject phenomena, including "*social rules* and *conventions*, *group languages*, *everyday agreements*, *collective beliefs* and *values*, and *genuinely collective emotions*" (Gilbert 2003: 55).

The constitutive element of a plural subject is a joint commitment. In a nutshell, a joint commitment is "a single commitment of two or more people" (Gilbert 2006: 126), who collectively espouse a certain goal "as one." In other words, a joint commitment "is an instruction to the parties to see to it that they act in such a way as to emulate as best they can a single body with the goal in question" (Gilbert 2014a: 33; see also Gilbert 2014e: 7). This formulation needs some unpacking. What joint commitments are, how they form, and what social consequences they entail are the main topics of this chapter. For the present moment, it will suffice to remember that any group of jointly committed people constitutes a plural subject.

5.1.2 Ontological considerations: neither singularist nor supra-individualist

Gilbert's reflections directly address the problem of social ontology. As she (1996g: 177) notes, "the philosophical analysis of society is bound to take up the ontological question regarding the nature of human social groups and their relationship with the humans who are their members." Plural subject theory explicitly contrasts with an individualist—or as

Gilbert often calls it, *singularist*—standpoint on sociality that seeks to reduce collective phenomena to individual intentions, analyzed in terms of their coordination (see Gilbert 1989: 12). At the same time, Gilbert equally takes her distance from ontologically supra-individualist positions. In her view, such a standpoint would not only pose important metaphysical problems for the social sciences but would also call into question the role of human intentionality in the construction of the social world.

Gilbert treats the distinction between singularism and holism as a problem of conceptual analysis. To what do we refer when we, in everyday conversations, use collectivity concepts? The singularist standpoint is based on a conceptual scheme that puts singular agents and their individual goals at the center of social analysis. Gilbert acknowledges the conceptual parsimony of singularist approaches, as they aim to analyze sociality without introducing any further entity beyond individual preferences, expectations, and so on (Gilbert 2014e: 1–4). Yet, she also notes that Ockham's razor must bow its head when theories fall short of the reality they seek to explain.

When it comes to our everyday understanding of the social world, Gilbert (1996b: 4) maintains that "reasoning on the basis of the agent's preferences and rationality is not as powerful a tool as is often assumed." In particular, the singularist standpoint cannot provide a basis for the "ever-present use of the collective 'we'" (Gilbert 2014e: 4). Nor it can make sense of the prescriptive dimension that appears to be interwoven with the use of collectivity concepts (see Gilbert 1989: 413–416; 2000c: 7–8; 2014e: 5), including, for instance, the fact that *our* decision entails *normative* expectations regarding *my* future behavior, independent of moral considerations (see Gilbert 1996e: 73–77). In her view, our understanding of collective realities needs to be grounded in a *holistic* concept (Gilbert 2000c: 3).

The mention of a holistic standpoint can arouse the suspicion that dubious ontologies such as a "social spirit" or a "group mind" are being introduced in the analysis. On numerous occasions, Gilbert seeks to dispel such misunderstandings (see e.g., Gilbert 1989: 430; 2000c: 3). Although the term plural subject can spark associations with ideas of subjectivity or consciousness, Gilbert (2014e: 9–10) underscores that she has "never intended to suggest that there is any collective or group consciousness that is somehow independent of the consciousness of any individual group member." The concept of joint commitment allows for the ascribing of a particular attitude, for instance, a belief, to a plurality of persons that will be the *subject* of that attitude (Gilbert 2009: 182). This does not imply that the plural subject that believes "is something that exists 'over and above' the individuals involved." Its existence remains "*a function of a way these individuals have been, and are*" (Gilbert 2014e: 10).

In this regard, Gilbert's holistic approach does not presuppose any heteronomic determinism in terms of "externally observable structures of systems" (Gilbert 1989: 13), either. Her philosophical standpoint is predicated on the idea that "viable sociological collectivity concepts will entail that facts about human collectivities, in particular about their actions, are constituted by facts about the ideas and acts of will of human beings" (Gilbert 1989: 417). Yet, for Gilbert,

> In order for individual human beings to form collectivities, they must take on a special character, a "new" character, in so far as they need not, *qua* human beings,

have that character. Moreover, humans must form a whole or unit of a special kind, a unit of a kind that can now be specified precisely: they must form a plural subject. (Gilbert 1989: 431)

This means that, to form a collectivity in our intuitive sense, the participants "must see themselves as bound together in a highly specific way" (Gilbert 1989: 13). The task ahead, therefore, is to elucidate the precise nature of that tie.

To tackle this key issue, Gilbert uses two closely interrelated methods. The first consists of a close analysis of our everyday collectivity concepts. I shall say more about this method below. The second is grounded in the detailed investigation, mostly in the form of thought experiments, of everyday interactions and small-scale, temporary social situations, such as discussing a poem with friends or going for a walk together. I will discuss the latter method in the following section.

5.1.3 Methodological considerations: microanalysis of everyday concepts and interactions

Gilbert (1989: 3) considers that the primary aim of her analysis is "to make explicit the structure of certain everyday concepts." Against the viewpoint of Durkheim (e.g., 1982: 73), who disputed the utility of everyday concepts for sociological analysis, Gilbert (1989: 4) argues that "social science could use a careful examination of everyday notions" through the lens of the "'analytic' branch of philosophy." Indeed, she maintains that the "intuitive concept of a collectivity picks out a phenomenon of the greatest interest" (Gilbert 1989: 10). The practical work of conceptual analysis can hardly be expressed in abstract terms. Broadly framed, this approach aims "perspicuously to describe the phenomenon to which the relevant everyday statements refer" (Gilbert 2014e: 3). Some examples should help clarify how Gilbert proceeds in her analysis.

The first-person plural pronoun "we" undoubtedly figures among the most basic concepts that we use in our everyday language to refer to some form of collectivity or group. Yet on closer examination, we can see that this pronoun can express at least two distinct social arrangements. Let us imagine the following situation involving three persons. Oliver meets Evelyne and Fabian in the library and asks them: "What are you doing?" Evelyne answers: "We are studying." Looking on the desk, Oliver sees that Evelyne is revising her environmental sciences notes, while Fabian is reading a biography of Marx. On a separate occasion, Oliver meets Evelyne and Fabian again, asks the same question, and obtains the same answer, but he notes that he has interrupted a discussion the two were having on post-colonial theory, the subject of a forthcoming exam. In the second occasion, it seems, the pronoun "we" was used in a stronger sense, suggesting that Evelyne and Fabian were sharing into an action. In the first case, instead, Evelyne used it in a weaker sense, indicating that she and Fabian were *both* studying (Gilbert 1989: 154–155, 168; 2006: 145).

The aim of conceptual analysis, in this case, would be to identify what exactly the differences are between these two uses of "we," what conception of collectivities they entail, and under what circumstances the strong sense can be legitimately used. The fact that not all uses of the strong sense are legitimate is suggested, for instance, by common situations in which someone uses the strong sense of "we" to imply a common intention that the other party denies: "What do you mean by *we*?" Evelyne might ask, distancing herself from Fabian after he, out of the blue, had put a hand on her shoulder and told Oliver, "Of course, *we* will help you move next week." Gilbert (1989: 178) speaks in this context of a "tendentious" use of "we" (see also Gilbert 2006: 145–146). In her book *On Social Facts*, Gilbert concludes that the "full blooded" or "central" sense of "we" in everyday speech "refers to a plural subject" (Gilbert 1989: 200). Gilbert often uses an asterisk—we*, us*, our*—to designate this specific acceptation.

Scenarios like the one sketched above are an integral part of Gilbert's method. As narrative inventions, their goal is not faithfully to reproduce an empirical reality but to describe logical possibilities and "reveal conceptual structures" (Gilbert 1989: 11). As such, they seek to highlight the concept "that is implicit in the judgments we are most immediately inclined to make about what counts as an X and what does not" (Gilbert 1989: 11). Using these methods, Gilbert comes to the conclusion that, at the core of all social groups, there is the general concept of joint commitment. In sum, her thesis is that "to understand the structure of joint commitment is to understand the deep or underlying structure of the smallest carrier of genuine sociality—the social atom" (Gilbert 2003: 41). It is therefore toward the conceptualization of joint commitment that I turn in the next section.

5.2 The Conceptualization of Collective Intentionality

5.2.1 A paradigmatic illustration: walking together

Gilbert's numerous vignettes and their analysis can take up a great deal of space. For the sake of concision, in this chapter I shall generally keep such examples to a minimum. Here, however, I will indulge in an abbreviated and simplified paraphrase of one of her most famous examples, as it will help to elucidate the more technical aspects of Gilbert's standpoint.

In her 1990 article "Walking Together: A Paradigmatic Social Phenomenon" (reprinted as Gilbert 1996g), she wonders what is it for two people "to go for a walk together?" She starts by imagining a single person, whom I shall call Karolina, walking on a road. After a while, Karolina notes that another person is walking besides her. At this point, their physical proximity does not seem a sufficient reason to say that the two are "walking together." Karolina does recognize the other person; it is her friend Piotr. It is a while since they had a chat, and, therefore, she would be happy if Piotr continued to walk alongside her. Piotr feels the same way. As far as they are concerned, however, these unexpressed personal goals do not put them in any way closer together.

Would the situation be different if their goals were out in the open? For example, each of them could state, "My goal right now is to go on walking in your company." If both take the affirmation of the other at face value, the answer must be, according to Gilbert, negative. To see how it is so, we might consider what we would expect if Karolina and Piotr were, in fact, taking a walk together. In that case, we can imagine that, should Piotr suddenly start to walk faster, Karolina, noting that she is being left behind, might shout: "Piotr, you have to slow down!" In the absence of special circumstances, we might feel that Karolina is *entitled* to rebuke Piotr in such a way. Conversely, we could say that Piotr has an *obligation* to rectify the situation. The same would be true if the roles were reversed. Thus, we could say that, in this situation, "[E]ach has a right to the other's attention and corrective action" (Gilbert 1996g: 180). The situation of "common knowledge" sketched above does not seem to provide any foundation for such entitlements and obligations.

According to Gilbert (1996g: 184), the situation would have been different if, upon meeting, Karolina and Piotr had "*join[ed] forces* with the other in accepting the goal that they walk in one another's company." To do so, a simple exchange would have sufficed. Imagine Piotr asking Karolina whether she minds if he joins her for a walk. "Not at all," she answers, "I should like to have some company." What has changed in comparison to the previous example? Remaining on a pre-theoretical level, we can consider that, now, Piotr and Karolina can justifiably say that "going for a walk together is our* goal." What Piotr and Karolina each did is to offer their will "to be part of a pool of wills that is dedicated, as one, to that goal" (Gilbert 1996g: 185). In other words, what their verbal exchange achieved is "binding together a set of individual wills so as to constitute a single, 'plural will' dedicated to a particular goal" (Gilbert 1996g: 185); they constituted a plural subject of that goal. Furthermore, each of them is now entitled and obligated to behave in a certain way "*qua* a member of the whole" (Gilbert 1996g: 186). Should Piotr suddenly break away from Karolina and start running in the opposite direction, she might, taken aback, shout at him: "Piotr, what are you doing?"

Against the backdrop of this vignette, we can now turn to a more formal and argumentative analysis of the concept of joint commitment. The first step in illuminating the concept of joint commitment is to clarify the idea of commitment in relation to a single agent. Then, we can identify what it is that changes when two or more people are jointly committed.

5.2.2 From personal to joint commitment

The notion of a *personal* commitment presupposes a fairly intuitive model of intentional action, according to which a single person "intends to do something and, being guided by that intention, behaves in such a way as to fulfill it" (Gilbert 2003: 46). Having so decided, this person can be said to be "thereby committed in some intuitive sense to do that thing" (Gilbert 2006: 127). This commitment does not have an obvious social dimension, for no other people need to be involved, "nor does it arise on the basis of some pre-existing moral requirement" (Gilbert 2014a: 31). A personal commitment is, consequently, a commitment that is created by one person alone as the result solely of that person's unilateral exercise of her will (Gilbert 2006: 128).

Following this reasoning, through the use of her will, a person binds herself to some course of action. Why is this the case? According to Gilbert (2006: 131), decisions give a person "sufficient reason to act in a certain way." As one might be said "to be *bound* [...] to do something one has sufficient reason to do" (Gilbert 2006: 129), it is rationality that requires one to act in accordance with one's decision. In this sense, decisions, as well as intentions or efforts, differ from inclinations, urges, or enthusiasm, for these do not involve commitments. These sentiments can give someone a disposition to do something, but they do not provide her yet with sufficient reasons to do it (Gilbert 2006: 131). In other words, one can be inclined (etc.) to do something without, in any intuitive sense, being subject to a commitment to do it (Gilbert 2000e: 20). For this reason, when it comes to one person's reasons for action, Gilbert (2000d: 52) considers that "commitments 'trump' mere inclinations."

The discussion so far draws attention to the normative force of commitment. Without much effort, we can imagine a person who, after failing to abide by a personal decision she made, perhaps while indulging a sudden urge, reprehends herself, in her inner monologue, for her weakness of will. Indeed, she might "understand herself to be *answerable* to herself"—and only to herself—for her lapse, or feel that "she *owed it to herself*" to follow a certain course of action (Gilbert 2006: 133). In short,

> If one violates a commitment to which one is subject, one has done what in some sense one was not supposed to do. One has to some extent and in some sense done something wrong—something open to criticism. (Gilbert 2003: 47)

This normative force holds true as long as the commitment is not rescinded. Yet, the subject of a personal commitment, as the sole creator of such commitment, is in a special position to put an end to it. What this person needs to do is simply to change her mind. In this sense, the author of a personal commitment has "*the authority* unilaterally to rescind her own decision" (Gilbert 2000d: 52). What is more, no one is in the same position: "I can persuade you to change your mind, but I cannot directly change it" (Gilbert 2008: 491).

We are now in a position to discuss how the structure of the commitment may change when it involves two or more actors. Remember, Gilbert (e.g., 2003: 49) defines a joint commitment as "a commitment of two or more people." As the example of Karolina and Piotr intuitively suggests, this idea does not simply express an "aggregate of personal commitments" (Gilbert 2000e: 21). Indeed, the people participating in a joint commitment remain "individual human beings" and yet "a joint commitment and hence a plural subject is in a sense unitary and indivisible" (Gilbert 2014c: 56). Thus, if we say that the subject of a (personal) commitment is the person bounded by it, "[I]n the case of a joint commitment, one can properly say that its subject comprises two or more people" (Gilbert 2006: 134–135). In a similar way, we can say that the jointly committed people "comprise the *creator* of the commitment" (Gilbert 2006: 135).

The unitary nature of a joint commitment is expressed in Gilbert's (1989: 303) metaphor, reminiscent of the frontispiece of Hobbes's *Leviathan*, of a group of people acting—or indeed having any type of intentional state—"*as a single body.*" Doing something as a single body is not a matter of all parties doing the same thing or participating in the same activity (Gilbert 1989: 155–157; 2000d: 54). Rather, it entails that the parties act as partners. That is,

> Two or more people are acting together if they are jointly committed to espousing as a body a certain goal, and each one is acting in a way appropriate to the

achievement of that goal, and each one is doing this in light of the fact that he or she is subject to a joint commitment to espouse the goal in question as a body. (Gilbert 2014a: 34)

As is the case for personal commitments, a joint commitment also has a normative force in the sense that it gives the participants sufficient reasons to follow the course of action dictated by the joint commitment and thus places constraints on their behavior (Gilbert 2000e: 24).

Indeed, as Gilbert (2003: 57) emphasizes, "[T]here is no need for a personal decision by each of the participants in favor of fulfillment of the joint commitment," as the joint commitment alone "is sufficient to rationalize behavior." Or, to put it even more bluntly: "*[G]iven a shared intention* [based on a joint commitment] *the corresponding personal intentions are redundant from a motivational point of view*" (Gilbert 2000e: 27). The flip side of this argument is that any joint commitment has important social consequences, since it conceptually entails certain obligations and entitlements among the parties involved (Gilbert 2000e: 17, 25).

5.3 The Consequences of Collective Intentionality

In the most general terms, on Gilbert's account (2009: 175) shared intention (that is, intentions rooted in joint commitment) entail "that each party to a shared intention is obligated to each to act as appropriate to the shared intention in conjunction with the rest." This means, first, that "each participant has an obligation not to act contrary to the shared intention" (Gilbert 2000e: 17) or, more straightforwardly, to "*conform* to the shared intention" (Gilbert 2009: 175). Accordingly, all parties to a shared intention are *entitled* to the others' "appropriate performances" (Gilbert 2000e: 17) and therefore have the standing to rebuke a participant who behaves in a way that is opposed to the shared intention (Gilbert 2000e: 17; 2009: 177). This observation also suggests that in case of a conflict between a personal and a joint commitment, reason requires the latter to prevail (Gilbert 2006: 158–159). The so-called obligation criterion presented in this paragraph does not actually preclude someone from acting contrary to the shared intention. The fact that one can fail to meet his or her obligations, however, does not in any way disprove the existence of such obligations (Gilbert 2009: 175).

The self-contained normative force of joint commitment thus gives rise to the possibility of a discrepancy or disjunction between individual and collective intentions. Contrary to singularist accounts that require each member of a collective to have the appropriate *personal* intentions, Gilbert (2000e: 27) maintains that "it is possible from a logical point of view for a shared intention to exist without the corresponding personal intentions." Shared intention is possible even if *none* of the individuals involved have a personal contributory intention (Gilbert 2009: 171–172). This insight is supported by the observation that each participant in a shared intention can privately form an opposite personal intention without making the shared intention void.[1]

The last statements should not be read as implying that a shared intention is never—or even cannot be—accompanied by personal contributory intentions of the participants. In fact, such intentions are possible and, arguably, common. The point, as Gilbert (2008: 491) emphasizes, "is not that generally speaking when there is a shared intention there are no such intentions. The point is, rather, that it is in principle possible correctly to ascribe a shared intention to the parties when one or more of them lack contributory intents."

Still, Gilbert (e.g., 2009: 174) notes that the possibility for a person to have personal intentions at odds with her joint commitment (and, potentially, to act on such personal intentions) should not be confused with the capacity unilaterally to withdraw from a joint commitment. Here lies a fundamental distinction between personal and joint commitments. If a person can, as discussed above, by a simple change of mind rescind her *personal* commitment to a certain course of action, she does not have the authority to do so with a *joint* commitment (Gilbert 2000e: 21). Why is it so? As the case of a personal commitment suggests, only the *subject* of the commitment is in the position to nullify it. If we think back to the example of Karolina and Piotr, we can see that the subject of their joint commitment to go for a walk together is neither Karolina nor Piotr alone, but the unit of them both. Accordingly, neither of them can rescind the joint commitment—only the two of them, *together*.

Following Gilbert (2000e: 29), we come to the conclusion that, once two or more parties enter into a joint commitment, "the single thing that constrains the practical reasoning of both parties is something over which neither party has absolute control." Thus,

> If one of the parties wishes to act contrary to the joint commitment, he can do so without fault only if the other parties have, in effect, waived their rights to conforming action, or, in other words, concurred with his decision not to conform. (Gilbert 2006: 148)

Gilbert (2003: 45) regards this "permission requirement" as an intrinsic feature of joint commitment—indeed, as a conceptual truth about shared intention (see Gilbert 2000e: 17). How does a person, then, put herself in a situation so full of important consequences? I will tackle this question in the next section.

5.4 The Constitution of Collective Intentionality

Gilbert devotes close attention to the formation of joint commitments, considering a number of options before settling on a specific account. For instance, she rejects the need for the parties to conclude an agreement in order to jointly commit themselves (Gilbert 2006: 116–118). Indeed, Gilbert (2014c: 49) recognizes a "close connection […] between joint commitments and agreements." Yet in her view, this connection goes in the opposite direction to the postulation of the agreement hypothesis, in the sense that "an everyday agreement can be understood as a joint decision, and a joint decision, in turn, can be construed as constituted by a joint commitment to uphold a certain decision as a body" (Gilbert 2014c: 49). How then does Gilbert proceed?

Gilbert's positive account of joint commitment formation rests, analytically, on four constitutive conditions that she deems collectively sufficient and individually necessary for the creation of a joint commitment, considered in its unity. These are the following: the participation of all parties, the specific expression of matching intentions, a condition of common knowledge among the parties, and a shared conceptual framework. Let us review them in order.

The first criterion posits that, in the absence of special conditions, all the parties involved in a joint commitment must participate in its creation or its extension, modification, etc. (Gilbert 2003: 49–50). Once the joint commitment is in place, each participant is committed through it. In this sense, each of them has an individual commitment "to promoting the object of the joint commitment to the best of his or her ability in conjunction with the other parties" (Gilbert 2003: 50). Yet, these individual commitments cannot exist on their own but derive from the joint commitment (Gilbert 2000d: 53). To this extent, they are not *personal* commitments; "they are not [...] the ultimate creation of the respective persons" (Gilbert 2003: 50). The individual commitments created through joint commitment are, thus, *interdependent*, in the sense that they must rise and fall together, binding all participants *simultaneously* (Gilbert 1996g: 185).

But what must the parties *do*, then, to create a joint commitment? The first step in this direction is the matching expression of a particular commitment of the will. This idea should be read as follows: In order to create a joint commitment, each of the participants must express, with words or with some form of communicative behavior, his or her *readiness* to be *jointly committed* with the others with respect to a certain intentional content (e.g., Gilbert 2003: 53–54; 2006: 138–140). If Piotr asks Karolina, "Do you feel like going for a walk?" and she nods and smiles at him, we can say that both expressed their readiness to be jointly committed to go for a walk together. At this point, however, the source providing them with a reason for acting will not be their personal expressions of readiness, but the joint commitment that so ensued. This requires the matching expressions of readiness to be "common knowledge." Here, the expression "common knowledge" is a technical term developed by game theorists (e.g., Lewis 1969) and designates a situation that involves "many levels of potential knowledge of another's knowledge" (Gilbert 2014c: 43; see Gilbert 1989: 186–197). To cut a long story short, "[I]f some fact is *common knowledge* between A and B [...], then the fact is entirely out in the open between them—and, at some level, all are aware that this is so" (Gilbert 2006: 121). (Gilbert sometimes adds an asterisk to open* to make this acceptation explicit.)

The account so far draws attention to the importance of interaction and communication for the creation of joint commitment. As Gilbert puts it,

> A typical context for the formation of a joint commitment of two people involves the parties in face-to-face contact, mutually expressing their readiness to be jointly committed, in conditions of common knowledge. As the parties understand, the joint commitment is in place when and only when each of the relevant expressions has been made. (Gilbert 2000e: 21)

Yet there is also a fundamental *conceptual* condition to the creation of a joint commitment. As the discussion above indicates, the parties understand that by expressing, *mutatis mutandis*, "the same thing," they commit themselves in a particular way: they give rise to a joint commitment (Gilbert 2003: 53). This demands that they have a *concept* of a joint commitment. Further, "[I]t also means that those who constitute a plural subject [via joint commitment] know that they do, and will thus think of themselves as *us**" (Gilbert 1989: 205).

It should be emphasized that this does not imply in any way that the members of the group must have a term for "we*," nor do the phrases "joint commitment" or "plural subject" need to be part of their language. Drawing on her favorite example, Gilbert notes:

> According to my proposal about walking together, one knows what a joint commitment is if one knows what it is to go for a walk with another person, since one goes for a walk with another person only if he and that other person are party to a particular joint commitment. One need not be able to spell things out. (Gilbert 2006: 139)

This last remark underscores, once again, the specificity of Gilbert's approach. Through her inquiry into our use of everyday collectivity concepts, she does not seek to uncover "under what conditions from a physical point of view are people doing things together," but, rather, "what thoughts or conceptions must be involved in order for people to count as (intentionally) [doing something] together" (Gilbert 1989: 165). As Gilbert (1989: 169) succinctly puts it, "It is not our dancing together, say, which 'creates' or is a precondition for the appropriateness of 'we'. Rather, it is the perceived appropriateness of 'we' which makes our dancing together possible."

Still, Gilbert's account leaves a fundamental question open: where does the concept of joint commitment (or plural subject) come from? As do other authors in the field of the philosophy of society (e.g., Searle 1996: 25–26), Gilbert seems to consider collective intentionality, with the conceptual apparatus that it requires, to be an innate human faculty:

> It seems reasonable to conjecture that the best way to get humans to do things together from the behavioural point of view, to dance and walk and talk and so on in a meshing and harmonious way, is to have them see themselves as parts of a plural subject or as joining forces, to see themselves no longer as, or as entirely, independent individuals. To put it crudely, if a benevolent creator were to make a set of rational agents like human beings, she would be wise to give them an innate concept of a plural subject. (Gilbert 1989: 167)

The conceptual irreducibility of joint commitment is one of the most contentious points in the debate between Gilbert and proponents of a singularist standpoint, notably Michael Bratman. Still, Gilbert's adamant defense of her position is predicated, among other things, on the incapacity of singularist standpoints to account for what she considers the intrinsic normative dimension of joint commitment (Gilbert 2008,

2014f). Since this question is so central to her account of collective intentionality, it is worth exploring in some detail.

5.4.1 The nature of collective obligations

As the discussion so far demonstrates, situations in which two or more people act (or, more broadly, intend) *together* are very common in our everyday life. And yet, while doing something together intuitively appears quite natural to us, it entails a normative dimension that seems to be grounded in nothing but the collective action itself. This may prompt some legitimate questions, such as,

> How can something that seems natural, relatively primitive, a matter of "brute fact" intrinsically involve something that seems to be of a different order: rights against persons and obligations toward them? How are the rights intrinsic to acting together possible? (Gilbert 2006: 115)

Gilbert's answer to these questions can be analytically separated into two parts, which, however, constitute two faces of the same coin. The first, more intuitive part focuses on the violation of a joint commitment and links its normative consequences to the "jointness" of such commitment. The second, conceptually more complex part, puts forward a positive understanding of rights and obligations and outlines their compatibility with the idea of joint commitments. Let us review them in order.

As discussed above, according to Gilbert's account a joint commitment cannot arise merely from matching personal commitments, and all parties involved in the joint commitment must participate in its creation. As the parties create what they may call "our*" commitment, they become "as a body" the subject of that commitment. But when one person involved in the joint commitment acts contrary to it in some way, who is the "victim" of her action? In light of the structure of joint commitments, it seems that all the participants, *qua* members of the joint commitment, are in this position, including the person who commits the violation. In fact, this person is not going against her personal commitment; "she is going against *their* commitment" (Gilbert 2000d: 55).

From this, it follows that "each party is answerable to all parties for any violation of the joint commitment" (Gilbert 2003: 49). Conversely, the parties in a joint commitment "gain a special standing in relation to one another's actions" (Gilbert 2000a: 40). Thus, as Gilbert argues,

> [I]t may seem appropriate to say that when I am subject to a joint commitment requiring me to do certain things, *all of the parties have a right* to the relevant actions from me, and correlatively, *I am under an obligation* to all of them to perform these actions. (Gilbert 2000a: 40)

In this sense, a joint commitment entails certain *normative* expectations among the participants—to be distinguished from *plain* expectations regarding what someone will (probably) do in the future. The parties to a joint commitment understand that, if they violate such a commitment, they may incur some form of (more or less institutionalized) sanction (Gilbert 2000a: 40) and that, conversely, they have the *standing* to demand certain actions or intentions from each other.

To better determine the nature of the "rights" and "obligations" inextricably interwoven into the fabric of a joint commitment, Gilbert draws on the work of the legal philosophers H. L. A. Hart (1955) and Joel Feinberg (1970). Following Hart, Gilbert distinguishes between two kinds of rights, namely *liberties* and *directed* rights. In the case of liberties, a right does not have a duty (or obligation) as a correlative. For instance, "Two people walking along both see a ten-dollar bill in the road twenty yards away, and there is no clue as to the owner. Neither of the two are under a 'duty' to allow the other to pick it up; each has in this sense a right to pick it up" (Hart 1955: 179). On the contrary, directed rights have the following form: "[O]ne person's right against a second person to an action of the second person is said to be equivalent to the second person's obligation to the right-holder to perform the action" (Gilbert 2008: 496). Gilbert characterizes the obligations of joint commitment as structurally equivalent with *directed* rights (Gilbert 2006: 35–41). Indeed, the obligation criterion discussed above, "could just as well have been labeled the rights criterion, as long as that is understood to refer to rights that are the equivalent of directed duties" (Gilbert 2008: 469).

In a second step, Gilbert grounds the deontic power of these directed obligations in the idea that they are "'owed' to special persons (who have rights)" (Gilbert 2006: 39). This means that "one has an obligation of the kind in question if and only if *one owes someone a particular action*" (Gilbert 2006: 39). Here, the use of the verbs "to owe" and "to own" need some further specification. Following Feinberg, Gilbert (2008: 497) considers that if a right-holder (per definition) is in a position to *demand* something—say, a specific future action from someone—he already *owns* that action in some intuitive sense. It follows that,

> Until the action is performed he is owed that action by the person concerned, thus being in a position to demand it of him prior to its being performed and to rebuke him if it is not performed. If it is performed, one might say that it has finally come into the possession of the right-holder in the only way that it can. (Gilbert 2008: 498)

When two or more people enter a joint commitment, their wills are simultaneously and interdependently bound as they are, jointly, the creator and subject of that commitment. As such, to whom do they *owe* conformity to a certain course of action? As Gilbert points out, none of the participants in the joint commitment *personally* "owns" the future actions of the others. Yet, any one of them is entitled to demand conformity, "as [the] co-creator of the joint commitment and co-owner of the actions in question" (Gilbert 2006: 155). Each member is thus in a position to say, using the first-person plural, "'That action is *ours*! Perform it!'" (Gilbert 2006: 155), or, using the first-person singular, "'Give me that, it's mine—qua one of us!'" (Gilbert 2008: 507).

By stressing the intrinsic normativity of joint commitment, Gilbert distances herself from any philosophical stances that would characterize the entailed obligations in terms of "moral requirements" (Gilbert 2014e: 5). For instance, in contrast to moral obligations, the obligation of joint commitment is absolute rather than context-sensitive and cannot be nullified by a change of circumstances—as is the case, for example, of the moral obligation to assist an unattended child, which can be superseded by the moral obligation to save a nearby old man from a sudden heart attack (Gilbert 1996a: 296–300; 2006: 159–161). Indeed, one may violate a joint commitment in order to save a life. However, "what our judgment tells us is precisely when we may *violate* or break an agreement" (Gilbert 1996a: 298). Thus, until a joint commitment is rescinded, its normative force remains in place. A similar line of argument can be applied to the case of coerced joint commitments, to which one or more parties are forced to enter, for instance under threat of violence (Gilbert 1996a).

Finally, Gilbert (2008: 507) considers that "it is possible for people jointly to commit one another to intend as a body to do something that considered in itself [...] is, for short, an evil act." Her position might bring to mind John Locke's considerations about honor among thieves. Unlike Locke, however, for Gilbert the source of the reciprocal abidance to their contracts among thieves is not merely convenience, nor is it a moral principle. Once again, the obligation in question differs from a moral requirement because it is rooted in the parties' joint commitment (Gilbert 2008: 507–508). Indeed, this obligation entitles the parties, among other things, to rebuke each other for not acting according to their evil plans.

These considerations demonstrate that Gilbert's approach is able to account for a large variety of social situations involving everyday face-to-face interactions. Gilbert's focus on small-scale settings is grounded in her search for the minimal form of sociality, which leads her to delve into the study of "the smallest possible social unit in sociological terms, the *dyad*" (Gilbert 2003: 55). Yet the structure that she seeks to uncover serves as a foundation for all sorts of social phenomena up to the scale of whole societies. This chapter therefore concludes with an outline of Gilbert's plural subject theory within the broader framework of social ontology.

5.5 Collective Intentionality and Social Ontology

To address larger and more complex social phenomena such as translocal communities or nations, it seems necessary to tackle two main issues pertaining to Gilbert's approach: the problem of authority and the possibility of "anonymous" joint commitments, that is, of plural subjects in which the parties do not and even cannot know each other or do not directly interact with one another.

At first sight, the issue of authority seems to constitute a problem for plural subject theory. As we have seen above, this approach presupposes the participation of all the parties in the constitution of their joint commitment. And yet in our everyday use of collective concepts, we often also say of a group that it did something when most of its members were not directly involved in that action. For instance, we may say that Switzerland devaluated its currency or that the Catholic Church condemned a recent war. In such cases, we have to assume a "primary" or "basic" case of joint commitment that serves as a foundation for a "secondary" one (Gilbert 2003: 49–50). Through a primary joint commitment of all the parties, a new person or body is created that is bestowed with the power "to create new joint commitments for them all by acting in specified ways" (Gilbert 2003: 49). In other words, if the members of a group "jointly accept that certain decisions of a certain few are to count as our* decisions [...], we can reasonably allow that the group itself has made the decision or performed the action in question" (Gilbert 1989: 206).

The examples of nations or of translocal communities such as the Catholic Church draw attention to the problem of transposing plural subject theory to larger populations. How can we conceive of a plural subject whose parties "do not all know each other, or even know *of* each other as individuals" (Gilbert 1989: 212)? The main obstacle appears to be the condition of "common knowledge" among the parties forming a plural subject (see above). A solution may be to tweak the concept of common knowledge by allowing for a "population common knowledge," that is, for the possibility that a certain content is out in the open* for all members of a certain population and that everyone is aware of this state of affairs (Gilbert 1989: 261–263). For instance, the fact that the planet is in danger was population common knowledge among those who worked on the 2015 Paris Agreement on climate change.

In light of this definition of population common knowledge, the creation of a plural subject by the members of a certain population requires that "all members of the population share a concept of the population" (Gilbert 2006: 175)—in our case, "those working toward the Paris Agreement." Furthermore, "[T]hese people must express their readiness jointly to commit with one another under the description in question" (Gilbert 2006: 175). As soon as they have evidence "from which they can infer that all such people have openly* manifested quasi-readiness to join in certain kinds of action with other members of the population" (Gilbert 1989: 212), a plural subject is constituted. The need for inferential reasoning here, however, suggests that this way of constituting a plural subject is more vulnerable to infelicities and thus less capable of binding the parties through their joint commitment. In this case, the line between a plural subject and other social phenomena becomes less distinct.

Indeed, Gilbert (1996d: 270) acknowledges that not all phenomena commonly studied by sociologists are plural subjects and that the label "social" is not only appropriate to plural subject phenomena. For instance, under a certain description, social classes do not constitute plural subjects. In fact, the famous exhortation that concludes *The Communist Manifesto*—"Workingmen of all countries, unite!" (Marx and Engels 1948: 44)—can be interpreted as signaling that the working class is not yet a plural subject, and that it should become one (Gilbert 1989: 227). Nevertheless, should the use of a concept of sociality be restricted to its most typical cases, there is, according to Gilbert (1989: 441), "little doubt that the plural subject phenomena are the most apt intuitively for the label 'social.'"

But can we actually identify this "label of the social" outside of the domain of philosophical speculation, that is, through the observation and analysis of real-life data? My answer to this fundamental question is a resounding yes, as I will demonstrate in the second part of this book. To do so, however, we need to build a bridge between the theoretical framework and the empirical case study. This will be the task of the next chapter.

6

Collective Intentionality and Empirical Research

6.1 Introduction

One of the aims of this study is to build a bridge between philosophical reflections and empirical research. This entails an evaluation of approaches to collective intentionality not only in terms of the intrinsic merit of their philosophical arguments, but also in light of pragmatic considerations pertaining to their usefulness in the context of data collection and analysis. As I have argued in Chapter 2, there are three interrelated issues that are particularly relevant in relation to this goal. I have named them the problem of public availability, the problem of distinctive constitution, and the problem of distinctive consequences.

To recapitulate, the first problem concerns the nature of collective intentionality as an epistemically public phenomenon the presence of which can be grasped, or at least reasonably inferred, on the basis of observations or other empirical data. The second and third problems are corollaries of the first. If collective intentions have some public aspects, we need to be able to distinguish them from other psychological or social phenomena, for instance by identifying some distinctive features in their communicative constitution or in their consequences for the collectively intending agents. In Chapter 2, I discussed Bratman's account of shared intentionality in light of these problems and concluded that it did not provide a solid foundation for a theoretical and methodological framework in the social sciences. In this chapter, I will discuss the accounts put forward by Searle, Gilbert, and Tuomela in a similar fashion.

In addition to that assessment, this chapter has a second purpose, namely to connect more closely the topic of collective intentionality to the study of religion. Unfortunately, I know of no specific study in this discipline that deals with collective intentionality in a way that would allow me to build directly upon previous insights. For this reason, I will take a detour through an approach that has some affinities with the matter at hand: speech act theory. As we have seen, speech act theory constitutes a stepping stone in the construction of Searle's view of (collective) intentionality, and a number of resources derived from it, such as the idea of direction of fit, also play a role in the work of other scholars. While the reception of this theory in the study of religion has been rather low key (see Grimes 1988, 2014; Hüsken 2007; Yelle 2006a, b), it has found a considerable audience among anthropologists.

The study of performative language entered as a "third force" in the anthropological debate between rationalists and symbolists in the study of magic and ritual in the

1970s, but almost succumbed to the rising tide of postmodern relativism surfed, among others, by linguistic anthropologists. However, scholars more inclined to espouse an "etic" perspective (see Mostowlansky and Rota 2016) used it to examine the formal aspect of ritual and the role of religious settings in the construction of social relationships and individual commitments. It is onto the mature stock of these approaches that I wish to graft the vigorous cuttings of a perspective rooted in collective intentionality. Indeed, I am hopeful that after a wave of relentless deconstruction (e.g., McCutcheon 1997; Fitzgerald 2001; Bergunder 2014), the study of religion is ready for new theoretical discussions (see, e.g., Stausberg 2009a; Schilbrack 2013, 2018).

In the concluding section of this chapter, I will bring together the philosophical and anthropological perspectives sketching three strategies to be deployed in the second part of this book. Let me note that, although I will present these strategies as the systematic result of theoretical reflections, I have developed them through a dialectical exchange between the ideal framework provided by the philosophy of collective intentionality and the practical collection and analysis of my empirical data. However, I do not consider this to be an issue, since the structure of the argument when presenting one's results does not need to follow the order of discovery.

6.2 Toward an Applied Framework

6.2.1 The public availability of collective intentions

The public availability of collective intentions is a crucial point for the development of an applied framework, since empirical research depends on the possibility of collecting and interpreting factual data. While data are not simply given and always depend on preliminary choices by the researchers, social-scientific research deals with realities that have characteristics independent of such a conceptual apparatus and, to quote Durkheim (1982: 2–3), "can only be ascertained through empirical investigation (as opposed to *a priori* reasoning or intuition) and, in particular, through 'external' observation by means of indicators."

In Chapter 2, I argued that Bratman's reductivist view of shared intentionality is not the best approach to construct a framework suitable for empirical research. Nevertheless, Bratman is very explicit in positioning shared intentions as a *public* phenomenon constituted by an interlocking web of corresponding individual intentions (Bratman 1999b: 134). This web is not situated in any individual mind and, therefore, according to Bratman, a single agent would not be in a position to have a shared intention. As he puts it, "[I]t takes at least two not only to tango but even for there to be a shared intention to tango" (Bratman 1999e: 117 n17). Continuing this line of thought, we can assess whether, according to the non-reductivist accounts developed by Searle, Tuomela, and Gilbert, a single agent can have a collective intention. I shall take a negative answer as a preliminary indicator in favor of the public nature of collective intentions or of some of their aspects. A positive answer would not automatically rule out the possibility that collective intentions are by nature public, but would make the interpretation more complicated since, in principle, at least some forms of collective intentionality, such as collective belief, could be kept completely private by the intending agent.

So it looks as if we are off to a bumpy start. By Searle's account, the capacity of a single agent to have a collective intention is not merely a possibility but, indeed, a conceptual necessity of we-intentions. This standpoint is consistent with his general understanding of intentionality as a biological feature of individual minds that, in principle, could be had by a brain in a vat (Searle 1983: 230; 2002b: 96). In his view, a collective intention has the same fundamental structure as an individual intention. Accordingly, a collective intentional state will be satisfied or felicitous depending on certain states of affairs in the world obtaining or being brought about. However, an infelicitous intention is an intention nonetheless. A brain in a vat hallucinating about the existence of the external world and we-intending to engage in a collective activity could still have a collective intention, albeit an infelicitous one.

In fact, all the examples that Searle offers in his contributions on the topic of collective intentionality involve realistic agents who are actually participating in a shared cooperative activity (such as preparing a sauce). However, with the exception of rare and rather cryptic hints, Searle does not specify what kind of relationship a we-intention creates or presupposes between the parties involved in such an activity. Indeed, the shortest answer seems to be: none. Searle's account of collective intention has been criticized for its solipsistic methodology, which does not address the intersubjective dimension of collective intentionality and its role in the constitution of social groups. Thus, taken at face value, Searle's account does not fare well with regard to the problem of public availability.

Tuomela's analysis of we-intentions is also predicated on a conception of collective intentionality as an intentional "mode." However, it introduces a number of interrelated conditions that connect and in fact subordinate the participatory intentions of the individual agents to the framework of their collective intention. In this sense, Tuomela presents the we-mode intention of an individual as conceptually dependent on a group. This allows him to conceptualize any individual we-mode attitude as an "individualistic slice" of a collective's joint intention. This characterization suggests that without a group reference, an individual could not have a we-intention. In Tuomela's original model, the interrelation of the we-intending individuals in a collective is founded on the subjective beliefs of the parties regarding the relevant conditions of their joint action (Tuomela and Miller 1988). Accordingly, Tuomela acknowledges that, at least in principle, an isolated agent can, on the ground of his false beliefs, have a we-intention— "In such a case a we-intention is not a 'slice' of a joint intention but at best of a believed joint intention" (Tuomela 2005: 341). Nevertheless, Tuomela regards such a situation as an exceptional case that appears to be barred by the communicative requirements of his more recent discussions of we-mode we-attitudes and the conditions of their creation, which introduce a new dimension "beyond mere mutual belief" (Tuomela 1995: 240).

Gilbert also distances herself from the idea that a single agent can have a collective intention (Gilbert 2014h: 99–100). In her view, an individual cannot be the subject of a joint intention, which is, by definition, the intention of a *plural* subject. Similarly, a joint commitment is by definition "a single commitment *of two or more people*" (Gilbert

2006: 126, my emphasis). Furthermore, Gilbert's account requires for the formation of a joint commitment that the parties in such a commitment openly express their readiness to be jointly committed with the others, with respect to a certain intentional content. In this regard, one can imagine borderline cases, for instance with respect to the limits of a joint commitment in a crowd of acclaiming people, where dissenting voices may not be readily hearable (Gilbert 2006: 178). Such cases, however, appear to pose a practical problem rather than a conceptual one.

In sum, on Gilbert and Tuomela's account, collective intentions appear as both a public and a group-dependent phenomenon that depends on some *in re* conditions obtaining in the world. These conditions provide us with further clues regarding the publicly available aspects of collective intentionality, notably in relation to its constitutive processes. I turn now to these aspects.

6.2.2 The distinctive constitution of collective intentions

Despite Searle's extensive and influential work on social ontology, he has surprisingly little to say about the creation of collective intentions. Arguably, since in his theory we-intentions are nothing more than mental states in (potentially isolated) individual minds, their formation is simply up to the single agent. Searle argues that intentional collective actions rest on a preintentional "sense of community" that allows people to identify "the other" as an actual or potential agent like oneself in cooperative activities. In addition to this so-called Background capacity of the mind, he considers that collective intentionality entails cooperation, and that the latter, in turn, implies a form of "common knowledge or belief" (Searle 2010: 49). However, he does not provide any further clarification on this matter. Instead, he underscores that, although human collective behavior often involves language, communication is not a necessary prerequisite of collective action. Yet his analysis does not answer the question of how the participants (and even less so an external observer) could conclude that coordinated activity results from we-intentions and not from coordinated personal intentions. Following Tuomela's terminology, this means that what Searle calls we-intentionality can be exemplified by both we-mode we-intentionality *and* by specific forms of I-mode we-intentionality (see Tuomela 2013: 85).

By contrast, one of the core distinctions between the I-mode and the we-mode mentioned by Tuomela is the fact that the constitution of we-mode we-attitudes "requires a 'communicative' change in the world—a relevant sign indicating agreement" (Tuomela 1995: 74). Tuomela refines this idea through the concept of an "authority system," that is of a procedure that has the generative power to create a social group. In this respect, his metaphor of a bulletin board as an authority system underscores the epistemic public availability of we-mode we-intentions, since it calls attention to the need for the participants to become aware of the information on the board as well of each other's participatory intentions.

Gilbert also frames the typical context for the formation of a plural subject as a communicative situation in which two or more people express their readiness to be jointly committed. In the absence of special conditions, all the parties involved in the joint commitment must participate in its creation and their exchange must take place in conditions of common knowledge; the joint commitment is established only when the relevant expressions of readiness have been made (Gilbert 2000e: 21). The exchange need not be verbal, but must be somehow codified to entail the necessary expression. Some of Gilbert's thought experiments also indicate that, in the appropriate context, the fact that someone refrains from challenging a procedure that would entail their inclusion in a joint commitment may be a sufficient communicative basis for the creation of a plural subject (e.g., Gilbert 1996c).

Once again, in comparison to the competing approaches, Searle's perspective lacks specificity and provides little information of interest for social-scientific research into the constitution of collective intentions. All in all, Searle's work is primarily concerned with the abstract conceptual problem of specifying the distinctiveness of we-intentions, but does not offer any further detail on the form of sociality that they entail. This is evident also from an examination of the postulated distinctive consequences of collective intentionality.

6.2.3 The distinctive consequences of collective intentionality

In Searle's account, collective intentionality entails by definition the idea of coordination and cooperation (Searle 2002b: 95). Unfortunately, Searle says virtually nothing on why or how collective intentions frame, improve, or otherwise affect such cooperation. It thus remains unclear whether all forms of cooperation require we-intentions. Conversely, it is not clear what consequences collective intentions entail for the we-intending agents and their relationships. This indeterminacy is surprising because in his social ontology, Searle underscores the constitutive deontic dimension of social institutions, which can both restrict and enhance the frameworks for action (e.g., Searle 2010: 91 and passim). Searle argues that this normative feature of sociality arises from the imposition of *collectively accepted* status functions on objects or people (e.g., Searle 1996: 40–43), but does not elaborate any further on this point.

A viable option may be to see such deontic powers as the result of the binding force of speech acts (e.g., Searle 2010: 123–132). In fact, in his theory of rationality, Searle (2001) draws on the specific commitment inherent to speech acts to develop an account of individual intentional action in which the motivational factor is not rooted in the agent's personal desires and beliefs but rather derives from desire-independent reasons for action. This idea, however, would need some tweaks to be carried over to collective cases. Discussing this issue, the Dutch philosopher Frank Hindriks (2009, 2013) suggests reinterpreting Searle's understanding of the collective imposition and acceptance of a status function in a way closer to Gilbert's notion of "joint commitment." Such an amendment would make his approach more fruitful for empirical research, too.

Indeed, one of the major appeals of Gilbert's plural subject theory is her philosophical account of the inherently normative dimension a joint commitment which takes the form of mutual rights and duties among the participants. According to Gilbert's "obligation criterion," each party to a joint commitment is obligated to abide by the collective intention and not to act contrary to it, unless the others waive their right to conforming action. *Ipso facto*, all parties in the joint commitment have a right to the others' appropriate performance as well as a standing right to rebuke those who do not behave conformably.

In several contributions and, more recently, in a book-length foundational inquiry on demand-rights (Gilbert 2018), Gilbert has developed a detailed analysis of the nature and origin of these obligations and entitlements. Gilbert clearly distinguishes the obligation of joint commitment from any form of moral obligation. She sees the former as a *directed* obligation, whereby a person "owes" an action to another person who, accordingly, has a standing right to demand it. This obligation arises from the structure of a joint commitment, whereby a group of "co-authors" together impose "*a particular type of normative constraint* on each one with respect to what it is open to him [sic] to do in the future, rationally speaking" (Gilbert 2018: 170).

As a co-creation of two or more people, a joint commitment cannot be rescinded unilaterally by one of them. When creating a joint commitment, the parties "pool their wills" in a way that commits them to emulating through their actions a single intending body and provides them with reasons for action that do not depend on corresponding personal intentions (Gilbert 2018: 161–168). Accordingly, the creation of a plural subject allows for the possibility—although not the necessity—of a disjunction between the personal and collective intentions of the parties. A joint commitment thus has a motivational force of its own, which can provide a reason for action independent of any participant's personal inclination.

In their consequences, the obligations of joint commitment overlap to a large extent with those of Tuomela's we-mode we-intentions. Tuomela distinguishes between different degrees of mutual obligation among the parties, depending on whether they hold a collective intention in the I-mode or in the we-mode. While the I-mode only involves aggregate private commitments, the we-mode implies a collective commitment that, once created, cannot be unilaterally dissolved. Such a commitment provides each participant with a reason normatively to expect an appropriate performance from the others. Furthermore, a collective commitment involves not only an obligation towards playing one's part in fulfilling the collective intention. It also commits one to making sure that the others can perform their parts, if necessary by helping, persuading, or even coercing them (Tuomela 2003b: 97; 2007: 37).

Through the years, Tuomela has proposed various accounts to explain the normative nature of collective commitments, without, however, providing a clear-cut picture. In his view, collective commitments entail a form of "technical" normativity akin to the "ought" inherent in speech acts (Tuomela 2007: 257 n31 and n32). Conversely, they do not entail a form of "proper" moral, legal, or prudential normativity, because the normative constraints apply only to group members *qua* group members, and not as private persons: the normativity of a collective commitment is a "group-social normativity" (Tuomela 2007: 27). In short, a collective commitment gives rise to "*sui generis* social obligations" (Hindriks 2018: 355).

The idea of collective acceptance in the we-mode, which consists in contextually accepting something "for the group," also entails that a person intending in the we-mode can accept a proposition *qua* a member of a group while simultaneously accepting a contrary proposition as a private person (Tuomela 2003a: 128–129). When acting for group reasons, the we-intending agents hand over to the group a part of their authority to act individually and become collectively committed to act "as if they were limbs of a collective body" (Tuomela 2013: 12). Accordingly, in line with Gilbert's take on joint commitment, Tuomela deems group reasons to be a source of desire-independent reasons for action.

6.2.4 Comparative assessment

The comparative discussion of Searle's, Tuomela's and Gilbert's non-reductivist philosophical standpoints in light of the three problems of public availability, distinctive constitution, and distinctive consequences provides us with important insights toward the development of a framework for empirical research. The most striking conclusion is probably that the most famous approach to collective intentionality, that is, the one put forward by John Searle, is together with Bratman's, the one that provides the fewest resources for such a project. Nevertheless, as I will demonstrate in the second part of the book, some aspects of his work can still serve as a source of inspiration for further reflection, notably his discussion of speech acts in relation to the production of desire-independent reasons for action.

Tuomela's and Gilbert's approaches, by contrast, offer heuristically interesting answers to our three main problems. In particular, their respective discussions of the we-mode and of joint commitments call attention to a number of communicative processes and normative social implications of collective intentions that are open to empirical investigation. I will come back to these in the last section of this chapter, in which I will sketch three practical strategies I use for the analysis of collective actions, beliefs, emotions, and aesthetics. Before I get to these practical results of my philosophical inquiry, I want to provide an intermediate link that can establish a preliminary connection between the issues of communication and normativity and the field of religion.

Indeed, some intuitions at the base of my work are not entirely unprecedented. In particular, relevant similarities can be found in the work of a number of social anthropologists who, in the 1980s and 1990s, availed themselves of the insights of analytic philosophy, most significantly of speech act theory, in their study of religious rituals. Thus, a detour through their work should allow us to advance on our way toward a workable fieldwork approach.

6.3 Speech Acts in a Ritual Setting

Due to the influence of Malinowski's (1934) pioneering work on the language of the Trobriand people and their "magic spells" (Duranti 1997: 215–218), speech act theory first found its way into social anthropology as an instrument to analyze magic and rituals. Performative theories of magic and ritual emerged at the end of the 1960s and were directed in particular against the rationalist and the expressivist standpoints in this field (see Horton and Finnegan 1973; Skorupski 1976). Anthropologists Ruth Finnegan (1969) and Stanley Tambiah (1973) were among the first authors to refer to Austin's theory of speech acts in the context of this debate, arguing that rituals and magical practices can be assimilated to performative utterances, which "simply by virtue of being enacted [...] achieve a change of state or do something effective" (Tambiah 2013: 181).

The search for a third way in the theoretical debate on magic and ritual led many anthropologists to embrace speech act theory. However, their positions remained somehow trapped in the dichotomy they wanted to overcome. Despite a consensus on the possibility of "doing things with words," scholars disagreed on *what* exactly words could do and *who*—the anthropologists or the people they studied—should have the last word on the matter (see Tambiah 1979).

By the 1980s, social anthropologists were increasingly skeptical of the universal applicability of speech act theory. Furthermore, in the same years, speech act theory attracted the criticism of linguistic anthropologists (e.g., Duranti 1993) and philosophers of language (Derrida 1988). Their main target, however, was not Austin's seminal work, but rather its subsequent elaboration by Searle, which was deemed incompatible with the ascendent postmodern paradigm. Linguistic anthropologists interpreted Searle's analysis of speech acts as an attempt to recast Austin's insights in psychological terms, whereas in their view, the ways in which languages are locally used and understood are embedded in specific social systems and reflect different modes of being in the world (Rosaldo 1982).

While these impasses caused some anthropologists to reject speech act theory, they prompted others to explore new ways in which to apply this approach in their work. Faced with the limits of an analysis of individual speech acts, a number of scholars paid increasing attention to contextual factors surrounding the "total speech act" (Hall 2000: 185). In the field of ritual studies, this meant focusing on the effects that the formal aspects of ritual have on speech acts.

Applying this perspective, Wade Wheelock (1982) observed that the reference to a fixed ritual script—that is, the repetition of encoded sequences and utterances—plays a fundamental role in understanding the scope of ritual language. Since the participants in the ritual are familiar with these elements, "[T]he actual uttering of the words tells no one anything they did not already know" (Wheelock 1982: 58–59). Rather, the speakers' aim is to complete a "shared, predetermined sketch of the entire situation" (Wheelock 1982: 64). Thus, the goal of ritual language is not to *inform*, but "*to create and allow the participation in a known and repeatable* situation" (Wheelock 1982: 59).

Increasing attention to the ritual setting offered a new insight into the connection between ritual language and social structure. In an influential contribution, Maurice Bloch (1974) argued that the symbols enacted in rituals cannot be understood without taking into consideration the particular mode of communication proper to ritual settings. Bloch noted that ritual communication is characterized by a higher degree of formalization than ordinary speech, a feature it shares with political oratory. Yet formalized language is "*impoverished* language" (Bloch 1974: 60) because the speakers are no longer free to choose between many different forms, styles, words, expressions, and syntactical forms.

In ritual settings, the highly stylized form of the speech acts limits the generative capacity of language: "[A]n utterance instead of being potentially followed by an infinity of others can be followed by only a few or possibly only one" (Bloch 1974:

62–63). And since formalized language leaves no room for contradiction, it cannot be analyzed in terms of its logical structures. This, however, does not mean that ritual language is meaningless. Drawing freely on Austin, Bloch postulated that while a formalized language loses the capacity to report facts, it increases its power "to influence people" (Bloch 1974: 67). This thesis has an important social corollary. Formalized language is closely linked to the exercise of authority and social control, because "one speaker can coerce the response of another" (Bloch 1974: 64). For this reason, in highly formalized ceremonies, individual intentionality (in the sense of volition) is limited to the initial act of "taking part" (Bloch 1974: 70), while the rest of the ceremony can be passively enacted.

The focus on the formal aspects of rituals and the effect formality has on speech acts brought about a reversal of the kinds of questions asked by social anthropologists. Instead of asking what it is people do when they do rituals, they wanted to understand what it is that ritual does to people. Against this backdrop, anthropologists questioned the role of individual feelings and intentions during ritual enactments, and their part in ritual success or failure. Austin's doctrine of the infelicities, and notably the so-called "insincerities," a subclass of the "abuses," provided an important source of theoretical reflection. In contrast to "misfires," "abuses" do not make a performance void, meaning that the act *is* performed, albeit unhappily. This observation suggests a distinction between the psychological and social dimension of speech acts (Austin 1979: 236). This intriguing asymmetry between inner states and outer expressions did not escape the eye of social anthropologists who sought to understand its consequences on a social level.

The full theoretical consequences of such a separation between private emotions and public obligation were spelled out in detail by Roy Rappaport (1979, 1999). Arguing against the one-sided emphasis on the symbolic aspects of ritual in most anthropological analyses, Rappaport drew attention to the important connections that exist between the formal characteristics of ritual actions and their performative implications. In his view, both performance and formality are constitutive of a ritual and are key to understanding its social effects, in particular with respect to the production of commitment.

Rappaport's main thesis can be summarized as follows: "[T]o *perform* a liturgical order, which is by definition a more or less *invariant* sequence of formal acts and utterances *encoded by someone other than the performer himself,* is *necessarily to conform to it*" (Rappaport 1999: 118). Rappaport holds forth that when a performer brings to life the canonical orders encoded in a ritual, he becomes "indistinguishable from those orders." Because the performer is the one who enacts these orders in the first place, he cannot reject them. Therefore, "*[B]y performing a liturgical order the performer accepts, and indicates to himself and to others that he accepts, whatever is encoded in the canons of the liturgical order in which he is participating*" (Rappaport 1999: 119). For instance, if dancing at the "kaiko" ceremonial among the Tsembaga Maring of Papua New Guinea is conventionally encoded as a pledge to fight in an oncoming war, the person who dances commits himself to fighting.

At first glance, this can seem paradoxical because the performer can be insincere or deceitful in his actions and sayings and, for instance, may simply refrain from showing up for the battle. Indeed, Rappaport acknowledges that liturgical performances cannot prevent such situations. However, they can ensure that other social consequences of the ritual remain unaffected by such infelicities. This is because it is "the visible, explicit, public act of acceptance and not the invisible, ambiguous, private sentiment that is socially and morally binding" (Rappaport 1979: 195).

As the example of the ritual dance indicates, liturgical orders cannot guarantee that the performer will honor his pledge. Finding oneself alone on the battlefield remains a definite possibility! However, Rappaport (1999: 124) notes that a ritual does not serve *"to ensure compliance but to establish obligation."* This conclusion explicitly draws on a corollary of speech acts highlighted by Searle:

> When one enters an institutional activity by invoking the rules of that institution one necessarily commits oneself in such and such ways, regardless of whether one approves or disapproves of the institution. In the case of linguistic institutions like promising and accepting the serious utterance of words commits one in ways which are determined by the meaning of the words. In certain first person utterances the utterance is the undertaking of an obligation. (Searle 1969: 189, quoted in Rappaport 1979: 195–196)

In a ritual setting, the performer binds himself to the rules or norms encoded in the liturgical order, whether or not he abides by them, and whether or not he personally approves of them (Rappaport 1979: 194). Thus, he makes himself accountable for failing to fulfill his commitment. Considering that a breach of obligation is fundamentally and universally perceived as immoral, Rappaport states that "morality, like social contract, is implicit in ritual's very structure" (1979: 198).

Although I do not understand my study as an extension of Rappaport's theory of religion, his insights on the performativity of ritual practices will play an important role in my analysis of the construction of collective attitudes among Jehovah's Witnesses. Indeed, I will show that particular features of ritual practices and ritual settings underscored by his work are not merely conducive to individual commitments but can facilitate the establishment of collective actions, beliefs, emotions, and aesthetic experiences. So, in conclusion, I shall spell out the practical strategies that I will deploy to discuss the creation of collective intentions in ritual contexts.

6.4 Three Strategies of Inquiry

In the discussion of the data collected in my fieldwork, I will draw on multiple resources, such as various historical documents and qualitative interviews, to underpin my arguments. Furthermore, I will construct my analysis by way of contrast with competing theoretical standpoints. All in all, however, I will put three main strategies to work.

Drawing on the philosophical assessment in the first part of this chapter, I presuppose that collective intentions require a public setting to be constructed; that is, something has to happen in and among the participants in a collective for such a group to collectively share an intention. Gilbert and Tuomela provide the clearest and most detailed accounts of this process and, despite their differences, both argue that a type of public communicative (ex)change is required for full-blown collective intentionality. Therefore, the first strategy in my empirical research will be to identify and analyze appropriate settings in which such public exchanges may take place. As I will demonstrate in the following chapters, Gilbert's and Tuomela's theories can be successfully combined with the insights presented above on the relationship between ritual settings and speech acts. Indeed, a detour through speech act theory will also allow me to integrate some insights from Searle's approach to the study of rational agency.

My second avenue of pursuit will consist in the analysis of collective commitments. Drawing on Gilbert's and Tuomela's accounts of the intrinsic normative features of social collectives, I will explore how individual agents describe their motivational structures. This will involve searching for desire-independent reasons for action that can be explained in terms of collective intentions. Accordingly, I will pay particular attention to possible signs of disjunction between what the agents (ought to) intend (believe, feel, etc.) on the basis of their collective or joint commitments as members of a group and what they personally intend. This form of investigation has some affinity with Rappaport's analysis of ritual speech acts. However, while Rappaport has called attention to the possible discrepancy between private intentions and public commitment, the approach that I will put forward distinguishes between collective and personal reasons for action.

Finally, treading once more in the footsteps of Gilbert and Tuomela, I argue that, for an external observer, to witness a rebuke—or the attempt to avoid a rebuke, for instance, by hiding or dissimulating one's behavior—represents an important clue that a collective intention may be involved in a social situation. Gilbert (2014e: 9) observes that, through the normative dimension of joint commitment, "[T]he social scientist can acknowledge the existence of rights and obligations of joint commitment while respecting the point that social scientific description should be free of the imposition of the observer's moral values and in that sense value-free." Nevertheless, rebuke in itself is not sufficient to conclude, with a degree of plausibility, that a collective intention is at play. There is no collective intentionality in me screaming at a stranger trespassing on my property, "Get off my lawn!" Thus, I will look for plausible markers that the rebuke in question is actually administered (or may be administered) in the name of the group to one of its members. This invites us to consider the various paths for empirical analysis sketched here as interrelated and mutually supportive.

At present, all this may sound very abstract. The next part of this study should bring more clarity and will demonstrate the heuristic value of this approach by examining how, in the case of Jehovah's Witnesses, a collection of people becomes a social group—a "we."

Part II

7

Empirical Orientation—The Jehovah's Witnesses

7.1 Introduction

The aim of this short chapter is to facilitate the transition from the theoretical reflections presented in the first part of the book to the empirical analysis developed in its second part. In the following four chapters, the Jehovah's Witnesses will serve as a case study to demonstrate how certain philosophical insights can be fruitfully applied to the study of a religious collectivity in terms of its members' collective actions, beliefs, emotions, and aesthetic experiences. As I have underscored in my general introduction, it is not my goal to retrace a detailed chronicle of this denomination from the nineteenth century up to today, nor to dwell on its teachings. As far as its theology is concerned, I will introduce some specific doctrines that are relevant to my analysis in due course. Here, suffice to say that the publications of the Watch Tower Society—the corporate body of the Jehovah's Witnesses—carry a millenarian message and announce the imminent advent of the Kingdom of God (who is known by his own unique name, Jehovah) on earth, although they no longer specify a precise date. However, a general overview of the origins, development and organizational structures of the Jehovah's Witnesses may prove useful to better situate certain important names and events in a broader context. Therefore, in the second section of this chapter I will sketch a very brief history of the Jehovah's Witnesses.[1] Throughout my summary, I will refer to the chapters in which a number of topics will be developed in greater detail.

In the third section of this chapter, I will introduce my methods and list the sources that I have used in my study. In addition to presenting the qualitative and quantitative data that I have collected from Jehovah's Witnesses in Switzerland and Germany, I will also discuss my treatment of the historical material and the importance of a historiographical perspective for my analysis. With this framework in place, the reader will be able to proceed with confidence to the empirical part of this study.

7.2 A Very Brief History of Jehovah's Witnesses

The denomination known today as the Jehovah's Witnesses emerged from the American neo-Adventist milieu in the 1870s. Its founder—and, indeed, the founder of a number of splinter groups—is Charles T. Russell (1852–1916). Russell was born in Allegheny, Pennsylvania, now a part of Pittsburgh, in a Presbyterian family. In his teens, he was already a full-fledged partner in his father's haberdashery store and rapidly became a successful businessman. Through a series of encounters with prominent Adventist figures, he became active in the theological debates of his time. In 1870, he started a small Bible-study group in his town and, in the following years, he contributed to various Adventist publications, before launching his own magazine, *The Watchtower*, in 1879.² In 1881, Russell founded the publishing company Zion's Watch Tower Tract Society to distribute the magazine as well as other religious pamphlets and books, including his successful *Millennial Dawn* series, later renamed *Studies in the Scriptures* (see Chapter 8). Three years later, the company was incorporated and, in 1896, its name was changed to Watch Tower Bible and Tract Society of Pennsylvania, Inc. To date, the Watch Tower Society³ still constitutes the main legal entity used by Jehovah's Witnesses, and its publications represent the fundamental references in matters of doctrine and practice for Jehovah's Witnesses around the world.⁴

By 1880, there were already about thirty local groups in the United States who identified themselves with the work of Russell. These local *ecclesiae*, as they were called, were only loosely in contact with one another and largely autonomous in terms of organization, practices, and biblical interpretations. Russell encouraged people who were unacquainted with each other to meet and edify one another as a way of building up their faith and even provided suggestions on how to organize their meetings (see Chapter 8). However, when he founded the Watch Tower Society and launched its magazine, Russell did not intend to constitute a new denomination nor to pursue a career as a religious leader. Accordingly, the name he chose for his followers was at first simply "Christians." In 1910, the name was changed to Bible Students, and in 1931, it was changed again to Jehovah's Witnesses. The name change in 1931 marks a pivotal moment in the development of a separate group identity under the presidency of Joseph F. Rutherford (1869–1942), who succeeded Russell at the helm of the Watch Tower Society in 1916.

Rutherford's election as President of the Society was controversial; both his theological innovations and his authoritarian leadership style caused a number of defections and schisms among the Bible Students. Rutherford's rise to power corresponds to a period of rising tensions between the organization and the surrounding world. In a number of publications and discourses, Rutherford openly attacked the ruling political powers, economic elites, and mainstream religions. Furthermore, under his direction, a number of demonstrations were staged with the explicit purpose of shocking the public. In some cases, these strategies resulted in open conflicts in the streets and the courtrooms of the United States. In Europe, Jehovah's Witnesses became the victims of violent persecution, notably in Nazi Germany and later in the USSR.

During the 25 years of his presidency, Rutherford enacted important organizational reforms. The gradual establishment of what he regarded as theocratic rule allowed him to exert stronger control over the local congregations and push them to standardize their practices, such as the use of the Watch Tower Society's literature (see Chapter 8). He also transformed the previously modest local conventions of Bible Students into great public events, assembling tens of thousands of people in a location over several days (see Chapter 10). These events were often the opportunity for major announcements, such as the introduction of the name Jehovah's Witnesses.

Besides the new name, Rutherford introduced many of the distinctive characteristics that are commonly associated with Jehovah's Witnesses today, in particular the house-to-house ministry, also known as field ministry (see Chapter 8). Today, active Jehovah's Witnesses, also known as publishers, invest several hours a month in disseminating the literature produced by the Watch Tower Society and spreading its message. To foster this missionary zeal, Rutherford launched a new magazine in 1919 and used a new mode of distribution to curb the power of local congregation leaders. Originally called *The Golden Age*, this publication was renamed *Consolation* in 1937, and since 1946 it has been distributed under the title *Awake!*[5] Furthermore, Rutherford was a pioneer in the religious use of new media, including the radio and the gramophone (see Chapters 8 and 9).

The decades that followed the Rutherford era were marked by a de-escalation of the Watch Tower Society's vitriolic rhetoric. Ethical concerns gradually replaced the focus on biblical prophecy, and an attitude of indifference toward worldly matters replaced the Society's previous rejection of the outside world. The presidency of Nathan H. Knorr (1905–1977) ushered in a period of growing bureaucratization of the organization's structures and a gradual fading of the charismatic authority of its president. From the early 1970s onwards, religious authority within the Watch Tower Society has been in the hands of a so-called Governing Body composed of a variable number of members (currently eight). Since the year 2000, when the fifth president, Milton G. Henschel (1920–2003), stepped down, the president of the Watch Tower Society is no longer a member of the Governing Body and takes care only of the "earthly concerns" of the organization. The Governing Body operates by means of six committees, introduced in 1975, which oversee various tasks, including the writing, translation and printing of all published material and the coordination of the Jehovah's Witnesses evangelical activities.

Shortly after the beginning of his tenure in 1942, Knorr swiftly introduced a number of reforms aimed at improving and strengthening the missionary work of Jehovah's Witnesses through new educational offers. The Watchtower Bible College of Gilead (commonly known as Gilead School), an instructional facility for overseas missionaries, was inaugurated in 1943. In the same year, at the congregational level, regular publishers started receiving weekly training to improve their rhetorical and argumentative skills as part of the so-called Theocratic Ministry School. Knorr was also responsible—together with his successor, Fredrick Franz (1983–1992)—for the realization of the *New World Translation of the Holy Scriptures*, the translation of the Bible currently in use, in a revised edition, among Jehovah's Witnesses (see Chapter 11).

The decades after the Second World War were also a period of global expansion and rapid membership growth. The number of countries in which Jehovah's Witnesses were active rose from 52 in 1942 to 206 in 1970. Today, Jehovah's Witnesses are (officially or unofficially) present in virtually every country of the world, and the number of active members worldwide rose from about 180,000 in 1947 to more than 8.4 million in 2020 (see Chapter 8). The numerical growth of Jehovah's Witnesses was accompanied by a constant expansion in the production of the two flagship magazines, *The Watchtower* and *Awake!* In 1960, *The Watchtower* already had a circulation of 3,750,000 copies. In 2021, the number of printed copies for each edition had reached 74,210,000, confirming

The Watchtower as the most widely circulated magazine worldwide, followed by *Awake!* with 68,097,000 copies.[6] The two magazines are currently published in 414 and 208 languages respectively. Since the launch of the multimedia website, jw.org, in 2012, however, the Society has found new ways of making its message available to both the general public and its members (see Chapter 11).

Today, the Watch Tower Society is a global organization. Its World Headquarters moved from Brooklyn, where they had been located since 1909, to Warwick, NY, in 2017. As of 2020, the Society had 87 branch offices worldwide, tasked with overseeing the activities of Jehovah's Witnesses in a given region. Each region is organized in circuits that bring together a number of congregations or assemblies. Each circuit has a circuit overseer, while a body of elders is responsible for the operation of a congregation. In my analysis, I will move back and forth between the global dimension of the Watch Tower Society and the local reality of the congregations. Indeed, what happens in the assemblies throughout the world is informed to a large extent by the Society's structures and its publications. Beside this, however, I maintain that it is at the scale of interpersonal interactions that collective intentions are formulated and that the Jehovah's Witnesses constitute themselves as a social collective, as a "we." This perspective is reflected in the methods that I have deployed in my research and the sources I draw on.

7.3 Methods and Sources

This study draws on a multifaceted set of data. The bulk of the empirical material was collected between 2014 and 2018 from five German-speaking congregations of Jehovah's Witnesses; four in Switzerland and one in Germany. On multiple occasions, I attended their biweekly meetings, during which I conducted participant observations and collected field notes. In these contexts, I also had the opportunity to engage in numerous informal conversations. Furthermore, together with my colleagues Fabian Huber and Evelyne Felder, I have conducted semi-structured interviews with seventeen members of these congregations. Table 7.1 provides an overview of these conversations. To protect their identity, their real names have been replaced with pseudonyms.

To make the reading of the interview excerpts easier, I have translated them from the original German or Swiss German into English and I have edited them for clarity, while paying attention not to alter the intended meaning of the speaker.

The participant observations and the qualitative interviews were complemented with two types of quantitative data. First, two members in each congregation were asked to keep track, over a period of eight days, of their media use. To do so, they were provided with a media journal in which they had to note which media they used, at what time of the day, and for how long. Second, 183 members of the congregations located in Switzerland completed a survey about their religious and media habits. The survey was administered in May 2016 via face-to-face paper-and-pencil interviews by my colleagues and myself, with the help of a team of students from the University of Fribourg. Our sample included 93 women and 89 men (and one n/a).

Without entering into details, our data allows us to sketch the following religious-social portrait of our sample. The average age of the surveyed Jehovah's Witnesses was 47

Table 7.1 Overview of the Interviewed Jehovah's Witnesses © Andrea Rota.

Pseudonym	Participation in the Field Ministry	Country	Age	Gender
Anna	Publisher	Switzerland	43	F
Emma	Publisher	Switzerland	44	F
Eric	Publisher	Switzerland	54	M
Eva	Auxiliary Pioneer[7]	Switzerland	21	F
Frank	Publisher	Germany	40	M
Fritz	Publisher	Switzerland	44	M
Gertrud	Publisher	Switzerland	71	F
Jörg	Auxiliary Pioneer	Switzerland	63	M
Lara	Publisher	Switzerland	24	F
Leonard	Publisher	Switzerland	37	M
Michaela	Regular Pioneer	Switzerland	22	F
Monique	Publisher	Switzerland	83	F
Olga	Regular Pioneer	Germany	28	F
Paul	Publisher	Switzerland	51	M
Richard	Publisher	Germany	65	M
Sofia	Publisher	Germany	42	F
Valentin	Regular Pioneer	Switzerland	28	M

and the distribution of age cohorts was as follows: 5.5 percent were 20 or younger; 34.5 percent were between the ages of 21 and 40; 35.5 percent were between 41 and 60; 24.5 percent were 61 or older. About three quarters of the respondents were married or in a relationship; among these, less than 10 percent had a partner who was not a Jehovah's Witness; half of the respondents had no children. On average, the surveyed Witnesses stated that, among their three closest friends, 2.75 friends were also Jehovah's Witnesses. Fifty-six percent of the respondents were children of Jehovah's Witnesses, while 13 percent joined the Witnesses prior to their twenty-first birthday; 23.5 percent did so between the ages of 21 and 41, and 7.5 percent between 41 and 60 years of age. Ninety-seven percent of the people surveyed reported attending congregational meetings twice a week and more than 90 percent participated in other activities of the Jehovah's Witnesses at least once a week (most probably in relation to their missionary work).

In addition to the data collected in a congregational setting, I conducted participant observations at a number of other events: I attended three regional conventions of Jehovah's Witnesses (two in Switzerland and one in Germany), a smaller district convention in Switzerland, and three celebrations of the Memorial of Christ's Death (two in Switzerland and one in the United States). Furthermore, I visited the Watch Tower Society's branch office in Selters (Germany) twice, where I was able to see the printing facilities and conduct extended expert interviews with members of the local public information department. Finally, in March 2016, I was invited to visit the Society's World Headquarters in Brooklyn, as well as the Watchtower Educational Center (Gilead School) in Patterson, NY. During my stay, I toured the studios where the Society's video productions (films, online broadcasting, animated series, etc.) are realized and conducted extended expert interviews with a member of the Society's central Office of Public Information and a member of the art department, which supervises the graphic design of the various Watch Tower media.

In my analysis, I also draw extensively on historical sources. As Zoe Knox (2011: 158) observes, the academic literature on the social, cultural, and political history of Jehovah's Witnesses is quite meager, with the exception of a number of studies on the persecution of members under the Nazi and Communist regimes (e.g., Gerbe 1999; Baran 2014), and on their legal struggles in the United States and in Canada (e.g., Penton 1976; Henderson 2010; Knox 2013).[8] Recently, this gap has been partially filled by a three-volume collaborative work on the history of Jehovah's Witnesses in Europe (Besier and Stoklosa 2013–2018) and by Zoe Knox's book on *Jehovah's Witnesses and the Secular World* (2018). However, concerning the topics considered in this book, the literature produced by the Watch Tower Society for its internal use and for missionary purposes remains, with rare exceptions, the only source.

The necessity of retracing specific historical aspects of the Watch Tower Society on the basis of its own literature may raise some methodological difficulties, since the presentation of some facts will be influenced by the Society's theology and practical interests (Knox 2011: 163–169). Within the framework of my research, however, I do not see this issue as particularly problematic. Quite the contrary! My goal in using this material is twofold. First, I want to show how some of the current organizational and ritual forms of the Jehovah's Witnesses came to be. For this purpose, several of the Society's internal publications are especially relevant, because one of their roles was (and still is) to communicate and explain reforms of organizational matters and of rituals to members of congregations worldwide. Second, I want to illuminate how the Watch Tower Society has presented itself and its activities to the public and, more importantly, to its own members. Over the years, the Society has developed a "canonical" view of its history. This historiography is reproduced, with small variations, in books, articles, and films that Jehovah's Witnesses are invited to study both individually and collectively. Accordingly, the analysis of this literature provides an important key for understanding how contemporary Jehovah's Witnesses relate (or are supposed to relate) their experiences with the (self-ascribed) divine mission of the Society.

Numerous Kingdom Halls (the Witnesses' places of assembly) have a physical archive of older Watch Tower publications, and for many years the Society has produced a CD, then a DVD, with a comprehensive index as well as an electronic archive of most of its books, booklets, yearbooks, tracts, magazines, and workbooks.[9] From 2012 onwards, these resources have been progressively moved online and are publicly accessible in numerous languages via the official Watchtower Online Library (wol.jw.org). Not all of the Society's publications are available on this website; most of the missing ones, however, can be found without much difficulty elsewhere in electronic form. In my research, I have often used and compared these various resources in order to reconstruct the relevant processes accurately, find the most telling passages to illustrate certain points, and to quote them as precisely as possible. To reference the Watch Tower publications, I use the same abbreviations used by the Society; for instance, the abbreviation "Bh 2005" refers to the 2005 edition of the booklet *What Does the Bible Really Teach?* When I was not able to find an official abbreviation, I coined one myself. The accompanying list of my primary sources includes a key to these abbreviations.

8

Collective Action—Advertising the King and the Kingdom

8.1 Introduction

In public and academic discussions, the first association that comes to mind when Jehovah's Witnesses are mentioned is usually their relentless missionary efforts. While there are other Christian groups engaged in house-to-house preaching in various parts of the world, notably the Latter-day Saints (Mormons), in Western Europe this form of ministry is a distinctive trait of the Watch Tower Society and its members. In the media and in everyday conversations, this activity is often considered an inconvenience and regarded with suspicion as a demonstration of the Witnesses' fanatical convictions. As a result, no one ever asks how the Witnesses themselves feel about going door-to-door to announce God's Kingdom and distribute the literature produced by the Watch Tower Society. Contrary to many stale and predictable polemical accounts of Jehovah's Witnesses' proselytism, this question offers a promising avenue of investigation, since it invites us to reflect on the motivational structures that underpins their zealous engagement.

In this chapter, I will discuss the missionary work of Jehovah's Witnesses, in particular their house-to-house ministry, as an example of joint action or collective intentional action. Taking a more individualist approach, scholars in the tradition of rational choice theory have emphasized the role of missionary activities in the constitution and consolidation of religious groups. In their analyses, they call special attention to the role of "costly activities" (costly, for instance, in terms of time invested) in discouraging free riders within the community. In my discussion, I will push back against this explanation and argue that an analysis of the Witnesses' field ministry in terms of collective intentions can provide new insight into the motivations and rationales behind this activity and can reveal a more complex commitment structure than the one suggested by the rational choice approach. More specifically, I will draw on the work of John Searle and Raimo Tuomela to defend the following thesis: Jehovah's Witnesses participate in the Watch Tower Society's preaching efforts on the basis of a collectively accepted, ritually instituted, "we-mode" intention that provides them with a rational reason for action that is independent of their personal inclinations.

The chapter will be structured as follows. In the next section, I will introduce the standpoint of rational choice theory in the sociology of religion, which will serve as a foil to my general discussion. Rational choice approaches can be articulated in various ways and combined with other perspectives (e.g., Boudon 1983; Stolz 2006, 2009). For the sake of my discussion, I will focus on the work of Rodney Stark and his closest collaborators, mainly because their research presents with great clarity a number of general philosophical premises regarding human action, rationality, and community building. In my discussion, I will highlight these features and examine the role that these theorists attribute to missionary work for the constitution of religious groups. Against this background, in the third section, I will start laying out my arguments by introducing a number of considerations on the history and practical implications of the Jehovah's Witnesses' missionary work. In the fourth section, I will switch to an empirical perspective and present quantitative and qualitative data from my research to illustrate how Jehovah's Witnesses apprehend their missionary engagement and evaluate their experiences in the field ministry.

All of my interviewees are active in the field ministry. Perhaps surprisingly, however, many of them indicate that they are not very fond of this activity, and some clearly would prefer not to do it. The main part of this chapter will be dedicated to making sense of their attitudes. To do so, in the fifth section, I will study how the Watch Tower Society frames its missionary work. I will argue that the field ministry is presented as a collective effort in which every contribution counts but none is individually sufficient. This observation raises the issue of determining how a discourse concerning a collective work can generate a proper joint action. In pursuit of a solution, I will call attention to the role of the so-called Service Meetings and to the performative aspect of the activities that take place during these encounters. Specifically, in the sixth section, I will focus on the question-and-answer study of the Watch Tower Society's publications, particularly of the magazine *Our Kingdom Ministry*. A sketch of the historical institutionalization of this practice will provide the background to some empirical considerations concerning its current features. To analyze the latter, I will avail myself of some of the implications of John Searle's speech act theory for the structure of human rationality and commitment. Drawing on Raimo Tuomela's treatment of joint action, I will then extend these reflections to the framework of collective intentional action. In my concluding remarks, I will summarize my findings and reflect on the status of my theoretical claims.

8.2 The Perspective of Rational Choice Theory

8.2.1 Foundational ideas

To speak about rational choice approaches to the study of religion means entering a very complex and varied field, and some preliminary choices regarding both the scholars and the topics to be discussed need to be made. In this section, I will deal with a particular "flavor" of rational choice theory in the sociology of religion, which gained prominence in the 1980s and 1990s (mostly) through the work of the sociologist Rodney Stark (1934–2022) and his closest collaborators: William Sims Bainbridge, Roger Finke, and Laurence R. Iannaccone. While some of these scholars refined their approaches in slightly different directions, their close and continued cooperation, their common research interests, and a number of general assumptions that they share about human behavior allow us to consider their work as constituting a coherent framework. Accordingly, the expressions "rational choice theorists" or "rational choice scholars" below will refer to these authors unless otherwise specified.

The work of rational choice scholars has been met with skepticism, particularly in Europe. Indeed, their premises and results have been thoroughly criticized on methodological (Voas, Crockett, and Olson 2002), empirical (Stolz 2004), psychological (Jerolmack and Porpora 2004), political (Gauthier 2019), conceptual (Bruce and Wallis 1984; Bruce 1999), philosophical (Bryant 2000), and ideological (McKinnon 2011) grounds. In light of such responses, one might ask whether it is still worth spending time discussing their ideas today. A number of reasons support an affirmative answer to this question within the scope of my research.

Despite the objections (some well founded, some rather hasty) of its detractors, the rational choice approach to religion is not trivial and offers plausible answers to empirical puzzles, including some important questions related to religious commitment and the internal dynamics of religious communities. Furthermore, rational choice scholars have used the case of Jehovah's Witnesses and their missionary work to illustrate and test their answers to such questions. Most importantly, however, the concepts of rationality and individual intentional action put forward by the authors in this field constitute an ideal foil to highlight some contrasting features of the framework developed in this study. In sum, my goal is to present selected aspects of rational choice theory in order to emphasize the distinctiveness of my approach to religious groups in terms of collective intentionality.

In the sociology of religion, the rational choice approach was developed in reaction to the secularization thesis that dominated scholarly debates for the better part of the twentieth century. With their earlier work, Stark and Bainbridge had wanted to demonstrate that secularization is not a modern phenomenon but rather a cyclical and self-limiting process that is always going on in all societies (Stark and Bainbridge 1985). At the turn of the millennium, Stark declared that the secularization thesis had been "laid to rest" (Stark 1999) and that a new paradigm had arrived, that "not only rejects each of the elements of the old paradigm [...] but] proposes the precise opposite of each" (Stark and Finke 2000: 31).

The main drivers behind this (self-proclaimed) paradigmatic revolution (Warner 1993) were the assessment of a theoretical deficit in the social scientific study of religion (Stark 2004) and the corresponding endeavor to develop "a general theory of religion" (Stark and Bainbridge 1987) that could deductively explain a large array of religious phenomena. The underlying concept stating what a theory *is* and how it should be framed was heavily influenced by the epistemology of Karl Popper (Stark 1997: 3–4).

> A theory is a set of statements about relationships among a set of abstract concepts. These statements say how and why the concepts are interrelated. Furthermore, these statements must give rise to implications that potentially are falsifiable empirically. That is, it must be possible to deduce from a theory some statements

about empirical events that could, in principle, turn out to be incorrect. (Stark and Bainbridge 1987: 13)

Accordingly, rational choice theorists have devised a set of concepts and a small number of axioms about human behavior from which to deduce empirically testable propositions (Stark and Bainbridge 1987: 15–21; Iannaccone 1997). Popper, however, was not the only source of inspiration for the development of their ideas. Among other authors, the American sociologist George C. Homans and the American economist Gary Becker are often acknowledged as important references (see, e.g., Stark 1997; Iannaccone 1997).

Homans was a staunch advocate of the explanatory power of deductive approaches and borrowed his axioms from behavioral psychology and elementary economics, noting that, at a fundamental level, these disciplines tend to converge since both "envisage human behavior as a function of its pay-off" (Homans 1961: 13). According to Homans, scholars of human behavior often have recourse to economic explanations to fill the gaps in their theories, although they rarely acknowledge it. In contrast to this, Homans offered a conception of social behavior "as an exchange of activity, tangible or intangible, and more or less rewarding or costly between at least two persons" (Homans 1961: 13), thus bringing the economic foundation of his analysis into the open.

If Homans's goal was to convince social scientists of the epistemic value of an approach to human behavior rooted in economics, Gary Becker's aim was, conversely, to persuade economists that it was possible to apply their specific disciplinary perspective to other aspects of human life beyond the exchange of goods in the marketplace. In a short manifesto entitled "The economic approach to human behavior," Becker defined the heart of this approach as "[t]he combined assumptions of maximizing behavior, market equilibrium, and stable preferences, used relentlessly and unflinchingly" (Becker 1976: 5).

The assumption of (conscious or unconscious) maximizing behavior goes back to the founders of liberal economic theory, notably Adam Smith (1977), and utilitarian philosophy who saw mankind, as Bentham (2000: 14) put it, "under the governance of two sovereign masters, *pain* and *pleasure*," in a constant endeavor to avoid the former and increase the latter. Various markets are assumed to coordinate individual efforts to this end. Finally, the assumption of stable preferences "provides a stable foundation for generating predictions about responses to various changes, and prevents the analyst from succumbing to the temptation of simply postulating the required shift in preferences to 'explain' all apparent contradictions to his predictions" (Becker 1976: 5).

Following the *homo economicus* axiom (see Febrero and Schwartz 1995), Becker argues that when social actors do not exploit apparently profitable opportunities, the economic approach reaffirms the actors' rationality and the stability of their preferences. To do so, it postulates "the existence of costs, monetary or psychic, of taking advantage of these opportunities that eliminate their profitability" (Becker 1976: 7), even though an outside observer might not immediately see these costs. Becker recognizes that this corollary renders the economic approach almost tautological in the same way that "postulating the existence of (sometimes unobserved) uses of energy completes the energy system, and preserves the law of the conservation of energy" (Becker 1976: 7).

In his view, however, this issue is secondary if the system is completed in a "useful way," that is, in a way that enables powerful predictions while remaining open to empirical refutation (Becker 1976: 7).

8.2.2 Towards a theory of religion

While rational choice theory developed over several decades, the general framework sketched above has constituted its underpinnings since the foundational article by Stark and Bainbridge, "Towards a Theory of Religion" (1980), later reprinted and extended as the second chapter of their general theory of religion (Stark and Bainbridge 1987: 25–53). Thus, the maximization axiom is built into the core of the theory, which assumes that "humans seek what they perceive to be rewards and avoid what they perceive to be costs" (Stark and Bainbridge 1980: 115). From this axiom, it follows that people imagine possible means to achieve the desired reward and choose "the one with the greatest likelihood of success in the light of available information" to guide their action (Stark and Bainbridge 1980: 117).

In some cases, however, it is not possible to obtain the desired reward or even to assess if the desired reward exists at all—for instance, if there is a life after death. In such cases, people will often accept, as a provisional substitute for the reward, what Stark and Bainbridge call a "compensator." A compensator is an explanation that posits attainment of the reward "in the distant future or some other nonverifiable context" (Stark and Bainbridge 1980: 121). Religious views on immortality constitute a paradigmatic case in point: since eternal life cannot be obtained here and now, "[T]he desire for immortality is not satisfied with a reward, but with an intangible promise, a compensator," the validity of which "must be accepted or rejected on faith alone" (Stark and Bainbridge 1980: 122). Thus, the concept of compensators introduces a form of Pascal's wager with different degrees of risk depending on the type of compensator.

Compensators can have various degrees of generality depending on the scope of the rewards to which they can provide a substitute. Among the most general compensators figure those that provide explanations for questions of ultimate meaning, such as whether life has a purpose. Stark and Bainbridge postulate the existence of such questions as an anthropological constant without, however, framing this claim as an explicit axiom. Furthermore, they consider as "self-evident" that some of these questions require a "supernatural answer." In particular, questions concerning the purpose (of life or the universe) would require the assumption of one or more conscious agents beyond the natural world. Religions can thus be conceptualized as "systems of general compensators based on supernatural assumptions" (Stark and Bainbridge 1980: 123). The fact that this discussion appears almost as an aside in their otherwise strict succession of axioms, definitions, and propositions is not innocent. What is expressed here is a fundamental premise of rational choice theory, namely, the stability of preferences, in this case the persistence of a religious demand.

Once the stability of the demand is postulated, the focus of the theory can shift to the supply side. The division of labor necessary for the production of complex rewards and compensators (Stark and Bainbridge 1987: 75–76) entails that "religious expression does not consist primarily of interaction between a lone individual and a god, but is anchored in social groups" (Stark and Finke 2000: 102). In particular, the need for supernatural rewards leads to the creation of social organizations "whose primary purpose is to create, maintain, and exchange supernaturally based general compensators," that is, religious organizations (Stark and Bainbridge 1980: 125).

Still, the interaction between the individuals and the organizations follows the same rational logic of maximization. The individual commitment to religious organizations—that is, the degree to which a person will comply with the requirement inherent in the explanations provided by the organization (Stark and Bainbridge 1987: 103)—will depend on "the net balance of rewards and costs humans perceive they will experience from participation" (Stark and Bainbridge 1987: 42). Should the costs exceed the utility, a person will move to a different religious organization; should no other organization be available, we can expect a drop in a society's religious life as measured, for instance, by regular attendance at religious services (Iannaccone 1991; Stark and Iannaccone 1994; Finke 1997).

Against this backdrop, one may assume that people usually avoid religious organizations that require high participation costs. However, already in the early seventies, legal scholar and religious freedom advocate Dean M. Kelley published a study noting that while most mainline Protestant churches in the United States were losing members, "stricter" denominations such as the Latter-day Saints and Jehovah's Witnesses were still going strong (Kelley 1972: 20–25). Two decades later, in a series of articles that became part of the rational choice canon, Laurence Iannaccone (1992a, b, 1994) sought to explain the correlation between the "strictness" and the "strength" of a church in economic terms.

Iannaccone's thesis is predicated on the idea that religious commodities are "inherently risky," because the existence of rewards such as eternal life and unending bliss "must be taken on trust" (Iannaccone 1992a: 125). This uncertainty would explain the emergence of religious institutions as means to increase (the appearance of) information and reduce fraud (Iannaccone 1997: 34). Congregational structures would provide trustworthy "testimonials" for the religious goods considering that "fellow members are more trustworthy than strangers" (Iannaccone 1992a: 126) and, as Stark and Finke (2000: 107) reason, "An individual's confidence in religious explanations is strengthened to the extent that others express their confidence in them."

Congregational structures also carry costs, however. In particular, they are vulnerable to group dynamics in which some people take advantage of others' efforts without contributing to the production of collective goods, such as a celebration (Iannaccone 1994: 1183–1184). Since these so-called free riders (Olson 1965) take more than they give, "their mere presence dilutes a group's resources, reducing the average level of participation, enthusiasm, energy, and the like" (Iannaccone 1994: 1884). Think, for instance, of a congregation in which only half of the participants join in singing the hymns. In light of these considerations,

> It would seem that religions are caught on the horns of a dilemma. On the one hand, a congregational structure which relies on the collective actions of numerous volunteers is needed to make the religion credible. On the other hand, this same

congregational structure threatens to undermine the level of commitment and contributions needed to make a religion viable. (Iannaccone 1992a: 127)

A congregation could limit this problem by screening out free riders. This strategy proves hardly practicable, however. According to Iannaccone (1994: 1187), an alternative solution is to introduce "entry fees" that "discourage anyone not seriously interested in 'buying the product.'"

In this respect, submitting members to various forms of social stigma—for instance, through a distinctive diet or dress code—makes it more costly for them to engage in activities outside the group. The same result can be achieved through higher demands in terms of financial or time investments (Iannaccone 1992b). In conclusion, increasing the strictness of the group (as defined here in terms of costly behaviors) discourages lukewarm congregants: "Potential members are forced to choose: participate fully or not at all," which causes levels of commitment and participation to increase (Iannaccone 1992a: 127).

8.2.3 The rational choice take on Jehovah's Witnesses' missionary work

In his original explanation of the positive correlation between "strictness" and "strength," Iannaccone was not directly concerned with the problem of church growth. However, his thesis was quickly integrated into a ten-point model, accounting for the success (that is, in rational choice terms, numerical growth) or decline of religious groups (Stark 1996). Due to their rapid global expansion since the end of World War II, Jehovah's Witnesses represent one of rational choice scholars' favorite empirical case studies to test their theories. Indeed, Stark and Iannaccone (1997) demonstrate that the structures and doctrines of the Watch Tower Society perfectly fit Stark's multilayered theoretical model. Drawing on this theoretical background and on the available historical data on the Jehovah's Witnesses' membership numbers, they conclude that by the end of the twenty-first century, there could be in excess of 190 million Witnesses worldwide (Stark and Iannaccone 1997: 154). Without entering into every detail of their analysis, it is worth noting that the missionary work of Jehovah's Witnesses accounts for various aspects of their success.

Most directly, the Witnesses' field ministry provides an important basis for the recruitment of new members via a voluntary labor force, which in the early 1990s accounted for a potential growth rate of up to 7 percent per year (Stark and Iannaccone 1997: 147–148). The missionary work also constitutes a framework for strong socialization of the younger members (Stark and Iannaccone 1997: 152–153). Most significantly, however, the Witnesses' "very high expectations concerning religious and missionary activity" contribute to discouraging free riding within congregations (Stark and Iannaccone 1997: 145). Together with other stringent requirements, such as the rejection of flag saluting and blood transfusion, door-to-door preaching participates in maintaining a relative tension between the group and the surrounding society, which fosters the individual religious commitment of the members and increases the credibility of the religious rewards (Stark and Iannaccone 1997: 144–146; Stark and Finke 2000: 48).

This analysis of Jehovah's Witnesses' structures found a favorable reception among some experts in the study of new religious movements, such as the Italian scholar of religion Massimo Introvigne (2004, 2015), who uses this framework to analyze the historical development of the Watch Tower Society. Other sociologists of religion reacted more critically, however. The rational choice predictions about the growth of Jehovah's Witnesses and other groups have been subjected to particular scrutiny (e.g., Cragun and Lawson 2010; Lawson and Cragun 2012). In this respect, David Voas (2010) reflects on the link between growth, missionary work, and commitment.

Voas notes that the Witnesses' global growth rate has slowed down since the 1980s, reaching 1.3 percent in 2005—a growth rate that is "only just keeping pace with that of the total world population" (Voas 2010: 119). According to his assessment, this slowdown is neither due to a decrease in fertility nor to a diminished missionary effort, but is rather the consequence of a "declining productivity of recruitment work," that is, of the number of hours necessary to generate a baptism (Voas 2010: 120). If the average American Witness in the seventies might have expected to convert at least two people during his career as a publisher, "[T]he current level of baptism is such that an ordinary Witness is unlikely to make any conversion in a lifetime of knocking on doors" (Voas 2010: 121).

A consequence of this trend could be a crisis of motivation and commitment among Jehovah's Witnesses, who would become increasingly inactive, leading ultimately to the collapse of the organization. Voas sees this risk as inherent in the role of missionary work within the Watch Tower Society:

> The proselytizing orientation of the [Jehovah's Witnesses] makes them vulnerable to decline when conditions become unfavourable. The rewards of membership are found in possessing and proclaiming the truth, rather than in access to rituals, emotionally uplifting worship, or a range of social opportunities. Meetings resemble training seminars more than conventional religious services. The difficulty is that if recruitment appears to be the *raison d'être* of activity, and then for extended periods not merely the individual publisher but the entire congregation experience no success, the consequential loss of morale could be substantial. (Voas 2010: 123)

While acknowledging that for some Witnesses the hardship of the field ministry may confirm their belief that our world is in Satan's grip, Voas maintains that for at least some of the members, the purpose of the field service must be real, and not merely symbolic. Therefore, "[I]f it becomes clear that the organization is losing ground, the willingness to sacrifice may also fade" (Voas 2010: 125). Voas thus turns the results of Stark and Iannaccone's analysis on their head and infers that *if rational choice theorists are right* in their claim that people expect to maximize the return of their investments, the future for Jehovah's Witnesses looks bleak. Nonetheless, he concludes, if the Watch Tower Society survives, "[I]t will not be because field service is efficient, but because it expresses and reinforces commitment [...] partly by creating a bond between publishers" (Voas 2010: 129).

My data does not allow me to make any statistical predictions regarding the future of the Watch Tower Society. However, it can shed new light on the form of commitment that underlies Jehovah's Witnesses missionary work—a kind of commitment, I will argue, that differs from the one implied by rational choice theory. The exploration of this issue constitutes the main topic of this chapter.

8.3 The Missionary Work of Jehovah's Witnesses

8.3.1 The institutionalization of the field ministry

To start our examination, it is important to present in some detail the origins and the practical implications of the Witnesses' field ministry. To do so, we have to go back to the inaugural period of the Watch Tower Society and first understand the plans of its founder, Charles T. Russell, regarding the diffusion of various publications.

In April 1881, *The Watchtower* published an announcement entitled "Wanted 1,000 Preachers." In it, Russell called attention to the opening of a vast field "for the employment of the time and talent of every consecrated man and woman to whom the Lord has committed a knowledge of His truth" (W, April 1881 [reprints]: 214). His plan was for these "Colporteurs or Evangelists" to go from town to town to distribute tracts and to sell copies of the book *Day Dawn* as well as subscriptions to the *Watchtower*. The Society offered to provide the tracts and the book for free so that the colporteurs could use the sale profits to cover their travel expenses. Apparently, the announcement drew some attention because a month later the magazine had to clarify that the Society was looking for "laborers [...] who will be working for heavenly wages, rather than for the price of a paper or book" (W, May 1881 [reprints]: 228).

As many *Watchtower* articles attest, Russell had the highest esteem for the class of colporteurs. Nevertheless, he strictly regulated their activities and severely punished those individuals who sought to rise to prominence, for instance through public preaching (Beckford 1975a: 7–8). From 1894 onward, a small class of traveling representatives of the Watch Tower Society, later known as Pilgrims, was responsible for overseeing the colporteurs' work as well as the activities of the *ecclesiae* (as the local congregations were called), making sure that the Society's directives were implemented at the local level (Beckford 1975a: 15–16, Jv 1993: 222–226). Today, this role is assumed by so-called circuit overseers.

The Society's centralized control over the activities and structures of the local congregations drastically increased under Rutherford. To achieve this goal, the new president profoundly reshaped the method of circulation of the Watch Tower publications. In 1919, Rutherford announced the launch of a new magazine titled *The Golden Age*—the title of this magazine will be changed to *Consolation* between 1937 and 1946 and finally to *Awake!* in August 1946. The distribution of *The Golden Age* was no longer confided to colporteurs. Instead, this task was assigned to voluntary workers within the local congregations (see the 1919 pamphlet *To Whom the Work Is Entrusted*, quoted in Jp 1959: 95).

Yet individual members could not order on their own account copies of the magazine to distribute. As a retrospective account published in *The Watchtower* explains, "Congregations desiring to participate in the new field service now opening up with the *Golden Age* campaign were asked to register as a service organization with the Society. Upon receiving such request, the Society theocratically appointed one of the local members to serve as the Society's appointee known as the 'director,' not subject to local yearly election" (W 1955, May 15: 298). With this move, Rutherford achieved two results simultaneously. On the one hand, he transformed the congregations in "sorting centers" for the literature destined to a given territory and, on the other hand, he started the progressive weakening of the office of the locally elected congregation leaders, known as elders (Blanchard 2008: 69).

In the following years, Rutherford phased in the modern house-to-house ministry and progressively extended the scope of this practice. By 1920, all members of local congregations who participated in the witnessing activities were required to turn in a weekly report on their efforts (Jp 1959: 96). In 1927, Rutherford sought to break the last resistance of local elders against the new door-to-door service by urging the "faithful" members to remove their reluctant leaders from office (W 1927, November 1: 326). The elders' role was finally judged "unbiblical" in 1932 and replaced with a service committee in which, by 1938, all the "servants" were directly appointed by the Watch Tower Society (Penton 2015: 87–89).

By the 1930s, participation in the field ministry had become a distinctive trait of the members of the Watch Tower Society (Jv 1993: 564). During that decade, the preaching work of Jehovah's Witnesses received a substantial boost thanks to one of Rutherford's most consequential theological innovations. Since Russell, the Watch Tower Society had identified its baptized members with the 144,000 members of the anointed class (or little flock) mentioned in the Book of Revelation, who are destined to enjoy everlasting life in heaven and rule with Jesus over God's kingdom. However, the Book of Revelation (Rev. 7: 9–10) also mentions a "great crowd" who do not belong to the anointed class but have survived the great tribulation. In 1932, Rutherford started to identify the great crowd with the growing number of sympathizers who attended Jehovah's Witnesses' meetings and conventions. These people, who would enjoy everlasting life on a paradise earth, were thus progressively brought into the Society (Chryssides 2016: 93–96). Today, the vast majority of Jehovah's Witnesses regard themselves as members of the great crowd or, as it is sometimes called, the "other sheep."

From a sociological point of view, Rutherford's interpretation provided a solution to the accelerating growth of the Watch Tower Society, whose members were about to surpass the fateful number of 144,000 (Chryssides 2016: 96). Furthermore, it encouraged a new and broader audience to read the Watch Tower publications (Blanchard 2008: 71). Between 1934 and 1938, a number of privileges and duties were extended to the new members. Among other things, already in 1932, the Society invited its anointed members to encourage the other sheep "to come along with them and to take some part in proclaiming to others that the kingdom of God is at hand" (W 1932, August 1: 232).

In sum, Rutherford's organizational reforms of the 1920s transformed the distribution of the Watch Tower literature from a work performed by a group of specialists to a task entrusted to all faithful members of the Society. A decade later, his theological reinterpretation of the great crowd in the Revelation of John simultaneously expanded the borders of the Society, widened the readership of its publications, and significantly increased the number of people available for the field ministry.

In the following decades, the Watch Tower Society implemented a number of measures to ensure the effectiveness of its work and extended its missionary reach on a global scale. The last major adjustments to the Watch Tower Society's missionary organization were introduced in the early 1970s when some of Rutherford's reforms were eventually rolled back. Elders were reestablished in 1971 (W 1971, November 15: 688–694), although their appointment remains under the control of the Watch Tower Society (Penton 2015: 323–325; Chryssides 2016: 137). Among the body of elders now presiding over a congregation, a service overseer is responsible for coordinating "the Kingdom-preaching work" of the congregants (W 1972, August 1: 460). The service overseer also keeps a detailed record of the congregation's preaching work and reports on it to the Society.

8.3.2 Practical implications of the field ministry

As the previous historical overview indicates, by the 1970s the fundamental structures of the missionary work carried out by Jehovah's Witnesses today were in place. For this reason, I will now shift from a diachronic to a systematic presentation of the field ministry. As indicated in Chapter 7, within the Watch Tower Society, regular baptized congregation members are also known as publishers or, sometimes, proclaimers. This appellation underscores their active role in the predication of the Kingdom, in particular through the house-to-house ministry and the distribution of Watch Tower literature. When they encounter a householder who expresses interest in their message, publishers are supposed to make return visits to engage this person in a discussion based on the Bible. Eventually, they should start a home Bible study with that person and direct him or her to one of the Jehovah's Witnesses congregations (Od 2015: 81–88). Other forms of preaching include "informal witnessing" in the workplace or in other public settings, calling on people at places of business, and so-called street work, that is, the distribution of literature to passersby. This last method has been revamped since 2015 thanks to the introduction of specially designed literature display carts (Km 2015, April: 2). In addition to their printed publications, throughout the years Jehovah's Witnesses have used a number of media in their field ministry, as I will detail in the next chapter.

There is no official minimum time requirement for ordinary publishers. Rather, the Watch Tower publications encourage them to set personal and realistic goals and to try and improve their field ministry depending on their life circumstances (e.g., Od 2015: 80; W 2015, February 15: 18). Nevertheless, Chryssides (2016: 137) mentions a quota of ten hours a month as a "normal expectation" from regular publishers. Publishers are required to fill out a report card each month detailing the number of publications distributed or videos shown, the number of return visits and Bible studies conducted, and the total number of hours spent in the field ministry (Od 2015: 74–55). Publishers who fail to submit their card for a month are considered "irregular"; those who fail to report for a period of six months, are "inactive" (Chryssides 2016: 137). Inactivity alone is never a ground for being excluded or "disfellowshipped." However, the Watch Tower publications regularly offer recommendations to elders and publishers on how to support and reintegrate inactive Witnesses (e.g., Km 1987, November: 2). Furthermore, inactive members are not counted in the official statistics released by the Watch Tower Society in its *Yearbook*.

In addition to the regular publishing work, the Watch Tower Society encourages its members who meet certain criteria to engage in the field ministry as pioneers—a modern form of the colporteurs of the past. Regular pioneers are appointed for one year and spend about 70 hours a month (or 18 hours a week) preaching, while auxiliary pioneers receive a renewable monthly appointment and spend between 30 and 50 hours a month in the field service (Jl 2012: 13; Mwb 2016, July: 8). Finally, special pioneers are expected to invest 130 hours a month in the missionary work and are often sent to open up new areas not yet reached by regular Witnesses. In some cases, they are granted a small reimbursement (Chryssides 2016: 138).

In sum, active Jehovah's Witnesses dedicate a considerable amount of time to their preaching work. For regular publishers, this implies arranging at least a couple of hours a week for the field ministry. For pioneers, the time investment is even larger. These observations prompt a number of questions. How do Jehovah's Witnesses manage to find the resources to balance their "secular" life and their missionary work? How do they perceive their involvement in the field ministry? What motivates them to take on such an endeavor? The empirical data presented in the next section provide some answers.

8.4 Individual Attitudes: Empirical Evidence

8.4.1 Preaching as a regular praxis and a lifestyle

Survey data on four Jehovah's Witnesses congregations in Switzerland show that, for the large majority of members, the field ministry is an integral part of the weekly schedule. When asked how often during the last three months they distributed flyers, brochures or tracts, 91.3 percent of the surveyed Witnesses responded that they had done so at least once a week or more often. None of them completely refrained from such activity. Further qualitative data collected in Switzerland and Germany help us to get a more nuanced picture.

All of the Jehovah's Witnesses interviewed mention their participation in the field ministry. Their time investment, however, varies depending on their life circumstances. "Of course, I still preach," says, for instance, eighty-three-year-old **Monique**. Then she adds: "I'm alone and I am no longer the youngest one, but I definitely have time. I preach between 20 and 30 hours each month." For **Frank**, on the contrary, time is scarce because he works from Monday to Friday. "Regarding the field ministry," he admits, "I have to make an effort. Right know the circumstances don't allow me to give as much as I would like." Some interviewees have reduced their working hours to have more time for the family and the ministry. Because of their engagement as regular pioneers, both **Valentin** and **Michaela** only work half-time. Finally, **Olga,** who also serves as a pioneer, states that because of her full-time job, she will spend her holidays as an international servant abroad for three or four weeks to reach her annual goal.

This display of commitment is sometimes accompanied by a degree of enthusiasm and a sense of urgency regarding one's mission. **Eva**, for instance, states that, "the more one participates [in the field ministry], the more one feels the joy." For his part, **Jörg**, who serves as an auxiliary pioneer, notes that, despite "everything that is going on in the world," many people remain indifferent to the message of Jehovah's Witnesses, and this gets him worked up:

> Try to imagine: You know that someone's house is on fire. I see this house burning. And I get there, and knock at the door [mimicking knocking sound], and you get out and I tell you, "Hey, your house is burning!" And you tell me, "I don't care." (**Jörg**)

Jörg explains that he strives to remain humble and emphasizes that people are free to choose whether they want to listen or not. "Jehovah only demands that we do our best," he concludes. Still, **Jörg**'s remarks already suggest a more complex attitude toward the field ministry, an attitude in which contrasting moods and experiences temper Jehovah's Witnesses' elation and engagement. Let us take a closer look at this ambivalent standpoint.

8.4.2 An ambivalent attitude toward the field ministry

Lara expresses her ambivalent attitude with respect to preaching in a very direct way. When asked about her experiences in the field ministry, she states that she has mixed feelings about it: "Very mixed feelings, I must say." She elaborates:

> On the one hand, it really brings you joy when the people [you meet] are happy to see you. Then, it is really pleasant when you can show them something from the Bible. That might sound clichéd, but it is really a good feeling. [...] [On the other hand] It is not so pleasant when people are very dismissive. Then it is, well, not the most enjoyable activity. But I think that with time one can get a thicker skin, so that getting a door shut in your face hurts less [laughs]. (**Lara**)

As **Lara**'s quote suggests, going from house to house preaching the coming of Jehovah's Kingdom can be arduous, and it is something that takes some time to get used to. However, many of my interviewees underscore that the feeling of discomfort when ringing someone's doorbell never goes away, even after several years, although one can perhaps manage it better. The following exchange with **Emma** and **Fritz** illustrates this point:

> **Emma:** Well, at the beginning [laughs] I said, "I'll do everything, but I won't do that [the field ministry]" [laughs]. Almost everyone says so [laughs]. Yes, but then I studied the Bible with a sister and it brings you such joy and you say, "What? That

is in the Bible? And that? And that?" that you suddenly think, "I want to tell that to the people." Of course, it is also a commandment in a sense, because Jesus said, "Go and preach," just as he did. That's clear. But the more you learn, the more joy it brings you. That does not mean that you don't get nervous. [...]

Fritz: It is also not human nature to go around ringing doorbells. But I want to underscore what my wife said. We do it out of conviction, and at the beginning it was more arduous, and today, too, it is not always easy.

Overall, the couple's statements present the door-to-door ministry as something that does not come naturally to most Jehovah's Witnesses. Furthermore, although the field ministry can lead to joyful feelings and experiences, it also constitutes a response to a biblical commandment that can serve as a source of motivation. Still, several Jehovah's Witnesses whom I interviewed indicate that an intrinsic personal conviction is not always sufficient to overcome the disquiet of the ministry; they emphasize the importance of working with other Witnesses to overcome this malaise. Such statements draw attention to a social dimension of the field ministry.

8.4.3 The social dimension of the field ministry

According to several of my interviewees, the fact that Jehovah's Witnesses usually preach in pairs constitutes the most enjoyable aspect of the field ministry and makes up for the difficulties one can experience in relation to the service. Indeed, for **Leonard** the companionship of other Witnesses is the core element that makes the field ministry a positive experience overall. He states:

I like it [The field ministry]. If you asked my wife, she would say that it's no fun. [...] I like it because I'm with a friend. For me that's the main thing. And, of course, to find people who are interested. But the chance that we really find someone who is interested is quite small. Even though I always look for the positive side in everyone and if someone gets ill-tempered, that's just how it is [...]. Overall, I do not consider it a burden. [...] But should it be that we do not have to do it anymore, I could live with that. Well, [we do not] "have to": we do not do it for a person but for our Creator, and for that reason it is not a burden. [...] I'm happy if I find someone who is interested, but I do not get frustrated if I was on the road eight hours and no one was interested. I was with a friend and I did something for my Creator Jehovah God. It's a matter of attitude. (**Leonard**)

Leonard's multilayered statement shows the interaction between attitudinal and relational aspects in the field ministry with regard to difficulties such as the general lack of interest or the rude reactions of some householders. These negative experiences are counterbalanced by the belief in the divine mandate of one's mission and by the enjoyment of a friend's company.

For other Jehovah's Witnesses, however, the role of a partner during the house-to-house ministry goes beyond the aspect of conviviality. Consider the example of **Paul**.

He states that he likes participating in the field ministry, but he recognizes that "it is not really easy." He continues:

> I mean, people do not usually go so gladly to ring at a door to talk about religion or even other things. [...] Sometimes we go as a group, and sometimes it is easier and sometimes more difficult. But at times it certainly requires a lot of effort. But what we often hear, what we have also experienced is that one realizes one gets strength [from others]. I am not sure that one could keep it up for a long time alone. (**Paul**)

Paul draws attention to the fundamental difference between serving in the ministry alone and doing it with someone else. In his view, the presence of other people gives each participant a strength that an isolated individual would not have. Eighty-three-year-old **Monique** also emphasizes this aspect. When asked whether she enjoys participating in the field ministry, her answer, after a moment of hesitation, is a "yes, but." She explains:

> In itself, it is not something that one would do. Don't you think? [...] There are only a few who find it is easy. Most say, "I'm not doing that" [laughs]. Well, we go in pairs, and I have recently met a person who asked me why we come in pairs. It is undoubtedly so that we don't lose our courage. Jesus already sent his disciples in pairs. Alone, with the current rejection and loss of interest, one would not go far. [...] Alone, one would lose courage. But, well, mostly I'm glad to do it. But when sometimes you don't feel like it, when you are ill, then you cancel. But it is not because in that moment you think, "It sucks" that you beg off. That's also the reason why we arrange to meet [for service] with one another. (**Monique**)

In this quote, **Monique** emphasizes both the strength and the motivation that derive from the fact of working in pairs. On the one hand, she states that a person alone would not find the necessary courage to face the widespread lack of interest among the householders; on the other hand, she indicates that the fact of planning to preach with someone else provides motivation to overcome one's reluctance when one lacks a personal drive.

What preliminary conclusion can we draw from these statements? On the whole, they convey that for many Jehovah's Witnesses the field ministry is an activity that can lead to positive experiences and joyful moments. However, it is often unpleasant, hard, and not something in which they would spontaneously engage—definitely not alone. Indeed, in this respect the collaborative preaching in pairs appears a crucial factor in motivating the missionaries. As for the efficacy of their practices, many Witnesses are aware that most people are not interested in their message and that most doors will remain closed.

Accordingly, my discussions with Swiss and German Jehovah's Witnesses invite us to make a more nuanced assessment of the Witnesses' attitudes toward their preaching activities and to go beyond generalizing statements such as the following by George Chryssides, who writes: "As well as being scriptural, Witnesses believe that house-to-house work is effective and that it encourages such Christian virtues as humility and endurance in the face of apathy" (Chryssides 2008: 75–76). As for "otherworldly rewards," the theology of Jehovah's Witnesses offers a specific view of their relation to the field service, which deserves a closer look. Thus, in the next section, I will discuss how the Watch Tower Society frames the missionary work of its members.

8.5 The Watch Tower Society's Framing of the Field Ministry

8.5.1 The field ministry as a collective duty and privilege

The Watch Tower Society's current interpretation of its members' missionary work is rooted primarily in the organizational and theological reforms initiated by Rutherford. Arguing against the passive cultivation of a "Christian character," Rutherford introduced a new conception of the individual relationship with God, insisting that such a relationship must find its expression through *action* (e.g., W 1926, May 1: 131–137), and notably through the annunciation of Jehovah's Kingdom. Accordingly, the Watch Tower publications present the preaching work as a biblical requirement of all true Christians (e.g., Jt 2000: 31; W 2008, January 15: 4), in accordance with Jesus's commandment to "Go [...], and make disciples of people of all the nations" (Mt. 28: 19). The Society also emphasizes its members' responsibility to help other men and women to attain repentance (e.g., Cl 2012: 161) and discusses the announcement of the Kingdom as a way to fulfill one's obligation to God (e.g., W 2004, September 1: 8–9). Still, the theology of Jehovah's Witnesses does not consider the missionary work as a means to earn personal salvation.

The columns of the Watch Tower magazines emphasize that the field ministry remains a voluntary service that Jehovah's Witnesses perform "by love for the Lord and his cause of righteousness" (W 1919, August 1: 230) and willingly accept "because they have freely chosen to become disciples of Christ, knowing fully the responsibilities that come with that privilege" (G 2001, July 22: 11). Indeed, already in early publications, the task of preaching was characterized as both a duty *and* a privilege, through which each Bible Student was called to play a part in the execution of God's work to destroy Satan's empire (W 1921, March 15: 94). More recent articles insist on the field ministry as a gift from God (e.g., W 2001, September 15: 20) and a unique privilege that only a few enjoy (e.g., Km 2001, September: 1).

While preaching is presented as a personal privilege and duty, it is not conceived of as the task of isolated individuals. Rather, the Watch Tower Society emphasizes that "no individual and no unorganized, scattered groups of individuals" could carry out this mission on their own (W 1986, June 1: 25), and sees it as its responsibility to provide its members with the necessary resources and structures to accomplish their ministry *together*. The Watch Tower Society explicitly considers itself the earthly part of Jehovah's organization (e.g., W 1919, August 1: 230; Pe 1982: 191–202) and presents its structures and activities as the contemporary expression of the same divine guidance that, according to its biblical interpretation, God provided to the Israelites and the early

Christian congregations (Fg 2012: 28–29). With respect to the preaching work, the Organization coordinates the efforts of its members and ensures that, "in fulfilling their commission, true Christians serve 'shoulder to shoulder,' or 'cooperate in [God's] service'" (W 2011, June 1: 14).

Individualist tendencies and overconfident attitudes in the field ministry are clearly discouraged. Jehovah's Witnesses are reminded that "modest people acknowledge their limitations and depend on God's help as they engage in the field ministry" and appreciate the assistance provided by the Society (W 2001, September 15: 20). Each member is therefore invited to accept and follow the Society's instruction to have a share—or to do their share—in the preaching work (e.g., W 2015, January 15: 18; Lvs 2017: 227–228). This perspective is reiterated in a recent reflection published by the Society on its own history:

> As we look back today over some 100 years and see how a small group of God's servants has grown into "a mighty nation," our heart does indeed "throb and overflow" with joy. May that joy and our love for Jehovah, "the Master of the harvest," impel each one of us to keep on *doing our share* in completing the greatest harvest of all time! (Kr 2014: 95, my emphasis)

In sum, the Watch Tower Society frames its role and mission in eschatological terms (Kr 2014: 59–67) as fulfilling the prophetic words of Jesus regarding the Good News of the Kingdom being preached "in all the inhabited earth" (Mt. 24: 14). Against this backdrop, the personal duty of all true Christians to advertise the King and the Kingdom becomes a share in a collective goal of Jehovah's Witnesses.

8.5.2 Individual failure and collective success

The general conception of the missionary work sketched above also influences the Watch Tower Society's way of presenting the history of its activities and their future developments. The Society explicitly recognizes the hardship of its members in relation to the field ministry and is aware of the sense of rejection that they may experience when knocking at people's doors. Yet, in numerous articles and book chapters, Jehovah's Witnesses are encouraged to demonstrate perseverance in the ministry and are provided with recommendations on how to keep a positive and humble attitude despite the adversities and even the persecution they may encounter (e.g., Bt 2009: 220–221; W 2012, June 1: 15). Most importantly, Jehovah's Witnesses are advised not to judge their worth or success as preachers based on the number of "new disciples" (as it is put in the Society's parlance) they make—despite this being the explicit goal of the missionary work (Cf 2009: 87–97). As the Society emphasizes, Jesus's eschatological message focused on the Kingdom being preached "in all the inhabited earth," and not on disciple-making. This prompts the following conclusion: "[A]s we preach the good news of the Kingdom, we keep in mind that even if we do not succeed in making a disciple, we do succeed in giving 'a witness.' Yes, no matter how people respond, we share in fulfilling Jesus' prophecy and have the honor to serve as 'God's fellow workers.' (1 Cor. 3: 9) What good reason to rejoice!" (Kr 2014: 95).

This rather sober picture of the field ministry, however, is just one side of the coin. In fact, if at the individual level the missionary work of Jehovah's Witnesses can, on occasion, fail to produce new converts, the image that the publications project of their *collective* effort is one of unconditional success. The articulation between the individual and collective dimensions of the missionary work are explicitly articulated, for instance, in the following book passage:

> With the passing of years, the zeal of Jehovah's Witnesses for the preaching of the good news has not abated. Even though many householders have told them quite firmly that they are not interested, there are large numbers who are grateful that the Witnesses help them to understand the Bible. The determination of Jehovah's Witnesses is to continue preaching until Jehovah himself gives clear indication that his work is completed. Instead of slacking off, the worldwide association of Jehovah's Witnesses has actually intensified its preaching activity. In 1982 the annual global report showed that 384,856,662 hours had been devoted to the field ministry. Ten years later (in 1992) 1,024,910,434 hours had been devoted to this work. (Jv 1993: 302)

In similar fashion, the Watch Tower Society regularly stresses the record-breaking circulation of its publications, the increasing number of languages into which its books, magazines and online content are translated, and the constant innovation in its preaching methods that enables it to reach more and more people (see next chapter). The results of these coordinated efforts are also regularly displayed in the Watch Tower publications: a profusion of articles and book chapters mentions and discuss the global growth of the organization (e.g., Re 2006: 63–65; W 2014, May 15: 27–27). Furthermore, a yearly statistical breakdown of the Society's members and their activities is a regular feature in the Society's *Yearbook*. These statistics showcasing the increasing number of Jehovah's Witnesses worldwide and the multiplication of their activities are not only instruments of external propaganda, but also serve a missionary discourse *within* the Society, as demonstrated by the fact that they are also quoted and commented in publications rarely read by non-Witnesses (such as most books and the Study Edition of *The Watchtower*).

In conclusion, the Watch Tower Society's presentation of its missionary work is twofold. On the one hand, the possible setbacks are mostly discussed at the level of the individual members with the intent to foster morale in the face of apathy, disinterest, adversity, or even persecution; on the other hand, success is mostly discussed in collective terms as the result of a concerted effort coordinated by the Society.

8.5.3 Service Meetings

The collective and coordinated nature of the Witnesses' mission is not merely a matter of rhetoric. Since the mid-1920s, active Jehovah's Witnesses have attended weekly meetings specifically designed to improve their public speaking and missionary work. The introduction of these meetings was concomitant with the progressive reliance on the distribution of literature by the members of local congregations and the introduction of the magazine *The Golden Age* (W 1919, September 15: 281). As a retrospective *Watchtower* article explains, "Prior to 1922, Jehovah's servants customarily gathered for a midweek Prayer, Praise, and Testimony Meeting. It was an occasion for singing, giving testimonies, and engaging in prayer" (W 1985, August 1: 18–19). However, on account of the growing importance of the house-to-house ministry, a portion of these meetings was progressively redesignated as a moment for discussing the preaching work (Yb 1975: 43–44).

In the beginning, the schedule and framework of the meetings were not formalized. In the following years, however, their structure was increasingly developed as an integral part of the so-called midweek-meeting. *The Watchtower* presented the goal of these encounters as follows:

> We believe that this unity of action will draw the friends closer together everywhere and will help them to more fully appreciate the wonderful privilege now enjoyed by them of announcing the kingdom, and will help the consecrated to enter more fully into the present joy of the Lord. In unity and in the spirit of the Lord there is strength. (W 1923, April 1: 105)

By 1926, these meetings were organized on a monthly basis under the name of Service Meetings (Jv 1993: 245). These encounters offered the opportunity to discuss methods for preaching and canvassing, including particular methods suggested by the Society (Bul 1926, March: 2).

By 1928, the Watch Tower Society urged each congregation of Bible Students to organize weekly Service Meetings to "discuss plans and ways and means of witnessing to the people in the territory assigned to the class" (Bul 1928, April: 4). Over the years, as the preaching work was extended to all Jehovah's Witnesses, a larger number of participants were expected to attend these encounters. In the 1940s, the Service Meeting was closely paired (while remaining distinct) with the so-called Theocratic Ministry School, a weekly encounter introduced in 1943 to provide publishers with further training for their public speaking and house-to-house ministry, and covering topics such as oratory skills, posture, and argumentative strategies (see Chryssides 2008: 130–131). Both meetings were usually held on the same midweek evening until December 2015. In January 2016, the whole midweek meeting was restructured and renamed "Our Christian Life and Ministry." Most of its fundamental features, however, have been maintained.

The development of the Service Meeting was accompanied by the publication of a magazine designed to provide guidance to the publishers. Already in 1919, in parallel with the introduction of *The Golden Age*, the Watch Tower Society started to publish a monthly folder called *Bulletin*. This publication contained, among other things, a series of suggestions on how to carry out the field ministry and served as a powerful instrument to standardize this activity across the United States and, later, in other countries. Indeed, with time, the instructions provided were meant as more than simple recommendations and presented as instructions to be followed by "all who want to be in strict unity and harmony with Jehovah's organization" (W 1933, November 1: 322).

The *Bulletin* and its direct successors, the *Director for Field Publishers* (1935–1936) and the *Informant* (1936–1956), also had another fundamental function: they provided a structure for the Service Meeting. This role was even more clearly outlined with the introduction, in 1956, of the magazine *Our Kingdom Ministry*, which included a program of each encounter down to the minute. For instance, the first Service Meeting presented in the new publication included,

> **5 min**: Welcome, text, comments. **10 min**: Talk on "Triumphing over Enemies by Kingdom Preaching" [...]. **10 min**: Discussion, by a selected group, of "Yearbook" material on Triumphing over Opposition [...]. **10 min**: Question-and-answer coverage of "Find the Scattered Sheep." **15 min**: Congregation servant cover by discourse "Kingdom Ministry Goals for 1957." **10 min**: Arrange locally [...]. (Km 1956, September: 2)

Where necessary, the magazine provides further specifications and instruction for each activity and the necessary written material to carry it out. A similar outline is also provided in the brochure that serves as a guide for the Christian Life and Ministry meetings, appropriately called *Meeting Workbook*.

As the passage from *Our Kingdom Ministry* quoted above suggests, a variety of activities are programmed during the Service Meetings and their successor, the Christian Life and Ministry meetings. In the following, however, I will focus on one of them: the question-and-answer study of the Watch Tower publications. Drawing on the analysis of this practice, I will argue that the Service Meetings and the publications used in them not only provide instruction, but also define a ritual setting that integrates individual participants into a collective mode of action. To support my analysis, I will reconstruct the institutionalization of this activity and call attention to its performative aspects.

8.6 The Contours of a Ritual Setting

8.6.1 The institutionalization of question-and-answer discussions

Question-and-answer discussions are one of the more recognizable and widespread features of Jehovah's Witnesses meetings. This method of discussing the content of the Watch Tower publications is used on a number of occasions. Thus, to understand its contemporary form and use during the Service Meetings, it is important to consider first how it was developed in other contexts, how it became integrated into the Service Meetings, and how it evolved over time.

In the historiography of the Watch Tower Society, the idealized beginning of their current congregation meetings is identified with the Bible study group founded by Russell in 1870 in Allegheny, Pennsylvania (Jp 1959: 14–15; Jv 1993: 236). However, it is following the publication of the first volumes of Russell's series *Millennial Dawn* in 1886 that local congregations started using the same books as the basis for their Bible home study. By 1895, this practice had spread to several cities under the name of "Dawn

Circles" and, in light of the reported success of these experiments, *The Watchtower* recommended "the holding of these Circles everywhere" (W 1895, September 15 [reprints]: 1868).

The Watchtower advocated an interactive form of study: the meeting leader would read aloud a passage from a book and then ask the participants to express themselves on the content presented to verify their correct understanding of the subject matter (W 1895, September 15 [reprints]: 1868). This framework and method would give rise to what was known as Congregation Book Study, a weekly meeting held until 2008 in private homes and devoted to the discussion of a Watch Tower book on the basis of questions provided in separate publications or in the book itself (Ta 1945: 186–189; Qm 1955: 100–104). (This meeting, renamed Congregation Bible Study, is now part of the Christian Life and Ministry meeting; see next chapter.)

The question-and-answer method of study was quickly extended to the Sunday meetings held in the congregations. In 1922, following a suggestion by some Pilgrims worried that "many of the friends are not getting the meat out of THE WATCH TOWER that they should" (W 1922, May 15: 146), the Society recommended devoting one of the weekly encounters to a systematic study of the magazine. To this end, *The Watchtower* started to publish study questions as an instrument to review selected articles. In 1932, the Society outlined the method used at its headquarters to conduct a study meeting, advising the congregations to adopt it:

> The meeting is led by a brother, usually the president of the Society when present. Three brethren who can read clearly and distinctly in English language are asked to sit in the front and in turn read one or two paragraphs at a time of the matter under consideration, and then the leader calls for questions upon the paragraphs read. Questions are propounded, and various ones called upon to express themselves in answer to the questions; and then the leader sums up by giving a brief and succinct explanation if further explanation is required. (W 1932, June 15: 191)

In the following years, all congregations were invited to focus only on the current issue of *The Watchtower* to "keep up to date" (W 1933, March 15: 82), and to sum up the matter by rereading aloud the paragraph under consideration. This last adjustment was explained by the lack of qualification of some meeting leaders to give a proper summation (W 1938, June 1: 194). In fact, through these measures, the Society aimed to replace personal preaching in the congregations with a centralized liturgy, the outline of which was provided in its publications (W 1935, December 1: 365; Jv 1993: 252). The results were not immediate, and the Society tried out various solutions, even suspending the publication of the study questions between 1939 and 1942 to avoid them being used as a pretext for long speeches by local leaders (W 1938, December 1: 366). The Society, however, never abandoned its goal.

In October 1942, study questions for the leading article were introduced anew at the bottom of each *Watchtower* column, in a tacit acknowledgement of repeated readers' requests to reintroduce this feature (W 1942, May 15: 146, 159). The Society also updated the procedure to conduct the *Watchtower* study meetings, presenting it in detail:

The study conductor of the *Watchtower* study will select a person to read the questions, and another capable reader to read the paragraph discussed. Those attending the meeting having comment to make on the questions will raise their hand, and the chairman will call on them to make a comment; not to read portions of the paragraph, but to express in their own words the thought they have on the question. Several comments should be made on each question. If certain scriptures in the paragraph are not quoted in the paragraph, and time permits, the chairman should ask those in the meeting to read these scriptures. After this is done, the summing up of the questions on the paragraph should be accomplished by reading the paragraph itself. (W 1942, October 1: 290)

The format presented here prefigures to a large extent the current arrangement of the *Watchtower* study in Jehovah's Witnesses congregations worldwide. The only major adjustment to this liturgical order was introduced in 1977, when the Society recommended reading the paragraph first and then asking the questions pertaining to it. Among other things, this change would allow the congregants to refresh their minds or to familiarize themselves with the content to be discussed and facilitate the participation of those who are shy or need more time to organize their thoughts (W 1977, February 1: 96).

The question-and-answer method developed for the *Watchtower* study provided the Society with indirect oversight of the discussions within each congregation and became the reference for the other meetings as well, including the Service Meetings. Indeed, progressively, question-and-answer moments became an important method to attain the more pragmatic goals of the Service Meeting of providing instruction to the growing number of publishers. In particular, the use of the question-and-answer method for the preparation of all publishers received a strong endorsement from the early 1940s in parallel with the other educational reforms promoted by the then President of the Society, Nathan Knorr (Org 1945). The recourse to question-and-answer discussions is explicitly and regularly recommended in the meeting outlines published in *Our Kingdom Ministry* since its first issue in 1956, and articles frequently included questions and answers that could be used for discussion as part of their rhetorical structure.

Starting in the early 2000s, *Our Kingdom Ministry* begun to provide lists of specific questions to be used to conduct question-and-answer discussions in relation to specific articles or videos. In the following years, printed questions for the study of most articles became a standard feature in the pages of the magazine. At the same time, the Society issued new instructions that insisted on the importance of sticking to the format provided in the magazine without introducing any "additional material" (Od 2005: 65).

Question-and-answer interactions also remain key moments in the midweek Christian Life and Ministry meeting, and both the *Meeting Workbook* that provides an outline for the encounter and the books studied on such evenings include various questions to be discussed. But why is this feature so prominent in Jehovah's Witnesses meetings? In the following section, I will argue that question-and-answer discussions are not merely a didactic instrument for studying the content of the Watch Tower publications, but a constitutive element of a ritual performance.

8.6.2 Empirical evidence

Participant observation in various congregations of Jehovah's Witnesses in Switzerland and Germany indicates an almost invariable core procedure for conducting question-and-answer discussions across the various meetings, including the Service Meeting and the Christian Life and Ministry meeting. First, a member of the congregation reads aloud a paragraph from *The Watchtower* or another publication—depending on the meeting—from the stage. Then, another member asks the public in attendance to answer one or two questions—included in the publication—that are related to the passage. The participants in the assembly can raise their hands to answer the questions. The name of a congregant is called from the stage, and that person receives a microphone so that everyone can hear his or her answer. The person leading the meeting usually offers short appreciative commentaries, such as "Yes, thank you; that's correct." In my observations, I have never encountered a case in which someone has been explicitly corrected from the stage, although on some occasions an elder or another knowledgeable member of the congregation was invited to provide a final comment on a specific question. After a few answers have been collected in this way, the congregation moves on to the next paragraph.

Although the answers may appear spontaneous, it does not take long before observers notice that most answers are more or less elaborate paraphrases of the text read from the stage a few moments previously. This is no mere coincidence. Various publications provide detailed instructions on how to prepare for these interactions at the Kingdom Hall. For instance, a passage from a guidebook for the Theocratic Ministry School offers the following advice:

> When you do this, first note the theme of the article, the key scripture and the boldface subheadings for the entire article. This gives you an overall view of the subject and will help you to appreciate the relationship of the details in the individual paragraphs. Now read the lesson through paragraph by paragraph, locating the answers to the questions and underlining just the key points for future reference. As you finish each paragraph, if you find that you cannot answer the question in your own words, it would be good to read the paragraph again so you can do so. (Sg71 1971: 36)

More recently, an animated cartoon for children has even been produced, which summarizes these fundamental steps for getting ready for a question-and-answer discussion.[1] In short, The Watch Tower Society encourages Jehovah's Witnesses through various media to prepare for each meeting carefully by reading the publications, looking in the text for answers to the given questions, making notes, and preparing brief comments in their own words.

Some scholars have emphasized that these question-and-answer discussions seek to prevent both the meeting leader and the individuals in attendance from advancing an individual interpretation of the texts, favoring instead rote learning and repetition of their content (Holden 2002: 67; Blanchard 2008: 115). In this sense, these authors emphasize the didactic aspect of these discussions, which, in their view, borders on a form of indoctrination. The same authors also suggest that the unitary thinking promoted by this practice—thinking whose content they assume each Jehovah's Witness fully assimilates—is conducive to the construction of Jehovah's Witnesses as a religious community. According to Holden:

> The rational procedures that the Witnesses have at their disposal for the operation of meetings help to create an atmosphere of uniformity which they regard as a tangible source of truth. [...] [T]hese meetings make possible more personal interaction and they are also one of the official channels through which the Witnesses organise their door-to-door ministry. Combined, these two 'functions' rekindle the Witnesses' consciousness of their unity and enhance their feelings of solidarity. The reinforcement of the Society's millenarian mission thus attaches the individual to the wider social group in the way propounded by Durkheim (1912). (Holden 2002: 68)

In a similar vein, Blanchard (2008: 107) argues that that the Watch Tower Society can be regarded as a community of readers in which specific reading habits are inculcated during the individual or collective study of the Society's publications.

While I acknowledge these authors' intuition concerning a link between congregational practice and the process of community building, I do not share their focus on the "learning" of content during the meetings, and I maintain that their reflections remain theoretically underdeveloped. How does a particular mode of meeting participation give rise to a feeling of solidarity? What kind of sociality is thereby formed and what kind of commitment does it entail? In addition, how do these forms of sociality and commitment help us to provide a rational explanation for the willingness of Jehovah's Witnesses to engage in the field ministry despite their more or less pronounced dislike for this practice?

Before beginning a systematic discussion of these questions, I need to point out another piece of empirical evidence based on my participant observation in several Witnesses' congregations, on follow-up discussions with my colleagues at the University of Fribourg with whom I attended various Witnesses' meetings, and on the quantitative analysis of various Watch Tower publications.

For an external observer, a striking feature of the question-and-answer discussion resides in the particular semantics and phrasing used during the exchange. While it is not unusual for Jehovah's Witnesses to share their feelings and experiences with the congregation, neither the first-person pronoun "I" nor the second-person pronoun "you" (in its singular or plural form) appears preponderant in framing the interaction. Instead, even the casual visitor will rapidly recognize that a significant number of answers provided by the congregants are uttered in the "we" form. This is not surprising if we consider that, in light of the way Jehovah's Witnesses prepare for and conduct this part of the meetings, the form of the question will provide a strong suggestion regarding the form of the answer.

A survey of all the questions printed in the 2015 study edition of *The Watchtower* shows that the large majority of the questions uses the third-person singular or plural (72 percent), as in "How did Jesus express love for his disciples?" (W 2015, November

15: 4) and "What events took place in 66 C.E.?" (W 2015, July 15: 14). The focus of *The Watchtower* on doctrinal and exegetical matters explains the predominance of these questions. Questions formulated in the second person (plural or singular) constitute approximately 10 percent of the total and often aim at eliciting examples (e.g., Give examples of 'a time to be silent'" [W 2015, December 15: 19]) or the expression of feelings (e.g., "How do you feel about Jehovah's love for you?" [W 2015, September 15: 22]). Sometimes, they address a particular group within the congregation, such as parents (e.g., "How can you protect your children from unclean entertainment?" [W 2015, November 15: 7]). About a fifth of the questions are formulated using the first-person plural pronoun "we," as in, "What lessons do we learn from the parable of the talents?" (W 2015, March 15: 24) or "How can we show faith in our daily lives?" (W 2015, October 15: 12). In addition, about 17 percent of the questions in the third-person form (plural or singular) also contain references to a "we," in formulations such as "Our conscience can have what bearing on our preaching?" (W 2015, September 15: 12), "What exciting prospect awaits us?" (W 2015, January 15: 12), and "What example did Jesus set for us?" (W 2015, June 15: 11). Thus, slightly less than a third of all questions contains a direct or indirect reference to a "we."

A survey of all the questions published in the magazine *Our Kingdom Ministry* in three distinct years—2005 (N=140), 2010 (N=152), and 2015 (N=60)—reveals an even larger proportion of questions in the "we" form.

The we form is used in 38 percent of the questions published (N=352). Furthermore, 30 percent of the questions in the third-person form (singular or plural) contain a reference to a "we"-group similar to the examples discussed in relation to *The Watchtower*.

So far, I have presented the historical development of the question-and-answer interactions in Jehovah's Witnesses meetings, the role of the publications in structuring such interaction, their basic form during various congregation meetings, and the form of the questions asked during these exchanges. To understand how these elements are conducive to the constitution of a joint mode of action within the framework of the Service Meetings, I will now introduce some of the theoretical approaches presented in the first part of this book. Since these approaches have already been discussed in detail,

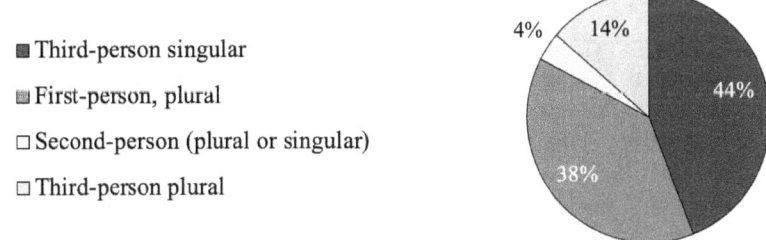

Figure 8.1 Question Formulation in the 2005, 2010, and 2015 Editions of *Our Kingdom Ministry* (N=352). © Andrea Rota.

I will limit myself to sketching their core ideas here. Incidentally, it is worth noting that rational choice theory does not pay particular attention to the structure of rituals, communicative or otherwise, and only assesses ritual forms in light of their more or less important "cost" (as estimated by the researcher) for the participants. Accordingly, rituals or other practices are regarded as "inert" objects in a cost–benefit evaluation with no capacity to otherwise affect the participants' motivational structures. My argumentation follows a different path, starting with a consideration of the role of speech acts in Jehovah's Witnesses' rituals.

8.6.3 Theoretical reflection

Speech plays a central role in almost all Jehovah's Witnesses congregational activities. While the meetings include ritualized gestures performed by all congregants, such as standing up for the opening and closing prayers and songs, utterances are omnipresent. However, the form of these utterances and the allocation and distribution of speaking time are regulated through the outline provided in advance in the publications and supervised by the congregations' elders. As for their content, the publications constitute, once again, an inescapable reference for all people in attendance. Still, because of its structure, the question-and-answer discussion is the practice of Jehovah's Witnesses that most paradigmatically presents a performative dimension as outlined in Roy Rappaport's (1979, 1999) theory of ritual.

In line with Rappaport's framework (see Chapter 2.4.), the liturgical order of the meeting in general and of the question-and-answer discussion in particular is "*encoded by someone other than the performer himself*" (Rappaport 1999: 118). Furthermore, the structure of the meeting is such that the utterances of the participants are "a *public act*, visible to both the witnesses and the performer himself" (Rappaport 1979: 194). Finally, because, according to speech act theory, the very fact of uttering a certain sentence entails specific obligations for the person who does so, the speaker cannot do anything but conform to the liturgical order of the meeting. To understand this last point better (and expand it beyond Rappaport's original insight), it is worth outlining some of Searle's reflections concerning the relationship between speech acts, commitment, and rationality.

In a nutshell, Searle maintains that every speech act intrinsically entails *rational constraints* on the person who utters it and commits him or her to conforming to a certain course of action (Searle 2002a: 319). Thus, every speech act has normative implications for the person uttering it. This is also true of plain statements, because the person who utters a statement is committed to the truth of that statement by, for instance, avoiding self-contradictions (Searle 2008: 173). For this reason, from each "is" statement, it is always possible to derive an "ought" (Searle 2008: 174; see also Searle 1964; 1969: 175–198; Hindriks 2013). Against this backdrop, Searle argues that speech acts provide a rational agent with reasons for action that are binding "just in virtue of the nature of the fact reported in the reason statement, and independently of the agent's desires, values, attitudes and evaluations" (Searle 2008: 165).

To unpack Searle's position, it is worth dwelling on some aspects of his theory, starting with his approach to human rationality. Searle develops his theory of rationality in action in open contrast to some main features of what he calls the Classical Model of practical reason, a model epitomized by Hume and more recently by mathematical decision theory (Searle 2001: 5–7). One of the fundamental assumptions of the Classical Model—Searle (2001: 7–32) discusses six of them—is that rationality concerns the selection of means to achieve our ends. The ends themselves, however, are outside of the scope of rationality and are "entirely a matter of what we desire" (Searle 2001: 1). As Bertrand Russell puts it, "Reason [...] signifies the choice of the right means to an end that you wish to achieve. It has nothing whatever to do with the choice of ends" (Russell 1983: 4, quoted in Searle 2001: 11). From this, it follows that unless you have a set of desires to start with, "there is no scope for reason, because it is a matter of figuring out what else you ought to desire [i.e., the appropriate means], given that you already desire something" (Searle 2002a: 314). Within this framework, "[T]here can be no reasons for action which do not arise from desires, broadly constructed," which means that "there cannot be any desire-independent reasons for action" (Searle 2002a: 314).

Against this dominant view, Searle argues that what sets human rationality apart from animal rationality is the capacity to create desire-independent reasons for action and to act upon them (Searle 2001: 31). Desire-independent reasons for action constitute external motivators that do not depend on internal attitudes but still provide rational grounds for action. To show how these reasons differ from common desires, Searle offers this comparison:

> I want chocolate and I want to keep my promise. What's the difference? *In the case of the promise the desire is derived from the recognition of the desire-independent reason, that is, the obligation. The reason is prior to the desire and the ground of the desire. In the case of chocolate the desire is the reason.* (Searle 2001: 170)

As this quote suggests, the creation of desire-independent reasons for actions is "always a matter of an agent *committing* himself in various ways" (Searle 2001: 167). The way these commitments are brought about is inherent to the structure of speech acts.

As discussed in Chapter 3, a speech act is constituted by a propositional content with a certain illocutionary force (Searle 1968). The illocutionary force determines the conditions of satisfaction for a given speech act, that is, the conditions under which the speech act will be felicitous. For instance, a promise will be satisfied (and the speech act will be felicitous) if it is kept, an order will be satisfied if it is executed, and an assertion will be satisfied if it is true. The same structure applies, with a few adjustments, to any intentional state: a desire will be satisfied if it is realized, an intention will be satisfied if it is carried out, and a belief will be satisfied if it is true (Searle 1983: 4–13). Against this backdrop, we can ask what it takes for a speaker, let us call him Simon, to make a simple statement like, "It is raining," and what consequences this speech act entails for him (Searle 1983: 26–29).

First, Simon must have the intention of uttering a certain sound sequence. This intention is satisfied when he articulates the phonemes "ɪt ɪz ˈreɪnɪŋ." However, the simple utterance does not yet amount to him stating that it is raining. Indeed, Simon might not mean anything by those sounds; maybe he is simply practicing his English pronunciation. For him to utter "It is raining" and actually mean that it is raining, he also must intend that the utterance should have conditions of satisfaction in the form of truth conditions—that it is raining. As long as Simon is only practicing his English pronunciation, the fact that the sky is entirely free of clouds is irrelevant; however, it is enough to make its statement infelicitous (that is, false) if he actually means it.[2]

Since Simon has freely imposed conditions of satisfaction (that is, truth conditions) on conditions of satisfaction (the utterance), he cannot be indifferent to the truth of the statement, because his claim is a claim to truth and he has thereby committed himself to sincerity. This does not entail that he cannot lie—for sure, he can state that it is raining while knowing that there is not a cloud in the sky—but this does not invalidate his commitment to truth. It is only because a statement entails such a commitment that it is possible to lie. In sum, by following the constitutive rules of (constative) speech acts, Simon has created a commitment for himself and thereby a desire-independent reason "for accepting the logical consequences of his assertion, for not denying what he has said, for being able to provide evidence or justification for what he has said, and for speaking sincerely when he says it" (Searle 2001: 175). For this reason to serve as a motivator for his action, he "does not first have to recognize an obligation and then figure out that he has a reason for action, because to recognize something as an obligation is already to recognize it as a motivator" (Searle 2001: 122).

Against this backdrop, let us get back to our case study and consider a simple example taken from the magazine *Our Kingdom Ministry*. Drawing on the observations in Jehovah's Witnesses congregations, it is possible to imagine how the following passage from an article entitled "Skillful Use of the Bible" may be treated in a meeting. The passage reads as follows:

> Skillful use of God's inspired Word enables us to proclaim and teach the truth clearly and expose the false teachings and traditions of men.—2. Tim. 2: 15; 1 Pet. 3: 15. (Km 2009, September: 2)

The printed question pertaining to this paragraph is "Why is the Bible so useful?" A number of answers could be offered, but no matter how they are phrased, these answers are bound by the structure of the question-and-answer discussion to (re)state the content of the passage.[3] Following Searle, we can see that answering the proposed question in the public setting of a congregation meeting is a multilayered action. In particular, it entails a commitment to upholding the premise stated in the question—namely, that the Bible is useful—as true. Furthermore, it signals the acceptance of a number of equivalences and implications suggested in the article, such as the fact that the Bible is God's inspired Word (see Searle 2001: 100–104). According to the analytical framework presented above, the speech act of answering the printed question provides the speaker with a desire-independent reason for action. In this specific case, he or she would have, for instance, a rational motivation for not denying the usefulness of the Bible or its divine inspiration.

In light of these considerations, let us go a step further and explore the relationship between the normative dimension of speech acts and the constitution of a (religious) social collectivity. So far, the theoretical framework has dealt with the individual commitment of a single speaker. When a congregant provides an answer during a question-and-answer discussion at a Jehovah's Witnesses meeting, he creates a commitment for himself; the other congregants are in a position to assess his commitment (by, for instance, pointing out a contradicting statement by the same speaker) but are not necessarily bound by his statement (see Searle 2001: 176). We can assume that, over time, each congregant will answer a number of questions, often concerning similar topics, thus committing themselves in a similar fashion. In this perspective, a religious community would consist of a number of men and women with similar individual commitments.

When it comes to defining a community, however, this conception is only partially satisfying, because it is easy to imagine a set of individuals with similar individual commitments who do not constitute a community in any intuitive sense—think, for instance, of the set of people driving in Switzerland right now: each person is committed to driving on the right side of the road, but this does not seem to connect them to one another in any special way. In the case of Jehovah's Witnesses, however, it is possible to identify a more holistic conception of community, one that relies not on individual but on *collective* intentions and commitments.

Following Raimo Tuomela, we can consider a collective intention—or "we-intention"—as an intention that the members of a group can express in chorus by means of locutions like "We shall do X" or "We will do X." However, for Tuomela, the subject of a collective intention is not the group itself but its individual members, who each "we-intend" to do X. Let us explore this idea from the perspective of a single member of a group G; let us call her Christina. For Christina to we-intend to do X means that she has accepted the statement "We shall do X" as true for herself. Therefore, since she considers herself to be a member of group G, she intends to do her part—for example, the partial action Y—to bring about the total action X and to help other members of G to do their part. Furthermore, Christina believes that the participation of other members of G is necessary to bring about X and that the other members of G will (at least try to) do their part of X; she also believes that her beliefs are mutually shared within the group.

Christina could have various reasons for participating in the collective action of group G. For instance, she could have a private interest in the group achieving its goal, or she could privately endorse the action of the group and therefore decide that it is worth participating in its activities. These scenarios would correspond to a form of collective intentionality that Tuomela calls *I-mode* we-intentionality. However, the previous paragraph suggests a stronger understanding of collective intentionality. According to this perspective, which Tuomela calls *we-mode* we-intentionality, Christina does not participate in the group action for private reasons but does so because she has integrated (that is, accepted) a *group reason* to do her part. This group reason is paradigmatically encapsulated in the expression "We will do X." As a private person, Christina does not need to endorse the group goals; however, as a we-mode we-intending group member, she has desire-independent reasons for action, provided by the group, that motivate her to act for the sake of the group—Tuomela speaks in this respect of a "for-groupness" criterion of we-mode collective intentionality. To put it bluntly, within this framework, Christina could rationally answer the question, "Why are you doing Y?" by saying, "Because *we* are doing X and *we* cannot do X unless I do my part and do Y."

How does this theoretical picture relate to the case of Jehovah's Witnesses? As we have seen, the Watch Tower presents its missionary work as a collective endeavor, and its publications make abundant use of personal pronouns and possessive determiners that point toward a "we"-group. In fact, we can find one such reference in the passage discussed above: "Skillful use of God's inspired Word enables *us* to proclaim and teach the truth clearly [...]" (Km 2009, September: 2, my emphasis). This statement logically entails the existence of a group goal—that is, "our goal" to proclaim and teach the truth clearly—toward which the skillful use of the Bible provides a means. To answer the question related to this passage implies a recognition of the existence of this collective goal.

To explore this entailment further, let us consider a more explicit example from another issue of *Our Kingdom Ministry*. The fourth paragraph of the article "Who Would Be Interested in This?" reads thus:

> Our magazines discuss the real meaning behind current events and direct attention to the Bible and God's Kingdom. They are the only magazines on earth that are "publishing salvation." (Isa. 52: 7) Therefore, we want to give them wide distribution. A good way to do that is by asking yourself, "Who would be interested in this?" (Km 2013, May: 2)

The question related to this paragraph is this: "Why do we want to give the magazines wide distribution?" In this case too, we can imagine a multitude of answers, such as, "We want to distribute them because they are 'publishing salvation.'" Such a statement, however, already entails the recognition by the speaker of a group goal (expressed by the pronoun "we") and a commitment to the truth of the statement—that is, that there is a will to distribute the magazines.

In a sense, it would still be possible to argue—although somewhat artificially—that, so far, the speaker is only committed to the existence of the collective goal and to no further course of action. However, since the speaker—by (re)stating the content of the paragraph—includes herself in the "we"-group, she cannot deny her commitment to contributing to the collective goal. Ideally, we can imagine the following practical syllogism playing out in the reasoning of the speaker: 1) "We intend to distribute the magazines"; 2) "I am one of us"; 3) "I will do my part in distributing the magazines." Indeed, the last sentence of the paragraph already suggests how the individual agent can start to do her part toward the collective goal.

A collective goal cannot be satisfied by a single member alone. If only one Jehovah's Witness distributes the magazines, and the others do not or cannot, the goal that "*we* distribute the magazines" is not collectively achieved, no matter how zealous and effective the single Witness might be—Tuomela calls this the "Collectivity Condition" of we-intentionality. For this reason, to formulate a we-intention, an individual must believe that the other members (or at least a sufficient number of other qualified members) will also similarly we-intend. Accordingly, Tuomela (1995: 176–177) speaks of the necessity of "a mechanism or procedure representing the process of the group members' [...] going from the multitude of 'I's' to a 'we'" (Tuomela 1995: 176–177). Tuomela (1995: 15) calls such a "group-will-formation system" an authority system. Despite its somewhat confusing name, an authority system is not concerned with controlling the activities of the members and policing their group commitments but rather with *creating* such group commitments.

According to Tuomela, for an authority system to work properly, a number of requirements must be met (see Chapter 4). First, the topic of the proposed collective action must be brought to the participants' attention in one way or another. Second, the set of potential and actual participants has to be publicly indicated. Third, the information about the intention to participate must be publicly available, at least within the group. If these premises are given, it is possible for a group of people collectively to accept a group goal. To illustrate how such an authority system works, Tuomela uses the example of a bulletin board. The board lists a number of particular goals for the group and invites the members to sign up to related activities. Appending one signature constitutes a sufficient act for the creation of a we-mode group intention: "The participants' having signed up, and thus agreed, gives each participant a group reason for participating in the agreed-upon action. Furthermore, it also gives a reason for each participant normatively to expect that the other participants indeed will participate" (Tuomela 2013: 132).

The ritual use of the magazines during Jehovah's Witnesses' question-and-answer discussions fulfills all the requirements put forward by Tuomela's Bulletin Board View. First, the topic of the group action is brought to the participants' attention through the magazines. The fact that the goal in question is a collective one is indicated by the use of pronouns in the first-person plural form. The topic is reiterated during the public lecture of the articles at the meetings, ensuring that all congregants are aware of it. Second, the set of the participants is publicly indicated. In most cases, it includes all Witnesses in attendance, although some restriction might be mentioned—in the case of the field ministry, for instance, there are explicit preconditions for the participation of unbaptized publishers (see, e.g., Od 2015: 69–71). Third, the speaker makes his intention to participate publicly available within the group by answering the question. Since the answer is expressed in the we-form, the other participants signal their intention to participate by refraining from challenging such an answer as valid for them.[4] Furthermore, since the group members are committed to realizing the group goal, their individual contribution can involve more than merely doing their part properly. In particular, their collective commitment gives them rational reasons to "help or even pressure others, if needed for X's successful coming about" (Tuomela 2013: 76). For instance, individual Witnesses have an intrinsic motivation to help other members in their ministry or to invite inactive members to find their way back to the congregation.

In conclusion, the question-and-answer discussions function as an authority system that creates desire-independent reasons for action to participate in collective activities and binds the congregants through collective commitments. Accordingly, it provides them with rational reasons to do their part, to help others in their contribution toward the achievement of the collective goals, and to rebuke other we-mode-thinking members who have deviated from the group's ethos.

8.6.4 Further considerations: expression of readiness and planned joint action

My analysis of the ritual structure of Jehovah's Witnesses' meetings underscores the role of the question-and-answer discussion in the constitution of the missionary work as a collective action. However, between the expression of a readiness to join in a collective action (Gilbert 1989: 180–184) and the completion of the action itself, there is still a "gap" (Searle 2001: 14–15). In particular, some mechanism is necessary to guarantee that the contribution of each participant will be coordinated. Another of the Jehovah's Witnesses' meetings serve this purpose, the so-called Meeting for Field Service. During this meeting, smaller groups of congregation members reunite, under the direction of a conductor, in a private home, at the Kingdom Hall or in another convenient place to prepare and organize the door-to-door preaching (Od 2015: 61–62).

This meeting can take place at different moments during the week and is sometimes held directly after one of the other meetings. Its recommended length, which used to be of about 10 to 15 minutes has been reduced in 2015 to five to seven minutes or even less if it follows another meeting (Km 2015, March: 3). The Meeting for field service is meant to "prepare the minds and hearts of the brothers and sisters for the work they will be doing" (Km 1986, May: 7). Regarding its content, it depends on the local circumstances, and there is no longer a recommended outline (between 1979 and 1991 a column on the first page of *Our Kingdom Ministry* provided a monthly outline). The possible activities and topics of discussion include "A video about the ministry from jw.org," "Ministry-related information from *The Watchtower*," or "How to help your field service partner be more effective at the door" (Km 2015, March: 6). Most importantly, however, "Before ending the meeting with a brief prayer, all should know where and with whom they are going to work" (Km 2015, March: 3). Accordingly, during this meeting, groups are organized, territories are assigned, and publishers make their own arrangements with their partner regarding, for instance, when and where to meet to preach (Km 2015, March: 5).

The Meetings for Field Service that I was able to observe in Swiss congregations had an informal character. After a regular meeting, small groups of people were seated on two rows of chairs facing each other, holding their respective agendas and comparing weekly schedules before settling on a day and a time to meet with a partner. The planning only took a few minutes. Furthermore, interviews with individual Witnesses call attention to the growing role of text messaging services such as WhatsApp in the organization of the field ministry (see Chapters 9 and 11). Despite the relaxed atmosphere, the meeting produces the desired effect of jointly committing (Gilbert 1989) two or more members of the congregation to go preaching together, with the motivational and deontic consequences that such a commitment entails.

8.7 Conclusion: Individual Attitudes and Joint Preaching

8.7.1 Rationality and commitment

In this chapter, I began by presenting the perspective of rational choice theory on religion. In particular, I called attention to its specific understanding of rationality as maximizing behavior and on the role that this approach attributes to "costly activities" such as Jehovah's Witnesses' intensive missionary work to strengthen religious communities. Rational choice scholars insist on the persistent demand for religious commodities and on the rational decisions of social actors who look for the best means to satisfy their desires. Under certain conditions, accepting higher costs appears to be the rational option leading to higher utility. The constitution of a group must therefore be interpreted as the results of individual commitments justified by the perceived individual benefits of participating in the group's activity.

The concept of rationality underlying rational choice theory falls within the scope of what Searle calls the Classical Model of rationality, as discussed toward the end of this chapter. Models of this kind conceive of rationality in terms of means to the satisfaction of desires. Searle highlights the paradoxes entailed in such a conception through the following example:

On the Classical Model, the soldier who throws himself on a live hand-grenade in order to save the lives of his fellow soldiers is in exactly the same situation, rationally speaking, as the child who selects chocolate over vanilla when picking a flavor of ice cream. The soldier prefers death, the child prefers chocolate. In each case, rationality is just a matter of increasing the probability of getting to a higher rung on the preference ladder. (Searle 2001: 168–169)

Stark and Finke (2000: 39) are aware of this critique and also discuss cases such as the one of the "heroic soldier." Such examples, they note, are often mentioned by their detractors to demonstrate that people do not always act rationally. To illustrate this point, they quote the British sociologist Anthony Heath, who writes,

The people who act out of a sense of duty or friendship cannot be accounted rational and cannot be brought within the scope of [the] rational choice [proposition]. [...] Rationality has nothing to do with the *goals* which [people] pursue but only with the *means* they use to achieve them. (Heath 1976: 79, quoted in Stark and Finke 2000: 39)

To this claim, Stark and Finke (2000: 39) reply that "unselfish" actions like the one of the soldier appear to violate the principle of rationality "only if we adopt a very narrow, materialistic, and entirely egocentric definition of rewards and ignore the immense variety of preferences and tastes." An "altruistic" act always implies, from the perspective of the actor, a net benefit: we indeed have to assume that in his cost/benefit calculation, the soldier sees the survival of his comrades as more rewarding than his own survival.

In his argument, Searle takes issue with the position of both rational choice theorists and critics such as Heath. On the one hand (and against rational choice scholars), he draws a distinction between the action of people who are motivated by their desire and those of people who act, for instance, out of a sense of duty or friendship. On the other hand (against the position exemplified by Heath's statement), he does not consider the latter to be irrational. Instead, drawing on his analysis of intentionality and speech acts, he demonstrates how people can rationally behave on the basis of desire-independent reasons for action that they impose on themselves. As Searle notes,

> The really hard part of practical reason is to figure out what the ends are in the first place. Some of these are desires, but some are rationally compelling desire-independent reasons for action. *For these, the reason is the ground of the desire; the desire is not the ground of the reason.* That is, once you see that you have a reason for doing something you do not otherwise want to do, you can see that you ought to do it and a fortiori, that you ought to want to do it. And sometimes, but by no means always, that recognition will lead you to want to do it. (Searle 2001: 126)

In this chapter, I used Searle's analysis to argue that the ritual setting of Jehovah's Witnesses' meetings, and most notably the question-and-answer discussion that constitutes a significant portion of such meetings, provides the foundation for the creation of such desire-independent reasons for action among the people in attendance. Through their participation in these interactions, Jehovah's Witnesses commit themselves to a certain course of action independent of their personal inclinations.

Considering the general dislike for the field ministry among the Jehovah's Witnesses I have interviewed, I argued that this form of commitment provides a rational explanation for their engagement in the missionary activities. Yet, in light of the structure of the meetings and the form of the speech acts performed during the question-and-answer discussions, I further argued that Jehovah's Witnesses' preaching activity can be considered a case of collective action and that the commitment at play is, therefore, a case of collective commitment. This conclusion brings me to the question of the relationship between collective intentional action and group formation.

8.7.2 Collective intentional action and group formation

As detailed above, the Watch Tower Society frames its missionary work as a collective effort in which every member of the organization is invited to share. The analysis of the Service Meetings allowed us to see how this framing of Jehovah's Witnesses' preaching is not merely a rhetorical device, but is transformed into a social reality through the use of performative speech. I have argued that the question-and-answer interaction constitutes an authority system—in Raimo Tuomela's sense—conducive to the formation of a collective intentional action in which each participant is "we-committed" to the realization of a collectively accepted goal by doing his or her part. Providing an empirical example of Tuomela's Bulletin Board View, this ritual performance has a generative power in the sense that it (re)creates a social group defined by the common goal of the members who "sign up" (see Chapter 4). Each time Jehovah's Witnesses discuss the field ministry in their question-and-answer discussions, they dynamically reconstitute or reaffirm the existence of their group around this joint goal. In this sense, participation in the field ministry does not merely act as an instrument to regulate the behavior of Jehovah's Witnesses but defines a constitutive rule (Searle 1969: 33–35)— or a set of constitutive rules, if we consider the specific guidelines for how the field ministry should be carried out—which contributes to defining the social ontology of a congregation (or even of the Watch Tower Society).

The collective nature of the joint intentional action set up in the congregational setting carries over to the practical implementation of the field ministry, particularly through the predication in pairs. Against a facile assessment of this practice as an instrument of social control (with one member of the dyad surveilling what the other does, and vice versa), both my empirical data and my theoretical reflections suggest another interpretation of the social effects of this practice. The fact of preaching in pairs requires a certain level of coordination among the publishers—at the minimum, where and when to meet and for how long, who will start the conversation with a householder, who will say what, etc. This common course of action is agreed upon during the Meetings for Field Service and can be adjusted communicatively on the way from one house to the next. Such planning ensures that not only the general goal of the field ministry but also the basic unit of action through which it is realized by each participant is a joint activity. Being collectively committed to the goal of going door to door with a partner provides, as many of my interviewees attest, an important motivational factor: since a collective commitment cannot be unilaterally broken, it provides the individual Witnesses with a normative reason to overcome their personal inclinations and find the courage to ring one more doorbell.

8.7.3 Explanation and justification

In this chapter, I provided an explanation for why Jehovah's Witnesses engage in their door-to-door ministry even when many find it highly unpleasant. Specifically, I have argued that certain ritual activities within their congregations provide the structure to establish desire-independent reasons for action that are conducive to a specific form of joint action. However, in the interviews that I conducted with Jehovah's Witnesses, all of them could provide various justifications for their missionary zeal, and the Watch Tower Society's publications provide an even longer catalog of answers. Was my theoretical detour really necessary? I would argue that it was. To see why, it is worth calling attention to Searle's distinction between justification and justificatory explanation.

According to Searle, there are different ways to explain intentional phenomena such as intentional actions, beliefs, desires, etc. For instance, there are causal explanations—as Searle (2001: 109) humorously puts it, a concussion can explain why "Jones believes he is Napoleon." Indeed, some cognitive theories of commitment and community formation strive to provide such causal explanations for human behavior (Sosis 2004; Norenzayan 2013). Within the framework of this study, however, I follow Searle in considering "that the peculiarity of intentional phenomena is that they are, in virtue of their very nature, also subject to constraints of rationality, and as part of those constraints they are subject to the demand for justification" (Searle 2001: 110). Causal explanations do not provide any reason that would justify, say, a particular belief or show it to be rational.

The statements found in the Watch Tower Society's publications regarding the reasons for engaging in the house-to-house ministry provide a justification for this activity in the sense that they indicate why preaching is the right thing to do. However, the reason "[W]hy *something should have been done or is a good thing to have been done* is not always the same as *why it was in fact done*" (Searle 2001: 110). For instance, I could justify my decision to attend a conference by stating that I recognize the importance of disseminating academic knowledge, although I did not act on that reason (instead, I just wanted to meet with a colleague for a drink). The fact that intentional phenomena are subject to normative rational constraints does not eliminate the need for causal constraints in the explanation: "One can give justifications of intentional phenomena that are not causal, but to the extent that the justification does not state a reason that was causally effective, it does not give an explanation of why the intentional phenomena occurred" (Searle 2001: 112). Accordingly, Searle (2001: 111) distinguishes between simple "justifications" and "justificatory explanations," where the latter specifies the reasons why an agent actually acted.

Justificatory explanations can be predicated on internal or external reasons. An internal reason is an intrinsic motivation of the agent. An external reason, instead, is a factitive entity in the world such as the fact that one has an obligation "that can be a reason for an agent, even if he does not know of that entity, or knows of it but refuses to acknowledge it as a reason" (Searle 2001: 114). For some (or even most) Jehovah's Witnesses, internal reasons such as the desire to serve Jehovah might be the actual justificatory explanation of their missionary zeal; however, I see no way to ascertain this fact with any certainty. In this chapter, I have sought a different justificatory explanation that does not rely on the direct justifications of individual agents and looks instead for external reasons for their actions. I have thus argued that the ritualized use of performative language during Jehovah's Witnesses meetings provides the congregants with desire-independent group reasons for action; that is, with external reasons that allow us to explain their action in rational terms while remaining agnostic regarding their claims.

9

Collective Beliefs—The Domestication of New Media

9.1 Introduction

In his book *Die Realität der Massenmedien*, Niklas Luhmann maintains that "What we know about our society, indeed about our world, we know from the mass media" (Luhmann 1996: 9, my translation). According to Luhmann, this statement is true for both our academic and our everyday knowledge of history and nature. In the case of Jehovah's Witnesses, Luhmann's observation also applies, in a sense, to the current development of God's plans for humanity. The first page of the booklet *What Does the Bible Really Teach?*—one of the Watch Tower Society's most widely distributed publications and a cornerstone of its contemporary missionary work—opens with the following exhortation:

> READ any newspaper. Look at television, or listen to the radio. There are so many stories of crime, war, and terrorism! Think about your own troubles. Perhaps illness or the death of a loved one is causing you great distress. You may feel like the good man Job, who said that he was "filled with dishonor and affliction."—Job 10: 15. Ask yourself: Is this what God purposed for me and for the rest of mankind? Where can I find help to cope with my problems? Is there any hope that we will ever see peace on the earth? The Bible provides satisfying answers to these questions. (Bh 2014: 3)

This passage indicates that various media are regarded as a window onto the world. The pictures, sounds, and texts they convey, however, are interpreted through a theological lens. On the one hand, they constitute a source of existential questions, to which the Bible is meant to provide an answer; on the other hand, they confirm a number of doctrines preached by the Watch Tower Society. For instance, the same booklet reassures readers that the tragic things they see on TV are part of a greater plan and explains that "[l]ong ago his [Jehovah's] Word, the Bible, foretold not only the bad things happening in our day but also the wonderful things that will occur in the near future" (Bh 2014: 86). Thus, the recurring news reports on wars, famines, natural disasters, and the spread of illnesses are seen as signs that we live in the end of times and that Satan's rule over the world and humankind—a situation that ensued from his defeat in Heaven and his banishment to the earth—will be over shortly (Bh 2014: 87–90).

While the media are presented as lending support to some of the Watch Tower Society's core beliefs, it would be wrong to conclude that the organization encourages their use unmindfully. On the contrary, the Society's treatment of various media is itself based on certain beliefs and judgements regarding their nature, function, and effects. The empirical focus of this chapter is precisely this framework for perception and assessment. In this regard, my analysis ties in with the developing hermeneutic approach to media in the study of religion. This kind of perspective has been developed in contrast to widespread deterministic views that predicate a direct effect of media on the masses of passive (religious) consumers (e.g., McLuhan and Fiore 1967; Schultze 1990) or that postulate a distinctive and all-powerful logic of the media affecting all other social spheres, including religion (e.g., Hjarvard 2013). To break out of the deterministic mold, numerous authors have emphasized how the production and use of media are linked to interpretative processes through which new technologies are adapted to specific contexts and goals (e.g., Keppler 2005; Ayaß 2007). From this perspective, media are regarded less as transformative agents than as "a set of concrete opportunities or threats to be weighed and figured into the pursuit of ongoing social objectives" (Marvin 1988: 232). Accordingly, their adoption in religious contexts ought to be analyzed against the background of the "assumptions and beliefs underlining these technological choices" (Campbell 2010: 44).

In this chapter, I will discuss the potential but also the limits of this hermeneutic approach and suggest some improvements regarding its application to the study of the dynamic relationship between media use and the constitution of religious collectives. At the core of the hermeneutic approach lies an inversion of perspective that the sociologists Elihu Katz and David Foulkes (1962: 387) put in the following terms: "[T]he question [is] not 'what do the media do to people?' but, rather, 'What do people do with the media?'" In what follows, I shall reconceptualize this idea in more collectivistic terms and ask, "What do religious *communities* do with media?" From a theoretical point of view, this reformulation demands a reflection on the concept of community and on the relationship between the beliefs and attitudes of individual members and the nature of collective agents. To discuss this point, I will focus on he framework developed by the theologian and media scholar Heidi Campbell, whose publications have been highly influential in the development of a hermeneutic perspective on media and religion, and show how recent philosophical insights into collective beliefs can be fruitfully implemented to improve some key aspects of her analysis.

In my argument, I will proceed as follows. First, I will situate Campbell's work in the contemporary debate on the topic of religion and media, reconstruct her theoretical background, and highlight some of her most innovative contributions. Then, I will apply Campbell's framework to the case of the Jehovah's Witnesses. Against this background, I will point out some theoretical and empirical problems raised by this analysis. In a nutshell, I will argue that Campbell's work, while being very effective for the analysis of the adoption of new technologies in religious settings, is predicated on a vague conception of the relationship between individual and collective media use and an interpretation that ultimately invites the adoption of an account of a religious community as a sum of people, each of whom individually professes the same evaluative beliefs—what is technically called a summative or aggregative conception of groups (see Chapter 2). In contrast to this position, I will introduce Margaret Gilbert's theory of joint commitment and plural subjects and defend the idea that a religious collective can exist autonomously from—although not necessarily in contrast to—the individual beliefs and practices of its members. To support this move, I will elaborate on the interpretation of the Jehovah's Witnesses' ritualized study of media discussed in the previous chapter. In my conclusion, I will argue that the ritual production of a plural subject upholding distinct collective beliefs is a constitutive feature of a religious collectivity—a proposition that can be paradigmatically illustrated by the study of the religious framing of media within the Watch Tower Society.

A final preliminary remark is in order. In this chapter, I will draw upon some philosophical reflections concerning collective belief. The conceptualization of belief is a knotty issue among philosophers and even more so among scholars of religion. It is not necessary to enter into these debates here. For my purpose, a general definition of belief as an "attitude we have, roughly, whenever we take something to be the case or regard it as true" (Schwitzgebel 2015) will suffice. As part of this definition, however, I will also include, in addition to descriptive or factual beliefs, evaluative beliefs, such as those expressed in sentences such as "I believe that this ice cream is good" or "I believe that killing is bad." This extension is in line with Gilbert's (e.g., 1987; 2002, see also below) use of belief, which is relevant for my discussion, and is supported by several philosophers and social scientists (e.g., Rokeach 1968; Price 1969: 435–436; Boudon 1995: 22; Engel 1996: 161); problems that might arise from this inclusion, for instance in the field of metaethics, need not concern us.[1]

9.2 Heidi Campbell's Religious-Social Shaping of Technology

My point of entry into the debate over the relationship between media, religious belief, and the constitution of religious collectivities is a particular approach known as the religious-social shaping of technology, which was developed about ten years ago by the American scholar Heidi Campbell (b. 1970). To highlight the originality of her perspective, it is useful to contrast it with the paradigm that dominated (and to some extent still dominates) the research on media and religion of recent decades.

9.2.1 Breaking the determinist mold

In the second half of the twentieth century, the analysis of the role of the media in society was strongly informed by deterministic views that did not see the media as neutral instruments of communication under the control of social actors but rather conceived of them as technological artifacts that, through their specific affordances, impose on their users their own mode of knowing (see Krüger 2012: 12). This perspective, encapsulated in Marshall McLuhan's famous formulation, "The medium is the message" (McLuhan 1994: 7), was developed in particular by the so-called Toronto

School of Communication (e.g., Innis 1951; Meyrowitz 1985). Scholars in this tradition were interested in the specific impact of the media on the individual consumer and, more broadly, on social behavior. Their analyses contributed significantly to mapping media changes through the centuries. With regard to the transformations of the media landscape of their time, however, their interpretations were often characterized by normative and pessimistic views connecting the rise of electronic media and mass media entertainment to the decline in rational discourse and ultimately of democratic society (see, e.g., Ong 1958; Postman 1985).

These conclusions were deeply intertwined with a theological discourse that presented (electronic) media as the expression of a hedonistic and consumerist society and as the object of "idolatrous practices" that constituted a threat to religion (Krüger 2012: 354–372). It is therefore unsurprising that the thesis of media scholars working within this paradigm was received positively by a number of religionists working in the academic research on religion and media (e.g., Christians 1997; Schultze 2002; see also Ferré 2003: 86–88). Indeed, while the idea of a deterministic impact of media on their users has generally been replaced, in media and communication studies, by approaches that are more refined, this perspective remains implicit in many contributions focusing on religion. A striking example is provided by the success, in the last decade, of the idea of the "mediatization of religion." This theory situates the contemporary religious change within the framework of a broader mediatization of society (Hjarvard 2008b, 2013). In a nutshell,

> Mediatization designates the process through which core elements of a social or cultural activity (for example, politics, teaching, religion and so on) assume media form. As a consequence, the activity is, to a greater or lesser degree, performed through interaction with a medium, and the symbolic content and the structure of the social and cultural activity are influenced by media environments and a media logic, upon which they gradually become more dependent. (Hjarvard 2008a: 13)

With regard to religion, the exact contours and consequences of this process remain contested and can vary from author to author (see, e.g., Hepp and Krönert 2009; Sa Martino 2013; Thomas 2016). In his systematic overview of this research paradigm, however, Oliver Krüger (2018) was able to identify a number of common premises. In particular, Krüger observes that, in addition to the unquestioned assumption of the ever-increasing media saturation of society, several scholars in this field conceive of media and religion as two autonomous and competing fields. In this sense, they not only disregard the complex historical and contemporary interpenetrations of these domains but also reproduce a normative stance that sees media use in a religious context as a contaminating influence on some unspecified "pure" form of religion.

In his assessment of mediatization theory, Krüger joins a number of scholars of media and religion who reject the claim that a particular medium has a determinate effect on society or religion and stress the importance of investigating how religious traditions frame the use of specific media technologies and how religious groups and individuals engage in various forms of media production and consumption (e.g., Barzilai-Nahon and Barzilai 2005; Neumaier 2016; Vitullo 2019). While this research agenda has been progressively developed since the mid-1990s (see Stout and Buddenbaum 1996), in the contemporary social study of religion it is inseparably linked with the more recent work by Heidi Campbell, which constitutes a reference for many young scholars and a basis for further theoretical reflection (see Rota and Krüger 2019).

9.2.2 From the social shaping of technology . . .

In her classic study *When Religion Meets New Media* (2010), Campbell calls attention to the negotiation processes that accompany the introduction of new media technologies into religious contexts. Campbell's primary source of inspiration is the groundbreaking work by the communication scholar Diane Zimmerman Umble (1992, 1996), who studied the introduction and use of the telephone among Old Order Mennonites and Amish in Pennsylvania. Zimmerman Umble showed how these communities, famous for their rejection of modern technology, progressively integrated the telephone into their everyday lives by negotiating a way of making and receiving calls compatible with their communal values. This resulted in the construction, from the 1960s onward, of shared telephone shanties to be used collectively by members of the same neighborhood. In a similar fashion, Campbell (2007) analyzed the negotiation processes that accompanied the diffusion of mobile phones among ultra-Orthodox Jews in Israel. In this case, the initial resistance to the new medium was overcome by restructuring the product to address religious concerns. The outcome was the development of a "kosher" phone that preserved the possibility of mobile communication while blocking all services such as Internet access or erotic hotlines that were deemed incompatible with the group's shared moral values. Against this backdrop, Campbell refined a systematic approach to study the intersection of religion and media.

Campbell's approach draws on insights provided by a broad research program known as the social shaping of technology, SST for short, which took form in the mid-1980s, particularly among British sociologists and media scholars (see MacKenzie and Wajcman 1985). The approaches federated under the SST umbrella are diverse (see Williams and Edge 1996) but are united in rejecting the "typical assumption that technological change is an independent factor, impacting on society from outside of society" (MacKenzie and Wajcman 1999: 5). In place of this deterministic presupposition, SST scholars substitute the idea that "there are 'choices' [. . .] inherent in both the design of individual artefacts and systems, and in the direction or trajectory of innovation programmes" (Williams and Edge 1996: 866). Accordingly, particular attention is paid to the analysis of the different paths of technological innovation and to the various factors that influence the reception of technology in society. In this respect, "SST stresses the *negotiability* of technology," highlighting, among other things, the scope for social groups "to shape technologies to their ends" (Williams and Edge 1996: 867).

The ways in which new technologies are molded by their users in order to fit better into the routine of their daily lives were explored in detail by the media and communication scholar Roger Silverstone and his collaborators in a series of research projects in the 1980s and 1990s that focused on British households. Silverstone and his team argued that the production and reproduction of technologies do not end with the disappearance of a new technology into the home but continue in consumption as a "transformative and transcendent process of the appropriation and conversion of meaning" (Silverstone and Hirsch 1994: 4). The family was regarded as a privileged framework within which such transformative dynamics take place, in the sense that new technologies are literally brought home and made—or not made—acceptable and familiar within the domestic sphere (Silverstone and Haddon 1996: 45). Households were seen as actively domesticating the products—as one would tame wild animals (Haddon 2007: 26)—by incorporating and redefining them in accordance with the household's own values and interests (Silverstone, Hirsch, and Morley 1994: 14).

When considered from the perspective of these evaluations and negotiations, the household can be conceived of as a "moral economy," that is as "a social, cultural and economic unit actively engaged in the consumption of objects and meanings" (Silverstone and Hirsch 1994: 6). More precisely, "The household is a *moral* economy because the economic activities of its members within the household [...] are defined and informed by a set of cognitions, evaluations and aesthetics, which are themselves defined and informed by the histories, biographies and politics of the household and its members" (Silverstone, Hirsch, and Morley 1994: 16).

From this perspective, each household communicates with the surrounding society while at the same time drawing on specific social, cultural, religious, and biographical resources to construct the bounded environment of the home as an autonomous (albeit not isolated) unit (Silverstone, Hirsch, and Morley 1994: 16–17). For this reason, the process of domesticating a new technological product within the moral economy of the household not only shapes the product itself but also contributes to the self-creation of the household. The acts of appropriation that constitute consumption and the social relationships thereby sustained and constructed are two sides of the same coin (Hirsch 1994: 195).

9.2.3 ...to the religious-social shaping of technology

While Silverstone and his colleagues focused on the appropriation of new technologies within individual households, other scholars extended the domestication approach to other spheres of society (see Haddon 2007: 27–28). In the same vein, by advocating an approach that focuses on the religious-social shaping of technology, Campbell, who draws explicitly on Silverstone, wants to emphasize how "spiritual, moral, and theological codes of practice guide technological negotiation" (Campbell 2010: 59).

In her book, Campbell discusses examples from Christianity, Judaism, and Islam. However, she is well aware that these traditions are not internally homogeneous and that within each of them there are a variety of theological, moral, and organizational options. For this reason, her unit of analysis is not entire religious traditions but specific communities within those traditions, conceived as "spiritual networks of relationships and practices" (Campbell 2010: 8; see also Campbell 2005: 21–40; 2013). In this respect, Campbell convincingly argues that, while individuals within the same religious tradition usually share certain beliefs and practices, "[I]t is the specific grouping to which they belong that often dictates their rules of religious life" (Campbell 2010: 15).

Echoing the case of the household, Campbell underscores that it is within the boundaries of a specific community that choices and reactions to new technologies are negotiated and that media are domesticated to fit a particular moral order. As she puts it, "Religious communities are unique in their negotiations with media due to the moral economies of these groups, and the historical and cultural settings in which they find themselves" (Campbell 2010: 58). Accordingly, Campbell invites us to regard a religious community as a "family of users" who, on the basis of shared beliefs and identity markers, "create a distinctive 'moral economy' of social and religious meanings that guide their choices about technology and rules of interaction with them" (Campbell 2010: 58). I shall come back later to this conception of a religious community. For now, the main takeaway is the acknowledgment that a study of the relationship between religion and media "involves asking questions about how technologies are conceived of, as well as used, in light of a religious community's beliefs, moral codes, and historical tradition of engagement with other forms of media technology" (Campbell 2010: 59).

To operationalize her theoretical stance, Campbell identifies four chief factors that shape the adoption of media technologies by a religious community: first, the role of the history and tradition of the community with respect to media, in particular, its relationship to text as a template for future negotiation with other media; second, the central beliefs and social patterns of the community and the way they inform its response to new media; third, the community's position toward authority and its consequences for the negotiation process; fourth, the communal framing and discourse legitimizing the use, adaptation, or rejection of a new media technology (Campbell 2010: 60–63; see also Hutchings 2017: 203–209). The different aspects of this analytical framework can be fruitfully used to analyze the case of Jehovah's Witnesses. In the following, however, I will concentrate on the way in which the Watch Tower Society frames the legitimate and illegitimate use of various media. Important aspects pertaining to Campbell's first three points will emerge as the result of this discussion. I will also deal with her first point in greater detail in Chapter 11, although from a different perspective.

9.3 Framing the Use of Media Technology within the Watch Tower Society

Campbell (2010: 134–161) distinguishes three discursive strategies through which a community frames its relationship with media: a validating discourse, a prescriptive discourse, and an officializing discourse. In the following, I will draw on various Watch Tower publications to illustrate these three communal framing strategies, paying special attention to the last.

9.3.1 Validating discourse: The history of Jehovah's Witnesses as a history of media

The history of the Watch Tower Society can be reconstructed, at least to a certain extent, as a history of media. Indeed, soon after his encounter with Adventist doctrines in 1869, its founder, Charles T. Russell, became active in the field of religious publishing, first as an associate of Nelson H. Barbour at *The Herald of the Morning*, and then, from 1879, as the editor of *The Watchtower*. Russell went on to establish the magazine as the primary means of spreading his theological ideas and to structure an organized readership. French sociologist Arnaud Blanchard (2008) identifies different phases after this first foundational period, leading to an increasingly centralized and strong control over the production, distribution, and use of printed media in order to ensure the diffusion of a standardized and invariable message.

Still, a focus on the role of media in the organization of the Watch Tower Society is not only a valid strategy for an academic analysis, it is also a constitutive part of the Society's own historiography and, thus, an integral element of its self-representation. Accordingly, the Watch Tower publications provide several examples of a framing that Campbell calls a validating discourse, that is, a discursive strategy through which religious groups define "how technologies validate group goals and serve as a way to affirm their communal identity" (Campbell 2010: 137). An early example is provided by the Society's annual report for the year 1920. In that year, the Society stopped outsourcing the manufacturing of its books and magazines to commercial firms and built its own printing facilities in Brooklyn, New York (Jp 1959: 112–115; Jv 1993: 577–579). *The Watchtower* presented the inauguration of the new printing shop in the following terms:

> After taking the matter to the Lord and watching earnestly for his leadings, in a short while found ourselves in possession of a well-equipped printing plant with several first-class presses; and in due time the Lord brought forth fully consecrated brethren to man those presses and to do the work, so that during the greater portion of the year all the work on THE WATCH TOWER, THE GOLDEN AGE, and many of the booklets, has been done by consecrated hands, but one motive directing their actions, and that motive being love for the Lord and his cause of righteousness. (W 1920, December 15: 371)

Relating this episode more than 70 years later, the book *Jehovah's Witnesses—Proclaimers of God's Kingdom* insists that the decision of the then president of the Society, Joseph Rutherford, to move to New York and start printing there was accompanied by unmistakable signs of God's favor (Jv 1993: 587).

Printed media, however, are not the only focus of the Watch Tower Society's historiography. In many retrospective accounts published by the Society, entire chapters herald its constant media innovation (e.g., Jv 1993: 554–602; Kr 2014: 68–77). These publications emphasize, for instance, the Watch Tower Society's groundbreaking use of cinematography in its 1914 *Photo-Drama of Creation*, its status as one of the pioneers of religious radio broadcasting (see below) and the way in which it later adopted all sorts of media technology, including phonographs, "sound cars" (vehicles with loudspeakers mounted on top), motion pictures, video and audio cassettes, floppy disks and CDs. They also highlight how, to meet the need for adequate typesetting in different languages in a globalized environment, Jehovah's Witnesses were at the forefront in the development of publishing software. Finally, the latest media innovation, the introduction of the refurbished multimedia website, jw.org, in August

2012, deeply influenced the way in which Jehovah's Witnesses (re)present themselves (see Chapter 11).

9.3.2 Prescriptive discourse: The media as instruments to announce the Kingdom

The Watch Tower Society's introduction of new media technologies into the religious life of Jehovah's Witnesses is very often connected to the search for new missionary opportunities. This brings us to Campbell's second framing strategy, which she calls a prescriptive discourse. Through a prescriptive discourse, "[R]eligious individuals and groups laud the embrace of technology because of its ability to help fulfill a specific valued goal or practice" (Campbell 2010: 136). The Society's early adoption of the radio to announce the news of the Kingdom constitutes a first telling example. While many Evangelical groups recognized the potential of this medium to spread their message (Lambert Bendroth 1996; Krüger 2012: 304–306), the Watch Tower Society was among the first religious actors to embrace the new technology (McLeod 2010; Krüger and Rota 2015; Rota 2018).

Already in 1922, one of Rutherford's public conferences was broadcast "to approximately 25,000 people who were 'listening in' on their receivers" (W 1922, April 15: 1922). However, the adoption of radio broadcasting also had to be validated. The columns of *The Watchtower* warned their readers against the widespread spiritic interpretation of the airwaves as a means of communicating with the dead (see Baudouin 2015) and replaced it with a biblical framing, presenting the radio as the realization of an Old Testament prophecy according to which God would one day allow mankind to use bolts of electricity to carry his message over great distances (W 1922, June 15: 180, quoting Job 38: 34, 35). Against this backdrop, the Society was able to push what it believed was "the most economical and effective way of spreading the message of the truth that has yet been used" (W 1924, December 1: 358).

From there, the radiophonic mission grew rapidly. In the early 1930s recordings of Rutherford's preaching were played on more than 400 commercial radio stations, potentially reaching five continents (Jv 1993: 122). However, Rutherford's scorching rhetoric against politicians, businessmen, and religious figures (Penton 2015: 96–97) quickly led to the joint effort of several institutions to restrict the Witnesses' use of the airwaves. Faced with growing restrictions, in 1937, the Society decided to suspend the broadcasting of his preaching on commercial stations and to reorient missionary work by adopting a different medium, the phonograph, which was promptly presented as an even less expensive and more effective means of evangelization than the radio (e.g., W 1936, November 15: 344; W 1937, February 1: 46)

More recent publications compare the success of the radio and the phonograph with contemporary preaching methods in terms of the same goal of stimulating missionary work. Indeed, the current adoption of the Internet as a central instrument in the field service is explicitly portrayed as a continuation of the earlier use of the radio (Kr 2014: 74). Thus, the introduction of the revamped website jw.org was also accompanied by a validating discourse meant to encourage Jehovah's Witnesses to use it in their field ministry. Consider this exhortation:

Direct People to the Website: Some who hesitate to converse with us or accept literature are willing to investigate Jehovah's Witnesses by looking at jw.org in the privacy of their home. So publicize the Web site at every appropriate opportunity. (Km 2012, December: 5)

Similarly, the Watch Tower publications incite Jehovah's Witnesses to use the Society's video clips and smartphone apps to present their message to householders (see Chapter 11).

9.3.3 Officializing discourse: Potentials and dangers of (new) media

On the whole, the discussion of the first two framings conveys a picture of a media-friendly organization. Nevertheless, it also suggests that the embracing of new media technologies by the Watch Tower Society was never indiscriminate. On the contrary, each new technology goes through a thorough evaluation that determines both its advantages and its potential dangers. This process results in the construction of a discursive frame that Campbell calls an officializing discourse that "seeks not only to promote designated uses of technology, but also to set defined boundaries for use in terms of theological beliefs and social values" (Campbell 2010: 144). Numerous articles in the magazines *The Watchtower* and *Awake!* as well as various books, videos, and other online content published by the Watch Tower Society involve such framing, which deserves closer scrutiny.

The case of television is, in this respect, emblematic. Despite its early use of video technology to create the above-mentioned *Photo-Drama of Creation* and other movies, until very recently the Watch Tower Society did not own a television channel or produce specific content for TV broadcast (see Chapter 11). Nevertheless, the small screen was a recurrent topic in its publications from the late 1950s. As Figure 9.1 shows, discussion of television in the pages of *Awake!* and *The Watchtower* was raised continuously up to the mid-1980s, following the diffusion of the medium into mass

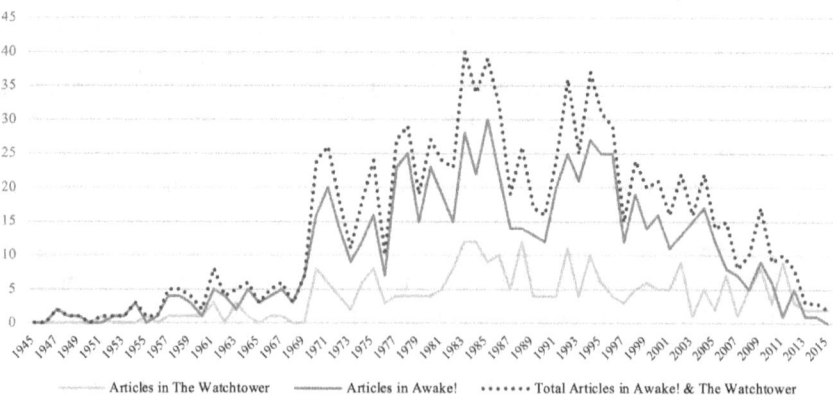

Figure 9.1 Number of Articles on Television per Year (1945–2015). © Andrea Rota.

culture, decreasing from the mid-1990s onwards, as the Internet progressively emerged as the new central concern.[2]

In her qualitative content analysis of the two Watch Tower magazines, Felder (2016: 23–25) notes that when discussing television, the articles often present it as a means to lessen the distance between nations and peoples as well as a source of information about global events. From the 1950s to the 1980s, a particular emphasis was also placed on the educational potential of TV. For instance, an Article in *Awake!* notes that television "makes available a variety of instructive material with a full view of the teacher and of any experiments or visual illustrations that he may provide," and prizes the fact that "[o]ne can learn about mathematics, various other sciences, basic household skills, languages and many other things on educational television" (G 1974, September 8: 8). On the following page, however, the tone of the article changes.

> But television is merely a means of communication. Whether it benefits you personally depends upon the type of programs that you watch. [...] Many things that appear on television create in the viewer a desire for material things that may have little practical value. [...] The trend of television toward the "new morality" is also a disheartening one. Startled viewers have seen shows that deal with homosexuality and lesbianism. Full frontal nudity has appeared on stations of the Public Broadcasting System. Comedy shows often feature off-color humor. (G 1974, September 8: 9)

When faced with such content, the reader is advised to change channel or to turn the TV set off.

Similarly, many articles discussing the topic of the Internet from the mid-1990s also begin by drawing attention to its many useful aspects, but in most cases the benefits are cast into doubt by a stronger emphasis on the possible risks associated with misuse of the technology, as the following example illustrates:

> ALL OVER THE WORLD, MILLIONS OF PEOPLE USE the Internet every day. Many log on to conduct business, to catch up on world news, to check the weather, to learn about different countries, to obtain travel information, or to communicate with family and friends in various parts of the world. But some—married and single adults as well as a surprising number of children—will be going on-line for a very different reason: TO LOOK AT PORNOGRAPHY. (G 2000, June 8: 3)

In line with these first examples, a cross-media analysis shows that the upfront rejection of a medium is rare; however, the positive aspects of using different media should not lull users into a false sense of security. The potential drawbacks mentioned in the Watch Tower Society's publications are numerous, but certain dangers are featured more prominently and consistently. Since the arguments are similar in their numerous iterations, some selected examples will suffice to convey an idea of the dominant interpretative patterns.

Being exposed to pornography or otherwise immoral content, as indicated in the previous examples, is one of the most notable perils associated with the use of various media. As the article about the Internet quoted above argues, pornography "can seriously affect your quality of life, warp your judgment, damage your relationships with others and, most important, ruin your relationship with God." Thus, readers are warned, "Whether featured in a book or a magazine or online, pornography is not for Christians. Avoid it at all costs!" (G 2000, June 8: 10). The Watch Tower Society's publications similarly warn readers to avoid media portraying or discussing the sphere of the occult. Jehovah's Witnesses' theology underscores the influence of invisible beings in humans' everyday life (Chryssides 2008: 101–102). While God's angels protect people from spiritual harm, the rebellious angels, or demons, who joined the side of Satan, seek to mislead them through various forms of spiritism. "The practice of spiritism," as the booklet quoted in the introduction of this chapter explains, "is involvement with the demons, both in a direct way and through a human medium" (Bh 2005: 100). Thus, in *Awake!*, we can read the following admonition:

> All who truly love Jehovah will stay away from books, movies, and computer games that are rooted in the occult or that promote occult practices and beliefs. "I shall not set in front of my eyes any good-for-nothing thing," says Psalm 101: 3. What is more, occult entertainment often glorifies violence and immorality, which "lovers of Jehovah" repudiate.—Psalm 97: 10. (G 2011, February: 6)

Quoting from the first letter to the Corinthians (10: 21, 22) the same paragraph sternly warns, "You cannot be partaking of 'the table of Jehovah' and the table of demons."

According to the theological views of the Watch Tower Society, the Devil also seeks to instigate mankind to rebel against God. Thus, "It is no coincidence that violence, often with occult themes, saturates the popular media" (W 2007, June 1: 6). For instance,

> Songs featuring increasingly violent lyrics "have moved into the mainstream of the music industry" [...]. Using filthy language, some songs glorify murder and rape, even of wives and mothers. (G 2012, August: 4)

Other media do not fare any better in this respect. Indeed, Satan "tries to estrange us from Jehovah by sowing a spirit of violence in our hearts, in part by way of questionable literature, movies, music, and computer games," and, for this reason, "[t]hose who cleave to Bible principles shield their mind and heart from all forms of entertainment that nurture a lust for violence" (W 2005, September 1: 29).

The consumption of inappropriate content is not the only risk associated with media use, however. In the eyes of the Watch Tower Society, electronic media that invite interactive use can lead to dangerous associations. Many articles warn parents about the risks their children might incur when visiting chatrooms or online forums (e.g., G. 2000, December 8: 20). In addition, young people are advised to be very selective in their online friendships to avoid bad company and superficial relationships.

Moreover, even without connecting with other users, media can harm communication. By offering time-consuming forms of entertainment (e.g., W 2013,

9.4 Media Use among Jehovah's Witnesses

The overview provided in the previous section demonstrates that the publications of the Watch Tower Society make use of all three discursive strategies defined by Campbell. However, while the prescriptive and validating discourses are geared toward regulating the use of media in relation to religious practices, it is the organizing discourse that appears to have the most far-reaching consequences for Jehovah's Witnesses everyday interaction with media. What can we say on this matter?

9.4.1 Evidence from quantitative data

Quantitative data on Jehovah's Witnesses' media use is scarce. In his groundbreaking study, *The Trumpet of Prophecy. A Sociology of Jehovah's Witnesses* (1975a: 142–144), James Beckford surveyed the use of media among the members of ten British congregations. However, his data, while interesting, is quite meager and ultimately inconclusive; furthermore, the data does not provide any information regarding newer media technologies, notably the Internet. To bridge this gap, in 2016, my colleagues and I conducted, with the help of a group of students, a survey in four German-speaking assemblies of Jehovah's Witnesses in Switzerland, filling out a total of 183 questionnaires through face-to-face interviews (see Chapter 7).

The data collected reveal that 72 percent of the Jehovah's Witnesses surveyed read a mainstream newspaper or magazine on a regular basis. Furthermore, 75 percent

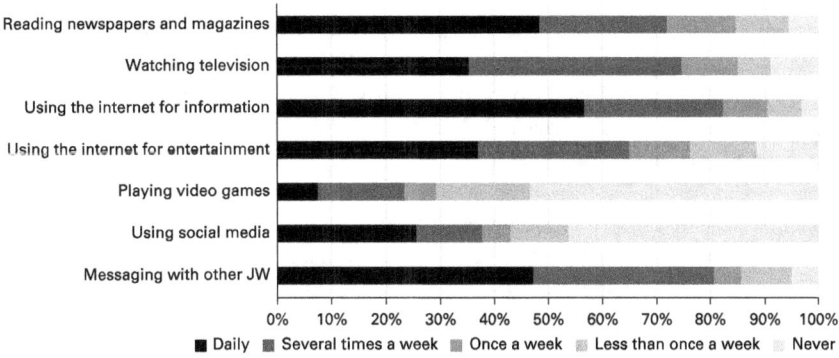

Figure 9.2 Media Use Frequency (N=183). © Andrea Rota.

declared that they watched television daily or several times a week. The Internet also belongs to the everyday media habits of most Witnesses, with 82.5 percent browsing it daily or several times a week to find information on various subjects—a datum that suggests Internet use in line with, if not slightly more frequent than, the Swiss national average. Sixty-five percent surf online regularly to look for entertainment. The use of video games is less widespread: only 29.5 percent of the Jehovah's Witnesses surveyed play video games at least once a week. This might be due in part to the average age of the people surveyed, which was 47. The use of social media platforms such as Facebook and Twitter is split into two uneven groups: 37.7 percent of the surveyed Witnesses affirm checking them daily or several times a week, while 46.5 percent never use them. By contrast, almost 86 percent of the respondents use WhatsApp or other messaging services to communicate with other Jehovah's Witnesses at least on a weekly basis.

On the whole, the warnings in the publications do not seem to deter from the use of electronic media in general. However, the surveyed Witnesses largely share the concerns expressed in the Watch Tower Society's publications about the potential risks of browsing the Internet. Pornography, violence, and wasting time are the three most cited dangers that the use of media in general can pose to (more easily impressionable) children and teens. Thus, from the quantitative data emerges the idea that the surveyed Jehovah's Witnesses do not reject media technology per se, but are concerned about its possible misuse. This view appears to be in line with the framing of media in the magazines and is confirmed by further data. Accordingly, the surveyed Witnesses tend to remain ambivalent regarding the influence of various media. Most of them consider that watching television, surfing the Internet, or using social media has neither a positive nor a negative influence on young users. Video games, which a majority perceives rather in a negative light, represent the only outlier among electronic media. Still, about 30 percent of the surveyed Witnesses remain undecided regarding the potentially harmful effects of video games.

9.4.2 Evidence from qualitative data

These results gain further coherence when compared with qualitative data. For example, **Lara** mentions watching TV on a regular basis. The popular series *The Big Bang Theory* (CBS, 2007–2019) is one of her favorite programs. Still, she would advise younger people to choose in advance what they wanted to watch on TV or online, instead of zapping from one thing to another: "For instance, on YouTube," she says, "you can jump from one video to the other and, suddenly, you have lost an hour!" Lara is also skeptical of social media and offers the following explanation for why she does not have a Facebook or Twitter account:

> I don't like that [using social media]. I mean, on the one side it is definitely very convenient. It has benefits, and I don't want to push it aside. But for me, personally, it would certainly be time consuming, and I don't like the frivolity that often prevails there [on social media]. I don't want to generalize, but there are many things that I consider superficial, such as when everyone posts "nice weather" [...]. It's not my cup of tea. (**Lara**)

While recognizing the possible advantages of social media, **Lara** does not trust herself to make wise use of the technology and, fearing she will waste her time, she prefers to refrain from using it.

A similar ambivalence emerges more generally with respect to the Internet and digital technology. **Leonard** states that the Internet is indispensable in many domains of life; it is a "super medium" that can transmit information very quickly and allows you to be flexible. However, its negative side is evident: "You can spread information that is not true or damaging. Also, pornography, violence, etc., are relatively easy to access." Thus, he concludes, "It has both sides, I would look at it pragmatically, I wouldn't say that it is all bad. You just have to be aware of what you're doing on the Internet." **Gertrud** presents a similar picture of digital media. They always have two sides, she notes. On the one hand, for instance, she likes being able to talk on Skype with her son who lives abroad; on the other hand, these media have a strong potential for addiction. According to an article she read, 10 to 15 percent of people need to be treated for media addiction at some time in their life.

The same addictive potential is also associated with video games. **Frank** addresses this topic speaking from his own experience. In the early 2000s, in a period during which he had distanced himself from the Watch Tower Society, **Frank** was a very active gamer, and was particularly active in playing the online role-playing game *World of Warcraft*. On the server where he played, he became, in his own words, "kind of a star." In 2007, **Frank** came back to the Jehovah's Witnesses and now regularly attends the semiweekly meetings. He still plays video games sometimes, but his attitude toward *World of Warcraft* has changed.

> The problem [...] is the things one has to deal with. *World of Warcraft* is a fantasy world. [...] And then there were also demons and ghosts and whatever. And then, that was it for me. OK, I don't want this anymore. [...] *World of Warcraft* is infested with the occult. And at the beginning that wasn't clear to me. [But] it became clearer and clearer to me. [...] That doesn't fit what we learn here in the Bible.
> (**Frank**)

Frank admits that it was not easy for him to quit playing *World of Warcraft*. At least five times a year, he says, he is tempted to install the game and see "what's going on." To this, he comments, "It is important to be disciplined. It is just a phase that lasts two days and as quick as it comes, it is also gone." As for the problem of occult content, this is not something confined to video games. **Frank** also notes that musicians such as *Kiss* or *AC/DC* play "very dark music" and their lyrics are "often about the Devil and his demons." To avoid such content, **Frank** rarely listens to the radio and uses instead a music streaming app where he can create his playlist. On this topic he concludes, "The media that I consume for entertainment is something that I must have 100 percent under control. I don't want to be exposed to something that I don't want to see."

Finally, **Jörg**'s comments bring home a similar point regarding television. For many years, he did not own a TV and, even though he now has one, he is less than enthusiastic about watching it.

> Nowadays you have about 150 TV channels. [...] And you can browse 150 channels and just find things that *pffff* [are not good]. A lot of crime thrillers, violence. And I am always wondering why people like these things [...] and want to see them. Ah, it disgusts me. [...] On TV we watch nature programs and sometimes you get a good movie like *Into the Wild*. [...] Otherwise, the things shown in movies are violence, sex, conspiracies, corruption. [...] I am not some kind of delicate flower in the corner, but I don't need to watch those things. And my wife doesn't either. We'd rather discuss something together, or to study something, for instance, in *The Watchtower*. (**Jörg**)

Nevertheless, **Jörg** would not say that watching TV is in itself harmful.

> No, no, it is not harmful. You just have to get a handle on it. Something comes up and you say, "I don't need to see this." Some violence or some, ah [almost disgusted], science fiction movie. [...] You know what's coming. And I have to make a distinction between what is useful to me and what brings me nothing. What can I watch? There's not much left. And when sometimes there's a nature movie [...] then I think that's a good thing. (**Jörg**)

After reviewing so much empirical data, we can now ask ourselves how these findings contribute to our understanding of the dynamic relationship between religion, media, and community.

9.5 Reassessing the Nexus of Religion, Media, and Community

9.5.1 A provisional appraisal

A comparison between the content of the publications and the quantitative and qualitative data collected among Swiss and German Jehovah's Witnesses indicates a remarkable consistency in the way different media and their use are framed and portrayed. In both the publications and the interviews, we find the idea that different media can be used in productive ways and provide enjoyable entertainment. This favorable perspective, however, is systematically tempered by the reference to various harmful consequences of media content and excessive media use. In particular, the quotes discussed above imply a belief in the capacity of media content to directly influence the audience—a power that the Devil ruthlessly exploits for his evil plans. The consequence of this belief, however, is not a complete rejection of media but an effort to control one's media use.

In light of this finding, we might follow Campbell (2010: 58) and define the community of Jehovah's Witnesses as a "family of users" who choose to come together in a shared (physical or ideological) space to create a distinctive moral economy "that requires them to make common judgments about the technologies they will appropriate or reject and rules of interaction with them." This conception, however, prompts several questions about the nature, production, and consequences of such "distinctive moral economy" to which Campbell's theoretical framework does not provide clear answers. How does this gathering lead to the formation of a moral economy? How does the moral economy guide the religious users' choices? How does it shape their practices? And how should we understand the image of a family of users? At the core of these questions lies the problem of the relationship between the collective "moral economy" of the group in question and the personal beliefs, attitudes, and practices of the individuals composing it. I maintain that to find a satisfying answer we have to meet two related challenges: a methodological and a theoretical one.

The methodological problem concerns the status of the interview and survey data. Our first instinct might be to take this data at face value and analyze it as an indicator of the personal beliefs and actual practices of Jehovah's Witnesses. Indeed, at first sight, there is no ostensible reason for not doing so. In fact, this appears to be the position of several prominent scholars studying Jehovah's Witnesses. Thus, Beckford (1975a: 144) notes that "[M]any Witnesses revealed in the course of conversation that they were highly selective in their choice of programme. They were uniformly reluctant, moreover, to visit the cinema and to attend dance-halls." In his view, "A tentative explanation for this pattern may be that the latter activities would expose Jehovah's witnesses [sic] to potentially corrupting influences over which they would have little control in a public setting, whereas in their own home they would be in a stronger position to insulate themselves against unwanted influence." Similarly, in his ethnographic research in Britain, Holden (2002: 130) observes that "although Witnesses are by no means the only parents to worry about the possible effects of television on children's behaviour, the Society still issues an authoritarian warning against unsuitable television programmes." Then, directly after, he quotes a Jehovah's Witnesses married couple who confirmed to him they would only watch programs "that would be suitable for their own children and that portrayed behaviour that they, the parents, would allow to take place in their own homes" (Holden 2002: 131). Finally, in his authoritative presentation of the history of Jehovah's Witnesses, Chryssides states,

> Although Jehovah's Witnesses may make occasional visits to the cinema and theatre, they prefer outings to be congregational rather than individual, and in any case, the amount of sex and violence that is regularly on release *leaves little that they would wish to view*. (Chryssides 2016: 175, my emphasis)

But is this really the case?

This question leads us to the theoretical problem regarding the conceptualization of a religious community. The idea implied in the scholarly assessments above is that Jehovah's Witnesses, having adopted for themselves the beliefs and values preached by the Watch Tower Society, orient their media habits accordingly. A community, therefore, is implicitly conceived as *a sum* or *an aggregate* of men and women, each individually having committed to certain beliefs and attitudes. According to this quite intuitive view, to say, for instance, that, as a community, Jehovah's Witnesses abhor violence in movies, would mean that each member of the community—or at least most—having assimilated the message conveyed in the publications, individually abhors violence in movies and, therefore, refrains from watching violent movies. In the following point, I will introduce two new empirical examples that will allow me to question this perspective.

9.5.2 Individual discrepancies

The first empirical example concerns **Emma** and **Fritz**, a married couple of Jehovah's Witnesses. When asked about his television-watching habits, **Fritz** states that he is "rather passionate about the news and documentary films." As for his wife, he implies, she has other preferences, but he would rather let her explain, which leads to the following exchange between the two:

> **Emma:** Other things [television programs]. [Laughs]
> **Fritz:** What kinds of things? [Laughs]
> **Emma** [emotionally]: Crime thrillers! [Laughs] Oh! [addressing the interviewer] You are recording that now? [Laughs]
> **Fritz:** Yes, that is recorded.

In the following conversation, Emma details her taste for crime thrillers. She explains that in addition to the popular German television series *Tatort*,[3] she enjoys watching English and Swedish crime thrillers, before inquiring again, "Eh! That's anonymous, right?"

In this interaction, Emma expresses a preference regarding media content that contrasts with the views put forward in the magazines of the Watch Tower Society. At the same time, her reaction reveals her unease when imagining that her statements might be made public. Commenting on his wife's reaction, **Fritz** notes that Jehovah's Witnesses have their flaws and weakness, too:

> This also shows that we are no saints. Everyone has his preferences and enjoys watching something. Personally, I also enjoy watching a disaster movie. Perhaps that does not fit the concept of Jehovah's Witnesses when one looks from the outside. But we are a community that goes to the movies. (**Fritz**)

In this statement, **Fritz** seeks to minimize what from the outside might be perceived as deviance. On the one hand, he stresses that Jehovah's Witnesses are not barred from going to the movies; on the other, he notes that to indulge in certain forms of entertainment is also "human." His remarks prompt a new exchange between the couple:

> **Fritz:** We should also live. [...] Everyone has his preferences, and they are also part of our lives. There is nothing wrong with that. Of course, we must be somewhat careful [...] if we go around preaching the love of Jehovah God and at home we watch a movie portraying a mass shooting, you know...
> **Emma:** That wouldn't be so believable.
> **Fritz:** Our credibility might be slightly questioned if somebody should ask or get to know what kind of movies we watch.

Emma: Or everything with an esoteric content. That is also taboo for us. [...] Because we know that we are observed. The people do not just listen to what we say but observe us.

The couple's assertions draw attention to a distinction between their public behavior as preachers of God's message and certain personal attitudes that might be perceived as incompatible with that behavior. The general public implied in **Emma**'s and **Fritz**'s last statements appears to be the world of non-Witnesses that surrounds them. Emma's preoccupation with her anonymity, however, also suggests a concern that other people might recognize her by her name. A second case will allow us to explore this aspect in a comparative context.

During an interview, **Anna** also describes her media habits. **Anna** subscribes to a daily newspaper and to a Sunday paper, and watches various news and current affairs shows on television. On Sunday evenings, she usually watches an episode of *Tatort*. Watching TV is also a regular activity in her family life, and **Anna** and her husband regularly use movies as an opportunity for discussion with their children. In addition to movies, **Anna** started watching the TV series *Breaking Bad* and *House of Cards* with her older son.[4] She recognizes that this choice may seem surprising and notes,

Well, I watch it now. If someone else does not watch it, that is OK. Now, I don't think that *Tatort* is that bad but, yes, *Breaking Bad* is probably somewhat at the limit. My younger son is not allowed to watch it. That's clear. Yeah. But, well, I wouldn't go and tell my congregation, "Hey, I watch *Breaking Bad*." I mean, you have some idea of who might also watch it, and you know with whom you can talk about such things. (**Anna**)

Anna's statement shows that she knows her private media habits do not correspond to the expectation of the Watch Tower Society and therefore she would refrain from mentioning them in a communal setting. At the same time, she is also aware that other Jehovah's Witnesses do watch similar TV series while also refraining from mentioning it openly at the congregational meetings, and she feels like she can share her viewing experiences with them, at least privately.

In sum, when it comes to their individual media use, **Anna**, **Emma**, and **Fritz** are evidently not always guided by the religious framing conveyed by the Watch Tower Society's literature. Furthermore, **Emma**'s embarrassment and **Anna**'s secrecy manifestly reveal their awareness that they are doing something they should not. Finally, they recognize, at least implicitly, that their fellow Jehovah's Witnesses (or at least some of them) would have a standing to rebuke them should they find out about their favorite series.

In light of these considerations, it might be tempting to analyze their statements in a normative sense. According to this way of thinking, **Emma** and **Anna** might be considered 'bad' or 'incomplete' Jehovah's Witnesses who have not yet fully assimilated the beliefs and moral system of the group. Or perhaps they would be regarded as weak or faulty members of the group who lack the willpower to act on their beliefs. These positions may well describe the attitude of the community toward them. However, they do not really advance our theoretical understanding of the dynamic nature of a religious collectivity. To move forward, I advocate analyzing the community of Jehovah's Witnesses using Margaret Gilbert's theory of joint commitment. In contrast to the aggregative or summative conception of a community presented above, her philosophical framework allows us to ascribe certain beliefs or attitudes to the community of Jehovah's Witnesses rather than to its individual members. In our case, this would mean that it is not each individual Witness who abhors violence in movies, but Jehovah's Witnesses as *a plural subject* who does.

9.6 Jehovah's Witnesses as a Plural Subject

9.6.1 Collective belief and joint commitment

In a nutshell, a plural subject is a group of people jointly committed to intending something as a body—that is, to emulate, by virtue of the actions of all, a single intentional agent (e.g., Gilbert 2014e: 7). I have provided a systematic discussion of this concept in Chapter 5. In the context of the present discussion, however, it is worth illustrating this idea through a thought experiment drawn from Gilbert's 1987 article "Modeling Collective Belief" (see also Gilbert 1996g). The example proceeds by first demonstrating the limits of a summative account for the definition of a group and then introducing a non-summative account.

Let us imagine a single person, Ansgar, reading a poem and finding it very moving. Ansgar is in a room with other people reading the same poem. The mere physical proximity of the people in the room or the fact that they are reading the same text does not seem to provide grounds for considering them a group or community in any intuitive sense. This conclusion would not change even if we assumed that all the readers personally believe that the poem is moving, for their attitude remains private. Would the situation be different if each of them had expressed their attitude openly to the others, that is, if the way each of them feels about the poem had become common knowledge among all of them? According to Gilbert, the answer must be negative. While each person would know what the other readers individually believe, "the fact that a *group* is involved does not play any obviously essential role in what is going on" (Gilbert 1987: 189). As Gilbert (1987: 189) notes, an analog of group belief can exist "in many populations which are not intuitively social groups. It is probably common knowledge in the population of adults who have red hair and are over six feet tall that most of them believe that fire burns, for instance." Thus, the summative account presented so far would be compatible with a set-theoretical approach to collective phenomena, but it seems only accidentally to refer to a phenomenon involving a group.

Following Gilbert, however, we can imagine a different situation. This time, Ansgar and the other readers meet at Diletta's house to talk poetry. After having read the poem aloud, they discuss its merits and conclude that the poem is very moving. No objection is raised regarding this reading of the poem and no one requests further commentary on it. A few moments later, Ricarda (who did not participate in the discussion) enters the room and asks if the poem is interesting, to which Diletta replies, "It is quite dull."

We can imagine upon hearing this statement Ansgar would retort, "But we thought it was very moving!" In this situation, Ansgar's rebuke would appear to be justified on grounds that cannot be accounted for on the basis of a summative conception of a group (Gilbert 1987: 192–193). What has changed concerning the situation sketched above is that through their communicative practice, the people convened at Diletta's house have decided to "let a certain interpretation 'stand' in the context of their discussion" as an attitude that can be ascribed "to the group as a whole" (Gilbert 1987: 191). Ansgar's right to rebuke Diletta "appears to be understood as grounded *directly* in the existence of a group view that contradicts what the speaker says," and does not require any external moral or prudential reason (Gilbert 1987: 193).

In line with Gilbert's terminology, we can say that the people participating in the poetry discussion have jointly accepted a certain attitude as that of their group and are thus jointly committed to upholding this attitude as a body. As such, they constitute the plural subject of that commitment. Furthermore,

> It is understood that when a set of persons jointly accepts that p [where p is any propositional content], then each of the individuals involved is personally obligated to act appropriately. Such action consists, roughly, in not publicly denying that p or saying or doing anything which presupposes its denial. (Gilbert 1987: 194–195)

Thus, the creation of a joint commitment entails important corollaries (see Chapter 5). First, as we have already seen, it creates a set of mutual rights and obligations. Each party in a plural subject is now entitled and obligated to behave in a certain way "*qua* a member of the whole" (Gilbert 1996g: 186). A violation of these obligations constitutes grounds for rebuke. Second, individual members cannot unilaterally break their joint commitment by simply changing their minds, because they are not individually the subject of the commitment they are revising. It is the group that constitutes the plural subject of such a commitment (Gilbert 2000e). Thus, an individual can abandon a joint commitment without fault only if the other persons have waived their rights to the conforming action. Third, the joint commitment would still hold—and its plural subject would continue to exist—even if one or more of the parties should no longer personally share the attitude that the group has jointly accepted. Indeed, we can imagine that, in the meantime, Ansgar has revised his personal attitude and now also considers the poem in question to be quite dull. (In fact, he might have had this opinion from the beginning, but being, say, shy or a conformist, he has refrained from stating it.) Nevertheless, when he rebukes Diletta, he speaks for the group. Thus, Gilbert draws this radical conclusion:

> [I]t is not a necessary condition of a group's belief that p [a given propositional content] that most members of the group believe that p. Indeed, given the above it seems that *it is not necessary that any members of the group personally believe that p.* (Gilbert 1987: 191)

At this point, it is important to avoid some common misunderstandings. Gilbert's conclusion does not mean that personal and joint attitudes *never* converge, just that they do not *necessarily* converge. In this sense, a plural subject cannot be simply reduced to individual intentions, and yet it does not constitute a new metaphysical reality. Accordingly, Gilbert's thesis does not seek to provide a measure of the *intensity* of individual commitments but rather to specify the *form* of commitment—namely, a *joint* commitment—at the core of group-building processes.

This theoretical discussion allows us to see the empirical cases of the previous section in a new light and to consider **Emma**, **Fritz**, and **Anna** as parties in a plural subject jointly committed to abhorring violence in movies independently of their personal attitudes on the matter. To support this view further, we can look for circumstances under which the interviewed Jehovah's Witnesses entered just such a joint commitment. Gilbert emphasizes that joint commitments are an essential element of everyday life, and a simple exchange between two people is sufficient to create one (Gilbert 1996g: 184). All it takes is for the parties openly to express their readiness to be jointly committed with each other concerning certain intentional content (Gilbert 1989: 180–184; 2006: 138–140). With respect to our empirical case, however, I maintain that the parties entered a joint commitment in a setting that involves the ritual use of media.

9.6.2 The ritualized use of media

Jehovah's Witnesses are openly invited to use the publications of the Watch Tower Society to deepen their understanding of the Bible. The study of these publications, however, is not only an individual activity but also, and foremost, a communal activity, taking place at the congregation meetings organized semiweekly at Kingdom Halls around the world. I have discussed this practice exhaustively in Chapter 8, but it may be useful to summarize and highlight some of its core features here.

At the weekend, each congregation of Jehovah's Witnesses meets for a public Bible discourse and then reviews an article from *The Watchtower*. In a second meeting, which is held on a weekday, the congregants receive instruction on the basis of various publications to organize their missionary work and improve their rhetorical and teaching skills. Until December 2008, a third weekly meeting, called Congregation Book Study, was held in smaller groups in a private location, usually a congregant's home, and was devoted to the study of one of the books published by the Watch Tower Society. In 2009, the Society decided to rename this meeting Congregation Bible Study and to integrate it into its congregations' midweek program (Km 2008, October: 1; Kr 2014: 174–176). In the following, I shall discuss a particularly telling example of such a Congregation Bible Study meeting.

As is the case with the collective study of *The Watchtower* and other publications, the Congregation Bible Study (and, previously, the Congregation Book Study) meeting is based on a question-and-answer discussion. The questions to be discussed are provided in the book itself, and the chapter or passage that will be discussed each week is announced to all members well in advance through the meeting workbooks. During the Congregation Bible Study, a book paragraph is read from the platform, followed by one or two questions related to its content. The participants can signal their readiness to answer the questions by raising their hands. Most of their answers, however, are more or less elaborate paraphrases of the text read from the platform. After a few answers have been collected, the congregation moves on to the next paragraph.

To understand better the significance of this process for the constitution of a joint commitment among participants in the meeting, let us consider a concrete example from the book *Keep Yourselves in God's Love* (Lv 2008), first used for Congregation Bible Study in 2009. In a chapter entitled "How to Choose Wholesome Entertainment," readers are admonished to "abhor what is wicked." Concerning the world of entertainment, the text notes that it can be broadly divided into forms of entertainment that Christians definitely avoid and others they may or not find appropriate; it then goes on to examine the first category:

> [S]ome forms of entertainment highlight activities expressly condemned in the Bible. Think, for example, of websites as well as movies, TV programs, and music that have sadistic or demonic content or that contain pornography or promote vile, immoral practices. Since such degraded forms of entertainment portray, in a positive light, activities that violate Bible principles or break Bible laws, they should be shunned by true Christians. (Lv 2008: 65)

The following question appears as a footnote to guide the communal discussion of this passage: "What forms of entertainment do we reject, and why?" (Lv 2008: 65). The form of the question and the content of the paragraph clearly point to the expected answer—that is, some version of the statement, "We reject degraded forms of entertainment because they violate Bible principles."

As for the second category, the book indicates that individual tastes may vary but stresses the importance of the making informed decisions based on the Bible (Lv 2008: 66-69). Indeed, already in the first chapter, it explains that "Jehovah wants us to benefit from his love forever," but also admonishes that "whether we will or not, [...] is up to us" (Lv 2008: 5-6). To do so requires "learning about Jehovah's personality and ways" in order to perceive "what the will of Jehovah is" (Lv 2008: 9). To illustrate this idea, the book addresses the use of media. It says,

> For example, the Bible contains no direct command telling us not to watch movies or TV programs that feature gross violence or sexual immorality. But do we really need a specific law against watching such things? We know how Jehovah views these matters. His Word plainly tells us: "[Jehovah] hates anyone who loves violence." (Psalm 11: 5) It also says: "God will judge sexually immoral people." (Hebrews 13: 4) By reflecting on those inspired words, we can clearly perceive what the will of Jehovah is. We therefore choose not to be entertained by watching graphic portrayals of the sort of practices that our God hates. We know that it pleases Jehovah when we avoid the moral filth that this world tries to pass off as harmless entertainment. (Lv 2008: 9)

The question associated with this paragraph is the following: "How can we know what is pleasing to Jehovah even in situations where there is no direct Bible law? Give an example" (Lv 2008: 8). Again, the question and the paragraph clearly delimit the form and content of the speech acts that will be considered appropriate answers.

To answer such a question in the public setting of a congregation's meeting not only amounts to a statement recognizing a certain state of affairs but can also be viewed as a speech act through which the speaker commits himself or herself to upholding certain evaluative beliefs regarding the appropriate forms of media entertainment. However, in light of Gilbert's framework presented above, I want to reaffirm and reinforce the argument that I presented in Chapter 8. As I have argued, the ritualized question-and-answer discussion of the Watch Tower Society publications can be regarded as a "group-will-formation system" in the sense of Tuomela (1995: 15). But the same practice also provides a suitable foundation for a joint commitment in the sense intended by Gilbert.

By answering the questions according to the form and content suggested in the publications, the utterances of a few congregants outline an attitude for the group and signal their readiness to enter into a joint commitment with the other participants to uphold certain beliefs.[5] The other participants tacitly do the same by refraining from challenging the collective position encapsulated in the answer. In this way, the members of the congregation are constituted as the plural subject of such a belief and are jointly committed to upholding it as a single body. Indeed, the joint commitment does not prevent individual Witnesses from showing poor judgment in their everyday decisions—a possibility that the publication quoted in this section recognizes (see Lv 2008: 68–69). However, in its constitution, the jointly accepted beliefs of the group are laid out explicitly, thus providing a ground for rebuking—or for offering counsel and guidance (see Holden 2002: 77–81)—to those who are known to deviate from them.

This perspective invites us also to reflect on the construction of religious authority within a religious collectivity. In the theology of the Watch Tower Society, the Bible is regarded as the infallible word of God and as the ultimate source of truth and authority. However, its interpretation is systematically mediated through the Society's publications. This means that in the case of Jehovah's Witnesses—as indeed in the case of many other religious groups—the accepted doctrinal positions are not established through public deliberations but rather through a fiat of the Watch Tower Society's Governing Body, based on its (evolving) interpretation of the Bible (Chryssides 2008: 18–19; Penton 2015: 253–256). The authority to make such decisions, however, depends on the acceptance of the Jehovah's Witnesses' congregations. In this sense, through the ritual study of the organization's books and magazines, Jehovah's Witnesses not only jointly commit to upholding certain beliefs but also jointly accept the validity of the biblical exegesis that they verbalize during their meeting, and thus, indirectly, jointly acknowledge the interpretative prerogative of the Watch Tower Society.

9.7 Conclusion

In sum, Margaret Gilbert's approach provides a philosophical foundation for the introduction of a more nuanced concept of religious collectivity and of the role of media in its constitution. Gilbert maintains that,

In order for individual human beings to form collectivities, they must take on a special character, a "new" character, in so far as they need not, *qua* human beings, have that character. Moreover, humans must form a whole or unit of a special kind, a unit of a kind that can now be specified precisely: they must form a plural subject. (Gilbert 1989: 431)

Accordingly, a set of individuals each having the same beliefs or attitudes provides neither a sufficient nor a necessary condition to constitute a group in any strong sense—not even a set of individuals each personally feeling themselves as belonging to a group seems to make the cut. In a similar way, a family of users gathered on the basis of similar individual media use does not yet constitute a unit of any special kind. Instead, the creation of such a unit requires the formation of a joint commitment, which can be achieved through a ritual means. Thus, following Gilbert (1987: 195), I would argue that "any set of persons who jointly accept some proposition thereby become a social group or collectivity, intuitively [...] if they were not one before."

With respect to the specific relationship between religion, media, and religious community, Margaret Gilbert's theory of joint commitment and its application to the analysis of empirical data allow us to attribute a certain evaluative belief—for instance, that violence on TV is despicable—to the plural subject of such belief while remaining agnostic on the beliefs of the individual congregants. In this sense, it is worth noting that Heidi Campbell closely associates the creation of a moral economy with a series of negotiation processes that can be interpreted as conducive to a joint commitment. However, in line with her research interest, her analysis sets a particular emphasis on the negotiation between religious groups and leaders and particular *media*, drawing attention to how such media are subjected to different rules to fit the moral order of the community. In this case, the community is considered to be preexisting; it is presupposed a priori.

By contrast, I would argue that the community is also generated by the imposition of such rules on how media should be used.[6] To use a distinction introduced by John Searle (1996), the rules in question are not regulative rules by means of which a community regulates its use of media, but constitutive rules, by means of which the community constitutes itself *as a community*. To use a simile, these rules are not like those at a theme park, forbidding its guests to dive in a pool (which presupposes the existence of the theme park); they are more like the rules of chess, without which chess would not exist. In this sense, the conception of collectivity becomes necessarily dynamic. While a joint commitment lasts until it is collectively dissolved by the parties taking part in it, it can be—and as the empirical case discussed here shows, it will be— continuously, regenerated and reproduced, allowing for both a reaffirmation of the unity of the already jointly committed members and the swift integration of new members into the plural subject.

In the empirical case discussed in this chapter, the constitutive rules in force shape the attitudes of the plural subject of Jehovah's Witnesses and provide grounds for policing the public behavior and discourse of the parties in such a plural subject. However, as long as such constitutive rules are not publicly challenged, diverging personal attitudes remain possible and, as the empirical data suggest, are tacitly known and tolerated by at least some of the members. From a methodological point of view, this indicates that "simply asking people for an opinion on some issue may well not be enough to elicit a personal belief" (Gilbert 1987: 196), since a person may answer in his or her capacity as a participant in a plural subject (see also Tuomela 1995: 324–331 for a similar conclusion).

In this respect, I must stress that by pointing out the possibility of discrepancies between the collective and individual attitudes among Jehovah's Witnesses, I do not want to imply that none of the Witnesses has personal feelings and beliefs that support his or her involvement in the group but only to indicate that such a convergence is not a logical necessity for the existence of the group. In fact, Gilbert indicates that a joint commitment can exert a certain psychological power over the parties in a plural subject at least in the sense that "the individual parties to a collective belief necessarily understand that their behavior is subject to a certain constraint, the obligation to speak and act in certain ways" (Gilbert 1987: 200). In this sense, she acknowledges that "it will be easier, and less internally stressful, to give voice to the view that p when it *is* one's personal view" (Gilbert 2002: 64). However, both her philosophical account and the empirical evidence presented in this chapter indicate that there is room for a contextual flexibility in the individual's orientation toward collective or personal evaluative beliefs (see also Tuomela 1995: 331 for a similar conclusion).

10

Collective Emotions—The Collective Excitement of Conventions

10.1 Introduction

Jehovah's Witnesses constitute a visible religious presence in cities worldwide. Particularly since the introduction, in 2015, of mobile literature carts, the sight of a small group of Witnesses distributing Watch Tower books and magazines in public squares, next to famous monuments, or near railway stations has become part of the everyday urban landscape in many countries. For most people, however, it is quite rare to observe a group of more than two to four Witnesses. Thus, as I noticed in many discussions with friends and colleagues, the name Jehovah's Witnesses usually evokes the image of isolated pairs of missionaries. Conversely, it is rarely associated with large crowds of people, such as the masses of Roman Catholics gathered on Sunday mornings in St. Peter's Square or the congregants assembled in an Evangelical megachurch. However, while it is true that the biweekly assemblies of Jehovah's Witnesses are far from multitudinous, several times a year the members of the Watch Tower Society fill convention centers, stadiums, and other public arenas for their district and regional conventions. These packed events, which reunite thousands and sometimes tens of thousands of Witnesses, are the empirical focus of this chapter.

This empirical example will serve as a case study to evaluate the analytical power of two different conceptions of collective emotions. The first is based on a particular interpretation of the sociology of Emile Durkheim—and specifically of his 1912 monograph *The Elementary Forms of Religious Life*. It is epitomized by the philosophical reflections of Anne Rawls and the microsociological approach of Randall Collins. In the study of religion, this perspective has been received and developed by a younger generation of academics, including the Swiss scholar of religion Rafael Walthert. These authors emphasize the role of shared emotional moods among individuals for the constitution of group solidarity and social order.

As I will argue, their conception of collective emotions is a summative one, meaning that a group is considered having a collective emotion when all or most of its members experience a certain emotion. Against this view, I contrast Margaret Gilbert's non-summative conception of collective emotions, which seeks to ascribe an emotional state to the group itself, independently of the emotional mood of its individual members. Gilbert's work on collective emotions has not yet found a broad reception in the social sciences and even less in the study of religion, despite some similarities with the better-known work by Arlie Hochschild on "emotion work." This chapter seeks to discuss critically the possible implications of Gilbert's approach for the study of religions and its potential applications in this regard.

At this point, some remarks regarding the concept of emotion are in order. While this is an extremely complex topic, the above-mentioned perspectives have some points of contact with universalist and constructionist positions in the philosophy and anthropology of emotion that may serve as a general orientation (see Harré 1986b; Reddy 1997; Corrigan 2004: 7–13). It is, of course, impossible to provide a detailed discussion of these positions here, but their core features can be summarized. In a nutshell, universalist approaches consider emotions to be a fundamental biological trait of human beings (and of at least some animals) that, in their basic form, remain similar across the world and through time.

While modern universalist theories disagree on the exact nature, scope, and function of emotions, they generally agree in considering them to be (the result of) bodily or preconscious cognitive processes that are experienced as distinctive bodily sensations or feelings in the brain (see, e.g., James 1884; Damasio 2013). Universalist traits can also be associated with the expression of emotions. This perspective was first advanced by Charles Darwin (1872), who studied the visible gestures associated with various emotions and maintained that because of their evolutionary origin as signaling mechanisms, emotional expressions are universally recognizable. This line of analysis has been developed by the psychologist Paul Ekman (1980) and popularized, for instance, by the TV series *Lie to Me* (Fox, 2009–2011) and the animated film *Inside Out* (Pixar 2015).

Constructionist approaches reject the universalist idea of emotion as a passively experienced and "involuntary phenomenon which, though capable of influencing intelligence, language and culture, [is] not itself essentially dependent upon these complex and historically conditioned factors" (Harré 1986a: 2–3). Instead, they consider cognitive, evaluative, and intentional aspects to be constitutive of emotions— an insight that can be traced back to Aristotle (see Lyons 1980: 33–35). Accordingly, constructionist theories propose that "emotions are characterized by attitudes such as beliefs, judgements and desires, the contents of which are not natural, but are determined by the system of cultural belief, value, and moral value of particular communities" (Armon-Jones 1986: 33). As social constructions, emotions are regarded as being "as variable as any other cultural phenomena" (Lynch 1990: 10–11). Pushing this idea even further, constructionism assumes that the capacity of experiencing particular emotions depends on learned cultural knowledge, which includes specific norms, standards, and expectations.

This position has several implications, some of which constitute a subject of debate within constructionism itself. In particular, it questions the understanding of emotion as something intrinsically connected to particular phenomenological feelings or bodily sensations, since it must be possible for an agent to acquire the constitutive elements of an emotion as an attitudinal cognition-dependent response (Armon-Jones 1986: 43). This does not necessarily mean that emotions are never accompanied by a feeling-sensation, but that such a feature is not a defining feature; rather it is a "contingent fact about emotions" (Armon-Jones 1986: 51). Without trying to settle this debate here, it is worth pointing out that this issue will reemerge below in the discussion of collective emotions, albeit in a different form.

Beyond these clarifications, there is no need here for a more precise definition of "emotion." Even within the field of the study of religion, a review of the different existing suggestions would only reveal a forest of assumptions and corollaries, none of which will play a particular role in my analysis (Corrigan, Crump, and Kloos 2000). When necessary, attention will be drawn to some explicit or implicit features of "emotions" in the work of the authors I quote. The issue of whether there are specific religious emotions is also moot. Without trying to defend this point in detail, I maintain that the postulation of such special emotions generally entails an apologetic perspective that aims either to defend religion as a *sui generis* reality (see Mariña 2004; Corrigan 2004: 4–5) or to devalue particular forms of "emotional" religion (see Fer 2018). Accordingly, I side with William James's (1998: 27) position that there is "no one elementary religious emotion, but only a common storehouse of emotions upon which religious objects may draw" and conceivably no specific or essential religious objects or acts. Riis and Woodhead (2010) have reformulated this idea in modern terms, framing religious emotions as any emotion in the context of a religious regime.

The structure of this chapter can be compared to an hourglass, with two theoretical bulbs connected by an empirical neck. In the first part, I will present a detailed discussion of the Durkheimian interpretation of collective emotions that I briefly mentioned above. The heart of this section is my presentation of the approach defended by the sociologist Randall Collins and it will constitute the foil for further discussions. To understand the presuppositions and implications of his work, however, it is crucial to understand its Durkheimian roots and the overarching epistemological debate in which it is embedded. A summary of *The Elementary Forms* and an assessment of Anne Rawls's "exegesis" of this book will serve these goals. A shorter presentation of Rafael Walthert's application of Collins's approach will provide a telling illustration of its analytical power in a religious context. In the second part of this chapter, I will analyze various empirical data pertaining to the conventions of Jehovah's Witnesses and assess the extent to which the theoretical framework introduced so far can be put to good use in understanding the role of collective emotions in relation to such events.

Without wanting to give away my conclusion here, I will argue that a different approach may be more fruitful. Thus, in the lower bulb of the metaphorical hourglass, I will first introduce the concept of emotion work put forward by Arlie Hochschild. Hochschild's analysis focuses on the effort that *individuals* put into adapting their feelings to a certain situation. Her attention to the normative dimension of emotion will provide a bridge to Margaret Gilbert's non-summative theory of *collective* emotions and to the idea of a group of people jointly committed to upholding an emotion as a body. To round out my analysis before the final discussion, I will examine in detail how the discourses and practices surrounding the Watch Tower Society's conventions can be considered conducive to producing such a joint commitment. The reader may be surprised at that point to find an in-depth discussion of the history of the conventions and of the way Jehovah's Witnesses prepare for them. Indeed, one might expect such information to be presented at the beginning, and not at the end of the chapter. For this reason, I want to emphasize that my historical discussion—and, more precisely, my historiographic analysis—is not meant (merely) to provide context for my case study but constitutes an integral part of my theoretical argumentation. My goal is to show how the conventions are constructed as "institutional events" (see Searle 1996), that is, as situations associated with rights and duties that regulate the way Jehovah's Witnesses collectively feel about them. This can be done only after the other elements of my reasoning have been put in place.

Finally, in my conclusion, I will summarize my findings concerning the heuristic fruitfulness of the approaches reviewed in this chapter and come back to the distinction between summative and non-summative accounts of collective emotion. I will close on a more specific note by discussing what this chapter contributes to the study of the role of collective emotions among Jehovah's Witnesses against the backdrop of previous studies.

10.2 Emotional Effervescence and Group Solidarity

10.2.1 Emile Durkheim's *Elementary Forms*

Emile Durkheim is among the founding fathers of the sociology of knowledge and, in the field of the sociology of emotion, he is often considered as one of the initiators of the constructionist paradigm (Fisher and Chon 1989). However, already in the mid-1970s, and more intensely since the 1990s, an alternative analysis of his work has emerged. Rejecting any reference to symbolic forms as the foundation of an analysis of sociality, a number of sociologists, philosophers, and scholars of religion have explored an interpretation of Durkheim's arguments that insists on the priority of the ritual, collective effervescence, and emotional bonding over all kinds of cultural factors. The study of Durkheim's classic work *The Elementary Forms of Religious Life* has played a central role in their reflections. The main thesis of the book linking religion to society is well known. Thus, I will only discuss a few selected passages pertaining to the role of emotional states in the development of religious beliefs and the construction of social order.

Drawing on multiple ethnographic reports on the totemic practices of Australian tribes, Durkheim famously came to the conclusion that the "manifestly religious" character of the totem (Durkheim 1995: 169) and the symbolic connection between totem and social system have one and the same source (Durkheim 1995: 208). In short, the moral obligation that the clan members feel weighing on them as an impersonal and external force has its source in the clan itself. This impersonal force, of which the totem constitutes a representation, ensures the moral cohesion of the clan and compels its members to act in a certain way with respect to sacred things. At the same time, and without the clan members being aware of it, the sacred nature of the totem is derived from the bestowal upon it of the society's authority, which sets it apart from the rest of the profane world.

However, Durkheim does not content himself with presenting this general analysis. Instead, he seeks to elucidate the concrete social mechanisms through which the moral authority of society is experienced and attached to the totem. Discussing the particular mode of living of the Australian tribes, he notes that while the different clans live scattered in small groups over long periods of the year, they regularly come together "at specified places for a period that varies from several days to several months" (Durkheim 1995: 216–217). When such a gathering, called a *corroboree*, takes place, each clan member experiences a state of high exaltation:

> Once the individuals are gathered together, a sort of electricity is generated from their closeness and quickly launches them to an extraordinary height of exaltation. Every emotion expressed resonates without interference in consciousnesses that are wide open to external impressions, each one echoing the others. (Durkheim 1995: 217–218)

According to Durkheim (1995: 220), a man in such a state of exaltation no longer knows himself and feels under the control of some external power. The social origin of such effervescence, however, is too complex for the "unformed [*rudimentaires*] minds" of the Aboriginal to grasp (Durkheim 1995: 222). Nonetheless, while the Aboriginal cannot know that "the coming together of a certain number of men participating in the same life releases new energies that transform each one of them" (Durkheim 1995: 222), he looks for the cause of such excitement. In the context of the corroboree, it is the totemic images that surround him that attract his attention. Consequently, it is to these images that the emotions that he feels attach themselves. It is in this way that the totem becomes the symbol that embodies the external "religious force" felt by the individual consciousness (Durkheim 1995: 223).

Importantly, the individual clan member does not experience this state of elation alone: "His companions feel transformed in the same way at the same moment, and express this feeling by their shouts, movements, and bearing" (Durkheim 1995: 220). During the corroboree, the bodily behavior of the participants changes, and the gestures and vocalizations of everyone "tend to fall into rhythm and regularity, and from there into songs and dances" (Durkheim 1995: 218). Durkheim explains this phenomenon by the necessity of the "collective emotion [*sentiment collectif*]" to find an ordered expression through "harmony and unison of movement" (Durkheim 1995: 218). It is through these synchronized movements that the individual minds, which are otherwise inaccessible to one another, can "come out of themselves," meet, and commune:

> For the communication that is opening up between them to end in a communion—that is, in a fusion of all the individual feelings into a common one—the signs that express those feelings must come together in one single resultant. The appearance of this resultant notifies individuals that they are in unison and brings home to them their moral unity. It is by shouting the same cry, saying the same words, and performing the same action in regard to the same object that they arrive at and experience agreement. (Durkheim 1995: 232–233)

Thus, the rhythmic movements perform two roles simultaneously: they reveal the mental states of others but also contribute to creating them: "It is the homogeneity of these movements that makes the group aware of itself and that, in consequence, makes it be" (Durkheim 1995: 233). Similarly, the homogenous and stereotyped movements serve to symbolize the social sentiments, but only "because they have helped to form them" (Durkheim 1995: 233).

Here, Durkheim is suggesting a relationship between a symbol and its referent which that is not merely conventional but objective and, in some sense, causal. The same is true with respect to the totemic emblem to which the social sentiments are attached and through which the society can perpetuate its consciousness of itself. While every object can in principle serve as a totem (Durkheim 1995: 230), the link between them and the collective feelings of the group is not merely conventional. Rather, "It tangibly portrays a real feature of social phenomena: their transcendence of individual consciousnesses" (Durkheim 1995: 233). Accordingly, Durkheim (1995: 233) warns, "we must guard against seeing those symbols as mere artifices—a variety of labels placed on ready-made representations to make them easier to handle. They are integral to those representations."

Durkheim's reconstruction of the dynamics through which social cohesion emerges has attracted the attention of a number of scholars who emphasize the logical primacy, in Durkheim's work, of concrete collective practices over collective beliefs and representations. This point has been strongly emphasized by the ethnomethodologist Anne Rawls (b. 1950), who reads the *Elementary Forms* as a radical epistemological proposal to challenge the dominant position among sociologists that takes collective beliefs and representations as the starting point for the analysis of social phenomena.

10.2.2 Anne Rawls's interpretation of *The Elementary Forms*

Rawls's interpretation of Durkheim aims to find a way out of what she considers an intrinsic inadequacy of constructivist approaches, which goes back to Kant's argument against the empirical validity of our categories of understanding. If the world can only be perceived in terms of human categories, a gap arises between thought and reality. Accordingly, in contemporary social sciences "social consensus and socially accepted definitions of meaning are treated as the true measures defining the limits of validity" (Rawls 1996: 431). In this view, socially constructed concepts are based on (and point toward) other socially constructed concepts in a potentially infinite regress.

To counter such a position, Rawls (2001: 34) draws on Durkheim to argue that "[n]arratives, myths, representations, beliefs and concepts are all dependent on the enactment of concrete practices for their genesis and recognizability." As she explains,

> The current belief that concepts construct the concrete world is, Durkheim would argue, the naïve view. The concrete world, while it may give rise to concepts through social construction, must first itself be socially constructed as a concrete witnessable world through concrete witnessable practices, before it can give rise to any feeling or concepts. If concrete practices themselves need to be socially constructed, then that social construction must be concrete. It cannot be merely conceptual and interpretative. (Rawls 2001: 36)

An epistemology based on enacted social practices stops the infinite regress by introducing a non-conceptual foundation (Rawls 2001: 42, 45)—that is, by providing "an empirical source for the categories" on which any complex form of social organization rests (Rawls 1996: 433).

According to Rawls (1996: 438), Durkheim's theory demonstrates that the basic categories of understanding are "perceived directly as social or moral forces during the enactment of social (religious) practice." These moral forces are experienced as emotions, notably in the form of collective effervescence or of sentiments such as respect, comfort, and well-being (Rawls 2001: 38; 2004: 170) and are literally capable of moving people both psychologically and physically (Rawls 2004: 163, 165).

Although people have different explanations of why they feel these emotions—for instance, the power of the totem—they experience them before, and independently of, any previous belief as a direct product of enacted ritual practice. As Rawls puts it,

> Collective effervescence is the effect that participants feel when moral forces act upon them. It does not exist as shared concepts in a group mind. It is directly felt by all as a physical reaction to the enactment of the rite. Moral force produces *collective* emotions that are common to all participants. [...] It matters little what people think, or believe. What matters is what they do. (Rawls 2004: 170)

In short, "Moral forces [...] are created by rites, that is, by sounds and movements, not by systems of belief" (Rawls 2004: 168).

Rawls insists that, in enacted practice, sounds and movements are causally efficacious because they place "the group in *simultaneous and homogenous movement*" (Rawls 2001: 41). By acting in unison, the members of a group "mutually *show one another* that they are all members of the same moral community and they become conscious of the kinship uniting them" (Durkheim 1995: 362; quoted in Rawls 2001: 40, emphasis added by Rawls). In such a context, the emotional experience is the same among all participants because it is the direct result of the movements enacted by everyone during the rite (Rawls 1996: 449; 2001: 49). More importantly, being the product of a collective enacted practice, this emotion can be directly known and validated personally and intersubjectively; and, as the direct perception of general (social) force, it can provide a foundation for general categories such as causality, emotionally experienced as ritual efficacy (Rawls 1996: 450; 2001: 60).

In sum, according to Rawls, Durkheim's thesis aims to demonstrate that emotions constitute the foundation on which human reason rests. By performing "visibly and hearably recognizable practices that produce identical internal feelings in all participants simultaneously" (Rawls 2001: 36), human groups generate moral forces that are internalized as categories and provide a basis for shared intelligibility and thus for the social lives of the groups themselves (Rawls 1996: 451; 2001: 36).

The consequences of this standpoint are far-reaching. Among other things, it counters the idea that the social sciences must necessarily deal with "the realm of human meanings and human freedom" (Collins 2004: 45) and opens the door to a model of causal explanation of human emotions, behavior, and cognition in the form of a universally valid mechanism (Collins 2004: 44). In his theory of interaction ritual chains, the American sociologist Randall Collins (b. 1941) has provided one of the more consequential applications of this corollary to the analysis of social dynamics. It is to this theory that I now turn my attention.

10.2.3 Randal Collins's microsociology of ritual interaction chains

Siding with the standpoint of ethnomethodology, Randall Collins maintains that "there is an irreducibly tacit element in cognition and communication" that makes it impossible to fully define roles and situations. For this reason, he argues that "what guides interaction [...] must be found on another level" (Collins 1981: 991). While ethnomethodologists seem to remain vague about the nature of this underlying level, mysteriously dubbed the "x-factor," Collins urges us to "take the plunge" and leave the cognitive plane to "recognize the x-factor as emotions" (Collins 2004: 105).

The foundation of such a claim is resolutely Durkheimian. According to Collins, Durkheim's analysis of situational interactions as presented in the *Elementary Forms* still constitutes the most useful account in explaining how ritual practices, by intensifying emotion and focusing cognition, can create and reproduce culture "without assuming any preexisting beliefs or moral standards" (Collins 2004: 39). However, while many of the insights in his theory of interaction ritual chains come from Durkheim's pioneering work, Collins emphasizes a change of perspective, or more precisely, of scale. Instead of focusing on the macro-level of societal integration, as many interpreters of Durkheim have, he advocates a microsociological approach inspired by his reading of Erving Goffman (1967).

For Collins, there are both epistemological and ontological reasons to pursue a program of "radical microsociology" (Collins 2004: 3). A microanalytical approach reveals a picture of social structures "as patterns of repetitive micro-interaction" that cannot be accounted for in terms of rules and norms (Collins 1981: 985). Accordingly, the concepts used in the analysis of social realities at the meso- and macro-level are mere constructs derived from "aggregating, comparing and abstracting micro-sociological evidence" (Collins 2010: 1). Abstractions such as the state, the economy, or culture "do not *do* anything" (Collins 1981: 989) and have no real existence beyond the collection of "individual people acting in particular kinds of microsituations" (Collins 1981: 988). Against this background, Collins argues that a sufficiently powerful theory at the micro level in the form of a micro explanatory mechanism will be able to "unlock some secrets of large-scale macrosociology" (Collins 2004: 3).

The micro perspective advocated by Collins is not a study of individual thoughts and behaviors but rather an analysis of situations, of momentary encounters among individuals that he discusses in terms of interaction rituals. During their existence, all individuals move through a series of interaction rituals that shape their path toward other interactions, forming the pattern of an interaction ritual chain. Through the repetition of such patterns, social structure emerges. Yet, moving beyond the simple description of emergent structures, Collins aims at identifying the underlying mechanism that steers individuals along those patterns. It is this mechanism that a theory of ritual interaction chains seeks to elucidate (Collins 1981).

The basic form of the mechanism can be described as an input–output model in relation to an interaction situation. On the input side, Collins (2004: 48; 2010: 2; 2014: 299) defines a small number of "ritual ingredients" that go into forming a successful interaction ritual. First, two or more people have to be physically co-present in one place so that they can, consciously or unconsciously, perceive the verbal and non-verbal microsignals that their bodies are emitting. Second, a barrier is needed to exclude outsiders from the ritual and prevent them from contaminating the participants' attention. Third, the participants in the interaction ritual have to share a common focus of attention, such as a topic of conversation or a speaker on the stage, and have to become mutually aware of each other's focus of attention. Fourth, they have to share a common mood or emotional experience. What emotion is experienced is less important than the fact that each participant experiences the same emotion (Collins 1993: 208; 2014: 300).

When these elements are reunited, the mutual focus of attention and the shared emotion enter into a positive feedback loop, reinforcing each other:

> As the persons become more tightly focused on their common activity, more aware of what each other is doing and feeling, and more aware of each other's awareness, they experience their shared emotion more intensely, as it comes to dominate their awareness. Members of a cheering crowd become more enthusiastic, just as participants at a religious service become more respectful and solemn, or at a funeral become more sorrowful, than before they began. (Collins 2004: 48)

This loop effect is made possible by the physiological dimension of emotions. Collins emphasizes that "[a]ll emotions have a physiological component, whatever cognitions or overt actions may also accompany them" and argues that "[t]he intensification of an emotion typically occurs as a strong and involuntary rhythmic flow of physiological reaction. Co-present individuals become caught up in a common emotional rhythm" (Collins 1993: 208). At the same time, "Movements carried out in common operate to focus attention, to make participants aware of each other as doing the same thing and thus thinking the same thing," thus providing the signals that serve as the basis for intersubjectivity (Collins 2004: 35). Indeed, it is not a shared semantic content but a shared rhythm that "enables each person to anticipate what the other will do" (Collins 2004: 120).

The physical copresence and the rhythmic entrainment of the bodies intensify the shared experience and bring about that strong collective emotion that Durkheim calls collective effervescence. When this effervescence "pervades the individual consciousness," the people assembled experience the feeling of being brought out of themselves into something larger and more powerful (Collins 2010: 3). For this reason, interaction rituals are "emotion transformers": "They take first-order emotions—anger, joy, sadness, etc.—and transform them into solidarity. They create new, higher-order social emotions out of more primitive emotions" (Collins 2014: 300).

A sentiment of solidarity is the first output of interaction rituals; this correlates with the intensity of the effervescence: "[t]he greater the entrainment, the greater the solidarity and identity consequences" (Collins 2004: 83). At the emotional level, interaction rituals also produce what Collins calls emotional energy. In contrast to collective effervescence, which peaks during an interaction, emotional energy is a long-term emotional outcome that can vary in duration and strength. High emotional energy is the result of intense interaction rituals that leave the individual "pumped up with confidence and enthusiasm" (Collins 2014: 300).

Emotional energy also has a cognitive dimension that is realized in the production of salient concepts that become raised above others by being emotionally overcharged (Collins 1993: 224–225). As a result of their emotional intensity, specific cognitions "spring easily to mind, and thus guide our thinking, and our planning for future action" (Collins 2014: 301). The emotional energy of the interaction is stored in collective symbols that are themselves a further output of the ritual. These symbols are the items or ideas on which the participants have focused their attention during the interaction ritual, and through their capacity to reinvoke the emotions of that situation, they come to represent group membership (Collins 1993: 212; 2004: 81).

Collins underscores that not all interaction rituals are successful. Interaction rituals can fail, and in that case "their effects fail" (Collins 2014: 300). On the input end, failed ritual will display "a low level of collective effervescence, the lack of momentary buzz, no shared entrainment at all or disappointingly little" (Collins 2004: 51). From this follows the lack of any output at the level of the group solidarity or even a negative effect, expressed as "a sense of a drag, the feeling of boredom and constraint, even depression, interaction fatigue, a desire to escape" (Collins 2004: 51).

Against this backdrop, Collins argues that emotional energy can be regarded as the "prime motivator of social life" (Collins 2014: 300), since people will subconsciously and emotionally seek and repeat successful interaction rituals while avoiding unsuccessful ones in order to "maximize their overall flow" of emotional energy (Collins 1993: 205). In this way, interaction ritual theory aspires to provide a way to predict how and why individual people move from one situation to the next" (Collins 2004: 44). For Collins, this approach complements and corrects the rational choice perspective discussed in Chapter 8 by calling attention to pre-rational motivational forces (see Collins 1997; 2010: 6).

Collins's approach has found various applications in the study of religion (e.g., Baker 2010; Barone 2010; Heider and Warner 2010; Wollschleger 2012; Wellman, Corcoran, and Stockly-Meyerdirk 2014). To provide an example of how Collins's theory illuminates a specific case study, in the next section, I will summarize some of the findings published by the Swiss scholar of religion Rafael Walthert (b. 1978) who applies Collins's approach to the case of the International Christian Fellowship, an evangelical congregation based in Zurich.

10.2.4 Rafael Walthert's analysis of Evangelical celebrations

The International Christian Fellowship (ICF) was founded in the 1990s in Zurich. Today, ICF congregations are present in a number of Swiss cities and in other locations around the world (Walthert 2010: 245–249). Up to 2,500 people take part in the Sunday celebration in Zurich, which constitutes the main manifestation of the community in the public sphere and is the "emotional highlight" for the participants (Walthert 2013: 100 n43). These events take place in a former industrial building and comprise a

30-minute sermon from the stage and various moments of stage play, live rock music, and joint singing. The sermon is usually in the form of a first-person account in which the preacher underscores the importance of actively choosing a moral course of action in everyday life (Walthert 2013: 98–99). Drawing on Collins's framework, Walthert shows how these celebrations can constitute "a means for [...] the inducement of individual religious commitment" (Walthert 2013: 100).

The celebrations are characterized by a high degree of enthusiasm, which can be measured "through the noise level and intensity of movement and utterances of the participants" (Walthert 2013: 103). Such emotional effervescence is fostered by the convergence of a shared focus of attention and a rhythmic interplay between the audience and the people on the stage. The preacher, who is on the stage for most of the ritual, is the main focus of attention, and his sermon includes several rhetorical devices meant to encourage interaction with the audience, such as yes-or-no questions that the congregants answer in chorus. Walthert (2013: 101) notes that "[o]nce rhythmic entrainment gets going, it seems to become increasingly easy for the preacher to induce further cheers through remarks and jokes that might not produce much laughter outside the ritual situation." Furthermore, a careful management of the setting through various technical means such as big video screens and spotlights minimize the risk of competing foci of attention and help to shape the emotional mood and the interaction within the assembly (Walthert 2013: 100–103; 2017: 24–27).

In view of this ritual orchestration, Walthert (2013: 102) underscores that the goal of the celebrations is not to produce emotion for the sake of it but to direct emotions in a certain way to convey a message and render it plausible (2010: 253). In particular, the ritual interaction focuses on the figure of the preacher as the symbol of both exceptional personal faith and exemplary membership of the community. The production and emotional reinforcement of this symbol gives the participants confidence in their beliefs, experiences, and decisions in the form of emotional energy, without the need for a "conscious commitment by the actors themselves" (Walthert 2013: 104). At the same time, the individuals "contribute as part of a rhythmically entertained collectivity to its formation" (Walthert 2013: 111) and thus produce "the unintended consequence of social solidarity" (Walthert 2013: 112) upon which the existence of ICF *as a community* rests.

The paradigm presented so far offers a powerful theoretical and epistemic framework for analyzing the ways in which individuals come to form groups and how a religious community is produced. In the following section, I shall discuss the benefits and limits of deploying it to understand the case of Jehovah's Witnesses.

10.3 The Conventions of Jehovah's Witnesses as Interaction Rituals?

10.3.1 The biweekly assemblies

The biweekly assemblies at the local Kingdom Hall are an integral component of virtually all active Jehovah's Witnesses' weekly schedule. My interviewees emphasize

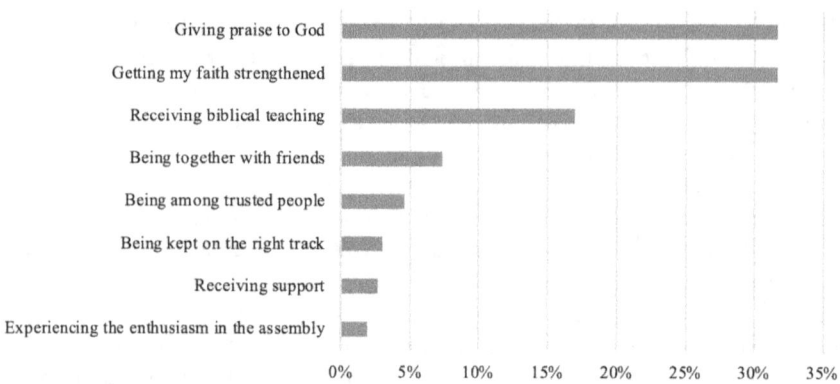

Figure 10.1 Most Important Aspects of the Assemblies (N=183). © Andrea Rota.

the importance of these reunions in their life and some present them as an invigorating situation that allows them to refuel their energy, for instance after a long day at work. No observer could describe the assemblies of Jehovah's Witnesses as moments of particular effervescence, however. On the contrary, the most prominent features in their general economy are long biblical discourses and the strictly organized question-and-answer discussions. The two short moments of collective singing that open and close each meeting are composed and dignified, with little to no room for improvisation and without any accompanying movements. Cheers and applause are not part of Jehovah's Witnesses assemblies.

This kind of schedule prompted sociologist David Voas (2010: 123) to comment that Jehovah's Witnesses meetings "resemble training seminars more than conventional religious services." While my interviewees would probably not share this assessment, the survey conducted among Swiss Jehovah's Witnesses reveals that, on an eight-item list, the experience of enthusiasm in the assembly is the least important aspect associated with the biweekly meetings.

Following Collins, however, we might want to look for other situations in which strong emotions are produced and shared, preferably related to settings in which a larger number of people come together. Indeed, Collins emphasizes that "[i]t is the big, intense religious gatherings that bring forth the emotion and the shift in membership attachment; as one settles back into the routine of smaller and less collectively emotional church services, and then drifts away from attending, the identification and the emotional energy also fade" (Collins 2004: 61).

10.3.2 Empirical evidence: The conventions as exceptional moments

Large gatherings are a recurrent part of the activities that the Watch Tower Society plans for its members. In addition to attending the Memorial for Christ's Death (see Chapter 11), which reunites the same-language congregations sharing a Kingdom Hall, Jehovah's Witnesses go to two semiannual circuit assemblies comprising about 20 congregations and an annual district (or regional) convention that brings together the circuits of a certain region, such as the German-speaking part of Switzerland. Virtually all of the Jehovah's Witnesses I interviewed speak of the larger conventions as events out of the ordinary, as the highlights of their year and, in some cases, of their life.

Twenty-one-year-old **Eva** provides a first, telling example. Since both her parents are Jehovah's Witnesses, she has attended numerous conventions since childhood and was baptized at a convention in the summer preceding our conversation. Speaking of her most recent attendance at a conference she says, "It was mega cool," adding, "Because last year I got baptized, I thought that no convention could be as beautiful as the last one [laughs]. But I can no longer stand by this idea. Every time, it gets better." **Richard**, who belongs to an older generation and is close to retirement, also shares a similar elation with regard to the conventions. When asked about his most important experiences as a Jehovah's Witness, he answers thus:

> I have experienced many wonderful things within the religious community; wonderful conventions that have left a profound impression on me and that sometimes left me with the feeling of walking on clouds on the way home—or of even not wanting to go back home at all. To this day, I can still remember a convention in [city name] when I was just married. Well, we [my wife and I] said, "We are not going back home; this is already paradise" [laughs happily]. (**Richard**)

In the same vein, forty-year-old **Frank** compares the conventions to a "taste of paradise" and exclaims, "Wow! You think that conventions cannot get any better, but then you always have the feeling that the latest convention is even better than the previous one."

The gleefulness of these retrospective accounts is mirrored in the excitement expressed at the prospect of the next convention. For my interviewees, their presence at the event goes without saying. Answering a question about his plans concerning the upcoming regional convention, **Leonard** says with a cheerful laugh, "Of course I'm attending!" and shares his expectations regarding this event: "There are always new publications at regional conventions: [...] flyers, DVDs, films, and so on. I am very happy about that!" In addition to the new publications, **Leonard** also looks forward to the "spiritual food," that is, the biblical teachings provided throughout the three-day program: "That's what invigorates us," he explains, "A three-day crash course every year. That's massive." He concludes by observing that these gatherings are the occasion to see numerous "acquaintances from the past who have moved to other places or something like that." Echoing Leonard's attitude, **Paul** explains that he has already booked the days off work for the convention. His expectations are also very similar: "The spiritual food, the teaching, the encouragement that we receive; there may be new magazines, new literature, a new book [...], and we always see people we know from other congregations, from other towns, and we always meet new people, which is always nice."

The social dimension of the conventions is an aspect upon which several of my interviewees put particular emphasis. **Michaela**, for instance, finds it very invigorating to see such a number of "comrades-in-arms" and underscores the special atmosphere that can be experienced in the conference venue. **Emma** conveys a similar feeling when she speaks about the last convention she attended and underscores the sense of unity among the attendants:

> As always, it is simply beautiful. It is beautiful when one sees 8,500 [people], or even more, simply all together. Everyone has the same goal, we all have our little troubles, but we all pray to Jehovah. We are there, we cultivate friendships with people that we cannot meet during the year. It is simply beautiful, and it does one good. We really get invigorated, and we are all sad when the three days are over. (**Emma**)

During the interview, her husband, **Fritz**, also shares his impressions of the convention. "This year," he says, "[the convention] touched me in a particularly deep way. For me personally, I was able to take home much that I did not expect to. And I grew closer to Jehovah God. And I have understood the Bible in an even deeper way."

10.3.3 Empirical evidence: Participant observation

In light of these statements of emotional investment and anticipation, it is time to look closer at the concrete unfolding of a regional convention. I attended circuit assemblies and regional conventions in Switzerland and Germany on multiple occasions between 2015 and 2018. In the following, I will draw on the field notes I took at the three-day regional conventions in 2015 and 2016 in Zurich, and in 2018 in Friedrichshafen. In Zurich, the venue of the convention was an indoor stadium, and the attendance was around 9,000 people; in Friedrichshafen, some 5,000 Jehovah's Witnesses gathered in a repurposed aircraft hangar. Despite these differences, the setting and the structure of the convention programs were quite similar. After a short description of these aspects, I will discuss the interactions and emotions observable among the participants.

Almost the entirety of a convention's program takes place on a stage—a delimited space on the stadium floor in Zurich and a platform at one end of the hall in Friedrichshafen—from which various speakers address the participants. All the attendees are seated: during the convention, only the speakers stand for a prolonged period of time, usually next to a table or behind a pulpit. On the day on which the baptism is administered, a pool is installed for this purpose. Finally, several large-screen monitors are used to show a close-up of the speaker(s) as well as several videos especially produced by the Watch Tower Society for each convention.

Conventions open with a greeting, some practical information, and music. All participants are invited to stand and join in with the singing; a prayer follows. Music and collective singing mark the beginning and the end of each part of the program. The core part of a three-day convention, however, is a series of panels, called symposia, covering different topics, such as biblical passages, personal attitudes, interpersonal relationships, children's education, missionary work, and the persecution of Jehovah's Witnesses in different countries. The talks in each symposium have different forms, ranging from sermons delivered by a single speaker to personal testimonies or interviews, to short staged dialogues. On several occasions, short videos serve as an introduction or illustration for the talks.

Regardless of the symposium's form, each intervention is scripted. The speakers are often from local congregations and can display different degrees of rhetorical skill. Each symposium includes up to six talks and lasts about ninety minutes. The transitions between two symposia are often limited to a short musical interlude and some practical information. In addition to the talks and discourses, the program also features an audio drama (or dramatic Bible reading), a video drama, and the baptisms. The video drama is an hour-long film on a biblical topic shown in one or more segments during the convention and is presented on the conference program as a particular highlight. The baptisms take place during the lunch break, each individual baptism taking about a minute. Conventions are the only event of the year at which Jehovah's Witnesses administer baptisms and the ritual is filmed and broadcast on the monitors in the venue. However, most of the participants who remain in the venue during the pause are concentrating on eating their packed meals and pay little attention to the ceremony.

The participants dress in formal attire and sit in silence for most of the convention; many bring pillows and footstools for comfort. During the symposia, most people look up scriptural references in their Bibles or Bible apps (see Chapter 11) and have a notebook or a tablet in their hand to take notes. The intensity of the actual note taking can vary greatly from one participant to the other, with some simply noting the biblical passages quoted in the talks and others doodling on their notepads. Isolated participants can be seen using their smartphones to exchange text messages or to check social media. Yawns and apparent fits of drowsiness are not uncommon.

In addition to the collective singing and the moments of prayer, for which the participants are invited to stand, the formal applause at the end of a symposium or after a video constitutes the only apparent collective (inter)action during the program. The moments of applause are clearly codified (for instance, there is no applause after the collective singing) and do not last longer than ten seconds. The only exceptions are the applause after the video drama and toward the end of the convention when applause can last up to 30 seconds. There is virtually no interaction between the participants and the speakers on stage, beside some chuckles following rare amusing remarks or entertaining video scenes. Rhetorical questions addressed from the stage are not met with an answer from the public, and no spontaneous reactions from the audience are noticeable. Outside of the venue, before and after the program, small groups of people gather to chat convivially or to attend to various practical tasks. On the second day of the 2018 convention in Friedrichshafen, about one third of the participants were still in the venue 20 minutes after the end of the program. During the closing songs, communications, and greetings on the last day, however, some participants were already preparing to leave.

In sum, to an external observer, conventions of Jehovah's Witnesses do not appear to produce any "buzz of excitement" (Collins 2004: 82) or any mutual entrainment among the attendees. Personally, I experienced the convention as a long and tedious event, in sharp contrast to the enthusiastic appreciation presented above—a sentiment shared by the colleagues who occasionally accompanied me. Of course, it would be methodologically questionable for me to infer that my perception must reflect that of the other participants or of Jehovah's Witnesses more generally. Still, these experiences were sufficient to awake that "sense of incredulity" that, following Jonathan Z. Smith (1982a: 61), requires from scholars that they check their sources more accurately.

10.3.4 Empirical evidence: A closer look

A closer look at the data from the interviews reveals that the attitude of at least some Jehovah's Witnesses regarding their conventions is more complex and characterized by a certain ambivalence. Sometimes, this ambivalence is a matter of small dissonances that are implied rather than expressed outright. For instance, **Michaela** expresses a particular appreciation for the video drama. Her reason for this, however, is as follows: "I am not a person who can stay focused for a long period and so it was always a nice diversion. I mean, with the pictures and stuff." Here, **Michaela** suggests that the conference's program can become monotonous and that, consequently, a little variety is welcome. Similarly, **Jörg** states that the last congress he attended was "fantastic," in particular because the program was shorter and there was more variety, that is, more videos and interviews, than in the past. This time, he notes, "Nobody went on talking forever."

In other cases, the ambivalence is more explicit. **Leonard,** for instance, remembers his attendance at conventions as a child.

> As a kid, it was demanding. [It is] even more demanding as a parent. I commend the parents who are there three days with the kids who get unruly. And, in the past, [the convention] was even longer. It was four days or five days. My mother experienced seven- or even eight-day-long conventions. [...] That was hardcore. [...] [Today] we are really happy about it. Of course, sometimes at three in the afternoon, you think to yourself: "This goes on for two more hours...," but that's normal. (**Leonard**)

Leonard draws attention to the more demanding side of the conventions. If remaining focused is an obvious challenge for children (and their parents), his last remark indicates that boredom or weariness may also be a problem for adults.

Some remarks by **Fritz** and **Emma** point in a similar direction. When I shared with them my experience as an outsider at the convention and asked what they thought of it, they had the following to say:

> **Fritz:** I am glad that you ask. For me personally, it is sometimes hard to remain seated for so long. So, I take the liberty of standing up and going outside. Then I can concentrate again. Everyone knows that, though. It is astonishing that we can sit there for three days in the first place. But I think that one waits to see what might be in store. And if you are happy about that, then you also remain longer. But it is somewhat demanding, yes. It is not a walk in the park.
> **Emma:** Yes, you are not so capable of assimilating new content after a while, because, despite your happiness, you get tired. At some point, you are full.
> **Fritz:** I speak now from my heart, I'm being very open: When I get tired at a convention, I have trained myself to close my eyes for five minutes and then I am receptive again. Previously, I have fought for hours with myself and have not been able to pick up a thing. And today I say, though it is my personal thing, close the eyes for five minutes, and then I am ready to go again.
> **Emma:** But many do this, especially after lunch.

The couple's comments draw attention to a tension between competing emotions or sensations. On the one hand, both **Emma** and **Fritz** mention sentiments of happiness and anticipation with respect to the conference and its content, and emphasize the importance of an attentive and receptive disposition during the program. On the other hand, they acknowledge that the conference setting and its length may induce adverse emotional moods. Finally, they explain the strategies they adopt to make sure that these latter sentiments do not overcome the former. In this sense, the upholding of the "positive" emotions mentioned by the couple appears to be connected to certain expectations they had of themselves, which they would only admit to having failed to meet when speaking from the heart.

This observation is supported by the following "admission" by **Richard**, who, after stressing time and again in reference to the conventions that "one can take home many beautiful thoughts and rejoice at what is said," adds this:

> It is possible that there is a topic that does not speak to me personally, and then I must confess, to my shame, that I switch off for a moment. Let's say, I have heard this thing a hundred times or that it is something that I don't particularly like, then I am not so focused. And then there are topics about which one thinks, "Too bad that it is already over." (**Richard**)

Richard notes that the program can contain precious pearls but can also be repetitive. Nonetheless, he rebukes himself over his own lack of concentration, thus indicating that his attentive disposition is linked to some normative presuppositions.

In sum, a closer look at the interviews calls attention to the convention as a situation in which various and divergent emotional moods coexist among the participants. At least some Jehovah's Witnesses experience a certain tedium during these events, which appears to contrast with the positive emotional semantics they used when first describing the gatherings. What is more, my interviewees appear aware of this discrepancy and admit to it with a measure of shame or regret, as if they had failed to feel in a certain way. At the same time, some of them note that the difficulty of remaining focused is not really a secret and that the fact that one might drift away or need a break is something "normal" that "many do," and something that "everybody knows" about. All these observations will be central to my analysis in the second part of this chapter. First, however, we have to consider how the empirical evidence from the convention affects its analysis in terms of interaction rituals.

10.3.5 Theoretical reflection: A first preliminary discussion

What preliminary considerations can be made on the basis of the empirical data presented so far? The results from my observations and the passages quoted in the previous sections indicate that for some Jehovah's Witnesses, participation in the convention can sometimes be challenging, in particular because of the repetitiveness of the program and the duration of the event. From the perspective of Collins's interaction ritual theory, several core elements on the input side are evidently lacking. The focus of attention is fuzzy, a result of the fact that the speakers change frequently, and because the actual contents of the talks and videos are quite diverse (while being very similar to the content discussed in the regular assemblies). Furthermore, the attention directed towards such focal points appears to be intermittent at best, with Witnesses admitting that they struggle to remain concentrated and that they occasionally experience a sort of ritual fatigue. To describe the applause and the collective singing as moments of collective effervescence would undoubtedly mean stretching the concept beyond the limits of plausibility. Still, no other form of rhythmical entrainment can be observed during the conventions. Indeed, conventions present some crucial characteristics that Collins associates with failed ritual interactions: "There is a low level of collective effervescence, the lack of momentary buzz, no shared entrainment at all or disappointingly little" (Collins 2004: 51).

The picture on the output side is more complicated. On the one hand, it is hard to pinpoint clearly shared symbols created during the ritual. The publications announced during the conventions could be a candidate, but it is difficult to evaluate how emotionally charged they are. The identification of particularly salient concepts is also problematic. When asked during the interviews about specific highlights of the last conference, my interviewees tend to mention rather general contents, such as "the personal life stories," "the publications," "the videos," "a better understanding of Jehovah," or the one-time event of their baptism. On the other hand, the self-reports of convention attendees emphasize a sense of solidarity, a heightened identification with the group, and the feeling of becoming invigorated.

Such emotional discrepancies in the ritual constitute a challenge for an analysis in terms of interaction rituals. One may be tempted to draw a comparison to special instances of interaction rituals that Collins calls "forced rituals," during which individuals "are forced to put on a show of participating wholeheartedly in interaction rituals" (Collins 2004: 53). This situation is typical of "power rituals" in which people are physically or otherwise coerced to attend and take orders. In such situations, order-takers are "required to give at least 'ritualistic' assent at that moment," while experiencing "a heavily mixed emotion" (Collins 2004: 113). Although forced rituals are empowering for the order-givers, order-takers experience an alienating loss of emotional energy, and since they cannot extract themselves from participating in the ritual, their resistance finds its expression in the privacy of the "backstage," where they can ridicule the order-givers and speak cynically about the dominant symbols (Collins 2004: 112–114).

However, Collins's take on power rituals is theoretically questionable and does not fit the empirical data on Jehovah's Witnesses. As Kemper (2011) notes in his detailed critique of Collins's power rituals, if such rituals alienate the order-takers and their (contingent) compliance is inauthentic, there can be no emotional bonding or solidarity between them and the order-givers. If power rituals can produce solidarity, they can only achieve it "among the participants on the same side of the power divide" (Kemper 2011: 184). From an empirical point of view, both the idea of coerced participation and the consequent alienation of the attendees from the Watch Tower Society (as the source of the biblical instruction provided at the event) do not appear plausible. In fact, the interviews reveal neither an attitude of cynical detachment nor a shared emotional mood (coerced or otherwise), but rather an attempt to navigate contrasting emotional moods. Having reached this conclusion, I see no point in trying and bend Collins's approach in new and creative ways to fit the data as other have done (e.g., Heider and Warner 2010). Instead, I suggest we turn to a different analytical standpoint.

10.4 An Alternative Account of Collective Emotions

We have reached here the neck of the metaphorical hourglass mentioned in the introduction of this chapter. The transition from one bulb to the other can be framed as the transition from a perspective that asks "How social factors affect what people feel" to one that focuses on "how social factors affect what people think and do about what they feel" (Hochschild 1979: 552). The latter approach has been particularly developed by the American sociologist Arlie Hochschild (e.g., 2003, 2012), who explicitly contrasts it with Collins's position (Hochschild 1979: 554; see also Collins 1981: 1001 n8).

10.4.1 A Change of perspective: Arlie Hochschild's emotion work

Similar to Collins, one of the main sources of Hochschild's approach is the work of Ervin Goffman. In her interpretation of Goffman's work, however, Hochschild emphasizes that when entering a new situation, it is not uncommon for people to have feelings that do not fit the context (for instance, feeling sad at a wedding). However, such feelings will be brought under control to reflect the definition of the situation. Indeed, Hochschild (1979: 552) insists on the socialized nature of feeling and calls attention to the omnipresence of shared "feeling rules," that is, of implicit social standards or guidelines "that direct how we want to try to feel" (Hochschild 1979: 563).

Feeling rules are not mere expectations regarding how we may feel in a certain situation but have a normative character expressed through the language of rights and duties—we might, for instance, speak of "having the right" to feel angry at someone (Hochschild 1979: 564). When our emotions contravene a rule, we are usually prompted to redress the situation by a call for an account or a sanction. In social situations, feeling rules establish a "sense of entitlement or obligation that governs emotional exchanges" (Hochschild 2012: 56) and determine "what is rightly owed and owing in the currency of feeling" (Hochschild 2012: 18). The display of appropriate feelings constitutes a way of paying tribute to others and contributing to the collective good of a smooth social interaction.

Hochschild (2012: 76–86) speaks of these transactions in terms of a gift exchange involving different forms of emotional management. On a fundamental level, what seems to be owed is a sincere display of feeling. In this case, "Payment is made in facial expression, choice of words, and tone of voice" (Hochschild 2012: 77). However, people can also "go a step further" and offer a more "generous gesture" by trying to transform their mood to genuinely feel a certain way (Hochschild 1979: 569). To illustrate this distinction, Hochschild suggests a comparison between the methods taught by the English and the American schools of acting. According to the English school, an actor ought to convey a particular emotion through a perfect mastery of facial muscles, bodily movements, and outward gestures. By contrast, the American school, which draws on the work of Konstantin Stanislavski, emphasizes the importance for the actor to mobilize the memory of a suitable emotional experience in order to guide the performance. Hochschild dubs the first technique "shallow acting" and the second "deep acting" (see Hochschild 1979: 558; 2003: 92; 2012: 35–42).

The theatrical metaphor has its limits, however. Hochschild observes that whereas on stage, "[t]he illusion that the actor creates is recognized beforehand as an illusion by actor and audience alike [...] in real life we more often participate in the illusion" (Hochschild 2012: 46). In a sense, real life deep acting involves deceiving not only others about one's feelings but also oneself (Hochschild 2012: 33). Accordingly, when people perceive a discrepancy between how they feel and how they want to feel (or ought to feel) in a given situation, they can respond by actively engaging in "emotion work." This term defines "the act of trying to change in degree or quality an emotion or feeling" (Hochschild 1979: 561). As such, emotion work calls for a "coordination of mind and feeling" (Hochschild 2012: 7) that differs from both an automatic response to inner sensation and superficial "face work" (Goffman 1967). For this reason, Hochschild emphasizes that "the very act of managing emotion" should not be regarded as something external to emotions, but as an intrinsic "part of what the emotion becomes" (Hochschild 2012: 27).

In sum, Hochschild's approach offers a distinctive standpoint on emotions that differs from the neo-Durkheimian view discussed in the first part of this chapter. With respect to the empirical case at hand, her perspective offers important insights into the normative dimension of emotions in social settings, as well as into the ways in which people try to bring their feelings in line with particular situations according to socially shared feeling rules. This provides a strong framework for making sense of the discrepant emotions expressed by my interviewees. All the same, when it comes to defining an alternative conception of *collective* emotions, Hochschild's analysis does not differ so sharply from the perspective of the other authors considered above. The reason is that, according to both perspectives, emotions by definition are something that *individuals* experience, even though they can have a collective or social origin.

For neo-Durkheimian authors, particular emotions, such as a sense of effervescence, are indeed the product of people gathered together in physical proximity. However, it is a fundamental element of their theory that these emotions are experienced by each participant (or at least by most of them) in the (interaction) ritual: it is the very fact that the emotional mood is deemed directly knowable by every individual and is intersubjectively sharable through synchronized rhythmic movements that makes its symbolic (that is, conceptual) expression superfluous (or secondary). By contrast, for Hochschild, personal emotions are always framed by preexisting social rules that shape the individual's emotion work—what is done to the emotion is a part of what the emotion is. Nevertheless, even from her perspective, an emotion remains something phenomenologically experienced by the individual. Thus, for a group genuinely to have a collective emotion would require each (or most) group members to experience such an emotion—through deep acting or otherwise.

In line with the general framework of my work, I suggest that a non-reductionist approach—in terms of collective intentions—can provide new insights in the domain of collective emotions, while also maintaining some similarities with Hochschild's standpoint. Accordingly, I will now turn to Margaret Gilbert's plural subject theory of collective emotions, which provides a non-summative account of collective emotions.

10.4.2 From shared individual emotions to collective emotions

Gilbert approaches the topic of collective emotions by following her usual method (see Chapter 5), that is, by interrogating the meaning of our everyday use of language. She notes that the *ascription* of various kinds of emotion to groups is a very common phenomenon. There is nothing unusual, for instance, in expressions such as "the congregation was ecstatic to hear the new preacher" or "the assembly was saddened by the sudden death of its pastor." When scrutinized, however, these ascriptions tend to be dismissed as mere figures of speech that cannot be taken at face value (Gilbert 2014b: 229–232). According to Gilbert, the main reason for writing off the idea of a *group* having certain emotions derives from a conception of consciousness and emotions that stresses their eminently *individual* nature. Thus, "[F]or a particular being to have a specific emotion is for *that very being* to be in a particular state of consciousness" (Gilbert 2014d: 19). More precisely, emotions are deemed to "essentially involve *feelings*, which are somewhat on a par with *sensations*" (Gilbert 2000b: 125).

Gilbert calls these "sensation-like" experiences "feeling-sensations" (Gilbert 2000b: 125). Metaphorical language appears to be the only possible way to describe these "feeling-sensations." Thus, "[P]eople talk of 'surges' of anger, of joy 'welling up,' of the 'sting' of jealousy, of 'pangs' and, for less vivid cases, 'twinges' of guilt," and so on (Gilbert 2014b: 232). If each emotion entails a "specific phenomenological state" (Gilbert 2014d: 20), then "it may seem obvious that while individual human beings can have feeling-sensations, groups cannot" (Gilbert 2014b: 232). Consequently, to speak of the emotions of a group could only mean to speak about the emotions of (some or all) members of that group.

To counter these critiques and develop a non-summative account of collective emotions correctly ascribable to a group, Gilbert adopts a three-pronged approach. First, she proposes a conception of "emotions" that does not rest on the idea of "feeling-sensations." Second, she demonstrates that various versions of summative accounts do not meet criteria sufficient to ascribe an emotion to a group. Third, she offers an alternative account of collective emotions based on the concept of joint commitment and her plural subject theory. In the following, I will summarize her argument.

Gilbert acknowledges the difficulty of providing an argument that would demonstrate that particular phenomenological states are *in no case* a feature of emotions. However, her goal is more modest, namely to show that the question of whether an emotion *necessarily* involves a feeling-sensation is at least open to debate. To do so, Gilbert first discusses the way in which we imagine emotions when we talk about them (Gilbert 2014d: 20). Drawing on John Dewey (1895: 16–17), Gilbert notes that, in many cases, references to emotions—for instance, being hopeful of success— express dispositions to action, rather than phenomenological states. Furthermore, Gilbert (2014b: 233) calls attention to the difficulty of pinpointing the qualities that are usually ascribed to emotions. In this regard, she draws inspiration from the philosopher

Martha Nussbaum, who defines emotions as particular "evaluative judgments" (Nussbaum 2001: 27).

Nussbaum notes that, at least in some cases, it is very difficult to define the corporeal or mental phenomena that belong (or do not belong) to an emotion. Referring to the example of grief, Nussbaum (2001: 57–58) says, "There usually will be bodily sensations and changes of many sorts involved in grieving; but if we discovered that my blood pressure was quite low during this whole episode, or that my pulse rate never got above sixty, we would not, I think, have the slightest reason to conclude that I was not really grieving." Moreover, Nussbaum observes that cultural and even merely situational factors also contribute to the variety of feelings associated with a given emotion and concludes that such plasticity and variability "prevents us from plugging the feeling into the definition as an absolutely necessary element" (2001: 60).

In light of the possible distinction between emotions and feeling-sensations, Gilbert proceeds to assess whether a summative account of collective emotions of the form, "[A] group has emotion E if and only if each of its members has emotion E" (Gilbert 2014d: 21) provides a sufficient basis to speak of the emotions of a group. Drawing on similar arguments as those used to reject summative analyses of collective beliefs (see Chapter 9), Gilbert concludes that such an account is not satisfactory and proceeds to present her alternative view of collective emotions. Relying on her concept of joint commitment, Gilbert puts forward the following central idea, where "E" stands for a given emotion, such as excitement, guilt, remorse, anger, fear, and so on: "Persons X, Y, and so on, (or: members of population P) are collectively E if and only if they are jointly committed to be E as a body" (Gilbert 2014d: 23).

As I have already discussed at length in previous chapters, a joint commitment brings a plural subject into existence and has a number of consequences for the parties involved. First, a joint commitment cannot be rescinded unilaterally and without fault by an individual member's change of mind. Furthermore, it obligates each of the jointly committed people to a specific course of action; conversely, it forbids them to openly contradict, through their words or actions, the intention to which they are jointly committed. This entails the following:

> A satisfactory account of collective emotions will account for the fact that the parties have the standing to rebuke one another for behavior that is not in the spirit of the collective emotion, and all of the accompanying standings, rights, and obligations just mentioned. (Gilbert 2014d: 23)

No summative account provides an adequate foundation to fulfill this criterion.

Gilbert's account specifies that for a group of people to "emote" in a certain way, they must be jointly committed to doing so *as a body*. This means that "the parties are jointly committed to emulate, by virtue of their several actions and utterances, a single subject of the emotion in question, in relevant circumstances" (Gilbert 2014d: 24). What is at stake in this emulation, however, is only "each party's *public performance*": "*what goes on in each mind and heart* is not at issue with respect to what the parties are committed to" (Gilbert 2014d: 24). In the case, for instance, of collective excitement, Gilbert stresses that:

[A] joint commitment *instructs* the parties to act in a certain way if it is manifest *from the content* of the joint commitment that the parties must act in that way if they are to fulfill it. It is evident, then, that the joint commitment constitutive of a case of collective excitement does not instruct the parties to be personally excited over the happening in question. [...] The joint commitment constitutive of a case of collective excitement over some happening does not instruct the parties to experience a "thrill" of excitement or any particular feeling-sensation or feeling. (Gilbert 2014d: 25)

Therefore, it is definitely possible that one or more parties in a plural subject will display the adequate "expressive" qualities of the emotion to which they are jointly committed, despite not (or no longer) personally being in that emotional state. The existence of a collective emotion based on a joint commitment within a group *does not rule out* the existence of the corresponding personal emotion among the group members, or among some of them (e.g., Gilbert 2000b: 136). Crucially, however, "[T]here is no logical necessity that those who together co-create a given collective emotion have the corresponding personal emotion before or while they are doing so" (Gilbert 2014d: 27).

This conclusion has two important corollaries. First, should a person enter into a joint commitment to emote in a certain way without herself having the corresponding personal emotion, it would be wrong to say that she or any other member of her group is faking an emotion: "No one is pretending to feel the personal emotion in question" (Gilbert 2014d: 28). Rather, each is correctly indicating their participation in the collective emotion. Consequently, the earlier analogy of an actor acting a scene does not easily apply to the case of collective emotions as defined here, despite there being a joint commitment to act a certain way. Second, the question of knowing whether, in the context of a group jointly committed to a certain emotion, individual members tend to develop the corresponding personal emotion is an empirical one (Gilbert 2014d: 29). For instance, it is not possible to exclude the possibility that some (or even most) Jehovah's Witnesses privately engage in forms of "deep acting"; however, this cannot be assumed from the onset.

10.4.3 Theoretical reflection: A second preliminary discussion

The theoretical perspectives discussed in this section shed new light on the empirical material presented above. Both Hochschild and Gilbert call attention to the possible discrepancy between the way someone feels and the emotions he or she is expected to display in a given situation. Both authors thus emphasize a normative dimension of emotion that becomes apparent in the case of non-conforming conduct or attitudes. However, when it comes to qualifying the source and scope of this normativity, important differences emerge in their standpoints. Hochschild puts forward an overarching picture of the *individual* self and insists on the influence of social rules on the way a person tries to feel in a certain situation; whereas Gilbert advances a strong concept of *collectivity*, whereby a joint commitment of the parties to emote as a body establishes rights and obligations among them concerning their outward behavior—for Gilbert, this provides sufficient grounds for speaking of a collective emotion, independent from the personal feelings of the participants.

The empirical examples from the interviews indicate that it is not uncommon for Jehovah's Witnesses attending a convention to experience emotions that do not correspond to those they consider they ought to have. In their own accounts, the awareness of this disjunction appears in the form of a more or less shameful "confession" and is often accompanied by a description of the strategies employed to redress the perceived discrepancy—for example, taking a break in order to regain their focus. How should we make sense of these statements? Were we to follow Gilbert's plural subject theory, the dissonances registered in the interviews would result from my interlocutor having entered a joint commitment to uphold certain emotions "as a body," while having in some cases (but not necessarily in all cases) a different personal emotional state.

To support this interpretation, we might note that not only the expected behavior of the Witnesses is common knowledge; the fact that behaving appropriately is not always easy also appears to be "out in the open." When my interviewees observe that it is "normal" for someone to look at his watch or indicate that "everybody knows" about the need for a little diversion during the convention, they are suggesting complicity in the avoidance of the accepted rules—which weakens the thesis of pervasive deep acting as Hochschild frames it. Nevertheless, an overt statement flatly declaring that conventions are boring would be a serious offense to the collectively accepted emotional etiquette, which also regulates the verbal expression of emotion. It is perhaps for this reason that, even in the interview setting, my interlocutors present their remarks as expressions of personal opinion. As Gilbert (1996f: 380) notes, in principle it is possible for an individual to frame a statement as a "private point of view" while at the same time remaining jointly committed to the attitude of the group.

To further develop this interpretation, I will now investigate how the joint commitment of Jehovah's Witnesses to emote "as a body" in a certain way with regard to their convention is produced. This will involve reconstructing the narrative framing of these gatherings within the historiography of the Watch Tower Society as well as the concrete practices that precede and follow such events.

10.5 The Framing of an Institutional Event

International conventions and the annual regional conventions play an important role in the narratives of Jehovah's Witnesses and the historical self-representation of the Watch Tower Society. Past conventions are often mentioned in magazine articles, *Yearbook* features, and book chapters. Drawing on these sources, this section calls attention to the *way* in which these gatherings are framed in the Society's literature. My goal, as I pointed out in the introduction to this chapter, is to show how the conventions are constructed as "institutional events," that is as situations constituted through the rights and duties of the attending Jehovah's Witnesses.

The tradition of organizing conventions is rooted in the early activities of the Watch Tower Society. Around 1876, Charles T. Russell and the Bible Students in Allegheny started commemorating the Memorial Supper (Chryssides 2008: 35). Ten years later a short article in *The Watchtower* invited the reader to join the *ecclesia* in Allegheny for a few days for a "general meeting," starting on the evening before the Lord's Day, to reinvigorate each other "as iron sharpeneth iron" (W 1886, March [reprints]: 834). These meetings became a regular event and grew in size until they were eventually accompanied by a week-long program. In 1892, the invitation was extended to "All who trust for justification in the great atoning sacrifice for sins given at Calvary by our Lord Jesus [...] particularly all such who are regular subscribers to *Zion's Watch Tower*" (W 1892, March 15 [reprints]: 1382).

In the following years, the "general convention" was moved to the summer and held each year in itinerant locations. By the beginning of the new century, in addition to general conventions, local conventions were also organized in the United States, Canada and Europe, and, by the 1940s, on every other populated continent (Chryssides 2008: 35; Jv 1993: 255). After World War II, the system of local, national, and international conferences was reformed through the introduction of a semi-annual circuit assembly and an annual district convention with a standardized title and program for each event (Jp 1959: 216, 237–238). While the program and the logistics of the conventions have been simplified over the years and their duration shortened to three days for regional conventions and one day for circuit assemblies, these gatherings remain of the utmost importance in the eyes of the Watch Tower Society. This is observable in the great care the Society takes, in its publications, to frame these gatherings as successful and emotional events.

Looking back on its own past, the Watch Tower Society presents the history of the conventions as a history of increasing success. Considerable appreciation of these events is already apparent in the report that *The Watchtower* published about the convention of 1892:

> The Convention for Bible Study and for commemorating our Lord's death recently announced to be held in Allegheny from April 7th to 14th just closed. It has been one of the most interesting of the kind ever held here or perhaps anywhere; for we may scarcely except the gatherings of the early Church in the days of the Apostles. (W 1892, April 15 [reprints]: 1392)

In addition to such emphatic accounts, numbers and statistics are presented as an objective measure of the success of any convention. For instance, it is not uncommon to read that the participants attending a particular event vastly exceeded the expectations and that the venues were too small for all to find a place inside (e.g., W 2016, May 15: 28).

In fact, Jehovah's Witnesses' conventions reached an enormous size in the 1950s (Jv 1993: 269–275), with record numbers of 253,922 delegates in attendance at the 1958 convention in New York. Reporting on the event, *The Watchtower* commented, "Certainly the great King of heaven, Jehovah God, and his reigning Son, Jesus Christ, rejoiced together with the holy angels to have God's kingdom preached by one mouthpiece to the largest visible audience on one occasion" (W 1959, February 15: 122). Finally, the global spread of the conventions and the growing number of delegates attending in different countries serve to highlight the impact of these events for the missionary work of Jehovah's Witnesses. The Society's *Yearbook* regularly provides reports on the success of conventions around the globe.

Still, the size and spread of the conventions are discussed primarily as the visible expression of their symbolic importance. The conventions held between 1922 and 1928 are regarded by the Watch Tower Society as nothing less than the seven trumpets of Revelation (Fm 1969: 209–247, 383–396; Yb 1975: 135–139), while numerous other events are chronicled as "milestone," "landmark," "memorable" or "momentous" conventions (e.g., W 2012, September 15: 28–32; Kr 2014: 72). Lastly, in addition to their collective significance, assemblies and conventions are discussed as pivotal moments in the personal life of individual Jehovah's Witnesses, especially as the baptism ceremony is performed at these events. In the *Yearbooks* and in other publications, moving personal stories and edifying anecdotes of baptisms from across the world abound (e.g., Yb 2002: 43–44; W 2005, April 15: 24–25).

It is thus not surprising that the presentation of the conventions in the publications of the Watch Tower Society often includes an evocation of the emotions generated by the event. In relation to the early conventions, for instance, attention is called to their moving conclusions during which a so-called love feast was celebrated. This love feast was meant to reflect the "feeling of Christian brotherhood" among the participants that was expressed through prolonged applause and songs, often accompanied by "tears of joy" (Jv 1993: 257).

The joy of true brotherhood is a common topos in the characterization of early and recent conventions, with articles and book chapters carrying titles such as "Conventions— Joyful Affirmations of Our Brotherhood" (W 2009, September 15: 8–9), "Jehovah Congregates His Joyful People" (W 2012, September 15: 28–32), or "Conventions. Proof of our Brotherhood" (Jv 1993: 254–282). Feelings of exaltation are also recurrent in the Society's accounts. For instance, the announcement of the name "Jehovah's witnesses" [sic] at the 1931 convention was reportedly welcomed "with a tremendous shout and a long applause" (Kr 2014: 47) and in 1950 a new interpretation of Psalm 45: 16 was met with "a tremendous and sustained applause along with shouts of joy" (Jv 1993: 263).

However, it is not only special announcements or deep organizational changes that are discussed as sources of great joy and infectious enthusiasm. Recurring features of the conventions, such as the celebration of the baptism, are presented in similar fashion:

> IF YOU have been serving Jehovah for decades, you have likely heard numerous baptism talks at our assemblies and conventions. Yet, no matter how often you have been present on such occasions, you likely still feel moved each time you witness the moment that those sitting in the front rows of the auditorium stand up to present themselves for baptism. At that instant, a buzz of excitement ripples through the audience, followed by a burst of heartfelt applause. Tears may well up in your eyes as you look at yet another group of precious individuals who have taken sides with Jehovah. What joy we feel at such times! (Lv 2008: 183)

Similarly, biblical dramas, publications, and other activities carried out during the conventions are portrayed as moments accompanied by uplifting feelings.

10.6 Constructing and Conveying Collective Emotions

10.6.1 A ritual framework

These historical accounts of the conventions are not merely bookish reports destined to be left on a shelf. Rather, they are the object of active study during the biweekly assembly of Jehovah's Witnesses. Accordingly, the topic of the conventions is treated within the same ritual setting and through the same communicative modalities described in Chapters 8 and 9. Furthermore, in the months preceding the yearly convention, in particular in April and May, an important part of the midweek meetings is used to prepare for the conference. Feature articles in the Watch Tower Society's publications—accompanied by specific questions to be collectively answered during the meetings—and special talks provide the foundation for such planning. Their role is not merely organizational and their content cannot and must not be separated from the ritual setting in which it is read and discussed.

In fact, I will argue that each year, during the convention season, Jehovah's Witnesses take the floor in their Kingdom Halls to (re)affirm their joint commitment to uphold certain emotions as the emotions of the group. As I will show through the analysis of the content published in the magazine *Our Kingdom Ministry* between 1995 and 2015, the service meetings and the field ministry are privileged occasions for the formation of a joint commitment to uphold "as a body" the emotions verbalized in my interviews.

10.6.2 Preparing the convention

Before each convention season, several articles published in *Our Kingdom Ministry* call attention to the special character of these events. Conventions are compared to a feast or a banquet (e.g., Km 2009, April: 4; Km 2015, April: 4) where spiritual food is served to the worshippers as was the case during the festivals and high days described in the Bible. For these occasions, "entire families traveled to Jerusalem to enjoy these happy conventions" (Km 2012, April: 3), including the family of Jesus, which "was happy to make any sacrifices to attend and benefit fully" (Km 2010, April: 5). Drawing on these lofty examples, *Our Kingdom Ministry* portrays the modern conventions as a break with the daily preoccupations and sorrows and as concretizations of an ideal world to come, in which "we will be able to step out of the harsh wilderness of Satan's world and enjoy spiritual refreshment and upbuilding association in our spiritual paradise" (Km 2014, April: 3).

The social dimension is discussed as a central feature of conventions: "With Jehovah's day drawing near, may we not forsake this opportunity to meet together for an interchange of encouragement!" (Km 2014, April: 3). Getting to reunite with friends and associates who live in other parts of the country is an explicit goal at regional conventions. The attendees are advised to arrive early each day at the venue in order to enjoy "fellowship with others" (Km 2010, April: 5). However, these expressions of fellowship must be limited to those moments when the program is not in session: "When the chairman kindly invites us to take our seats before the music starts, we should end our conversations and be seated for the beginning of the program" (Km 2008: April: 5).

The formal program thus constitutes the core of the conventions, and articles in *Our Kingdom Ministry* regularly emphasize the importance of attending the conventions and doing so for the full length of the event. Accordingly, Jehovah's Witnesses are frequently reminded to plan their conference attendance in due time. The magazine also offers detailed descriptions of the overall logistics of the conventions and regularly provides a "convention reminder" with standard recommendations regarding, among other things, program times, parking, hotel reservations, and safety precautions. The elders of the congregations are advised to devote some time during a service meeting to reviewing this reminder (e.g., Km 2014, April: 2–5).

In addition to the practical aspects, a number of articles also stress the "need to prepare our heart" (Km 2002, May: 5) for the convention. This preparation entails consulting the program in advance and pondering some of the program points during personal study and the weekly family worship evening. At the convention, the hours before the beginning of each session should be used similarly. Later, during the convention, the attendees are encouraged to take notes and to review them with family and friends afterwards, in order to better remember the convention's main points. Beside this informal form of "debriefing," in the weeks or months following the conventions, the schedule of the service meeting can include some time dedicated to the discussion of the convention's highlights and the possible application of the insights gained to the field ministry and life more generally (e.g., Km 2003, April: 2).

Against this backdrop, the months preceding the conferences are framed as a period of "eager anticipation" (e.g., Km 1999, May: 3), a sentiment that the publications ascribe to their readers collectively with statements like, "How glad we are that the 'Faith in God's Word' District Conventions will be starting soon!" (Km 1997, May: 5) or, "We look forward with keen anticipation to this opportunity to bless Jehovah 'among the congregated throngs' (Ps. 26: 12)" (Km 2005, April: 5). The positive emotional experience is also confirmed retrospectively when discussing past conferences. For instance, a 2012 article in *Our Kingdom Ministry* reads: "How excited we were when a new book by that name was released at the 2010 'Remain Close to Jehovah!' District Convention!" (Km 2012, May: 2)

10.6.3 Sharing the excitement

The sentiment of excitement concerning the conventions is not meant to be confined to the internal discussions of the group but is rather intended to be shared with the public. For Jehovah's Witnesses, the conventions constitute privileged occasions for their missionary work. During the event and while traveling to its location, they are invited to "share the truth with others" through acts of "informal witnessing," such as talking to people at a restaurant (Km 2010, April: 6). In addition to these informal contacts, during the three weeks preceding a regional convention, the Watch Tower Society invests in an intensive campaign with the intent of inviting the public to attend. To this end, the Society prints special invitations that Jehovah's Witnesses distribute door-to-door or through public witnessing.

During these weeks, the task of circulating the invitation has priority over other missionary activities (Km 2012, April: 6). Similar to the other aspects of the field ministry (see Chapter 8), this task is not left to the initiative of individuals, but is conceived of as a coordinated effort. Accordingly, question-and-answer discussions—as well as other congregational activities—are used to clarify the methods to be employed during this task, while also providing the foundation for the constitution of a collective emotional state:

> How Will We Offer the Invitation? In order to cover our territory, we may need to be brief. We might say something like this: "Hello. We are sharing in a global effort to distribute this invitation. Here is your copy. You will find more details on the invitation." Be enthusiastic. When sharing in the distribution on the weekends, you should also offer the magazines when appropriate. (Km 2012, April: 6)

The question associated with this paragraph is the following: "How will we invite others to attend the convention?"

Our Kingdom Ministry regularly reassures its readers of the effectiveness of this work, relating stories of Witnesses rejoicing at seeing someone they invited at the convention, as well as testimonies of first-time attendees who took up their invitations (e.g., Km 2015, April: 4). Conversely, those who are disappointed in the lack of results of their efforts are reminded that "regardless of how many respond [...] our diligent efforts during the campaign will bring praise to Jehovah and reflect his generosity" (Km 2014, April: 4). In sum, an enthusiastic disposition constitutes the expected emotional posture during this activity, and a positive feeling is presented as the collective reward for such an attitude. "After the campaign concludes, how happy we will be to know that we participated enthusiastically and that as many people as possible joined us at the spiritual banquet that Jehovah provided!" (Km 2015, April: 4).

10.6.4 Regulating emotional behavior

In light of these observations, the question then arises as to why the atmosphere observed during the conventions is so unenthusiastic. The answer is twofold. First, the display of elation and joy during the conference is clearly codified. Spontaneous expressions of excitement are not considered appropriate behavior and are to be kept under control. For example, a joyful moment such as the baptism ought to be treated with the appropriate degree of seriousness: "It is not a time for outbursts, for partying, or for hilarity. But neither is it a somber or grim time" (W 1995, April 1: 30, quoted in Km 2000, May: 6).

Second, the selection of emotions discussed so far does not exhaust the list of emotions collectively upheld in relation to the conventions. While the overall sentiment associated with these events is a joyous one, the emotional attitude of the participants during the program is framed in terms of gratitude or appreciation. These sentiments should find a suitable expression in the behavior of the attendees. Besides "being present each day and savoring every morsel of spiritual food that is served" (Km 2009, April: 5), the participants can, for instance, show appreciation by being punctual (Km 2000, May: 5), listening in silence to the musical interludes (Km 2015, April: 5), and reviewing with their children "[T]he kind of Christian behavior that is expected of them at all time and in all places" (Km 2002, May: 4).

Paying particular attention to good manners and behavior during the program, as well as in the breaks between sessions, is explicitly expected of all attendees, both children and adults (Km 1997, May: 4). During the program, a respectful demeanor is also expressed by refraining from disturbing or inconveniencing the other participants. While friendly discussions are encouraged at the margins of the conferences, they should stop as soon as the program begins. For the same reason, "The use of cellular phones, pagers, camcorders, and cameras should not be allowed to cause distractions during the program" (Km 2000, May: 5). During the conventions a form of "restraint" should help all attendees to focus on the program:

> We would never want to become "dull in our hearing" when listening to God's Word. (Heb. 5:11) Let us therefore be resolved to show due respect by listening attentively as the sacred pronouncements from Jehovah are discussed at our upcoming district convention. (Km 2000, May: 5)

The Watch Tower Society appears to be aware of the fact that remaining concentrated can be a challenge, as indicated by advice given in *Our Kingdom Ministry* on how to increase listening skills, for example by taking notes and looking up every biblical reference (e.g., Km 2011, April: 4).

The exhortation to pay attention and the corresponding recommendations of conduct are not meant as mere personal advice, but rather reflect a normative expectation in relation to the group's behavior. This is demonstrated by the presence of generalized forms of rebuke within the magazine, such as the following:

> Last year many adults and youths were again observed walking aimlessly through the corridors, milling around outside, and visiting with others while the program was in progress, rather than listening to what "the faithful and discreet slave" had provided for our benefit. Jesus promised to give us spiritual food at the proper time. (Matt. 24: 45–47) Therefore, we ought to be present to benefit from that food and not show a lack of appreciation. (Km 1997, May: 3–4)

To ensure that everyone remains focused on the program—or at least behaves accordingly—is not only a matter of individual responsibility but also a collective task: "If it becomes necessary for one of the attendants to give anyone counsel in these matters, it should be accepted as a loving provision from Jehovah. (Gal. 6: 1) All need to remember that the reason we put forth effort to attend the convention is so that we may 'listen and learn'" (Km 1997, May: 3).

10.6.5 Theoretical reflection: A third preliminary discussion

The passages from the Watch Tower publications discussed in this and the previous section show how the conventions are emotionally framed during the midweek meetings of the Jehovah's Witnesses—again, my argument relies on the analysis of such meetings as presented in Chapters 8 and 9. These sections demonstrate how, during the period preceding a convention, the magazine *Our Kingdom Ministry* provides its readers with specific instructions on how to plan their attendance and how to organize the missionary work surrounding the event. Most importantly, they support the thesis according to which the collective study of the magazine serves as a communicative framework for establishing a collective emotion, namely a joint commitment to uphold a certain attitude "as a body." During the service meetings, a distinctive emotional semantic register conveying a sentiment of enthusiasm, joy, and expectation is mobilized and collectively adopted by the people attending the assemblies—indeed, these are the very same semantics that can be found, directly or indirectly, in the statements of my interviewees. As collective emotions in Gilbert's sense, these attitudes have a prescriptive dimension. This mean they are connected to certain normative expectations regarding the external behavior of the individual parties to the joint commitment.

A critical reader may still want to read the excerpts presented above as examples of "very sophisticated [...] techniques of deep acting" (Hochschild 2012: 49) through which the Watch Tower Society institutionally manages how Jehovah's Witnesses feel, and not as the textual basis for the production of a joint commitment. I am not sure that it is possible to provide a definitive determination either way, since the answer depends on the acceptance of different conceptions of emotions, groups, and the self. However, to explore this distinction further, we may consider conventions themselves as ritual settings and ask ourselves what would be subjectively considered a ritual failure with respect to the expected emotions.

Hochschild addresses this question through the example of a bride who, on the day of her wedding, does not feel as happy as she thinks she ought to feel. Only after a phase of profound distress does she manage to realign her feelings with the situation. Hochschild notes that, in the eyes of the bride, the ritual is almost a failure because she sees the unity between the event and having the proper feelings as a condition of its success (Hochschild 2012: 59-63). If attaining such unity is something that some of my interviewees strive for, falling short of this goal (as they admit is sometimes the case) is not seen as something that necessarily compromises the ritual—at least as long as their behavior does not contradict the expected emotional display. Thus, in the case of Jehovah's Witnesses conventions, I argue that the perceived ritual success does not consist in shaping one's personal feelings but in successfully upholding a collective emotion "as a body." In this sense, the (re)affirmation and (re)constitution of Jehovah's Witnesses as a collective agent also incorporate the dimension of collective emotions.

10.7 Conclusion

10.7.1 Two approaches to collective emotions: An empirical and theoretical assessment

Throughout this chapter, I have used the example of Jehovah's Witnesses regional conventions as a case study to discuss the epistemological premises of two distinct approaches to collective emotions and to evaluate their analytical potential. On the one hand, I have detailed the standpoint of the neo-Durkheimian tradition championed by

Rawls, Collins, and Walthert, among others. On the other hand, I have presented Gilbert's "plural subject" theory of emotions in dialog with Hochschild's take on emotion work. These two perspectives diverge from one another on crucial points. First, they are predicated on different conceptions of emotion and on different assumptions regarding the relationship between emotional states and sociality. The authors in the neo-Durkheimian tradition understand emotions as specific and universal mental and bodily states that serve as foundations for human cognitive functions and are directly accessible by individuals. As such, emotions can be influenced by the co-presence of other individuals, but social factors are not *per se* part of the emotions themselves—indeed, emotions provide an explanation for the emergence of society. By contrast, both Hochschild and Gilbert emphasize the cognitive dimension of emotions and, although in different ways, call attention to their inherent social and normative dimension.

Second, the two approaches involve distinct understandings of the *collective* nature of collective emotions. The neo-Durkheimian perspective implies an aggregative or summative understanding of collectivity, since it is the direct experience of the same emotion among the members of a group that allows them to realize, through synchronized movements, their cognitive and moral unity. A non-summative conception of collective emotion—that is, the ascription of a certain emotion to a group but not necessarily to each of its members—requires that we abandon the idea of individual phenomenological experience as constitutive of emotional states. This is the position adopted by Gilbert and by some constructionist anthropologists (see the introduction of this chapter), who consider feeling-sensations to be contingent and not intrinsic properties of emotion. This perspective openly challenges our common-sense understanding of emotions.

The application of either approach to the empirical case of Jehovah's Witnesses conventions presents challenges, although I would argue that the neo-Durkheimian perspective, as epitomized by Collins's work, is confronted with a more serious set of difficulties. On the one hand, data from participant observation does not reveal the forms of emotional entrainment and bodily synchronization that provide a basis for intersubjectivity. On the other hand, both observational and verbal data indicate that the participants experience diverse and sometimes divergent emotions. As discussed above, the attempts to make room for this kind of divergence within Collins's theory are problematic, either because they question the primacy of direct emotional experiences over role-taking in structuring a situation, or because they imply asymmetric power relations that would alienate the participants.

The alternative approach discussed in this chapter clearly fares better in accommodating a variety of individual emotional responses. By calling attention to the cognitive and normative dimensions of emotions, both Hochschild and Gilbert allow for the possibility of a discrepancy between the emotional states (or emotional display) expected in a situation and the individual emotions of the participants. Nevertheless, Hochschild's and Gilbert's positions differ substantially on their treatment of the participants' emotional commitments. While both scholars agree that the correct display of the appropriate emotion is a fundamental implication of the normativity of emotions, Hochschild goes a step further by underscoring how feeling rules prompt people to try to modulate how they feel (phenomenologically) in a given situation. Furthermore, in Hochschild's account, individuals are confronted with anonymous emotion norms that they adopt in conjunction with their reading of the situation. In this respect, they are "bound to the norm by standards of individual rationality on the one hand, and by anonymous social pressure emerging from the other group members' compliance on the other hand" (Salmela 2013: 174). By contrast, from Gilbert's standpoint, the source of the prescriptive emotion norms within the group is the joint commitment of the group members. In this case, the individual members' emotional behavior rests on a group rationality and can, *but does not have to*, match the private emotional state of the individuals.

From a methodological point of view, the case of Jehovah's Witnesses conventions indicates that observational data alone do not allow us to distinguish deeply enacted emotion from collectively upheld emotions—or, for that matter, from expressions of assumed "natural" emotional states. Furthermore, at least in some cases, the statements expressing a discrepancy between expected and experienced emotions could be interpreted in terms of individual deep acting *or* as the result of a joint commitment. However, in addition to specific verbal clues, such as references to personal opinion, a broader look at the ritual framing of the conventions convincingly tips the scale in favor of the latter approach. In particular, the conventions are set in a narrative frame that establishes them as institutional events, accompanied by a specific ritual communication that serves as an "authority system" (Tuomela 1995, see Chapters 4 and 8) conducive to a strong collective commitment to certain emotions.

In sum, the discussion in this chapter has shown that the neo-Durkheimian theory presented in the first part is a suitable instrument for studying, for instance, the role of collective emotions in an Evangelical celebration. However, this approach seems less effective at analyzing events such as Jehovah's Witnesses' conventions. Thus, I am inclined to conclude that this result invites us to acknowledge the existence of different forms of religious collectivities, one predicated on aggregated individual emotions in the case, for instance, of Evangelical Churches, and one predicated on collective emotions (and other collective intentions) in the case of the Jehovah's Witnesses. This conclusion challenges most academic analyses of the role of emotions within the Watch Tower Society.

10.7.2 The emotional conventions of Jehovah's Witnesses

The lack of strong emotions among Jehovah's Witnesses is a recurring topic in the academic literature on the Watch Tower Society. The sociologist David Martin (quoted in Beckford 1975a: 203) describes the Witnesses as "full of religious zeal but devoid of religious emotion." In his classic study *The Trumpet of Prophecy*, James Beckford shares this view and affirms that "[t]he highly affective quality of the bonds uniting members of other minority religious groups is patently lacking in the Watch Tower movement" (Beckford 1975a: 86). In his view, this is proof of the rationalistic character of the Watch Tower Society, which finds expression in the "unemotional and didactic atmosphere" of Jehovah's Witnesses meetings (Beckford 1975a: 203)—an assessment shared by David Voas (2010: 123). The same remains true for the national and international conventions, which are not considered to be of much value as evangelistic devices:

> It is doubtful whether many "outsiders" attend these gatherings, and the programmes of lectures, demonstrations, baptisms, dramatic performances and song do not seem to be designed to arouse the curiosity of newly interested people so much as to reinforce the convictions of initiates. (Beckford 1975a: 51)

Against this backdrop, Beckford concludes his analysis of the history and sociology of Jehovah's Witnesses by advancing the view that, probably, "Biblical literalism, evangelicalism and unemotionality are a better recipe for long-term, organized activism than heightened emotion and syncretism" (Beckford 1975a: 219).

In this chapter, I have demonstrated that collective emotions are definitely not irrelevant to the lives of Jehovah's Witnesses and for the existence of the Watch Tower Society as a religious community. However, the form of collective emotion at play is not the Durkheimian effervescence that likely constituted the implicit reference for Beckford and other scholars. Rather, it is a collective emotion in the form of a ritually produced joint commitment among the parties of a plural subject—or, following Tuomela, a we-mode we-emotion. This collective emotion does not entail the deep shaping of individual feelings but contributes to the constitution of Jehovah's Witnesses as a collective agent through their effort to uphold it "as a body." It is in this sense that Jehovah's Witnesses collectively share the excitement of *conventions*—in both senses of the word.

11

Collective Aesthetic Experiences—
The Feeling of the Bible

11.1 Introduction

The first meeting of Jehovah's Witnesses I attended as a part of my research was no ordinary meeting. On that day, congregations worldwide were celebrating the annual Memorial of Christ's Death, the most sacred event for Jehovah's Witnesses. The liturgy of that evening (and of each subsequent memorial that I attended) could be roughly divided into two parts. After a song had been sung by the congregation, which was followed by a prayer, the first part consisted mainly of a 35-minute sermon explaining the meaning and form of the ceremony. During the second part, unleavened bread and red wine were passed along the rows of seated people. However, no one in attendance consumed the emblems. As was made clear in the sermon, the partaking of the bread and wine is a privilege reserved for the anointed class comprising the 144,000 people who, as foretold in the book of Revelation (Rev. 5: 9, 10; Rev. 14: 1, 3), will rule in heaven with Christ after the end "of the current system of things." The vast majority of Jehovah's Witnesses do not share this heavenly hope, but rather look forward to eternal life on a paradise earth (see Bh 2014: 74). A few short announcements, a song, and a prayer concluded the Memorial.

That evening, one of my colleagues and I were expected as guests in a congregation, and two places were reserved for us. We each also received a copy of the songbook, and my musically inclined colleague was immediately able to take part in the singing. However, as soon as the sermon began, it dawned on us that we had forgotten to bring a more essential book, as the congregants were often invited from the platform to refer to the scriptures. My colleague and I whispered in agreement that, as participant observers, we had made a rookie mistake. Or, had we? In fact, we quickly realized that it would have been impossible for us to keep up with the pace at which the people in attendance looked up passages in their Bibles. A few seconds after a verse was mentioned, the books in the congregants' hands were opened to the right page and, as the passage was read aloud, everyone was following the printed words. A moment later, everyone had turned to the next quoted text with a few quick movements of their fingers.

When I attended the Memorial at the same congregation two years later, the situation was different. In the meantime, I had not improved my Bible-handling skills. However, I had installed an app produced by the Watch Tower Society called *JW*

Library on my smartphone. The app allows the user to download a large number of publications, including the songbook, which my accompanying colleague used to sing along. The app also contains a digital version of the *New World Translation of the Holy Scriptures*, as used by the Jehovah's Witnesses. As the appointed elder, Bible in hand, was explaining from the platform the reasons for Jesus's death and the meaning of his ransom sacrifice, I was able to follow along by tapping on the colored squares corresponding to the books of the Bible, and then on the boxes with the number of the chapters, before quickly scrolling down to the right verse. More important than my achievement, however, is the fact that most members of the congregation were also tapping on the screens of their tablets or smartphones. Within two years, the way in which a large number of Jehovah's Witnesses materially approached the scriptures had fundamentally changed.

This chapter draws on the profound transformation of the material approach to text among Jehovah's Witnesses to discuss a theoretical question, namely the role of aesthetic experiences in the formation and perpetuation of religious collectivities. Since the 1990s, the aesthetics of religion has gained prominence in the study of religion, with some authors suggesting that this perspective could provide a new foundation for a systematic approach following the collapse of the phenomenology of religion (Cancik and Mohn 1998; Mohn 2004). The aesthetics of religion draws its core ideas from various sources and includes a growing number of subfields, such as material religion (e.g., Meyer et al. 2010; Bräunlein 2016), embodied religion (e.g., Csordas 1994; Krüger and Weibel 2015), and museums and religion (e.g., Wilke and Guggenmos 2008; Buggeln, Paine, and Plate 2017). Providing an overview of this blossoming field would go beyond the scope of this study. For this reason, in the second section of this chapter, I will focus on the work of one of the most influential authors in this field: anthropologist and scholar of religion Birgit Meyer. While Meyer's work cannot be considered representative of all currents in the aesthetics of religion, her approach is especially interesting because it pays particular attention to the collective dimension of religious-aesthetic experiences and introduces a number of concepts useful for grasping the constitutive role of media within religious communities. However, Meyer's theory also presents some problematic aspects that invite further reflection.

To stimulate such reflection, I will discuss the Jehovah's Witnesses' relationship to the printed word and the effects of what can be considered a digital revolution within the Watch Tower Society, prompted by the 2012 launch of a renewed version of its official website, jw.org. It is hard to overstate the impact that this online presence had on the (self-)representation of Jehovah's Witnesses, both in the public space and within their organization. The webpage's logo, a blue square with the letters "JW.ORG" in white, is now displayed in front of Kingdom Halls worldwide, on the Witnesses' literature carts, and on the back covers of the Watch Tower magazines. To put the significance of digital technology into context, in the third section, I will provide a historical overview of the Watch Tower Society's material production of magazines and books, focusing on the printing and binding of Bibles. In the fourth section, I will examine the evolution of the Society's online presence and investigate the use of digital media among Jehovah's Witnesses. Asking not what, but *how* they read, I will discuss their aesthetic evaluation of electronic media and printed publications, calling particular attention to the special status attributed to the print Bible. The question of the use of digital Bibles in the congregation will provide the bridge to the theoretical reflection on *collective* aesthetics within the framework of collective intentionality that I will put forward in the fifth section. There, I will introduce a contrasting empirical example and examine it in light of Margaret Gilbert's distinction between plain and normative expectations, which will lead to my conclusion.

11.2 Religion as Mediation: Critical Considerations

Among the recent efforts to conceptualize the material and aesthetic dimensions of religion, the idea of religion *as* media deserves particular attention because it has proven quite popular among social anthropologists and scholars of religion alike. Canadian communication scholar Jeremy Stolow coined the expression "religion *as* media" in a review essay published in 2005. In it, he welcomes the increasing number of studies devoted to the interaction between religion and different media. However, he also notes that an instrumentalist paradigm of media practices dominates the research in this field, which reduces the reception and use of media by religious actors to mere passive assimilation. Against this backdrop, Stolow advances that "the most fruitful studies often turn out to be those which proceed, not from the instrumentalist formula, 'religion *and* media' [...] but rather from the idea of 'religion *as* media'" (Stolow 2005: 125). According to Stolow, the expression "religion *and* media" is pleonastic:

> Whether as the transmission of a numinous essence to a community of believers, the self-presencing [sic] of the divine in personal experience, or the unfolding of mimetic circuits of exchange between transcendental powers and earthly practitioners, "religion" can only be manifested through some process of mediation. (Stolow 2005: 125)

Thus, in all places and times, exchanges with and about "the sacred" are always bound to the use of material things, sensible objects and bodily practices.

Within the European study of religion, anthropologist and religious scholar Birgit Meyer (b. 1960) played a fundamental role in developing and promoting this approach through her numerous talks and publications and her editorial work as a board member of the journal *Material Religion*. In this section, I will focus on her work as a partial but telling illustration of a broader research paradigm. First, I shall summarize the core idea of her approach before taking, as a second step, a closer look at the epistemological and methodological premises that lie at its foundation.[1]

11.2.1 Birgit Meyer's approach: The fundamental ideas

Birgit Meyer's productive academic career extends over more than 25 years. Nevertheless, it draws the contours of a coherent and well-defined program. Meyer's approach can be presented in four successive steps. Starting from a critique of the historical neglect of media in the scientific study of religion, she develops a conception of religion as a process of mediation. From there, she advocates a research focus on the social practices validating specific media as suitable mediators with a transcendent realm. Finally, she stresses the role of shared aesthetics for the constitution of religious groups. Let us consider these points in order.

At the root of Meyer's approach lies an articulated critique of the "implicit bias against media in the study of religion" (Meyer 2011b: 28). Meyer underscores that this bias is the consequence of a "mentalistic" understanding of religion, which is typical of the Protestant tradition. Grounded in Cartesian dualism, this view framed religion in terms of inner convictions, ideas, and personal feelings, and correspondingly devaluated all outward practices and forms—including media and other material artifacts (Meyer 2011b: 28–29; 2014: 207–208; see also Asad 1993: 27–54). First devised in opposition to the sacramental ritualism of the Catholic Church and its use of images, this argument supported colonialist and missionary endeavors in their critique of "fetishism" and "traditional" religions around the world (Meyer 1999; 2006a: 438–439).

The iconoclastic impetus inherited from the Reformation developed into the anti-aestheticism of Protestant theology in the nineteenth century, epitomized by Friedrich Schleiermacher's aversion to aesthetic representations as substitutes for true religious experiences. Meyer insists on the long-lasting effects of these conceptions in the scientific study of religion. Among other aspects, she notes that the Protestant dismissal of religious media as preventing a direct relationship with God obscured the nature of the Bible *as a medium*, and favored a meaning-centered analysis of so-called holy books, which was "preoccupied with immaterial ideas—imagined as 'hovering above pages and ink'" (Meyer 2015: 335). Therefore, in the history of the discipline, material forms, organizational structures, bodily practices, and media have received only marginal attention.

Pushing back against these tendencies, Meyer et al. (2010: 210) contend that "there is no such thing as an immaterial religion." Further, Meyer (2011b: 23) understands media "as intrinsic, rather than opposed to religion." Her argument is predicated on a specific understanding of religion:

> I take that "religion" refers to particular, authorized, and transmitted sets of practices and ideas aimed at "going beyond the ordinary," "surpassing" or "transcending" a limit, or gesturing toward "the-rest-of-what-is" [...]. (Meyer 2014: 215)

Meyer, however, does not postulate the transcendental entity, to which religion points, as a self-revealing, ontologically objective reality—as does, for instance, Rudolf Otto (2004). Instead, she maintains that the experience of a divine presence results from the use of multiple media "through which the 'beyond' becomes accessible or the 'invisible' is 'shown'" (Meyer 2015: 337; see also Orsi 2012). In this respect, her concept of media includes modern mass media, other "older" media, as well as the body. This understanding of "religion as mediation" provides the foundation for a comprehensive research program.

I propose to place at the center of scholarly inquiries the very tangible ways through which humans "fabricate"—by mobilizing texts, sounds, pictures, and objects and by engaging in practices of speaking, singing, being possessed, and so on—a sense of the presence of something "beyond." [...] Which materials are used and how are they authorized as suitable? Through which acts does a sculpture, a building, or any other object become a harbinger of spiritual power? What steps are involved in procedures of sacralization? How is the human body included and addressed? Which sensorial registers are invoked? How are these procedures authorized and controlled and what kinds of relations ensue? Finally, how does a religious fabrication inspire belief? (Meyer 2014: 214)

Meyer (2015: 337) stresses that religious individuals or groups must not necessarily share the concept of religion as mediation. On the contrary, they often present their experience as immediate contact with the sacred. Nonetheless, the sense of immediacy is the product of social processes through which media are made to "disappear." The adoption of a new medium in religious contexts thus cannot be reduced to the mere instrumental espousal of a new technology. Instead, it must be considered in light of the social practices and power structures that sanction its status as a mediator and, thus, make it "invisible" by transforming "a mediated representation into an immediate presence" (Meyer 2006a: 437).

The authorization processes involved in the use of (new) media in relation to religious mediation practices belong to what Meyer calls "sensational forms."

Sensational forms [...] are relatively fixed, authorized modes of invoking and organizing access to the transcendental, thereby creating and sustaining links between religious practitioners in the context of particular religious organizations. (Meyer 2006b: 9)

Accordingly, on the one hand, sensational forms shape religious mediation, directing the sensory engagement of the participants with the transcendental. On the other hand, they make present the postulated reality that they mediate (Meyer 2014: 217; 2015: 338). Hence, individually felt religious sensations proceed, in fact, from formalized and authorized practices that foster them and "enable their reproducibility" (Meyer 2010a: 754). Furthermore, the religious subjects incorporate the sensational forms of their group through socialization. As part of the group *common sense*, sensational forms become unperceived and unquestioned embodied dispositions in the habitus of the group members (Meyer 2006b: 22; 2015: 338).

Stressing the inescapably collective foundation of religious experiences and sensations (Meyer 2006b: 9), Meyer draws attention to the role of "a shared corpus of songs, images, symbols, rituals, but also a similar clothing style and material culture" (Meyer 2006b: 24)—in short: a common aesthetic style—in the constitution of religious collectivities. Sharing a common aesthetic style generates feelings of togetherness and modulates "people into a particular, common appearance, and thus underpin[s] a collective religious identity" (Meyer 2006b: 24).

On the basis of this insight, Meyer (2006b: 20) proposes to reevaluate the "religion-media-community nexus." To do so, she draws inspiration from Benedict Anderson's

(1983) famous concept of "imagined communities," while questioning its underlying mentalistic bias (Meyer 2009: 3–6). In this regard, Meyer seeks to go beyond questions of representations and meaning to "scrutinize how the binding of people into imagined communities actually occurs and is realized in a material sense" (Meyer 2009: 6). She states the following:

> Indeed, in order to [...] be experienced as real, imaginations are required to become tangible outside the realm of the mind, by creating a social environment that materializes through the structuring of space, architecture, ritual performance, and by inducing bodily sensations [...]. In brief, in order to become experienced as real, imagined communities need to materialize in the concrete lived environment and be felt in the bones. (Meyer 2009: 5)

Meyer puts forth the concept of "aesthetic formations" to stress the material and corporeal dimension of the social bonds. As she explains, the shared aesthetic "tunes" the senses of the members and "induces a sensory mode of perceiving the world that produces community" (Meyer 2009: 7). However, she prefers the term "formations," to "communities" because it conveys simultaneously the idea of a "social entity" and its related "process of forming" (Meyer 2009: 7).

Birgit Meyer's approach to the study of religion, media, and community is innovative and thought-provoking. Nonetheless, a closer look at her work raises questions regarding some of the fundamental assumptions that guide her analysis. In the next section, following the structure sketched so far, I shall illuminate these underlying premises and discuss their methodological and theoretical consequences.

11.2.2 Birgit Meyer's approach: A closer look

In the first place, Meyer's definition of religion deserves closer scrutiny, since it deeply informs her whole research program. In the context of the ongoing post-colonial debates over the very possibility of defining religion, Meyer's position is characterized by a measure of pragmatism. Distancing herself from a radically discursive approach to "religion" that would leave the term without any actual referent in the world, Meyer (2015: 336) maintains that, "all scholars can do is to speak about religion self-reflexively, from a standpoint and a quest to know that is historically situated." Indeed, it is on the basis of her assumed perspective that she looks to gain new insight into her research objects. For this reason, it is important to spell out the different strands that constitute her frame of reference and some of the consequences that they entail.

The close imbrication of media and religion in Meyer's work can be traced back to empirical and philosophical sources. On the one hand, as Meyer underscores, it is her study of Pentecostalism and Ewe religion in Ghana that prompted her to adopt the definition of religion as mediation and stimulated the development of the concept of sensational forms (personal correspondence, 27 October 2017). On the other hand, the concept of mediation in Meyer's work has its roots in the work of Dutch philosopher Hent de Vries, whose influence she acknowledges in several of her publications (e.g., 2006b: 13; 2009: 11).

In short, de Vries argues that the global resurgence of religion at the end of the twentieth century and the rising importance of communication technologies during the same period are intrinsically interconnected, to the point that media and religion have become virtually interchangeable (de Vries 2001: 19). De Vries draws this idea from Derrida's essay "Faith and Knowledge" (1998). Derrida's position is detailed further in his article "Above All, No Journalists!" (2001), which is included in a volume edited by de Vries. In these texts, Derrida presents a twofold argument. First, he maintains that today, the global reach of various religious traditions depends on their use of media technologies. Second, he argues that the idea of mediation is fundamentally a Christian one: it is the figure of the Christ that introduces the idea of mediation and, with it, the necessity of spreading the Good News. From this, he concludes that to be present on the world stage, all religions must bow to a hegemonic Christian frame of reference. It is against this backdrop that de Vries synthetically formulates his influential research program centered on the process of mediation and mediatization "without and outside of which no religion would be able to manifest or reveal itself in the first place" (de Vries 2001: 28).

De Vries's program has not received universal praise. For instance, the anthropologist Charles Hirschkind (2011) notes that de Vries's argument requires the acceptance of a convergence between a theological idea of mediation—the Christ as the intermediary between humanity and God—and a sociological one, that is, the widespread use of media technologies. In Meyer's work, de Vries's mediation concept is treated mainly as an instrument to shift the research on religion away from an excessive emphasis on the categories of meaning and belief (Meyer 2004: 94–95; see also Engelke 2011: 98). Accordingly, Meyer does not explicitly wish to import all the philosophical baggage that this concept carries with it (personal correspondence, 27 October 2017). Nevertheless, I would argue that even her more sober and practical use of the concept is subject to the criticism formulated by Hirschkind and implicitly perpetuates the Christian understanding of religion that underpins de Vries's approach. This seems particularly at odds with Meyer's repeated criticism of the Protestant bias of much scholarly work on religion, as her framework, to put it bluntly, would replace one religiously founded bias with another.

This issue arises at the junction between empirical research and theoretical analysis. As Meyer (2006a: 435) notes, scholars in the fields of anthropology, religious studies, media studies, and philosophy have pointed out "that religion and media are entangled in complicated ways." For scholars working with the distinction inherited from Enlightenment philosophy, this empirical observation, she says, is potentially puzzling because it subverts "facile oppositions such as spirituality and technology, or faith and reason" (2006a: 435). However, the "puzzlement" can be resolved by considering that the "positing of a distance between human beings in the world and the divine realm" constitutes "a characteristic feature of religion [which] can only be overcome through mediation" (Meyer 2006b: 435). Thus, in her argument, Meyer appears to resolve what I consider to be an empirical problem—the relationship between religion and media—by positing both a postulated transcendence and the need for mediation as self-evident constituents of "religion." Yet, the discussion of de Vries's approach allows us to see, at least in part, the genealogy of this conception.

A further branch in this genealogy appears when we consider Meyer's approach toward specifying some of the attributes of the (postulated) transcendent reality. Drawing on de Vries' (2008) "deep pragmatism," Meyer (2015: 336) argues that, "[S]peaking about religion is doubly complicated, in that it involves a negative concept that seeks to access a phenomenon that is elusive *by nature* [my emphasis], involving something 'other' or 'alter' that exceeds the ordinary (Csordas 2004: 164) or, in short, alludes to 'the rest-of-what-is' (Van de Port 2010)." Despite its elusiveness, however, the encounter with the transcendent can be qualified with reference to particular sensations and bodily attitudes:

> Religious sensations are about human encounters with phenomena or events that appear as beyond comprehension, in a word: a sublime, that induces [...] a simultaneous sense of beauty or terror. Such encounters invoke sensations of awe vis-à-vis a transcendental entity, that by definition resists being fully known and yet makes itself felt in the here and now, in the immanent. (Meyer 2006b: 10)

Meyer (2006b: 10) insists that these sensations are not the human response to an irreducible numinous reality, nor do they originate from an unmediated individual experience. Instead, they are the products of authorized practices and objectivations within a religious group that organizes the "feelings of 'awe, wonder and the like.'"

According to Meyer, this fundamental shift opens the door to a study of religion that is sensitive to the importance of emotions, while focusing on the standardized techniques used to induce them. Drawing on Robert R. Marret's (1929) anti-intellectualist view of a universal human religious sense grounded in specific emotions, Meyer (2016: 17) conceives the idea of "awe" as "a powerful emotion," which results from "standardized methods that yield the fabrication of some kind of excess":

> Religion is the domain *par excellence* that offers standardized procedures to generate in religious practitioners—over and over again—a sense of wonder and amazement: the production of a sacred surplus. (Meyer 2016: 18)

In sum, Meyer frames the relationship with the (postulated) transcendent reality in terms of an enrapturing experience, and "religion" as the domain of this experience. Accordingly, Meyer's approach appears as a "socialized phenomenology." The ontological reality of the numinous is replaced with a socio-constructivist approach that emphasizes the collective creation of specific emotions related to the sacred; yet, the religious quality of these social productions still depends on the personal response of individuals to the transcendent—on their experience of a sense of wonder and amazement—which, in principle, remains shielded from direct observation.

This observation draws our attention to further theoretical and methodological issues. Even if we accept that the idea that religion and media are per definition "co-constitutive" (Meyer 2006a: 436), we are still confronted to the question of knowing *how* practices of mediation "make it possible to experience—and from a more distanced perspective one could say: produce—the transcendental" (Meyer 2006b: 13; see

Engelke 2010). Meyer's answer to this problem is provided by her concept of "sensational forms" as socially or culturally authorized forms that "*induce in people*, in a repeated and repeatable manner, sensations of reaching out that they experience as real" (Meyer 2014: 218, my emphasis). However, despite Meyer's emphasis on this concept in her more systematic articles, one has to turn to her ethnographic work to get a sense of how sensational forms might "do the job." In this respect, Meyer's analysis of the role of mass-produced Jesus pictures and practices of "visual piety" (Morgan 1998) in Ghana provides further insight into her theoretical framework.

Drawing on Webb Keane's (2007) concept of "semiotic ideologies," Meyer (2010b: 103) notes that "the conceptions of the relation between persons and things are grounded in historically and culturally specific settings." For instance, culturally different "modes of looking" (Meyer 2011a: 1041) that constitute an integral part of sensational forms can be acquired through the process of socialization and become "embodied dispositions in the habitus" (Meyer 2015: 338). Beliefs and practices revolving around the "power of pictures"—such as the fear of the demonic possession of pictures among Pentecostals in Ghana (e.g., Meyer 2008: 95–101)—involve conceptions of visuality in relation to the agency of "things" that differ from those of Western cultures. Such alternative modes of looking involve a distinct bodily and sensory dimension that can blur the line between a representation and what it represents, and invites us to grasp certain images as "an embodiment of a spiritual presence," without reducing them to "mere symbols of something else" (Meyer 2006b: 19).

The goal of Meyer's critique of an analysis of religion in terms of symbolic representations is not meant to reorient empirical research toward the analysis of (socialization) practices. Her goal is rather to transcend the idea of representation and meaning to focus on form and experience. However, to the extent that the experiences under scrutiny are studied through textual accounts, interviews, or their depiction in popular culture (e.g., Meyer 2010b, 2011a), it is hard, if not impossible, to separate the actual experiences from the communicative structures through which they are framed. Indeed, one might argue that, if people learn how to look at a picture, they also learn how to speak about how they look—even more, how they *are supposed* to look—at a picture.[2] This observation does not undermine the usefulness of the concept of sensational forms per se. However, it questions the possibility of directly grasping, for instance, "how Jesus pictures can induce spiritual experience" (Meyer 2010b: 117).

The primacy of form and experience over meaning (and, thus, communication) is also constitutive of Meyer's approach to "aesthetic formations," which, in her view, provides a framework to understand, following Durkheim (1888: 257), "the bonds which unite men one with another." In her view (2009: 9), community proceeds from a "shared sensory mode of perceiving and experiencing the world," revolving around "shared images and other mediated cultural forms." The concept of "sharing," however, must not be interpreted as an intellectual—or even an intentional—act.

> This sharing, it needs to be stressed, does not merely depend on a common interpretation of these forms and an agreement about their meaning (as asserted by interpretative or symbolic anthropology), but on the capacity of these forms *to*

induce in those engaging with them a particular common aesthetic and style." (Meyer 2009: 9, my emphasis)

How, then, do mediated cultural forms *induce* a common aesthetic and style, and thus the feeling of belonging to a community?

To answer this question, Meyer appeals to the work of French sociologist Michel Maffesoli (1993). Meyer (2009: 9) draws a parallel between her concept of aesthetic formations and Maffesoli's notion of "aesthetic style" as "'forming form' that gives birth to the whole manner of being, to customs, representations and the various fashions by which life in society is expressed." In particular, Meyer (2009: 9) highlights Maffesoli's interest in the "role of shared images in forging links between individuals, [and] organizing them into communities" within postmodern societies. Furthermore, she acknowledges Maffesoli's attention "to the ways in which shared images mobilize and thrive upon shared sentiments, inducing modes, and moods, of feeling together." Still, despite the Durkheimian undertones of Maffesoli's analysis and the affinity between the concept of style and the Bourdieusian notion of habitus, the conceptual move from "shared images" to the constitution of community remains vague. Unfortunately, even a closer reading of Maffesoli's baroque essay does not really provide further insight into the matter.

In the end, Meyer fails to provide a clear bridge between the aesthetic experiences (somehow) induced by sensational forms in individuals and the constitution of a collective, even if we accept her implicit summative definition of "community" as a group of people each having the same or a similar aesthetic experience. At this point, speculative reflection seems to reach its limit. To gain a deeper understanding of the role of shared aesthetic experiences in the constitution of religious collectives we need to turn to empirical data on which we can then build new theoretical insights. Let us then consider some aspects of the aesthetics of Jehovah's Witnesses.

11.3 Materializing God's Word: The Case of Jehovah's Witnesses

The aesthetics of Jehovah's Witnesses does not offer obviously spectacular features for the scholar to work with. As I have discussed in the previous chapter, their singing and bodily practices are quite subdued. When meeting, Jehovah's Witnesses are asked to wear elegant but modest clothing. The interior of the Kingdom Halls is reminiscent of a hotel seminar room, with rows of plain chairs, a platform with a simple pulpit, and, sometimes, a decorative plant; there is no cross—a symbol that Jehovah's Witnesses abandoned in 1936—and the walls are decorated only with a Biblical verse that changes every year. As French sociologist Arnaud Blanchard (2008: 124) suggests, the austere ambience of the Witnesses' meeting places draws even more attention to the Watch Tower media—in particular, the magazines and books—and the Bible as the most visible markers of religious life. Thus, a study of Jehovah's Witnesses' aesthetics is almost predestined to focus on the Witnesses' material relationship with the printed page and, in context of the recent changes in the Watch Tower Society's media landscape, their perception of electronic media.

11.3.1 Brief overview of the existing research

Of course, the growing importance of digital religious media is not a phenomenon limited to the case of Jehovah's Witnesses, but one that can be observed across various religious traditions and Christian denominations. Unsurprisingly, this trend first attracted the attention of theologians and Christian religious practitioners concerned by the increasing use of electronic editions of the Bible and various "Bible apps"—that is, software applications to read the Bible on tablets and smartphones (e.g., Beaudoin 1997; Barrett 2013; van Peursen 2014).

The study of Bible apps and their use is an emerging field of research in the scientific study of religion. The impact of these applications on individual modes of reading and structures of religious authority are among the most prominent research questions (Wagner 2012; Hutchings 2014, 2015b). Another avenue of research focuses instead on the subjective reception of electronic Bibles among frequent users. On the basis of an online survey, Hutchings (2015a) enumerates the perceived advantages and disadvantages of reading the scriptures on an e-reader, tablet, or computer. Among the most appreciated aspects of the new technologies, users mention their convenience and the facility of accessing and studying the Bible. Conversely, the erosion of the Bible's unique status and the loss of a meaningful relationship with the physical book are among the most frequently mentioned negative effects.

The latter aspects are at the core of Katja Rakow's (2017) study on the "the limits of 'Bibleness' of different Bible media." Rakow borrows the term "Bibleness" from the religion scholar Timothy Beal, who uses it to designate the particular "cultural iconicity" of the Bible and its capacity to project "a solid, bookish singularity, unity, oneness, and authority" (Beal 2015: 222). Drawing primarily on Christian blog posts, Rakow categorizes the different practice contexts that frame people's ascription of advantages or disadvantages to digital Bibles. In this respect, she distinguishes between a commemorative use of the Bible as a material carrier of memories, a semantic-hermeneutic use related to its study and interpretation, and a performative usage of the Bible as a material object in devotional or liturgical settings.

My research on the aesthetics of media among Jehovah's Witnesses presents similarities to the work of Hutchings and Rakow. However, there are also important differences concerning the empirical framework of my study and the form and goal of my analysis. In contrast to the authors quoted above, my data do not originate from random Bible readers. My sample only includes members of the Watch Tower Society. Using both quantitative and qualitative data, I can provide an accurate picture of the media habits of Swiss and German Jehovah's Witnesses and detail the debates that accompanied a media change they experienced more or less at the same time. The coherence of my sample allows me to situate it in a broader context, first by considering the history of the Watch Tower Society's media production, and second by comparing the reactions produced by the introduction of electronic Bibles to the responses to the adoption of other electronic media.

Regarding my theoretical and methodological approach, I refrain from any speculative statement on the affordance of various media (e.g., Ong 1982; Plate 2015, quoted in Rakow 2017). Instead, I persistently adopt a hermeneutic perspective. Nevertheless, my goal is not simply to reconstruct the worldview of my interviewees, but rather to prepare the floor for a theoretical discussion of the relationship between (shared) aesthetic experiences and the constitution of a collective agent in the sense detailed by the philosophical discussion on collective intentionality.

11.3.2 Printing books, tracts, and magazines

In its own historiography, the Watch Tower Society sees its publishing work as the continuation of the work done in the Christian communities of the second century, which were at the forefront of the early codex production, and links it back to Moses's and the apostles' responses to God's command to write (Jv 1993: 575). However, regarding the material realization of the magazines, tracts, and books that it distributed, the Watch Tower Society under Russell depended almost completely on commercial printers and binders. It is under the presidency of Rutherford that the Society sought to produce its own publications.

This decision was a response to contingent problems in the printing industry in the wake of the First World War; however, the new mode of production also played into Rutherford's plans to centralize the activities of the Bible Students. The purchase of the first rotary press, installed in 1919 in the Society's workshop in Brooklyn (Jp 1959: 90), coincided with the launch of the magazine *The Golden Age* and with the progressive introduction of the systematic door-to-door ministry as the privileged means for distributing the Watch Tower literature. Through the in-house printing of its literature by voluntary workers, the Society was able to lower the production cost and break free from numerous commercial ties (Blanchard 2008: 65–68).

In the 1920s, the Watch Tower Society extended its printing activities to other countries, and a rapid multiplication of the printing facilities in the United States and abroad accompanied the global expansion of Jehovah's Witnesses after the Second World War (Jv 1993: 583–593). The expansion of publishing was also enabled by important technological innovations. Among other things, a team of computer experts started developing publishing software to meet the need for adequate typesetting in different languages, releasing their Multilanguage Electronic Publishing System (MEPS) in 1986 (Jv 114: 596–597). This new digital solution and improved electronic tools for translation allowed the simultaneous publication of Watch Tower literature in 66 languages by 1992 (Jv 1993: 598). As I will discuss below, the Watch Tower Society was more reticent regarding the introduction of electronic publications and the use of the Internet to distribute its literature. Its work on publishing software, however, suggests that when the decision was made to switch to these new technologies, the necessary personnel and resources were, at least to a certain extent, readily available.

Over the years, the Society printed a staggering variety and an impressive number of publications. Yet, the production of Bibles follows a particular trajectory that deserves a closer scrutiny.

11.3.3 Printing Bibles

From the beginning of the nineteenth until the early decades of the twentieth century, many Western countries saw the foundation of so-called Bible societies, whose initiators took it upon themselves to spread the Good News by publishing and distributing copies of the scriptures to the population (Gutjahr 1999). While today the Watch Tower Society arguably belongs in the list of such institutions (see, e.g., Wikipedia, *sub voce* "Bible society," April 2021), this categorization does not necessarily apply to its early years of activity. In fact, the Zion's Watch Tower Tract Society did not publish any Bibles at the time of its foundation in 1881 nor at the time of its incorporation in 1884. Rather, it purchased and redistributed those released by various Bible societies (W 1880, November: 71; Si 1990: 321).

In the early 1890s, Russell's company gradually entered into the world of Bible publishing, first by arranging for special printings of the second edition of *The New Testament Newly Translated and Critically Emphasized* prepared by the British biblical scholar Joseph Rotherham (Jv 1993: 605), and then by purchasing the rights to publish in the United States the twelfth revised edition of the same translation in 1896 (Si 1990: 323). During the same year, a reference to the Bible was officially included in the name of the company, which became the Watch Tower *Bible* and Tract Society of Pennsylvania, Inc.

In the first decade of the twentieth century, the Society intensified its Bible publishing activity by releasing various translations of the scriptures under its name, aimed particularly toward the readers of the *Watchtower*, namely the *Holman Linear Parallel Edition* of the Bible in 1901 and the *Emphatic Diaglott* by Benjamin Wilson in 1902, which included the Greek text of the New Testament accompanied by an interlinear word-to-word translation in English and a full translation in the margin. Finally, in 1907, the Watch Tower Society published a Bible Student's Edition of the *King James* version that included in the appendix a 550-page-long collection of short exegetical comments along with references to Watch Tower publications (Jv 1993: 606). As a later publication states, "This excellent Bible served Jehovah's Witnesses for decades in their public preaching work" (Si 1990: 323).

This editorial work attests the Watch Tower Society's early effort to create a closer connection between its name, its publications and their scriptural foundation—a connection that is not merely intellectual but also physical. A missing element in this strategy concerned the material production of the Bibles, which was still outsourced to commercial companies. In 1927, the Society moved to fill this gap by printing and binding *The Emphatic Diaglott* in its factory in Brooklyn (Si 1990: 323). A new edition, "beautiful in appearance, bound in dark blue leatherette, flexible binding, gold embossed" (G 1942, September 30: 28), was released in 1942 and was reprinted for many years before being replaced by the *Kingdom Interlinear Translation of the Greek Scriptures*, first released in 1969 (W 1969, November 15: 689–690). Between 1942 and 1977, the Watch Tower Society acquired the rights to print three other editions of the Bible. In 1942, the complete *King James* version was released, accompanied by a concordance especially designed to help Jehovah's Witnesses in their field ministry. The 1901 version of *The American Standard Version* and the *Bible in Living English* followed in 1944 and 1972, respectively. These last two translations were particularly appreciated because, on most occasions, they used "Jehovah" to render the name of God (Si 1990: 323–324).

The systematic introduction of the name Jehovah is one of the main features of the Watch Tower Society's own translation of the Bible, the *New World Translation of the Holy Scriptures* (Ns 1961: 23), work on which started in 1946. The goal was to produce a literal but easily understandable translation which, in the Society's view, "was not colored by the creeds and traditions of Christendom" (Jv 1993: 608–609). The work on the New Testament was carried out between 1947 and 1949 by a group known as the New World Bible Translation Committee under the auspices of the Society's then president, Nathan Knorr. The *New World Translation of the Greek Scriptures* in English was officially published in August 1950 (W 1950, September 15: 316). From 1953 to 1960, the Watch Tower Society went on to publish its English translation of the Hebrew Scriptures in five volumes. After a review of the whole translation, the integral *New World Translation of the Holy Scriptures* was published in one green hardback volume in 1961 (W 1961, September 1: 576).

In the following years, the new translation was regularly advertised in the pages of the magazine with words of praise for both its quality and its beautiful appearance:

> Do you know someone who does not have his own copy of the Bible? No one should be without it. Especially now that this best book of all times can be read in the modern language of our day. The *New World Translation of the Holy Scriptures* is a complete Bible, printed on thin Bible paper and bound in a beautiful gold-embossed green cover. Concordance, appendix, maps and diagrams. Available in English and Spanish. Send only $1. (W 1967, December 1: 736)

The production and publication of an original translation of the Bible allowed a deeper harmonization between the scriptures and the other Watch Tower Publications and provided a uniform basis for the Witnesses' interpretation of the scriptures (Blanchard 2008: 124–129). However, through its distinctive title, language, and format, the new translation also helped to materialize and make more visible the specificity of this interpretation by means of a recognizable artifact. In the 1960s, the Society's magazines and yearbooks reproduced numerous accounts that emphasize the success of the new Bible in the field ministry (e.g., W 1962, July 1: 414), while more recent articles romanticize the impact of the Witnesses carrying their "green Bibles" in various parts of the world (e.g., Yb 2001: 176).

After the first edition, the *New World Translation* underwent multiple revisions and was printed in different formats including several "deluxe editions" and an eighteen-volume English braille version (1983–1989). Furthermore, the *New World Translation* was disseminated in various media, including audio cassettes (1978–1990), diskettes, floppy disks (1992, 1994), MP3 files (2004), and DVDs (sign language, 2006). However, all these media were targeted toward specific groups and never had the same reach as the printed book, despite impressive production numbers. The printed page enjoyed an uncontested position of primacy in the personal and congregational biblical study of Jehovah's Witnesses (see Blanchard 2008: 131–140). For this reason, the ongoing process of digitalization in the Watch Tower Society already represents, in and of itself, a media revolution.

However, to fully grasp the magnitude of the transition to digital media, it is important to understand how the printed page is manipulated in practice. For this reason, and since I discussed the use of the magazines and other media in some detail in the previous chapters (see, in particular, Chapters 8 and 9), I will begin the next section by providing further information on the specific practices associated with the individual and collective reading of the Bible among Jehovah's Witnesses. I then will outline the process that led to the introduction of the revamped webpage, jw.org, and discuss its impact on the Witnesses' media habits.

11.4 Tell Me *How* You Read...

11.4.1 Individual and collective study of the Bible

In the theology of the Watch Tower Society, the 66 books of the canonical Protestant Bible represent the ultimate and authoritative reference for all aspects of religious life and everyday conduct. The Society does not claim to possess any special revelation and asserts the principle of *sola scriptura* (Jv 1993: 120). The Bible in its entirety is regarded as the infallible and inspired word of God. While its overriding theme is the coming of Jehovah's Kingdom, the Bible "reveals the past, explains the present, and foretells the future" (It-1 1988: 310). Accordingly, the Bible is considered historically accurate and in line with (and, indeed, a precursor of) the contemporary scientific knowledge of the world; yet its greater value is in the field of prophecy, as attested by a large number of events regarded as foretold by the scriptures. Finally, the Bible's teaching, examples, and doctrines are viewed as a source of practical counsel and guidance in the various domains of life as well as the reference to answer deep existential questions.

For all these reasons, Jehovah's Witnesses are constantly encouraged to include personal study of the Bible in their individual daily practice. To incentivize daily Bible study, the Society's *Yearbook* published, from its first issue in 1927 until 1985, a collection of "daily texts"—short Bible passages accompanied by a comment drawn from *The Watchtower* of the previous year. Since 1986, the daily texts have been published yearly in a separate book entitled *Examining the Scriptures Daily* (which is also featured prominently on the home screen of the *JW Library* app, see below).

Despite this insistence on daily personal Bible reading, within the Watch Tower Society the interpretation of the Bible is not a private matter. As one among many similar passages admonishes,

> The Scriptures warn against isolating ourselves. We should not think that we can figure out everything by independent research. Both personal study and regular attendance at the meetings of God's people are needed if we are to be balanced Christians. [...] [N]o one arrives at a correct understanding of Jehovah's purposes on his own. We all need the aid that Jehovah lovingly provides through his visible organization. (Wt 2002: 26–27)

Thus ultimate exegetical authority does not reside with the individual, but with the "faithful and discreet slave," an expression (based on the parable of the faithful servant) used today to designate the Society's Governing Body (Penton 2015: 233–240). The faithful slave conveys their insight through the Society's magazines, books, and other media. Thus, although Bible readings and the discussion of biblical passages are regular features of Jehovah's Witnesses' meetings, congregational study of the Bible is mostly mediated through various publications and prepared speeches.

The structure of a weekend meeting (Od 2015: 56–57), which includes a public Bible discourse and the study of a *Watchtower* article, provides a clear illustration of the publications' role in relation to the biblical exegesis. In principle, the Bible discourse is meant for the general public (that may include non-Witnesses) and touches upon various topics. It is held by one of the congregation's elders or by a guest speaker, such as a circuit overseer. Independently of the subject matter, the speaker usually constructs his argumentation by drawing on biblical passages. Thus, from time to time, he will mention a verse from the Bible and invite the congregants to look it up in their Bibles. The speaker will then repeat the passage to locate—saying, for instance, "That's Luke 21, verses 10 and 11"—and, after waiting two or three seconds, will start quoting from the scriptures. The members of the congregation are quick to find the right page and read along in their Bibles.

During the second part of the meeting, the *Watchtower* study takes the form of a question-and-answer discussion (see Chapter 8). However, this magazine, which deals more closely with doctrinal topics, frequently refers to biblical passages meant to support a particular argument—or to which, alternatively, the article provides an explicative comment. The article is read aloud from the platform. On most occasions, when a biblical passage is mentioned, a member of the congregation is invited to read it aloud using a microphone. The other members of the congregation usually follow along in their Bibles.

Finally, the Bible plays an important role in the Witnesses' house-to-house ministry. Directly quoting from the Bible is often recommended to demonstrate the scriptural foundation of the Society's teachings (e.g., Bt 2009: 134–135), answer existential questions (e.g., W 2014, August 15: 12–14), fend off criticism (e.g., Rs 1989; Cf 2007: 105), provide practical advice (e.g., Be 2001: 159), and address many other ends. Most importantly, however, Jehovah's Witnesses are meant to encourage others to read the Bible and deepen their understanding of the scriptures. To achieve this goal, they propose and are trained to conduct free home Bible study programs. As in the other settings discussed above, during such lessons, the scriptures are not read following the order of the books in the Bible, but are approached thematically by choosing selected passages to illustrate, argue, or challenge a particular subject or idea. In this context as well, access to the source material is mediated via various Watch Tower guidebooks.

As I suggested in the introduction to this chapter, the use of digital supports to read the Bible has increased rapidly over a period of just a few years. It is now time for a closer look at the process underpinning this transformation.

11.4.2 The transition to digital media

The exponential rise in the Watch Tower Society's use of digital media in recent years is associated closely with the launch of a completely refurbished version of its jw.org website in August 2012. Without going into too much detail, it is worth retracing the steps that led to what would be a major transformation in the Jehovah's Witnesses' media landscape. As I have dealt with this transition elsewhere (Krüger and Rota 2015; Rota 2018, forthcoming), here, I will limit myself to a summary of the milestones in this process.

As with many other religious groups, the Watch Tower Society launched its online presence a few years after the arrival of the World Wide Web in the early 1990s. However, the three domains registered between 1997 and 2001—watchtower.org, jw-media.org, and jw.org—did not reveal any clear strategic perspective on how to use the new medium. In contrast with this modest online presence, however, the Internet has been a recurrent topic of discussion in Watch Tower publications. Between 1995 and 2015, the term "Internet" appears 660 times in *Awake!* and 170 times in *The Watchtower*.

A quantitative and qualitative analysis of these mentions shows a process of "domestication" of the new medium (Campbell 2010) in line with the examples discussed in Chapter 9. Although many articles provide factual information on the World Wide Web and its relevance in various social domains, the Internet is often associated with several threats. For instance, 20 percent of the mentions in *Awake!* associate the net with the threat of "false friends," while in 16 percent of cases, the magazine alerts readers to the devastating effects of pornography on one's personal and family life. Violent content, addiction, and time loss are just some among the further insidious aspects of the online world. Similar warnings are issued in the pages of *The Watchtower*.

However, the analysis also shows a changing attitude toward the Internet. In the pages of *Awake!* only 12 percent of mentions of the Internet appear between 2011 and 2015. Similarly, the most vehement denunciations of online pornography and false friends in *The Watchtower* were issued in the first decade of the new millennium. This evolution can be interpreted as a sign of the progressive normalization of the Internet in the professional and private lives of most people by the end of the decade. For the Watch Tower Society as well, it was clear that the new medium had become an integral part of the everyday activities of its members, who nevertheless received clear instructions on its proper (that is, normatively expected) use.

In 2012 the three Internet domains owned by the Watch Tower Society were merged in a fully revamped jw.org website. This new online presence constitutes the paradigm of a domesticated Internet that can be put to good use for the Watch Tower Society. From the homepage, visitors can access an exhaustive "About us" section and a "Newsroom" section with information on the organization's worldwide activities and legal battles. Furthermore, a localization function allows users to find addresses of Kingdom Halls around the globe and request a free home Bible study. The magazines and a large number of books and brochures are available to download in various formats, along with a growing volume of multimedia content, including videos, animated features, illustrated Bible stories, dramatic Bible readings, and audio dramas. Since October 2014, the website also hosts a monthly TV program called *JW Broadcasting*. Nevertheless, the Bible remains the most prominently featured content. The first tab of the main navigation menu redirects the viewer to a series of biblical resources geared for families, teenagers, and children, while the first link on the homepage opens an online version of the study edition of the *New World Translation* of the Bible.

Shortly after the launch of the new website, the magazine *Our Kingdom Ministry* jubilantly announced the introduction of a modern and effective means to spread the Good News. It also drew attention to the availability of online content in about 400 languages—"more than any other Web site"—allowing it to "give a witness to 'all the nations'" (Km 2012, September: 3). However, missionary work was not the only purpose of the portal:

> Make Good Use of It: The redesigned jw.org Web site is not just for the purpose of witnessing to unbelievers. It has been designed for use by Jehovah's Witnesses too. If you have access to the Internet, we encourage you to get acquainted with jw.org. (Km 2012, September: 3)

Using the Internet for Jehovah's Witnesses' spiritual benefit is the major innovation of the Society's reimagined web presence. While the recommendation quoted above still relies on the initiative of individual Witnesses, after a short period, its use has been systematically integrated into the structures of both congregation meetings and individual praxis.

The first visible consequence of this change affected a core element in the media landscape of the Jehovah's Witnesses: the magazine *Awake!* and the public edition of *The Watchtower*. In 2013, the number of pages in each issue of these publications was halved, falling from 32 to 16.[3] This reduction was justified in part by the goal of producing the magazines in even more languages—the number of translations of *The Watchtower* went from 195 in December 2012 to 204 in January 2013. However, the new web platform also enabled the Society to move part of the content online.[4] It is less clear to what extent the website's launch can explain the decrease in the number of issues of both magazines published each year (see the note to the Primary Sources).

The availability of multimedia content on jw.org has also introduced a variety of new religious media into the weekly program of the Jehovah's Witnesses. Particularly with the introduction of the Christian Life and Ministry midweek meeting in 2016 (see Chapter 8), audio recordings, videos, animated content, and *JW Broadcasting* segments have become a recurrent feature of Witnesses' congregational life. Thus, projectors and, more recently, flat-screen TVs have become integral elements in Kingdom Halls, along with a Wi-Fi Internet connection. During the meetings, multimedia content is discussed in the same way as magazine articles and book chapters.

Finally, the Watch Tower Society took a further major step in the world of digital media through the introduction of an application for smartphones and tablet computers called *JW Library*.[5] The app—for iOS, Android, and Windows—was launched in October 2013 and provides online and offline access to a large and multilingual library of Watch Tower books, magazines and meeting workbooks, as well as, in recent versions, numerous audio recordings, videos, animations, and *JW Broadcasting* segments. The app also prominently features a digital version of both the *New World Translation of the Holy Scriptures* and the book *Examining the Scriptures Daily*. The Society promotes the use of the application in various ways. For instance, the article "Are You Using JW Library?" (Mwb 2016, May: 2) explains that "*JW Library* makes it very convenient to do personal study and follow along during congregation meetings. It is also useful for the ministry, especially when witnessing informally." Other publications encourage using it to show short videos when door-to-door preaching (Mwb 2016, June: 2).

Several of my interviewees attested to the Watch Tower Society's efforts to promote its new media among Jehovah's Witnesses. **Leonard**, for instance, concludes our conversation by stressing that when it comes to the media used by Jehovah's Witnesses, the website jw.org "is on everyone's lips right now [...] and there are campaigns especially designed to call attention to jw.org and to all the other things that come with it." For **Jörg**, the trend is clear: "Well, that's the future, and the Watch Tower Society builds on the Internet," he says, and then emphatically adds, "With every click, every day or every year, it's incredible what's going on, on jw.org."

Among my interviewees, this enthusiasm is widely shared. However, closer inspection of the religious use of electronic media among Swiss and German Jehovah's Witnesses reveals a more complex picture. In particular, it indicates that their assessment of new technologies, compared with "old" print media is dependent on the context of their use. This is particularly true for the use of digital versions of the Bible.

11.4.3 Religious media habits: Evidence from quantitative data

Evidence from the survey conducted in four Swiss congregations indicates the importance of various media in the lives of Jehovah's Witnesses.[6]

According to the declarations of the surveyed Jehovah's Witnesses, 94 percent read the Bible daily or several times a week. The Bible is also by far the most frequently consulted religious reference on a weekly basis. Furthermore, the traditional media that have shaped the history of the Watch Tower Society are still featured prominently in the religious media habits of the Swiss Witnesses. Among the men and women interviewed, more than 81 percent read religious books and magazines daily or several

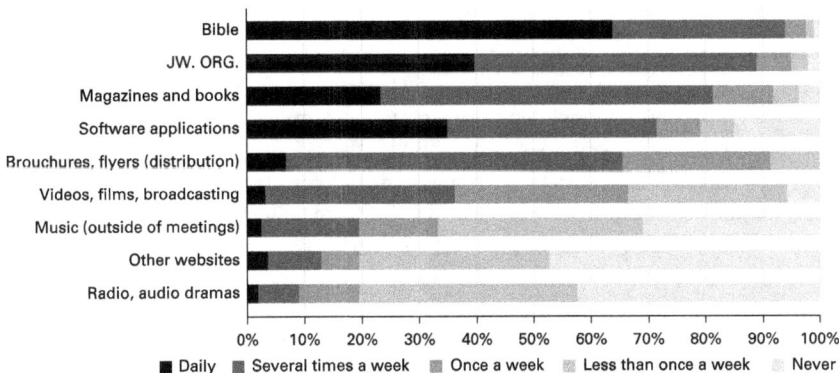

Figure 11.1 Frequency of Religious Media Use (N=183). © Andrea Rota.

times a week, while more than 91 percent distribute brochures or flyers at least once a week in contribution to their field ministry.

The survey data, however, also demonstrates the far-reaching effects of the Organization's recent digital turn for its members. The website jw.org is the second most frequently used medium in the above-mentioned list. Close to 90 percent of the Witnesses polled visit the website daily or several times a week, while other websites do not seem to play any relevant role in the religious lives of most. Tablet and smartphone apps are also part of the new media landscape of Jehovah's Witnesses, being used daily or several times a week by 71.5 percent of interviewees. Religious videos, films, and online television broadcasts are also watched, at least on a weekly basis, by 66.5 percent. The use of other media trails behind these figures.

This data, however, does not provide any information on the format in which magazines, books, and the Bible are read, nor on the settings in which various media are used. To fill this gap, my colleagues and I asked ten Jehovah's Witnesses (five men and five women) in four Swiss congregations and one German congregation to keep an eight-day media diary (Möhring and Schlütz 2010: 157–161; Naab 2013). These individuals were required to note precisely how much time they spent using various religious and "worldly" media.[7] Regarding their use of religious media, they were required to note the media and the formats they used, how much time they spent using each medium, and, if they were not alone, with whom they used each medium. The relatively low number of Witnesses surveyed invites cautious interpretation of the results. However, the analysis of the completed media diaries still provides interesting insights.

On average, the surveyed Jehovah's Witnesses spent about 840 minutes (fourteen hours) over a period of eight days using religious media, in large part within the congregational setting. While this is a considerable amount of time, it is worth noting that the same individuals spent, on average, a little less than 36 hours over the same period using worldly media. As for the type of media used as part of one's religious life, about 72 percent are electronic media and 28 percent are print media. This result deserves closer scrutiny. Figure 11.2 shows the average use of all religious media mentioned by more than three people.

The diaries indicate that, among all religious publications, the Bible is the one that is read the most, with an average of about four hours over an eight-day period. The scriptures are followed by the Watch Tower magazines, workbooks, and flyers, with an average use of roughly two hours and 45 minutes over the same period.[8] Across all religious publications available in print or electronic form, the use of electronic formats is clearly prevalent, although only one participant exclusively uses the electronic versions of the magazines, books, and the Bible. The switch to electronic format is the most widespread with respect to the magazines. When it comes to the Bible, most participants use it both in electronic and print form. While no one reads the Bible exclusively in print anymore, two participants study the scriptures only in electronic form. Among the purely electronic media, the website jw.org is the one utilized most often. On average, the participants spent two hours and fifteen minutes on the website over an eight-day period. The only medium not produced by the Watch Tower Society that is mentioned in at least three diaries is WhatsApp. The primary religious use of the popular messaging application is the planning of the field ministry.

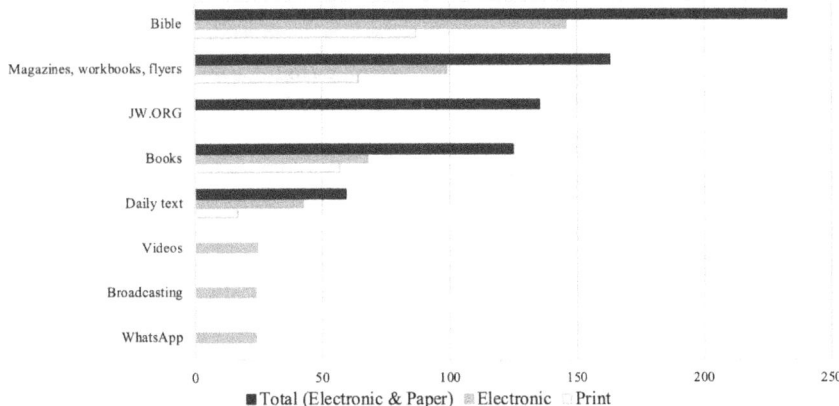

Figure 11.2 Average Religious Use of Media (in minutes over eight days; N=10). © Andrea Rota.

These results demonstrate, once again, the rapid and sweeping adoption of new media technologies for religious purposes among Jehovah's Witnesses. Nevertheless, every process of adoption (or rejection) is always an interpretative process. This can be illuminated by the statements collected during the interviews. In the following analysis, I will first focus on different contexts in which Jehovah's Witnesses use Watch Tower media, and then draw attention to the ways in which my interviewees perceive the Bible.

11.4.4 Transitioning to electronic media in the field ministry and congregational life

As the history of the Watch Tower Society demonstrates, media innovation has always played an important role in the life of Jehovah's Witnesses, in particular when it comes to their door-to-door ministry (see Chapter 9). Therefore, it is not surprising that the encouragement to use the website jw.org in the field ministry alongside videos and other multimedia content did not cause any major concern. In fact, my interviewees welcome new media as useful new instruments to spread the Good News of the Kingdom. In this regard, **Sofia** observes that in recent years, people are increasingly stressed and have less time for discussion. Preaching strategies have therefore had to be adapted. As she puts it, "[T]oday, no one simply reads a book. But a flyer? Definitely yes. And today, perhaps one doesn't even read a flyer. But a website? Definitely yes. Media habits have changed overall. That's something that we perceive, too."

Other Witnesses emphasize that the new media technologies allow them to overcome barriers in their preaching, particularly when meeting people who speak a foreign language. For instance, the website makes it easy to provide articles in a foreign language to someone without having to place an extra order with the congregation. As **Eric** states,

Say I meet someone who speaks Portuguese, and he is interested in an article [and asks], "Do you have it in Portuguese?" Previously, I would have said, "I will order it," and it was a huge logistical effort. And today, I go to the website in Portuguese, I print it out, I staple it together, and I say, "There it is." **(Eric)**

In addition to the advantages of digital media, this example also provides an indirect indication of the perceived limits of digital media and suggests that paper still plays a major role in the field service. In fact, several of my interviewees consider that leaving something to read with the people they meet is an integral part of their ministry that cannot be replaced by electronic media. **Valentin** underscores this idea with a touch of humor: "If you go and meet new people," he says, "you often bring printed magazines so that you can offer them to people. You cannot leave them the iPad."

The use of electronic media in the context of congregation meetings and for personal study reveals further aspects of this transitional phase. In fact, the interviews suggest that electronic media are integrated in different cross-media habits, and the use of a device such as a tablet often rests on pragmatic grounds. Among other reasons, my interviewees underscore the capacity of electronic media conveniently to store several publications. This allows them to carry books and magazines with great ease to the Kingdom Hall or to save space at home, where old issues of the magazines may otherwise accumulate. Many also appreciate the possibility of listening to articles and chapters while jogging, completing the household chores or during a moment of relaxation. Several Witnesses also note that the electronic media are tailored to fit the structure of the congregation meetings and make it easier to follow the activities by clicking on the hyperlinks.

Nevertheless, some of my interviewees remain attached to the printed material. This choice is related to deep-rooted media habits. Among others, **Leonard**, who, out of convenience, usually brings his tablet to the Kingdom Hall, notes that at a recent congregation meeting he had a printed *Watchtower*, because he actually prefers to scribble down quick notes in the margins rather than clicking around on the tablet. **Emma** describes the familiarity of handling the magazines as follows:

Personally, I have to say, I remain old school. I was always a bookworm. I must have the pages in my hand, and to prepare for a meeting, I have to write down my notes and use my colors [to highlight]. Of course, I also use the other one [the tablet]. In the field ministry, if a family has a child, you show a three- or four-minute video. [...] But personally, I still need the paper. [...] But we can choose. **(Emma)**

Anna also describes herself as "old school" in relation to media and does not like to "go around looking for things" on a tablet. By contrast, her whole family prefers the new technologies and would never go back to the printed publications. In this respect, she comments, "It's okay. Everyone should decide whether that's something for them or not." Finally, for **Paul**, the preference for paper is a health issue, because the screen is not good for his eyes: "My wife has the magazines on the iPad, and she makes her notes there," he says, "[but] I prefer not to look at a screen the whole day. But it's a question of taste."

In sum, the preference for one medium or another appears to depend on habits, context, and convenience. As long as there is a choice among options, the criticism of the new technologies seems to be limited. The few critical comments that I was able to record were always in the form of second-hand reports. For example, **Valentin** relates having heard that some people do not really like the interactive component with videos and pictures and would prefer the classic study of *The Watchtower*. "But," he adds, "It's quite rare, I have to say. The majority is excited for the new media." Does this assessment extend to digital versions of the Bible?

11.4.5 The feeling of the Bible

Regular reading of the Bible is a media habit common to all my interviewees. As it is the case for the Watch Tower publications, the choice of physical format varies across interviewees and often depends on the situation; considerations regarding the usability and portability of electronic media also play a role. However, in comparison to the other media discussed thus far, many of my interviewees express a preference for the printed book, which is not directly based on its practical functionality. This preference is sometimes associated with a vague feeling of "bookishness" or "Bibleness."

For **Emma,** this feeling is difficult to describe; she states that it is a type of warmth, but she could not really put the idea into words. Laughing, she exclaims, "Ah! I don't know. I cannot imagine Jehovah with a tablet. I want a Bible in the hand." Attempting to articulate a similar feeling, **Richard** recalls someone saying that one of the worst possible things in the world is a book burning, because "you burn the soul with the book," whereas you can simply delete digital information. There is a physical aspect of books that is important to him, which is why he prefers to take the print Bible with him to congregation meetings. He says:

> You know, I prefer to read the Bible when I have it in front of me. It is hard to describe [laughs]. One gets the feeling that the one is alive and the other [the electronic medium] is dead. You know? One medium is alive. You browse it. It's just a feeling, but that's how I feel. (**Richard**)

For many of my interviewees, this feeling is also related to visual habits connected to the print Bible. **Olga**, who is particularly thoughtful about this, states,

> When I go from home to home, I prefer to use the Bible as a book because with the book, I remember, "Oh, wait, there is something about that in that book down left [on the page]. Let me have a quick look." That's something that you don't have in the electronic version. You don't have this visual memory. For this reason, I find the traditional way better. [...] But, in fact, I often use the electronic version. Actually, too often. It's good that we talked about that. I should use it [the printed book] more often [laughs]. (**Olga**)

Olga's realization in the second part of the quote reveals yet another aspect associated with the use of the print Bible. As **Olga** implicitly suggests, the capacity to find a passage in the Bible quickly requires a certain degree of skill that the use of electronic media could compromise. Many of my interviewees are concerned about this issue. **Eric** addresses this point explicitly:

> What I want to maintain is my dexterity with the Bible. And that it is something you have to take care of because if you are always [gestures as if typing on a virtual keyboard], at some point you lose the feeling, I think. And then I'm looking for a way that is right for me [...]. I mean, I always have the Bible with me at the meetings so that during the presentation, I can look things up. It has better haptics. (**Eric**)

For **Sofia**, this issue affects her choices in the education of her eight-year-old and 14-year-old children, who are not yet allowed to read the Bible on a tablet at congregation meetings: "I believe that the learning effect lasts longer if my hands are occupied with the information." She explains, "The brain needs dimensions to grasp something, and to know whether a book of the Bible is at the end or at the beginning is a part of that." However, it is **Leonard** who uses most expressive formulation to convey this point:

> This is my personal opinion. It's something of a pity. Now, *The Watchtower* and *Awake!*, that's okay. There is no problem, you can have them electronically. But the feeling of the Bible, and to have it in your hand, and to open it, and do so rapidly. You don't want to unlearn that. You unlearn it if you always click on the Psalms on the tablet and there it is, [Psalm] 73. Afterward, you know, of course, that the book of Psalms is somewhere in the middle [of the Bible], but you have to search far longer for it. I notice myself that if for a week or two I only use the tablet, then it gets harder physically to use the Bible. You simply unlearn quickly. And I find it a pity when it comes to the Bible. (**Leonard**)

This quotation provides a good summary of several key aspects. First, **Leonard** prefaces his statement as a personal opinion connected to his experiences and preferences. I would argue that this preface can be extended to the quotes from my other interviewees regarding the Bible. Second, he distinguishes between the Bible and the magazines, noting the specific character of the former. Third, he associates this specificity with both a feeling and a specific skill that he considers valuable. Lastly, he reflects that electronic media place the perpetuation of this skill at risk and considers this to be a negative result of their introduction.

Yet the material aspect of the print Bible and the feelings associated with its physical features reportedly have practical consequences beyond the individual choice of which format to use to read the scriptures. In particular, many of my interviewees stress the particular efficacy of the book during their missionary work. **Eva**, who regularly uses her tablet to show the Society's video clips, insists that she does not want to discontinue using the print Bible in her ministry because "it is the book that the people immediately recognize as the Bible." In particular, among older people, she assumes "it might not be that well-received if I read a Bible passage aloud using a tablet." **Gertrud** also concedes that she could show the scriptures on a tablet but does not want to because "the Bible is an authority." This point is assertively conveyed by **Jörg** as well:

> I would never go from house to house and read a Bible passage from the iPad. I go from home to home and I have the Bible with me and I open it, and I say, "There it is, read it with me." [...] It makes a stronger impression if one has a Bible in hand rather than only such a flat thing, an iPad, even though I am quite at ease with the iPad. [...] But no. [...] For us, the Bible is like a sword. A weapon. And we use it to convey the truth. And if we do not use it, if it is an iPad, that goes against the grain. (**Jörg**)

Jörg underscores a demonstrative aspect of the print Bible, which projects an authority and a dignity that a tablet would not and could not have.

For the same reason, **Jörg** also refrains from using a tablet to read the Bible from the platform, although for any other aspect of the congregation meetings, he reads the scriptures on his iPad. Several of my interviewees draw the same distinction. They often ascribe this attitude to the unreliable nature of electronic devices, such as their battery life. **Richard**, for instance, expresses concern that he might be logged out from his tablet during a speech. In a telling statement, however, **Fritz**, comes back to the special status of the printed book. He states:

> For about a year, I have only used a tablet for congregation meetings. When I have a task on the platform, however, I still prefer to take the [print] Bible in the hand. [I do it] because it conveys, well, warmth, when you have a book in your hand instead of a tablet. [...] I notice the difference with the tablet in the congregation. For me, it is way more sterile, so to speak. When I go to the platform and have a task, I have the feeling you convey more warmth when you have a book in your hand. [...] On the other side, with a tablet one can find information faster. Or quickly look something up. (**Fritz**)

This quotation provides another good summary of some important ideas. First, it underscores that the status of the print Bible is something that my interviewees are not completely able to rationalize and which they therefore express through the semantics of feelings. Second, it highlights a recurrent association between the form and the content of the Bible in which the authority, truth, etc. of the content is considered to be manifested in and through the physical format. Finally, it indicates that the specific status of the printed book remains situational and varies according to context. The above-mentioned association is decidedly more prominent in public or liturgical settings, while it is of secondary importance for personal study or participation in congregation meetings.

After reviewing so much empirical data, it is time to come back to an analytical perspective. To do so, in the next section, I will start with a provisional appraisal of my findings so far. Using an approach similar to that used in preceding chapters, I then will introduce a contrasting empirical case that challenges this appraisal, thereby setting the groundwork for my theoretical discussion.

11.5 Shared Aesthetics and Collective Expectations

11.5.1 A provisional appraisal

In the first part of this chapter, I discussed Birgit Meyer's idea of religion as mediation. Without repeating my critique here, it can be argued that, following her approach, four steps are required to articulate the relationship between aesthetic experiences and religious collectivity. First, in defining religion, Meyer assumes that religion is predicated on the need to mediate between a postulated transcendental reality and the immanent world. Second, she clarifies that legitimate forms of mediation must be authorized, or fixed, in what she refers to as sensational forms. Third, she states that shared sensational forms produce a shared aesthetic and induce a shared sensory mode. Fourth, she equates a community—or aesthetic formation—to a group of people sharing a sensory mode. I take this to mean that an aesthetic formation comprises several people, each with the same (or at least a highly similar) aesthetic experience.

Importantly, the topic of "community" appears twice in Meyer's approach. The first time occurs in her second point, when she defines sensational forms as "relatively fixed, authorized modes of invoking and organizing access to the transcendental, thereby creating and sustaining links between religious practitioners in the context of particular religious organizations" (Meyer 2006b: 9). A second reference to "community" appears in her fourth point, in which she introduces the concept of aesthetic formation. As I understand her argument, a sensational form is a stepping-stone toward the constitution of an aesthetic formation. Therefore, it is at the level of the "shared sensory modes" that one would find the ultimate constitutive element of a religious collective. In the following discussion, I will turn her argument upside-down and argue that the idea behind the notion of aesthetic formation is fundamentally a summative one, which leads to a weaker form of "togetherness," whereas the concept of sensational form can be brought in line with a stronger conception of a *collective* aesthetic of religion.

To do so, I will proceed as follows. After a short review of the empirical evidence collected so far, I will introduce a contrasting case that calls into question what can be regarded as *prima facie* arguments in favor of Meyer's approach. Then, to provide theoretical support for my alternative view, I will introduce and discuss the distinction between plain and normative expectation. Applying this distinction, I will finally come back to my empirical material and draw my conclusion.

In the second, empirical part of this chapter, I have presented a historical overview of the Watch Tower Society's relationship with print media, and I have called attention to the centralization of all aspects of the Society's media production, including the production and binding of various Bibles and the realization of a distinctive translation of the scriptures. Throughout the twentieth and twenty-first centuries, the Watch Tower Society has produced and distributed Bibles on various media. Nevertheless, the print Bible remained the main reference for ordinary Jehovah's Witnesses. Based on this analysis, I have argued that the transition to digital media represents a major transformation in their media landscape—more so than the introduction of other media for missionary purposes as discussed in Chapter 9.

Evidence from quantitative and qualitative data suggests that the religious use of digital media is now an integral part of the media habits of most Jehovah's Witnesses. Most Swiss and German Jehovah's Witnesses greeted the shift toward digital media with openness and even enthusiasm, appreciating the possibility of freely choosing among different media formats for their study, preaching, and participation within the congregation. However, the switch to digital versions of the Bible is proving more challenging than the introduction of the magazines in an electronic format. While the use of electronic magazines and books is mostly dictated by pragmatic considerations, several interviewees described the special status they attribute to the print Bible. In particular, the use of the printed book is associated with specific feelings, reading habits, and skills considered valuable in their own right.

Indeed, the recurring reference to a "feeling of the Bible" appears to fit an analysis in line with Birgit's Meyer approach. For this reason, it is now particularly interesting to discuss a case in which a specific choice regarding preferred media elicited discord within a congregation. I call the following example "the case of Frank," even though, as I will illustrate, **Frank**'s predicament was probably not an isolated incident.

11.5.2 Dealing with technological change: The case of Frank

Forty-year-old **Frank** was among the early users of a tablet computer in his congregation and recalls that initially, the new device raised some eyebrows: "It was slightly complicated," he says with a laugh. "It was even very complicated." According to **Frank**, for the congregants, the tablet was unusual. "They could not make sense of it." Older Witnesses in particular, who were displeased by what they regarded as an expression of materialism, repeatedly tapped him on the shoulder during the congregation meetings, and made "stupid comments." **Frank** recounts,

> A comment, for instance, was, "Naa, that's no Bible. You must hold a Bible in your hand." So, I said, "Well, I'm not reading the newspaper [...]. In my Bible, there are the same words as in yours." I mean, it is from the same Society, that is, from jw.org. [...] And it was not just one [person]. And every time, the arguments were the same. Just because it is an electronic medium, they forgot that the book that is in an electronic form is the same. Others were less critical. They simply said that they worked for so long with the printed book that they cannot imagine doing anything else than browsing it and quickly opening it [at the right place]. But as one can see here [on the tablet], after all, it works quite efficiently [laughs]. (**Frank**)

Continuing his account, **Frank** plays down these episodes and indicates that this attitude was not generalized: "It was just a couple of people. But to hurt someone, one nail is enough." In the meanwhile, he concludes laughing, "[T]he majority of the congregation has an iPad."

The statements of other interviewees confirm that the reaction experienced by **Frank** was not an isolated episode. **Richard** also mentions the comments from some older members of his congregation regarding the use of mobile devices at the Kingdom Hall. He explains:

> Sometimes, there are people who have very closed minds and who did not consider it as a good Christian instrument. And when there is an older member in a congregation, or two or three, who still have this frame of mind, then they can make an impact. They can say [whispering], "That's not right; that's not good." Then it can be that a congregation does not accept it [the new instrument]. **(Richard)**

Nevertheless, **Richard** also notes that, as with other technological innovations, it is often simply a matter of time before people notice that these new devices are "something cool."

In a similar vein, **Jörg** notes that the use of tablets from the platform conflicted with long-held expectations:

> You can imagine. When for one hundred years, you are used to going to the platform with the Bible, and suddenly someone comes with a thing that you only have to click on. That is a big deal. What they [the people using the tablet] said was also good, it was also from the Bible, but they did not have it in their hands. **(Jörg)**

The matter was serious enough for the Watch Tower Society to send an official note regarding the use of electronic tablets to all congregations, asking the elders to read it from the platform. As **Jörg** recalls,

> That [the use of tablets] was a talking point that was addressed officially from the platform: "Hey, if someone comes forward [to talk from the platform] with an iPad, that is just how it is, you have to accept it. Because it was a little frowned upon, you know? When you spoke from the stage to the brothers, you used to simply have the Bible in your hand or some documents. And then the Society sent a letter specifically to say that if someone comes forward with an iPad or another electronic device, that it is fine. It is completely accepted now, completely accepted. **(Jörg)**

The letter in question, a leaked copy of which can easily be found on the Internet, notes that electronic devices have become increasingly common and that the Governing Body leaves the use of such devices from the platform to the individual discretion of each participant. Furthermore, the letter states that the use of tablets is not a matter for which elders must establish a rule, as long as the devices do not distract the audience, such as through notification sounds.

Let us summarize the main points of these views. My interviewees report negative reactions to the early use of tablet computers within the congregation. These reactions are often ascribed to older people and involve the use of a digital version of the Bible.

In particular, when the Bible was used to address the audience from the platform, that is, when it is visible and publicly displayed as a source of authority, the fact of reading it from a tablet was criticized as inappropriate. Behind the criticism, we again find the association between the medium and its content. This equivalence appears to be widespread. However, it is not universally upheld, as the rebuttal made by **Frank** above demonstrates. In it, **Frank** explicitly argues for a distinction between medium and content. Furthermore, my interviewees attribute the skepticism to the force of habit—a point emphasized by the emphasis placed on the complainants' age or stubbornness. They also note that the unfavorable judgments were expressed by a small minority, although some people could constitute influential "pockets of resistance" within a congregation. Their opinion, however, did not reflect any collectively accepted position. In fact, the official response of the Watch Tower Society indicated that the organization's position in the matter was collective toleration and individual autonomy.

How can we account for this case in theoretical terms? And what does it teach us on the topic of collective aesthetics and on the role of collective aesthetics in the constitution of a religious community?

11.5.3 Plain and normative expectations

My argument draws on the special status ascribed to the "Holy Book" and the reprimanding of the early digital Bible readers. Let us consider the first aspect. The widespread appreciation for the print Bible among my interviewees can be considered an indication of a shared aesthetic experience related to the use of the book and to its perceived authority—something that we may indeed regard as an aesthetic formation. However, it is important to note that when they were prompted to explain the "special feeling" of the Bible, my interviewees referred to their personal reading habits and experiences (as *potentially* distinct from those of other Witnesses). In this sense, it seems fair to say that *each of them* has a similar aesthetic relationship with the book.

As I have discussed at length in the first part of this study, and as I have shown in other chapters, the presence of analogous personal intentions provides a criterion that is too weak to speak of a *collective* intention—in this case, a collective aesthetic experience. One of the reasons is that the people in any random group could each have an aesthetic relationship of this kind with the Bible. Indeed, as demonstrated by the aforementioned studies by Tim Hutchings (2014, 2015a) and Katja Rakow (2017), this type of aesthetic evaluation can be found in a sample of Bible readers from various denominations and backgrounds, without these readers constituting a group in any intuitive sense. Furthermore, not all my interviewees seem to share this aesthetic appreciation to the same degree. This brings me to the second aspect: the reprimand.

The "case of **Frank**" is interesting for several reasons. As one of the first users of a digital Bible in his congregation, he faced scorn from some of his co-religionists. However, the fact that the disapproving voices were isolated suggests that **Frank** was not violating a clearly sanctioned order. Indeed, when commenting on similar cases, other interviewees do not mention any specific "authorized modes" of reading the Bible as explanations for such a disapproval, but rather invoke force of habit among older Jehovah's Witnesses. In this sense, it does not seem that **Frank** was reprimanded "in the name of the group." Moreover, **Frank**'s account conveys his surprise when faced with a rebuke. This is in sharp contrast with the accounts discussed in Chapter 9 (the "violent TV series" case), in which my interviewees actually assumed that their behavior, should it become public, would be reprimanded. What is the difference between these two cases? An answer to this complex question can be sketched by distinguishing between different reasons for expecting certain behaviors during an interaction and different legitimations for someone's right to rebuke another person. These questions are highly controversial among philosophers in the field of collective intentionality. However, once again, I will side with Gilbert, because her approach provides useful tools to advance our discussion.

When we say that we expect someone to do something, we can mean different things. When I say, for instance, that I expect my friends Anja and Till to arrive later at our dinner party tonight because they always do, I am making a statement about what is likely to happen in the future based on past instances of a similar conduct. But when I say that I expect you to be politer with me tomorrow, I may imply more than a simple prediction. Indeed, I probably intend to put a constraint on your behavior or to assert that I believe that you *ought* to behave in a certain way. Gilbert (1989: 347) refers to the kind of expectations that only entail regularity in behavior as *plain* expectations, and we may refer to the other kind as *normative* expectations.

Gilbert introduces this distinction in her discussion of the concept of "social convention" in which she critically discusses David Lewis' (1969) theory of conventions (Gilbert 1989: chap. 6; 1996e, 2014g). David Lewis's account of conventions is based on the individualistic analysis of personal inclinations within the framework of game theory. In a nutshell, Lewis considers conventions to be solutions to coordination problems where there is no clear preferred outcome at the onset and where the parties, through repetition, come to adopt a regular behavior that they expect—in the plain sense—all other parties to adopt and that they consider the preferred behavior on the condition that all other parties also regularly conform to it (see Gilbert 1996e: 63–68; 2014g: 211–212).

Gilbert pokes several holes in Lewis's theory. Most importantly, she notes that "the mere claim [...] that there is a commonly known, generalized plain expectation that people will do their parts in a certain practice does not seem to capture that aspect of social conventions which makes a social convention a 'moving force'" (Gilbert 1996e: 77). Intuitively, a convention exerts pressure on the parties, which might be regarded as an intrinsic motivation to conform to the convention. Gilbert provides the following general account of this idea:

> If one party fails to conform to a given convention, this offends against the other parties, as such. They are then in a position to rebuke him for this failure, and may appropriately cite the fact that their group has the convention as a complete justification for their rebukes. (Gilbert 2014g: 210)

The question, then, is whether generalized plain explanations provide sufficient justification for the sense of "offense" that one intuitively experiences when someone in a group violates a convention. Gilbert's answer is negative. Assuming that no other condition is introduced, consider the following case: Each morning, I prepare a cup of coffee for my wife before leaving home for work, and she now has a plain expectation in this respect. One morning, I am particularly late, and I do not have the time to prepare her coffee. Intuitively, my wife may reasonably be surprised or disappointed and might even estimate that I have behaved badly, but she does not seem to have any grounds to rebuke me. By contrast, if my wife and I were jointly committed to have breakfast together as our "morning ritual," she may rightfully require an explanation as to why my being late should free me from this convention.

In the real-world case of **Frank** that I discussed above, his detractors in the congregation appear to express their surprise and disappointment after their plain expectations regarding their preferred way of reading and using the Bible are not met. **Frank's** surprise, in turn, would express the reaction of someone who feels unjustly rebuked. This example also provides a telling, although perhaps unexpected, indication of what I would call a collective aesthetic in a strong sense. In such a case, we would expect to find an indication of a collective or joint commitment to experiencing, say, the touch and sight of the Bible in a certain way. Or, to be more precise, to behaving publicly in a way that would not contradict the fact of the group having such an aesthetic experience—independently of whether the individual members personally have it. In this framework, deviant behavior would be rebuked for collectively accepted *normative* reasons and in the name of the "we" that collectively perceives the Bible a certain way.

It is possible to argue that such a collective aesthetic with respect to the Bible's materiality was instituted by the letter sent by the Governing Body. With its recommendation, the collectively accepted source of authority among Jehovah's Witnesses introduced a convention that clearly entails a normative dimension, although this normative dimension is framed in terms of tolerance for different preferences. In the case of many Witnesses, personal preferences regarding how to read and use the Bible have not changed, to which many examples quoted in the previous section attest. Furthermore, their inferences regarding the Bible's status based on their aesthetic experiences with the book also remained unaltered. However, the letter made it clear that the congregation should not have any expectation (plain or normative) regarding the medium that each member adopts to read or otherwise use the Bible, including during congregation meetings or when speaking from the platform. Thus, I argue that the Jehovah's Witnesses *as a collective* (in the strong, non-summative sense) do not have a *specific* but rather a multifaceted collective aesthetic regarding the Bible, even though most Witnesses individually share a similar aesthetic relationship to the Bible—or, to be more precise, since their phenomenological experiences remain opaque to the social sciences, express their aesthetic experiences in a similar way.

If, after the collective acceptance of the letter's content, other congregation members were to openly denounce **Frank** for using a tablet to read the Bible, he, as well as all other members of the congregation, would have a right, and even a duty, to rebuke his critics. This observation opens a path for reformulating Meyer's concept of sensational form. I would argue that a collectively (Tuomela) or jointly accepted (Gilbert) sensational form provides a sufficient foundation for a *collective* aesthetic that creates and sustains links between religious practitioners and thereby establishes them as a religious collectivity, without the need to postulate any further power of sensational forms to induce personal aesthetic experiences.

11.6 Conclusion

The empirical results in this chapter appear less clear-cut than those of other chapters. Coupled with theoretical reflections, they allow us nevertheless to draw some relevant conclusion for the field of the aesthetics of religion and, more specifically, with regard to the idea of collective aesthetic experiences in a religious setting. In recent years, concern with the aesthetics of religion has allowed the scientific study of religion to redress a number of biases inherited from its Protestant roots that had made it harder to conceive of artifacts and media as relevant research objects. Furthermore, by stressing the social and bodily production of "the sacred," and, thus, the humanly constructed character of religion, the aesthetic approach may, as Christoph Uehlinger (2015: 405) notes, "shield off the critical study of religion against potential phenomenological inclinations."

Still, I would argue that despite its innovative insights, the aesthetics of religion, at least in the form advocated by Birgit Meyer and other scholars, has not yet completely severed its ties with the old paradigm in the study of religion. Rather, it still finds itself in a transitional phase in a way that may remind us of Jacques Waardenburg's (1978) "new style phenomenology." In his attempt to nudge the study of religion away from the classical phenomenological approach, Waardenburg (2017: 4) openly warned scholars that the "hang towards 'reification' tends to make us think that, when we speak of religions or religion, we have to do with things in themselves; whereas these 'things' really are our images and ideas." Against this backdrop, he insisted on the importance of studying religion on the basis of empirical data collected through the methods of the historical, social, and cultural sciences (see Waardenburg 1993). However, Waardenburg was not yet ready to abandon the category of experience. Waardenburg (1979: 448) argued that "religion is bound to empirical realities, but sees these realities as transparent in view of certain significations that are assumed to have an absolute origin or to be 'revealed.'" Thus, Waardenburg, drawing on Husserl, sought to reconstruct the intentionality and subjective meaning beyond the religious expressions, which remained for him at the core of religion.

Most contemporary approaches to the aesthetics of religion no longer seek to grasp the individual aesthetic experience, but, just like Waardenburg, still identify that (socially produced) individual experience as the marker of religion. One may even argue that while the object of study of these approaches is the public side of religion, it is still the private, inaccessible side that constitutes the "endpoint" of religion. From this framework, it follows that an account of *collective* aesthetic experiences is inevitably an aggregative one: it is not the social production of the experience that defines its collective nature, but the sum of individual experiences of the group members.

The approach that I have put forward in this chapter draws on the work of Margaret Gilbert to redefine the idea of a collective aesthetic experience as an intentional attitude held by a plural subject rather than by its individual members. In this respect, all that counts for the researcher—but, indeed, also for the religious actors—is the observation of a collective normative adherence to a certain public display that conforms with the aesthetic experience that the religious actors are jointly committed to uphold. This perspective entails renouncing any reference to direct personal experiences in the conceptualization of religion, at least in its collective form.

12

Conclusion

The aim of this book was twofold: to provide a new way to conceptualize collective religious agents, drawing on the insights of the philosophical debate on collective intentionality, and to develop and implement a strategy to make these philosophical ideas fruitful for the analysis of empirical data. Overall, I wanted to demonstrate the value of a philosophical approach for the study of religion, and the relevance of empirical inquiry as an outlook for the philosophy of religion. Without forcing the reader to go through all the details of my argumentation, I want to use these last pages to summarize and discuss some of my main ideas and address some open questions.

12.1 Conceptualizing Religious Collectivity Anew

Against the backdrop of an increasing empirical and theoretical interest in individualized forms of religiosity, in this study I wanted to find new philosophical resources to discuss the actions, beliefs, emotions and aesthetic experiences of religious collectives. My aim has been to conceptualize collective religious actors in a way that would not reduce them to the sum of their members' personal attitudes, nor reify their collective nature as a distinct metaphysical reality. Altogether, I have suggested employing the instruments of collective intentionality to clarify when it is possible to say that a group, a "we," has an intention, as opposed to a collection of people individually having that intention—and what the difference between these two entails. It is not my intention to recapitulate here the various positions developed by the philosophers discussed in this study. However, I want to call attention to the concrete way in which their ideas have been brought into play in my analysis.

In practice, my strategy has been multilayered and selective. Selective, because in the vast and complex debate on collective intentions, I had to identify and sort out those concepts and arguments that promised the greatest heuristic value for my project, and recast them in a way that may prove useful to scholars of religion and other social scientists. This led me, in the first part, to favor a non-reductivist approach to the conceptualization of collective intentionality. My strategy has been multilayered, as the effective deployment of such philosophical resources in the second part of my study required me to attach them to a broader analytical framework, one that included a number of ideas which, while related to the field of collective intentionality, do not directly derive from it. Thus, in my analysis, the full potential of a collective intentionality approach is unlocked in three incremental steps that can be summarized as follows.

In my argumentation, I have pushed back against the idea of a community as a given "state of nature," as something pristine. Likewise, I have opposed a concept of "religious group" that merely relies on the subjective imaginings and feelings of (more or less isolated) individuals. In my opinion, there is an important heuristic value in regarding a religious collectivity as an epistemically objective social fact (see Searle 2010: 17–18) that is dynamically constructed through human interaction. To grasp this reality "in the making," I have put forward a performative approach inspired by Rappaport's (1979) theory of ritual. While the contours of the concept of performativity are not sharp (see Austin 1962; Searle 1968), this notion has the advantage of calling attention to the generative power of communicative exchanges, in particular to their ability to produce and reproduce (inter)personal commitments. This idea, however, needed some refinement, in particular with respect to the nature and form of such commitments and the underlying dispositions of the agents entering into them.

In Chapter 8, Searle's (2001) work on the relationship between speech acts and rationality constituted a stepping stone to advance my reflection on these matters. His emphasis on the capacity of speech acts to create desire-independent reasons for actions, which function as normative motivational sources for the individual, allowed me to introduce a theory of commitment that preserves the rationality of the agents without casting them as mere calculating *homines economici*. My appeal to rational agents is not motivated by moral or anthropological reasons—I do not believe that humans, individually or in groups, always act rationally. (In fact, the idea of people behaving rationally only makes sense if we accept the possibility that they may also act irrationally.) However, the presupposition of the agents' rationality constitutes a fundamental methodological requirement if one seeks to make sense of their intentional behavior (see, e.g., Barker 1984; Smith 1982b; Lincoln 2003).

Unfortunately, Searle does not directly draw on these insights in his theory of collective intentionality, which remains, in many aspects, underdeveloped. However, other philosophers working in this field have introduced more sophisticated frameworks, which transpose similar—although not identical—reflections on normativity to the case of group agents. For all practical purposes, the discussion of Searle's position has helped me to integrate into my analysis the work of Raimo Tuomela and Margaret Gilbert. Despite important differences in their philosophical positions, both of these authors regard the creation and perpetuation of a collective or joint commitment among a group of agents as an integral element of collective intentionality. This kind of commitment differs from the personal commitments of individual agents in several ways. In particular, once it has been (collectively) created, such a commitment binds each participant in a way that none of them can rescind unilaterally. Thus, the parties in a collective intention have a reason to expect (in a normative and not merely predictive sense) a certain form of behavior from each other. Likewise, they have a justification to rebuke—but also, under certain circumstances, a duty to help—those who do not act conformingly. Furthermore, on Tuomela's and Gilbert's accounts, a collective intention provides the participants with collective reason for action that can—*but need not*—overlap with their personal intentions.

The theoretical outcome of my analysis is a concept of religious collectivity that differs from several other attempts at formulating the collective dimension of religious actions, beliefs, emotions, and aesthetic experiences. As I have spelled out in the second part of this book, most approaches to these issues focus on the personal intentions (beliefs, emotions, etc.) of the individual members of a group and gravitate toward a summative account of such a group. Roughly speaking, they tend to define what is collective based on what is similarly shared by each individual *personally*. Indeed, this is probably the most intuitive understanding of what a group is. Scholars have also noted that extending a belief from an individual to an entire group (or culture) that the individual personally identifies with (or is externally associated with) is a common cognitive process (e.g., Sperber 1997; Boyer 2013; see Bae 2016). What is more, this is also the way individuals themselves tend to speak about a given belief of their group—even when, upon investigation, one may find that they do not personally hold said belief.

Scholars are certainly aware of the problems related to this conception of religious collectives. However, one may argue that in the absence of a clear alternative, many fall back on this schema. For instance, Beckford indicates that it is not usually permissible to presuppose a uniformity of belief among the members of a group as large as the Jehovah's Witnesses. However, he considers that, in this particular case, one is justified in doing so because the Watch Tower Society "has always relied on the written word as the dominant medium for communication, and [...] its leaders have invariably insisted that Jehovah's witnesses *learn* its doctrines and learn how to present them methodically to other people" (Beckford 1975a: 103). On these grounds, Beckford argues that, in the case of Jehovah's Witnesses, the terms "teachings" and "religious beliefs" can be used interchangeably (Beckford 1975a: 103). As I interpret it, this passage overstates the power of religious socialization to shape the minds of individual Witnesses for practical purposes: It allows the author to speak collectively of the beliefs of Jehovah's Witnesses on the assumption that they are shared equally by all (or at least most) of them. From an empirical point of view, Beckford's thesis remains undecided (in particular, if each individual repeats what he or she has learned he ought to repeat). From a theoretical perspective, it provides yet another variation of a summative account of a religious collective.

If we stick to the example of belief, the collective intentionality framework that I have developed and deployed throughout this study allows us to attribute a certain set of beliefs to the Jehovah's Witnesses *collectively*, while remaining agnostic regarding the beliefs that each Witness individually holds in his or her heart (or brain). Let me emphasize once again that this does not mean that, within a group, personal and collective beliefs never converge—just that they do not do so *necessarily*. The same holds true for other collective intentional states such as collective intentions, emotions, or aesthetic experiences. In short, on my account, a religious collectivity is not defined by a convergence of personal attitudes. Rather, a religious collectivity conceptually depends on two or more people collectively intending (believing, emoting, experiencing, etc.) something as a body.

There is a blunter way to phrase this idea. In the absence of a form of collective intentionality, it is not possible to speak of a religious collective in the sense outlined in this study. Let me, however, prevent another possible misunderstanding. While this book aims at making a strong proposition, it is not my intention to claim that the theoretical framework put forward in this study makes other approaches to or concepts of a religious group superfluous, nor that my analysis covers all possible or even all relevant social forms of religion. This should be obvious, but it is probably worth reaffirming. Indeed, an important part of the debate on collective intentionality is aimed at distinguishing collective agents from other aggregative social forms, the analysis of which may yield important results. Indeed, though there is no collective intentionality in a group of people stuck on the highway because each of them individually decided to leave home early to avoid traffic, understanding these kinds of phenomena may help policy makers prevent many road accidents (see Boudon 1977).

In the end, however, I am convinced that the collective intentionality framework I have advanced in this study captures and analyzes an essential facet of contemporary religious life in many societies across the world and is worth being further developed and applied in the study of religion. To what extent the philosophical presuppositions at work in my analysis are, in the end, dependent on a Western frame of reference, and to what extent they can be relevant to the understanding of other cultures are questions that deserve detailed discussion, which, unfortunately, I cannot start here. However, I am inclined to see this primarily as an empirical issue rather than as a conceptual (or even metaphysical) one.

12.2 Approaching Empirical Research Anew

My detailed analysis of collective intentions among Jehovah's Witnesses in Switzerland and Germany provides preliminary but strong support for my previous claim. In the second part of my study, I have demonstrated how the Jehovah's Witnesses constitute (themselves as) a religious collectivity operating through a collective mode of action and sustaining collective beliefs, emotions, and aesthetic experiences. In addition to advancing the academic knowledge regarding various aspects of the Witnesses' religious life and organization, my inquiry has shown numerous ways to operationalize a philosophical framework in the context of an empirical research project. In this section, I want to summarize three interrelated strategies and briefly illustrate them in relation to the case of the Jehovah's Witnesses.

In the first part of my study, I have argued that in order to investigate collective intentions in practice, it is methodologically indispensable to find at least some aspects of such a phenomenon that are public in nature. While most—if not all—authors regard standard cases of collective intentions as an intersubjective phenomenon, Tuomela and Gilbert provide the clearest picture of collective intentions as the outcome of communicative interactions. Tuomela introduces the idea of an authority system, that is, of a "procedure representing the process of the group members' [...] going from the multitude of 'I's' to a 'we'" (Tuomela 1995: 176–177). In my analysis, I have argued that the meetings of Jehovah's Witnesses, and, more specifically, the question-and-answer discussion that constitutes one of the central aspects of their liturgy, essentially fulfill the criteria of an authority system identified by Tuomela. In a nutshell, through the recurring use of the first-person plural ("we," "our," "us"), the Watch Tower Society's publications bring the topic of a collective intention to the attention of the congregants, who, by performing speech acts that are highly constrained by the ritual structure of the interaction, express their collective acceptance of such a collective intention. This framework, I have argued, is also sufficient to account for the creation of a joint commitment as defined by Margaret Gilbert.

This analysis diverges from most accounts of the Jehovah's Witnesses' meetings in that it does not merely call attention to their role in the socialization of the individual Witnesses (although it does not deny it either); rather, it underscores how they provide a framework to establish a set of joint intentions and thus to constitute the Jehovah's Witnesses as a collective religious agent. As a paradigmatic case, the liturgical order of the Jehovah's Witnesses' meeting can be used as a reference to explore and compare other forms of authority systems in religious contexts. For instance, Wolterstorff (2017: 68) observes that the use of "we" and "us" is pervasive in the Orthodox liturgy and expresses the unity of all participants, that is, the unity of all those "who are fully conforming to the script." Still, not all forms of collective intentionality (and, thus, not all forms of authority system) necessarily depend on the explicit use of the pronoun "we," as many examples provided by Gilbert and others demonstrate. In sum, the concrete example of the Jehovah's Witnesses' meetings can offer researchers some useful clues as they seek to orient their attention in the field; at the same time, the philosophical debate outlined in the first part of this study supplies an abundance of resources to go beyond this particular case and analyze the specificities of a variety of empirical realities. It will be the task of the researchers to be "theoretically sensitive" to the inputs provided by their research subjects.

Indeed, when I started analyzing my empirical data, I was puzzled by what I regarded as a series of bizarre dissonances. For instance, people professing a zealous involvement in activities that they claimed not to like or speaking enthusiastically of gatherings which they found exhausting. However, "[I]t is the perception of incongruity that gives rise to thought" (Smith 1978: 294). Instead of accepting these findings as examples of cognitive dissonance (Festinger 1957), I was prompted by my philosophical readings to examine them considering the collective intentionality debate. From a problem, the discovery of such disjunctions (Gilbert) became an important instrument of analysis, leading me to the investigation of "group reasons" for action (Tuomela). This approach has allowed me to identify a complex motivational architecture that connects the individual to the group and, indeed, underpins the group's capacity to act, believe, etc. Several clues in my data indicate that an even more detailed analysis would be possible, for instance by including the various forms of collective commitment among family members or friends in a given group. Such an approach would potentially reveal an array of reinforcing or contradictory desire-independent reasons for action that might help illuminate the dynamic frictions and alliances within a religious collectivity, including those that could potentially lead to reforms, schisms, and the creation of new religious collectivities.

Such disjunctions were, furthermore, revealing of the normative dimension of collective intentionality as it follows from Gilbert's and Tuomela's theories. This dimension finds its most visible expression in the form of rebukes—or in their counterpart, the effort to avoid being rebuked. The cases that I have analyzed show that it is often possible for a normative reason for action at the level of the group to coexist alongside diverging personal intentions. This is indeed one of the most powerful aspects of the approach that I advocate for the conceptualization of religious collectivities. Nevertheless, in undertaking further research, more attention should be paid to what one might call the dark side of collective intentionality. For instance, since the participants in a collective intention are collectively entitled to demand conforming behavior from each other, forms of control can arise to the detriment of the individual. Furthermore, the construction of a collective agent entails the delimitation of a more or less vast set of people who are not part of it, potentially reinforcing forms of social and symbolic boundary making. These empirical questions remain, but ultimately, in the case of the Jehovah's Witnesses, or more generally with respect to socially controversial groups, I am persuaded that an approach in terms of collective intentionality would provide a more nuanced analysis than most of the currently available alternatives. I hope that other scholars of religion will also take up this invitation.

12.3 Addressing (the Study of) Religion Anew

In conclusion, what avenues does my thesis open for the study of religion, in addition to those that I have already outlined above? I am certain that the reader who has come so far already has his or her views on this matter. Let me, however, sketch a few ideas that might serve as seeds for future reflection and inquiry.

On the most practical level, my analyses offer a solid factual and methodological foundation to all scholars who wish to explore the media landscape of Jehovah's Witnesses as a means for understanding the dynamics of their organization. This is a particularly fascinating endeavor at the moment, because the Watch Tower Society is constantly implementing new digital technologies. For instance, in the summer of 2018, the Society introduced a series of interactive "Online Bible Study Lessons" on its website, jw.org. These lessons serve principally as a mission instrument, but they also raise the question of how they may impact traditional face-to-face Bible study—an issue of which the Society is aware.

Consider another example: When I first interviewed some members of the public information department at the Watch Tower branch office in Selters (Germany) in 2014, I was surprised to find out that my interlocutors were not able to name the members of the Governing Body of the Jehovah's Witnesses. Their individual identities seemed to be irrelevant. However, since the introduction, the same year, of the Society's online broadcasting offering, the leaders of the Society regularly appear as hosts on the program, and their faces and names are potentially viewed by millions of Witnesses on a monthly basis. Does this change represent a form of re-personalization of charisma? Future research may tell us.

Finally, it is worth underscoring that my research was conducted before the global COVID-19 pandemic. As in the case of most other religious organizations worldwide, the Watch Tower Society had to react quickly to protect the health of its members while ensuring that many, if not all, of its activity could continue, albeit under a different form. The quick introduction of video-conferencing software enabled local congregations to organize their biweekly meetings remotely, as well as larger events such as the Memorial of Christ's Death and the regional conferences. How this technological innovation will be domesticated in the long term, and what effect it will have on the Society's structures certainly constitute important research questions.

More theoretically inclined scholars of religion may have good reasons to send me politely angry emails to address the way in which I have interpreted and, to a certain extent, challenged the positions of leading figures in our field—from Rodney Stark, to Heidi Campbell, to Randall Collins, to Birgit Meyer and others. With or without the need for such a direct exchange of correspondence, I hope that my critical examination of the work of these authors will stimulate theoretical discussion in the study of religion and demonstrate that "there is life in the old dog yet" (Stausberg 2009b: 1). The debate must not necessarily revolve around the topic of religious collectives. Although this was my specific interest in this study, my intellectual involvement with these prominent scholars was also meant to probe various epistemic positions in our discipline.

This, meta-theoretical assessment, I believe, is not an idle academic exercise. Quite the contrary, it is an essential part of the study of religion as a self-reflective discipline; one that is able to unpick the underlying premises of its inquiry without barricading itself behind a *sui generis* conception of religion and without falling victim to siren voices that seek to reduce this effort to an attempt at self-deconstruction (see Schlieter 2010, 2020). The current state of the debate on scholarly forums such as the German-speaking mailing-list *Yggdrasill* clearly indicates the urgency of such systematic reflection.

In addition to addressing epistemological questions, this study can also be read as a contribution to the ongoing debate on the ontology of religion (e.g., Stausberg 2010; Schilbrack 2017). Overall, it demonstrates the complexity behind the notion of collective intentionality as a stepping stone toward a full-blown social ontology and calls attention to other theories besides the widely quoted work of John Searle. Furthermore, it invites the exercise of prudence when introducing a bridge between personal and collective forms of religion within a social ontology framework. Let me briefly spell out this point with an example.

In recent years, Jeppe Jensen has introduced the concepts of "e-religion" (external) and "i-religion" (internal) to designate the public-social and mental-cognitive dimensions of religion, respectively (Jensen 2014: 41–43). Jensen regards we-intentionality as a fundamental connector between these two levels in that it enables the collective externalization into the social world of some fundamental traits of "human nature" (Jensen 2016a: 215). Jensen combines this insight with a distributive and mimetic understanding of collective cognition to explain how e-religion, in turn, influences i-religion. According to this perspective, narratives, artifacts, and rituals have the capacity of "cloning minds" (Jensen 2016a: 221) in a way that synchronizes the individual modes of thinking, feeling, etc.

Against this background, Jensen (2016a: 218) argues, for instance, that it "makes sense to study beliefs in texts, because the same beliefs are replicated (more or less) in minds, and beliefs are what they are because they are products of minds." This is not the place for me to engage in a detailed discussion of Jensen's thesis. What interests me here is the fact that Jensen's argument introduces a mechanism that allows him to conceive the individual (mental or cognitive) and the social (collective-institutional) dimensions of religion as mirror images of one another. However, what I found most interesting in my study is precisely the possibility of a disjunction between, say, personal and collective beliefs. Without wanting to venture too far into the domain of the cognitive sciences, I would suggest that a deeper exploration of this discontinuity (see Searle 1984: 74) might prove as heuristically fruitful as the search for an "explanatory continuum" (Jensen 2016a: 213).

Finally, a last piece of food for thought may come from pondering what my philosophical ruminations and empirical analysis may hint at but, in the end, *do not* provide, namely a theoretical account of a specific form of *religious* collectivity. If we regard a definition as the "shortest possible version of theories" (Jensen 2003: 63), we have to conclude that, in classical Aristotelian terms, my framework circumscribes a *genus proximum*, that is, "collectivity," but does not clarify the *differentia specifica*: "religious." The reader must rest assured that I will not attempt a last-second acrobatic twist to solve this issue here. However, it is worth spending a few more lines to muse on some possible paths to pursue the reflection on this matter. Three main definitional strategies come to mind.

A first option would be to conflate religion and collectivity. This could mean arguing either that every form of collectivity is *per se* religious or that religion is in itself something collective. Neither of these positions seem very satisfactory. The former has an appealing Durkheimian ring to it, but to maintain some plausibility it would require abandoning the specific concept of "collective agent," which this study seeks to illuminate. The second one would bracket the possibility of individual forms of religion or, perhaps, regard them as neuroses (Freud 1993). This does not seem to follow from the theoretical framework that I have put forward: the fact that people can join forces, say, in adoring an idol *together* does not exclude the possibility of their adoring it individually. Of course, the fact of adoring *together* would have important consequences, as I have demonstrated in this study, but not with respect to the problem of defining religion.

As a second option, we could compile a list of *religious* intentions (worshipping, etc.) or intentional contents (ancestors, etc.). These solutions, however, appear equally impracticable, since this would amount to an extensive definition of religion, which would raise conceptual problems—which are the criteria for including a concept in the list?—and prove very impractical.

Let us explore a third, hopefully more viable, possibility—one that is implicit in my work. As in the case of other categories used in the study of religion, such as emotion, beliefs, or experiences, the search for an unequivocal character that would set *religious* intentions apart from other instances of the same kind is bound to run into trouble. A partial solution is to shift the focus from any intrinsic feature to a particular mode of construction. Thus, we may argue that religious collective intentions and, accordingly, religious collectivities, are phenomena that can be identified through the presence of a *ritualized* authority system that is embedded in an externally codified liturgical script. Admittedly, this strategy does not completely solve the problem. For instance, as many social anthropologists have argued (e.g., Bloch 1974), the line between religious and political rituals is not always clear-cut. However, this move has the advantage of avoiding essentializing religion while leaving the door open for further specifications, for instance in the form of a stipulative definition.

To conclude, instead of considering further subordinate options, we may ask what can be learned from this definitional effort? Let me point out two things. It appears that religion, whatever "it" is, shares several features with other human phenomena—among others, the possibility of assuming collective forms through collective intentionality. Pointing out that religious collectivities are but one "garden variety" of social facts among others could be an important task for the study of religion. This is somewhat ironic when one considers the numerous political, juridical and, indeed, religious attempts that have been made to unequivocally define their specificity. This consideration, however, does not constitute an argument to affirm that our effort to theorize religion should simply stop. Rather, it calls attention to the fact that any academic attempt at defining religion only gains its meaning and heuristic value from the research questions that it helps illuminate. To elaborate such a questions to further theorize the relevance of religious collective agents in the study of religion will certainly be a stimulating challenge that I hope other colleagues will be interested in taking up *jointly*.

Primary Sources

The primary sources referenced in this study are quoted in accordance with the abbreviations used by the Watch Tower Society in its indexes. In the few cases in which it was not possible to find an official abbreviation, I coined one myself; in the following list, these abbreviations are identified by an asterisk (*). If not otherwise noted, all publications listed are issued by and attributed to the Watch Tower Society without further specification of the author. All links to online resources have been verified on 17 November 2021. If not otherwise indicated, all quotes from the Bible come from the 2013 edition of the *New World Translation of the Holy Scriptures*.

Magazines

W: *The Watchtower* (1879–today)[1]
G: *Awake!* (1919–today)[2]

When it was founded in 1879, *The Watchtower* was a monthly publication. From 1892 onwards, it appeared twice a month. From 2008, however, each monthly edition has been printed with a different public in mind: the first edition of each month, called the "public edition" is intended to appeal especially to non-Witnesses with its simpler language and more accessible content. The other edition, which is published on the 15th of each month, is a "study edition" that Jehovah's Witnesses will use at their congregation meetings and has a circulation of about 14 million copies. In 2013, the number of pages of the public edition was reduced from 32 to 16. Between 2016 and 2017, the public edition was published every two months; as of January 2018, three issues appear each year. In 2006, the magazine *Awake!*, previously issued twice a month, became a monthly publication; as of 2016 it is published every two months. In 2013, it went from 32 to 16 pages.

Newsletters and Meeting Workbooks

*Bul: *Bulletin* (1919–1935)[3]
*Dir: *Director for Field Publishers* (1935–1936)
*Inf: *Informant* (1936–1956)
Km: *Kingdom Ministry* (1956–2015)[4]
Mwb: *Our Christian Life and Ministry–Meeting Workbook* (2016–today)

Books and Brochures

Be 2001: *Benefit from Theocratic Ministry School Education*
Bh 2005: *What Does the Bible Really Teach?*
Bh 2014: *What Does the Bible Really Teach?*
Bt 2009: *"Bearing Thorough Witness" About God's Kingdom*
Cf 2007: *"Come Be My Follower"*
Cl 2012: *Draw Close to Jehovah*
Fg 2012: *Good News from God!*
Fm 1969: *Then Is Finished the Mystery of God*
It-1 1988: *Insight on the Scriptures*, Volume 1
Jl 2012, 2014: *Who Are Doing Jehovah's Will Today?*
Jp 1959: *Jehovah's Witnesses in the Divine Purpose*
Jt 2000: *Jehovah's Witnesses—Who Are They? What Do They Believe?*
Jv 1993: *Jehovah's Witnesses—Proclaimers of God's Kingdom*
Kr 2014: *God's Kingdom Rules!*
Lv 2008: *Keep Yourselves in God's Love*
Lvs 2017: *How to Remain in God's Love*
Ns 1961: *Let Your Name Be Sanctified*
Od 2015: *Organized to Do Jehovah's Will*
*Org 1945: *Organization Instructions for Kingdom Publishers*
Pe 1982: *You Can Live Forever in Paradise on Earth*
Qm 1955: *Qualified to Be Ministers*
Re 2006: *Revelation—Its Grand Climax at Hand!*
Rs 1989 [1985]: *Reasoning from the Scriptures*
*Sg71 1971: *Theocratic Ministry School Guidebook*
Si 1990: *All Scripture Is Inspired of God and Beneficial*
Ta 1945: *Theocratic Aid to Kingdom Publishers*

Yearbooks

Yb: *Yearbook of Jehovah's Witnesses* (1927–today)[5]

Videos

"Prepare Your Comment." 2014. Retrieved from www.jw.org/en/bible-teachings/children/become-jehovahs-friend/videos/prepare-your-comment-meetings/

Other online content

"Fewer Pages, More Languages." s.d. Retrieved from www.jw.org/en/jehovahs-witnesses/activities/publishing/fewer-pages-more-languages/
"JW Library." Retrieved from www.jw.org/en/online-help/jw-library/

Notes

Chapter 1

1. As I will discuss below, in the sociological literature there is a variety of terms to indicate religious collectivities—communities, collectives, groups, organizations, etc. All these terms have specific connotations that are not necessarily relevant to my analysis. For this reason, I will use them interchangeably. Further relevant specifications will result from my analysis.
2. A non-exhaustive list includes academic studies on topics such as the origins and early developments of the movement (e.g., Blandre 1980; Conkin 1997; Dericquebourg 2016), its global expansion (e.g., Lawson and Cragun 2012), its social, political, and juridical transactions in various societies (e.g., Côté 1993; Rink 2002; Henderson 2004; Couchouron-Gurung 2011; Knox 2018), its stance on blood transfusion (Singelenberg 1990; Ratjar 2013, 2016), and its (failed) prophecies (Singelenberg 1989; Chryssides 2010). It is worth noting that the implementation of some studies, including mine, has been facilitated, at least to some extent, by a more open attitude on the part of the Watch Tower Society vis-à-vis academic researchers since the turn of the millennium (see Wah 2001). Thus, comments regarding the extreme difficulty of interviewing Jehovah's Witnesses or accessing their facilities that appear in some older scholarly articles (e.g., Séguy 1966; Dericquebourg 1980) should not be unreflectively transposed onto today's reality.
3. An interesting exception is provided by Dericquebourg's (1986) behaviorist analysis of the Witnesses' religious life, in which he argues that their doctrines tend to underplay the importance of personal faith and that their religious practices seek to bracket the recourse to the individual's conscience in favor of the repetition of certain standardized behaviors.

Chapter 2

1. Sawyer (2002) goes as far as seeing Durkheim as a proponent of emergentism *ante litteram*. I will have more to say about Durkheim's approach to the constitution of social collectives in Chapter 10.
2. Attentive readers of Bratman's work will notice that, for the sake of simplicity, I am drawing here on a preliminary version of his basic model (Bratman 1999e: 118–119), which nonetheless conveys most of its key features.

Chapter 4

1. For reasons of space and clarity, this description corresponds to a vastly simplified version of Tuomela's very sophisticated formal model of social action (see Tuomela 1984: 91).

Chapter 5

1. As this is quite counterintuitive, an example might be in order. As Gilbert (2008: 491–492) discusses at greater length, two individuals, let us call them Vanessa and Martin, can be jointly committed to climbing together to the top of a hill. If, after an hour's walk, Martin should privately decide to stop, the shared intention based on the joint commitment would not become void. Indeed, Vanessa will most probably react with surprise when, halfway to the top, she sees Martin suddenly turn back, and she will feel entitled to an explanation (for a similar example, see also Gilbert 2000e: 18).

Chapter 7

1. Since the information that I will present is quite general, I will refrain from encumbering this section with precise references. I advise the readers who wish for a comprehensive, systematic, and chronological account to refer to Chryssides (2016), Penton (2015), and Beckford (1975a), or to the overviews in languages other than English mentioned in the general introduction. These studies constitute the main sources of my summary in this chapter.
2. Initially entitled *Zion's Watch Tower and Herald of Christ's Presence*, the magazine went through a few name changes over the years. Since 1939, its complete title is *The Watchtower Announcing Jehovah's Kingdom*. To avoid confusion, I will systematically refer to this magazine using its customary shortened title, *The Watchtower*, in my text, and use the abbreviation "W" in the references.
3. Throughout this work, I will refer to the Watch Tower Bible and Tract Society of Pennsylvania, Inc, using the terms "the Watch Tower Society," "the Society," or "the organization."
4. While the Watch Tower Society constitutes both a juridical and a religious entity, the relationship between these two dimensions is quite complex and cannot be detailed here (Chryssides 2008: lxiv–lxvii; 2016: 141–144; Penton 2015: 294–303).
5. While I will usually refer to this publication with its current title, its official abbreviation in the references is "G," for *The Golden Age*.
6. See the list of primary sources for further specifications regarding the circulation of these magazines.
7. Auxiliary and regular pioneers are active Jehovah's Witnesses who invest a larger amount of time per month in the field ministry (see Chapter 8).
8. Conversely, there is an overabundance of (autobiographical) reports written by ex-members and of pseudo-scientific analysis put forward by anti-cult movements. For methodological reasons, I will refrain from using these publications as sources for my discussion.
9. These CDs and DVDs, which include advanced full-text search tools, are not meant for the public. However, the public information department of the Watch Tower Society's branch office in Selters has kindly provided me with copies of them in both German and English.

Chapter 8

1. See "Prepare Your Comment" (2014), available at: www.jw.org/en/bible-teachings/children/become-jehovahs-friend/videos/prepare-your-comment-meetings/
2. To mean something does not yet suffice to communicate it. However, while the level of communication may be relevant to emphasizing the *public* nature of commitment entailed in speech acts, the level of meaning suffices for grasping Searle's argument without overcomplicating it.
3. Note that I not claiming that the written sentences in the magazine or the printed questions are in and of themselves speech acts. However, the structure of the interaction in the meeting prompts the participants to utter speech acts, the form and content of which are to a large extent (although not completely) dictated by the form and content of the sentences and questions in the magazine.
4. If we go back to our example, it would indeed be logically possible to imagine a congregant listening to an answer and then exclaiming, "What do you mean by '*we* will distribute the magazines?' I did not agree to distribute anything!" This would entail, however, that the person in question rejects his status as "one of *us*," at least with respect to the group constituted by the collective goal of distributing the magazines. Conversely, once a person has agreed, directly or indirectly, to a collective goal, he or she cannot unilaterally rescind her commitment because, through the authority system, she has "has given up part of her authority to act to the group" (Tuomela 2013: 43) and it is up to the group to return it back to her.

Chapter 9

1. I thank Frank Hindriks for discussing this point with me.
2. The data presented in this picture have been provided by Evelyne Felder. I am grateful to her for allowing me to use them here.
3. *Tatort* (literally: "crime scene") is a police procedural television series (Das Erste, 1970–present) produced and broadcasted by various networks in Germany, Austria, and Switzerland. Each episode takes place in a different city in one of these countries.
4. The TV-series *Breaking Bad* (AMC, 2008–2013) narrates the struggles of a chemistry teacher turned criminal and his career in the violent world of drug trafficking. *House of Cards* (Netflix, 2013–2018) is a political thriller portraying a Washington congressman's rise to power through intimidation, violence, and corruption.
5. In this respect, it is worth noting that, in line with the data discussed in Chapter 8, in the publication that serves here as an example, the "we" form is used in the formulation of 47 percent of the study questions; four percent of the questions that use a different pronoun also use the direct object pronoun "us" or the possessive pronoun "our" in their formulation (Lv 2014).
6. I am not claiming here that the rules specifically concerning the use of media are in some way central to the constitution of a group. The point is rather that the analysis of these rules allows us to discuss, *exempli gratia*, the central process in the constitution of a collective—i.e., the creation of a joint commitment.

Chapter 11

1. Birgit Meyer has generously commented upon an earlier, much longer draft of this section. For that, I thank her wholeheartedly. Of course, I am solely responsible for the analysis presented in these pages, also because, on some occasion, she and I had to agree to disagree.
2. It may not be a coincidence that a very similar narration relating how a picture of Jesus had the power to avert a home robbery can be found in a brief sent by an American Methodist pastor to David Morgan (1998: 163), as well as in a testimony made in a Pentecostal-charismatic church in Ghana (Meyer 2011a: 1046–1047).
3. The study edition of *The Watchtower*, introduced in 2008, continues to be a 32-page magazine.
4. See www.jw.org/en/jehovahs-witnesses/activities/publishing/fewer-pages-more-languages/
5. The Watch Tower Society launched two other software applications for smartphone and tablet computers: *JW Language* and *JW Sign Language*. The first app is meant to be used in the field ministry to preach to people who speak foreign languages; the second one is meant to help preach to and teach to people with hearing impairments.
6. Evidence from the media diaries and from qualitative interviews clearly indicates a very limited religious use of media that are not produced or distributed by the Society.
7. In the instructions for the people participating in the study (originally in German), religious media were defined as follows: "By *religious media* we mean all the media that you use and that you consider relevant for your religious life. This includes also communication media (e.g., telephone, Skype...)." Worldly or everyday media were defined as follows: "By *everyday media [alltägliche Medien]*, we mean all the media that you use but that do not have any relevance for your religious life."
8. The daily text deserves a special mention; although the reading of the short text takes on average between seven and eight minutes a day, all but one participant read it several times a week—most of them daily—which indicates a widespread and well-established domestic praxis.

Primary Sources

1. This publication has had various titles since its foundation in 1879: *Zion's Watch Tower and Herald of Christ's Presence* (1879–December 1908); *The Watch Tower and Herald of Christ's Presence* (1909–1 October 1931) and, from October 1931 to the end of 1938, *The Watchtower and Herald of Christ's Presence* (15 October 1939–December 1938). Since January 1939, its complete tile is *The Watchtower Announcing Jehovah's Kingdom*.
2. This publication was founded in 1919 with the title *The Golden Age*. In 1937 it became *Consolation*. Its current title, *Awake!*, was introduced in 1946.
3. The title of this publication was *Bulletin* from 1919 to 1930, when it became the *Watch Tower Bulletin*. A year later, and until October 1935, the title was changed again to *Bulletin for Jehovah's Witnesses*, which was then renamed *Director for Field Publishers*. The abbreviation *Bul encompasses the first three titles.
4. The magazine or workbook was entitled *Kingdom Ministry* from 1956 to 1975. From January 1976 to the end of 1981, the title was changed to *Our Kingdom Service*. Finally, from 1982 to 2015, the title of the magazine was *Our Kingdom Ministry*.
5. Between 1927 and 1934, this publication was entitled *Yearbook of the International Bible Students Association*.

References

Alonso, F. M. (2018), 'Reductive Views of Shared Intention', in M. Jankovic and K. Ludwig (eds), *The Routledge Handbook of Collective Intentionality*, 34–44, London: Routledge.
Amit, V. (2020), 'Rethinking Anthropological Perspectives on Community: Watchful Indifference and Joint Commitment', in B. Jansen (ed.), *Rethinking Community Through Transdisciplinary Research*, 49–67, Cham: Palgrave Macmillan.
Ammerman, N. T. (1997), *Congregation and Community*, New Brunswick: Rutgers University Press.
Ammerman, N. T. (2018), 'Foreword: From the USA to Europe and Back', in C. Monnot and J. Stolz (eds), *Congregations in Europe*, v–xvi, Berlin: Springer.
Anderson, B. (1983), *Imagined Communities: Reflections on the Origin and Spread of Nationalism*, London: Verso.
Armon-Jones, C. (1986), 'The Thesis of Constructionism', in R. Harré (ed.), *The Social Construction of Emotion*, 32–56, Oxford: Basil Blackwell.
Asad, T. (1993), *Genealogies of Religion: Discipline and Reasons of Power in Christianity and Islam*, Baltimore: The Johns Hopkins University Press.
Austin, J. L. (1962), *How to Do Things with Words*, Oxford: Clarendon Press.
Austin, J. L. (1979), 'Performative Utterances', in J. O. Urmson and G. J. Warnock (eds), *Philosophical Papers*, 233–253, Oxford: Oxford University Press.
Ayaß, R. (2007), 'Kein Vergnügen an den Medien? Moralkommunikation in der Medienrezeption', in M. Klemm and E.-M. Jakobs (eds), *Das Vergnügen in und an den Medien. Interdisziplinäre Perspektiven*, 271–296, Frankfurt am Main: Peter Lang.
Bae, B. B. (2016), 'Belief and Acceptance for the Study of Religion', *Method & Theory in the Study of Religion*, 29 (1): 57–87.
Baker, A. (2016), 'Simplicity', in E. N. Zalta (ed.), *The Stanford Encyclopedia of Philosophy [Online Edition]*, Stanford: Metaphysics Research Lab, Stanford University.
Baker, J. O. (2010), 'Social Sources of the Spirit: Connecting Rational Choice and Interactive Ritual Theories in the Study of Religion', *Sociology of Religion*, 71 (1): 432–456.
Baran, E. B. (2014), *Dissent on the Margins: How Soviet Jehovah's Witnesses Defied Communism and Lived to Preach About It*, Oxford: Oxford University Press.
Barker, E. (1984), *The Making of a Moonie: Choice or Brainwashing?* Oxford: Basil Blackwell.
Barone, C. (2010), 'A Neo-Durkheimian Analysis of a New Religious Movement: The Case of Soka Gakkai in Italy', *Theory and Society*, 36 (2): 117–140.
Barrett, M. (2013), 'Dear Pastor, Bring Your Bible to Church', *The Gospel Coalition*, 18 August (2013), Available online: www.thegospelcoalition.org/article/dear-pastor-bring-your-bible-to-church/ (accessed 17 November 2021).
Barzilai-Nahon, K. and G. Barzilai (2005), 'Cultured Technology: Internet and Religious Fundamentalism', *The Information Society: An International Journal*, 21 (1): 25–40.
Baudouin, P. (2015), *Machines nécrophoniques*, Paris: Millon.
Bauman, Z. (2000), *Liquid Modernity*, Cambridge: Polity Press.

Bauman, Z. (2001), *Community: Seeking Safety in an Insecure World*, Cambridge: Polity Press.
Baumann, M. (2009), 'Templeisation: Continuity and Change of Hindu Traditions in Diaspora', *Journal of Religion in Europe*, 2 (2): 149–179.
Beal, T. K. (2015), 'The End of the World as We Know It: The Cultural Iconicity of the Bible in the Twighlight of Print Culture', in J. W. Watts (ed.), *Iconic Books and Texts*, 207–224, Sheffield: Equinox.
Beaudoin, T. (1997), *Virtual Faith: The Irreverent Spiritual Quest of Generation X*, San Francisco: Jossey-Bass.
Beck, U. (1986), *Risikogesellschaft: Auf dem Weg in eine andere Moderne*, Frankfurt am Main: Suhrkamp.
Becker, G. S. (1976), *The Economic Approach to Human Behavior*, Chicago: University of Chicago Press.
Beckford, J. A. (1972), 'The Embryonic Stage of a Religious Sect's Development: The Jehovah's Witnesses', in M. Hills (ed.), *A Sociological Yearbook of Religion in Britain*, 11–32, London: SCM Press.
Beckford, J. A. (1973), 'Religious Organization', *Current Sociology* [Special Issue].
Beckford, J. A. (1975a), *The Trumpet of Prophecy: A Sociological Study of Jehovah's Witnesses*, Oxford: Basil Blackwell.
Beckford, J. A. (1975b), 'Two Contrasting Types of Sectarian Organization', in R. Wallis (ed.), *Sectarianism*, 70–85, New York: John Wiley & Sons.
Beckford, J. A. (1985), *Cult Controversies: The Societal Response to New Religious Movements*, London: Tavistock publications.
Bentham, J. (2000), *An Introduction to the Principles of Morals and Legislation*, Kitchener: Batoche Books.
Bergunder, M. (2014), 'What Is Religion? The Unexplained Subject Matter of Religious Studies', *Method & Theory in the Study of Religion*, 26 (3): 246–286.
Besier, G. and K. Stoklosa, eds (2013–2018), *Jehovas Zeugen in Europa – Geschichte und Gegenwart*, Berlin: Lit Verlag.
Bessy, C. (2011), 'Repräsentation, Konvention und Institution: Orientierungspunkte für die Économie des Conventions', in R. Diaz-Bone (ed.), *Soziologie der Konventionen: Grundlagen einer pragmatischen Anthropologie*, 167–202, Frankfurt am Main: Campus.
Binder, W. (2013), 'Social Ontology, Cultural Sociology, and the War on Terror', in M. Schmitz, B. Kobow and H. B. Schmid (eds), *The Background of Social Reality. Selected Contributions from the Inaugural Meeting of ENSO*, 163–181, Dordrecht: Springer.
Blanchard, A. (2006), 'Le monde jéhoviste des imprimés', *Archives de sciences sociales des religions*, 134 (2): 37–62.
Blanchard, A. (2008), *Les Témoins de Jéhovah par leurs imprimés*, Yaoundé: PUCAC.
Blandre, B. (1980), 'Le Jour de Jéhovah. La crise économique de 1873 et la relance du millénarisme par Russell', *Revue de l'histoire des religions*, 197 (2): 191–200.
Blandre, B. (1987), *Les Témoins de Jéhovah, un siècle d'histoire*, Paris: Desclée de Brouwer.
Blandre, B. (1991), *Les Témoins de Jéhovah*, Turnhout: Brepols.
Bloch, M. (1974), 'Symbols, Song, Dance, and Features of Articulation. Is Religion an Extreme Form of Traditional Authority?' *European Journal of Sociology*, 15 (1): 54–81.
Bochinger, C., M. Engelbrecht and W. Gebhardt, (2009), *Die unsichtbare Religion in der sichtbaren Religion: Formen spiritueller Orientierung in der religiösen Gegenwartskultur*, Stuttgart: Kohlhammer.
Boudon, R. (1977), *Effets pervers et ordre social*, Paris: PUF.
Boudon, R. (1983), *La logique du social*, Paris: Hachette.

Boudon, R. (1995), *Le juste et le vrai*, Paris: Fayard.
Boyer, P. (2013), 'Why "Belief" Is Hard Work: Implications of Tanya Luhrmann's "When God Talks Back"', *HAU: Journal of Ethnographic Theory*, 3 (3): 349–357.
Bratman, M. (1999a), *Faces of Intention: Selected Essays on Intention and Agency*, Cambridge: Cambridge University Press.
Bratman, M. (1999b), 'I Intend that We J', in *Faces of Intention: Selected Essays on Intention and Agency*, 142–161, Cambridge: Cambridge University Press.
Bratman, M. (1999c), *Intention, Plans, and Practical Reason*, Stanford: Center for the Study of Language and Information.
Bratman, M. (1999d), 'Shared Cooperative Activity', in *Faces of Intention: Selected Essays on Intention and Agency*, 93–108, Cambridge: Cambridge University Press.
Bratman, M. (1999e), 'Shared Intention', in *Faces of Intention: Selected Essays on Intention and Agency*, 109–129, Cambridge: Cambridge University Press.
Bratman, M. (1999f), 'Shared Intention and Mutual Obligation', in *Faces of Intention: Selected Essays on Intention and Agency*, 130–141, Cambridge: Cambridge University Press.
Bratman, M. (2006), 'Dynamics of Sociality', *Midwest Studies in Philosophy*, 30 (1): 1–15.
Bratman, M. (2007), 'Shared Valuing and Frameworks for Practical Reasoning', in *Structures of Agency. Essays*, 283–310, Oxford: Oxford University Press.
Bratman, M. (2009a), 'Modest Sociality and the Distinctiveness of Intention', *Philosophical Studies*, 144 (1): 149–165.
Bratman, M. (2009b), 'Shared Agency', in C. Mantzavinos (ed.), *Philosophy of the Social Science: Philosophical Theory and Scientific Practice*, 41–59, Cambridge: Cambridge University Press.
Bratman, M. (2010), 'Agency, Time, and Sociality', *Proceeding and Addresses of the American Philosophical Association*, 84 (2): 7–26.
Bratman, M. (2014), *Shared Agency: A Planning Theory of Acting Together*, Oxford: Oxford University Press.
Bräunlein, P. J. (2016), 'Thinking Religion Through Things. Reflections on the Material Turn in the Scientific Study of Religions', *Method & Theory in the Study of Religion*, 28 (4–5): 365–399.
Bruce, S. (1999), *Choice and Religion: A Critique of Rational Choice*, Oxford: Oxford University Press.
Bruce, S. and R. Wallis (1984), 'The Stark-Bainbridge Theory of Religion: A Critical Analysis and Counter Proposals', *Sociological Analysis*, 45 (1): 11–27.
Bryant, J. M. (2000), 'Cost-Benefit Accounting and the Piety Business: Is Homo Religious, at Bottom, a Homo Economicus?', *Method & Theory in the Study of Religion*, 12 (1): 520–548.
Buggeln, G., C. Paine and B. Plate, eds (2017), *Religion in Museums: Global and Multidisciplinary Perspectives*, London: Bloomsbury.
Campbell, H. (2005), *Exploring Religious Community Online: We Are One in the Network*, New York: Peter Lang.
Campbell, H. (2007), '"What Hath God Wrought?" Considering How Religious Communities Culture (or Kosher) the Cell Phone', *Continuum: Journal of Media & Cultural Studies*, 21 (2): 191–203.
Campbell, H. (2010), *When Religion Meets New Media*, New York: Routledge.
Campbell, H. (2013), 'Community', in H. Campbell (ed.), *Digital Religion. Understanding Religious Practice in New Media Worlds*, 57–71, London: Routledge.
Campiche, R. J. and A. Dubach, eds (1992), *Croire en Suisse(s): analyse des résultats de l'enquête menée en 1988/1989 sur la religion des Suisses*, Lausanne: L'Âge d'Homme.

Cancik, H. and J. Mohn (1998), 'Religionsästhetik', in B. Gladigow, M. S. Laubscher, H. Cancik, H. G. Kippenberg and G. Kehrer (eds), *Handbuch religionswissenschaftlicher Grundbegriffe*, Stuttgart: W. Kohlhammer.

Chalmers, D. (1995), 'Facing up to the Problem of Consciousness', *Journal of Consciousness Studies*, (2): 200–219.

Chant, S. R., F. Hindriks and G. Preyer (2014), 'Introduction: Beyond the Big Four and the Big Five', in S. R. Chant, F. Hindriks and G. Preyer (eds), *From Individual to Collective Intentionality: New Essays*, 1–9, Oxford: Oxford University Press.

Chatton, W. (2002), *Reportatio super sententias: Liber I, distinctiones 10–48*, edited by G. J. Etzkorn and J. C. Wey, Toronto: Pontifical Institute of Mediaeval Studies.

Chaves, M. (2004), *Congregations in America*, Cambridge: Harvard University Press.

Christians, C. G. (1997), 'Religious Perspectives on Communication Technology', *Journal of Media and Religion*, 1 (1): 37–47.

Chryssides, G. D. (2008), *The A to Z of Jehovah's Witnesses*, Lanham: The Scarecrow Press.

Chryssides, G. D. (2010), '"They Keep Changing the Dates": Jehovah's Witnesses Changing Chronology', CESNUR 2010 Conference, Turin.

Chryssides, G. D. (2016), *Jehovah's Witnesses: Continuity and Change*, Burlington: Ashgate.

Collins, R. (1981), 'On the Microfoundations of Macrosociology', *American Journal of Sociology*, 86 (5): 984–1014.

Collins, R. (1993), 'Emotional Energy as the Common Denominator of Ritual Action', *Rationality and Society*, 5 (2): 203–230.

Collins, R. (1997), 'Stark and Bainbridge, Durkheim and Weber: Theoretical Comparisons,' in L. A. Young (ed.), *Rational Choice Theory and Religion*, 163–180, London: Routledge.

Collins, R. (2004), *Interaction Ritual Chains*, Princeton: Princeton University Press.

Collins, R. (2010), *The Micro-Sociology of Religion: Religious Practices, Collective and Individual*, ARDA Guiding Papers Series. Available online: www.thearda.com/rrh/papers/guidingpapers/collins.pdf (accessed 17 November 2021).

Collins, R. (2014), 'Interaction Ritual Chains and Collective Effervescence', in C. von Scheve and M. Salmela (eds), *Collective Emotions*, 299–311, Oxford: Oxford University Press.

Conkin, P. K. (1997), *American Originals: Homemade Varieties of Christianity*, Chapel Hill: The University of North Carolina Press.

Corrigan, J. (2004), 'Introduction: Emotions Research and the Academic Study of Religion', in J. Corrigan (ed.), *Religion and Emotion. Approaches and Interpretations*, 3–31, Oxford: Oxford University Press.

Corrigan, J., E. Crump and J. Kloos (2000), *Emotion and Religion. A Critical Assessment and Annotated Bibliography*, Westport: Greenwood Press.

Côté, P. (1993), *Les transactions politiques des croyants: Charismatiques et Témoins de Jéhovah dans le Québec des années 70 et 80*, Ottawa: Les Presses de l'Université de Ottawa.

Couchouron-Gurung, C. (2011), *Les Témoins de Jéhovah en France. Sociologie d'une controverse*, Paris: L'Harmattan.

Couldry, N. and A. Hepp. (2017), *The Mediated Construction of Reality*, Cambridge: Polity Press.

Cragun, R. T. and R. Lawson (2010), 'The Secular Transition: The Worldwide Growth of Mormons, Jehovah's Witnesses, and Seventh-day Adventists', *Sociology of Religion*, 71 (3): 349–373.

Csordas, T. J., ed. (1994), *Embodiment and Experience*, Cambridge: Cambridge University Press.

Csordas, T. J. (2004), 'Asymptote of the Ineffable. Embodiment, Alterity, and the Theory of Religion', *Current Anthropology*, 45 (2): 163–185.

D'Andrade, R., ed. (2006), *Anthropological Theory*, 6 (1) *[Special Issue 'Searle on Institutions']*.

Damasio, A. (2013), 'The Nature of Feelings: Evolutionary and Neurobiological Origins', *Nature Reviews Neurosciences*, 14: 143–152.

Darwin, C. (1872), *The Expression of the Emotions in Man and Animals*, London: John Murray.

Davie, G. (1994), *Religion in Britain Since 1945: Believing Without Belonging*, Oxford: Blackwell.

de Vries, H. (2001), 'In Medias Res: Global Religion, Public Spheres and the Task of Contemporary Comparative Religious Studies', in H. de Vries and S. Weber, *Religion and Media*, 3–42, Stanford: Stanford University Press.

de Vries, H. (2008), 'Introduction: Why Still "Religion"?', in H. de Vries (ed.), *Religion: Beyond a Concept*, 1–98, New York: Fordham University Press.

de Vries, W. (2016), 'Wilfrid Sellars', in E. N. Zalta (ed.), *The Stanford Encyclopedia of Philosophy [Online Edition]*, Stanford: Metaphysics Research Lab, Stanford University.

Demerath, N. J., P. D. Hall, T. Schmitt and R. H. Williams, eds (1998), *Sacred Companies. Organizational Aspects of Religion and Religious Aspects of Religion*, Oxford: Oxford University Press.

Demerath, N. J. and A. E. Farnsley (2007), 'Congragations Resurgent', in J. Beckford and N. J. Demerath (eds), *The SAGE Handbook of the Sociology of Religion*, 193–204, Los Angeles: SAGE.

Dericquebourg, R. (1980), 'Le Béthel, ordre religieux jéhoviste?' *Archives de sciences sociales des religions*, 50 (1): 77–88.

Dericquebourg, R. (1986), 'Le Jéhovisme: une conception comportementaliste de la vie religieuse', *Archives de sciences sociales des religions*, 62 (1): 161–176.

Dericquebourg, R. (2003), '[Review of] Andrew Holden, Jehovah's Witnesses. Portrait of a Contemporary Religious Movement', *Archives de sciences sociales des religions*, 124 (3): 153–154.

Dericquebourg, R. (2016), 'The Rise of Prophetism in an Industrial Society. Market Rationality and the Economy of Charisma. A Propos de Charles Taze Russell', *Acta Comparanda. Subsidia*, 3: 223–244.

Derrida, J. (1988), *Limited Inc*, Evanston: Northwestern University Press.

Derrida, J. (1998), 'Faith and Knowledge: The Two Sources of "Religion" at the Limits of Reason Alone,' in J. Derrida and G. Vattimo (eds), *Religion*, 1–78, Cambridge: Polity Press.

Derrida, J. (2001), 'Above All, No Journalists!', in H. de Vries and S. Weber (eds), *Media and Religion*, 56–93, Standford: Standford University Press.

Dewey, J. (1895), 'The Theory of Emotion. (2) The Significance of Emotions', *Psychological Review*, 2: 13–32.

DiMaggio, P. and W. Powell (1991), 'Introduction', in W. Powell and P. DiMaggio (eds), *The New Institutionalism in Organizational Analysis*, 1–38, Chicago: University of Chicago Press.

Duranti, A. (1993), 'Truth and Intentionality. An Ethnographic Critique', *Cultural Anthropology*, 8 (2): 214–245.

Duranti, A. (1997), *Linguistic Anthropology*, New York: Cambridge University Press.

Durkheim, E. (1888), 'Introduction à la sociologie de la famille', *Annales de la Faculté des Lettres de Bordeaux* 10: 257–281.

Durkheim, E. (1982), *The Rules of Sociological Method*, New York: The Free Press.
Durkheim, E. (1984), *The Division of Labour in Society*, Basingstoke: MacMillan.
Durkheim, E. (1995), *The Elementary Forms of Religious Life*, New York: The Free Press.
Ekman, P. (1980), *The Face of Man: Expressions of Universal Emotions in a New Guinea Village*, New York: Garland STPM Press.
Engel, P. (1996), 'Croyances collectives et acceptations collectives', in A. Bouvier, R. Boudon and F. Chazel (eds), *Cognition et sciences sociales*, 155–173, Paris: PUF.
Engelke, M. (2010), 'Religion and the Media Turn: A Review Essay', *American Ethnologist*, 32 (2): 371–379.
Engelke, M. (2011), 'Response to Charles Hirschkind. Religion and Transduction', *Social Anthropology* 19 (1): 97–102.
Febrero, R. and P. Schwartz (1995), 'The Essence of Becker: An Introduction', in R. Febrero and P. Schwartz (eds), *The Essence of Becker*, xvi–li, Stanford: Hoover Institution Press.
Feinberg, J. (1970), 'The Nature and Value of Rights', *Journal of Value Inquiry*, 4: 234–257.
Felder, E. (2016), 'Die Deutung des Fernsehens und sozialer Medien bei den Zeugen Jehovas. Qualitative Inhaltsanalyse der Zeitschriften "Wachtturm" und "Erwachet"!', BA Thesis, University of Fribourg.
Fer, Y. (2018), 'An Affective (U-)turn in the Sociology of Religion? Religious Emotions and Native Narratives', in V. Altglas and M. Wood (eds), *Bringing Back the Social into the Sociology of Religion*, 142–168, Leiden: Brill.
Ferré, J. P. (2003), 'The Media of Popular Piety', in J. Mitchell and S. Marriage (eds), *Mediating Religion. Conversations in Media, Religion and Culture*, 83–92, London: T&T Clark.
Festinger, L. (1957), *A Theory of Cognitive Dissonance*, Evanston: Row.
Finke, R. (1997), 'The Consequences of Religious Competition. Supply-Side Explanations for Religious Change', in L. A. Young (ed.), *Rational Choice Theory and Religion. Summary and Assesment*, 47–65, New York: Routledge.
Finnegan, R. (1969), 'How to Do Things with Words: Performative Utterances among the Limba of Sierra Leone,' *Man (New Series)*, 4 (4): 537–552.
Fisher, G. A. and K. Koo Chon (1989), 'Durkheim and the Social Construction of Emotions', *Social Psychology Quarterly*, 51 (1): 1–9.
Fitzgerald, T. (2001), *The Ideology of Religious Studies*, Oxford: Oxford University Press.
Freud, S. (1993), 'Zwangshandlungen und Religionsübungen', in *Gesammelte Werke VII*, 129–139, Frankfurt am Main: Fischer Verlag.
Gauthier, F. (2014), 'Intimate Circles and Mass Meetings. The Social Forms of Event-Structured Religion in the Era of Globalized Markets and Hyper-Mediatization', *Social Compass*, 61 (2): 261–271.
Gauthier, F. (2019), *Religion, Modernity, Globalisation. Nation-State to Market*, London: Routledge.
Gebhardt, W. (1999), '"Kalte Gesellschaft" und "warme Gemeinschaft". Zur Kontinuität einer deutschen Denkfigur', in G. Meuter and H. R. Otten (eds), *Der Aufstand gegen den Bürger*, 165–184, Würzburg: Königshausen & Neumann.
Gebhardt, W. (2010), 'Flüchtige Gemeinschaften: Eine kleine Theorie situativer Event-Vergemeinschaftung', in D. Lüddeckens and R. Walthert (eds), *Fluide Religion. Neue religiöse Bewegungen im Wandel. Theoretische und empirische Systematisierungen*, 175–188, Bielefeld: Transcript.
Gerbe, D. (1999), *Zwischen Widerstand und Martyrium: die Zeugen Jehovas im Dritten Reich*, München: Oldenbourg.
Gilbert, M. (1978), 'On Social Facts,' PhD Thesis, Oxford.

Gilbert, M. (1987), 'Modeling Collective Belief', *Synthese*, 73 (1): 185–204.
Gilbert, M. (1989), *On Social Facts*, Princeton: Princeton University Press.
Gilbert, M. (1996a), 'Agreements, Coercion, and Obligation', in *Living Together. Rationality, Sociality, and Obligation*, 281–311, Lanham: Rowman & Littlefield Publishers.
Gilbert, M. (1996b), 'Introduction. Two Standpoints—The Personal and the Collective', in *Living Together. Rationality, Sociality, and Obligation*, 1–20, Lanham: Rowman & Littlefield Publishers.
Gilbert, M. (1996c), 'Modeling Collective Belief', in *Living Together. Rationality, Sociality, and Obligation*, 195–213, Lanham: Rowman & Littlefield Publishers.
Gilbert, M. (1996d), 'More on Social Facts', in *Living Together. Rationality, Sociality, and Obligation*, 263–278, Lanham: Rowman & Littlefield Publishers.
Gilbert, M. (1996e), 'Notes on the Concept of a Social Convention', in *Living Together. Rationality, Sociality, and Obligation*, 61–88, Lanham: Rowman & Littlefield Publishers.
Gilbert, M. (1996f), 'On Feeling Guilt for What One's Group Has Done', in *Living Together. Rationality, Sociality, and Obligation*, 375–390, Lanham: Rowman & Littlefield Publishers.
Gilbert, M. (1996g), 'Walking Together: A Paradigmatic Social Phenomenon', in *Living Together. Rationality, Sociality, and Obligation*, 177–194, Lanham: Rowman & Littlefield Publishers.
Gilbert, M. (2000a), 'Collective Belief and Scientific Change', in *Sociality and Responsibility. New Essays in Plural Subject Theory*, 37–49, Lanham: Rowman & Littlefield Publishers.
Gilbert, M. (2000b), 'Collective Remorse', in *Sociality and Responsibility. New Essays in Plural Subject Theory*, 124–140, Lanham: Rowman & Littlefield Publishers.
Gilbert, M. (2000c), 'Introduction: Sociality and Plural Subject Theory', in *Sociality and Responsibility. New Essays in Plural Subject Theory*, 1–13, Lanham: Rowman & Littlefield Publishers.
Gilbert, M. (2000d), 'Obligation and Joint Commitment', in *Sociality and Responsability. New Essays in Plural Subject Theory*, 50–70, Lanham: Rowman & Littlefield Publishers.
Gilbert, M. (2000e), 'What Is It for *Us* to Intend?', in *Sociality and Responsability. New Essays in Plural Subject Theory*, 14–36, Lanham: Rowman & Littlefield Publishers.
Gilbert, M. (2002), 'Belief and Acceptance as Features of Groups', *Protosociology*, 16: 35–69.
Gilbert, M. (2003), 'Ths Structure of the Social Atom: Joint Commitment as the Foundation of Human Social Behavior', in F. F. Schmitt (ed.), *Socializing Metaphysics. The Nature of Social Reality*, 39–64, Lanham: Rowman & Littlefileld Publishers.
Gilbert, M. (2006), *A Theory of Political Obligation: Membership, Commitment, and the Bonds of Society*, Oxford: Clarendon Press.
Gilbert, M. (2007), 'Searle and Collective Intentions', in S. L. Tsohatzidis (ed.), *Intentional Acts and Institutional Facts: Essays on John Searle's Social Ontology*, 31–47, Dordrecht: Springer.
Gilbert, M. (2008), 'Two Approaches to Shared Intention: An Essay in the Philosophy of Social Phenomena', *Analyse & Kritik*, 30 (2): 483–514.
Gilbert, M. (2009), 'Shared Intention and Personal Intentions', *Philosophical Studies*, 144 (1): 167–187.
Gilbert, M. (2014a), 'Acting Together', in *Joint Commitment. How We Make the Social World*, 23–36, Oxford: Oxford University Press.
Gilbert, M. (2014b), 'Collective Guilt and Collective Guilt Feelings', in *Joint Commitment. How We Make the Social World*, 229–256, Oxford: Oxford University Press.

Gilbert, M. (2014c), 'Considerations on Joint Commitment: Responses to Various Comments', in *Joint Commitment. How We Make the Social World*, 35–57, Oxford: Oxford University Press.

Gilbert, M. (2014d), 'How We Feel: Understanding Everyday Collective Emotion Ascription', in C. von Scheve and M. Salmela (eds), *Collective Emotions*, 15–31, Oxford: Oxford University Press.

Gilbert, M. (2014e), 'Introduction', in *Joint Commitment. How We Make the Social World*, 1–19, Oxford: Oxford University Press.

Gilbert, M. (2014f), 'The Nature of Agreements: A Solution to Some Puzzles about Claim-Rights and Joint Intention', in M. Vargas and G. Yaffe (eds), *Rational and Social Agency. The Philosophy of Michael Bratman*, 215–255, Oxford: Oxford University Press.

Gilbert, M. (2014g), 'Social Convention Revisited', in *Joint Commitment. How We Make the Social World*, 207–228, Oxford: Oxford University Press.

Gilbert, M. (2014h), 'Two Approaches to Shared Intention', in *Joint Commitment. How We Make the Social World*, 94–128, Oxford: Oxford University Press.

Gilbert, M. (2018), *Rights and Demands. A Foundational Inquiry*, Oxford: Oxford University Press.

Goffman, E. (1967), *Interaction Ritual*, New York: Pantheon Books.

Gomez-Lavin, J. and M. Rachar (2019), 'Normativity in Joint Action', *Mind & Language*, 34 (1): 97–120.

Grimes, R. L. (1988), 'Infelicitous Performances and Ritual Criticism', *Semia*, 41: 101–122.

Grimes, R. L. (2014), *The Craft of Ritual Studies*, Oxford: Oxford University Press.

Gutjahr, P. C. (1999), *An American Bible. A History of the Good Book in the United States, 1777-1880*, Stanford: Stanford University Press.

Haddon, L. (2007), 'Roger Silverstone's Legacies: Domestication', *New Media & Society*, 9 (1): 25–32.

Hall, K. (2000), 'Performativity', *Journal of Linguistic Anthropology*, 9 (1–2): 184–187.

Harré, R. (1986a), 'An Outline of the Social Constructionist Viewpoint', in R. Harré (ed.), *The Social Construction of Emotion*, 2–14, Oxford: Basil Blackwell.

Harré, R., ed. (1986b), *The Social Construction of Emotion*, Oxford: Basil Blackwell.

Hart, H. L. A. (1955), 'Are There Any Natural Rights?', *Philosophical Review*, 64 (2): 175–191.

Heath, A. (1976), *Rational Choice and Social Exchange*, Cambridge: Cambridge University Press.

Heelas, P. and L. Woodhead (2005), *The Spiritual Revolution: Why Religion Is Giving Way to Spirituality*, Oxford: Blackwell.

Heider, A. and S. Warner (2010), 'Bodies in Sync: Interaction Ritual Theory Applied to Sacred Harp Singing', *Sociology of Religion*, 7 (1): 76–97.

Henderson, J. J. (2004), 'The Jehovah's Witnesses and Their Plan to Expand First Amendment Freedoms', *Journal of Church and State*, 46 (4): 811–832.

Henderson, J. J. (2010), *Defending the Good News: The Jehovah's Witnesses' Plan to Expand the First Amendment*, Spokane: Marquette Books.

Hepp, A. and V. Krönert (2009), *Medien – Event – Religion. Die Mediatisierung von Religion*, Wiesbaden: VS Verlag für Sozialwissenschaften.

Hero, M. (2010), *Die neuen Formen des religiösen Lebens: eine institutionentheoretische Analyse neuer Religiosität*, Würzburg: Ergon Verlag.

Hervieu-Léger, D. (1999), *Le pèlerin et le converti. La religion en mouvement*, Paris: Flammarion.

Hindriks, F. (2005), 'Rules & Institutions. Essays on Meaning, Speech Acts and Social Ontology', PhD Thesis, Erasmus University Rotterdam.
Hindriks, F. (2009), 'Constitutive Rules, Language, and Ontology', *Erkenntnis*, 73 (2): 253–275.
Hindriks, F. (2013), 'Collective Acceptance and the Is-Ought Argument', *Ethical Theory and Moral Practice*, 16 (3): 465–480.
Hindriks, F. (2018), 'Institutions and Collective Intentionality', in M. Jankovic and K. Ludwig (eds), *The Routledge Handbook of Collective Intentionality*, 353–362, London: Routledge.
Hirsch, E. (1994), 'The Long Term and the Short Term of Domestic Consumption. An Ethnographic Case Study', in R. Silverstone and E. Hirsch (eds), *Consuming Technologies. Media and Information in Domestic Spaces*, 194–210, London: Routledge.
Hirschkind, C. (2011), 'Media, Mediation, Religion', *Social Anthropology*, 19 (1): 90–97.
Hitzler, R. (1998), 'Posttraditionale Vergemeinschaftung', *Berliner Debatte Initial*, 9 (1): 81–89.
Hitzler, R., A. Honer and M. Pfadenhauer, eds (2008), *Posttraditionale Gemeinschaften: Theoretische und ethnografische Erkundungen*, Wiesbaden: VS Verlag für Sozialwissenschaften.
Hitzler, R. and M. Pfadenhauer (1998), 'Eine posttraditionale Gemeinschaft. Integration und Distinktion in der Techno-Szene', in F. Hillebrandt, G. Kneer and K. Kraemer (eds), *Verlust der Sicherheit? Lebensstile zwischen Multioptionalität und Knappheit*, 83–102, Opladen: Westdeutscher Verlag.
Hjarvard, S. (2008a), 'The Mediatization of Religion. A Theory of the Media as Agents of Religious Change', *Northern Lights*, 6 (1): 9–26.
Hjarvard, S. (2008b), 'The Mediatization of Society. A Theory of the Media as Agents of Social and Cultural Change', *Nordicom Review*, 29 (2): 102–131.
Hjarvard, S. (2013), *The Mediatization of Culture and Society*, New York: Routledge.
Hochschild, A. (1979), 'Emotion Work, Feeling Rules, and Social Structure', *The American Journal of Sociology* 85 (3): 551–575.
Hochschild, A. (2003), *The Commercialization of Intimate Life: Notes from Home and Work*, Berkeley: University of California Press.
Hochschild, A. (2012), *The Managed Heart. Commercialization of Human Feeling*, Berkeley: University of California Press.
Holden, A. (2002), *Jehovah's Witnesses: Portrait of a Contemporary Religious Movement*, London: Routledge.
Homans, G. C. (1961), *Social Behavior. Its Elementary Forms*, New York: Harcourt, Brace & World, inc.
Horton, R. and R. Finnegan, eds (1973), *Modes of Thought: Essays on Thinking in Western and Non-Western Societies*, London: Faber & Faber.
Hüsken, U. (2007), 'Ritual Dynamics and Ritual Failure', in U Hüsken (ed.), *When Rituals Go Wrong: Mistakes, Failure, and the Dynamics of Ritual*, 337–366, Leiden: Brill.
Hutchings, T. (2014), 'Now the Bible Is an App: Digital Media and Changing Patterns of Religious Authority', in K. Granholm, M. Moberg and S. Sjö (eds), *Religion, Media and Social Change*, 143–161, London: Routledge.
Hutchings, T. (2015a), 'E-readings and the Christian Bible', *Studies in Religion*, 44 (4): 423–440.
Hutchings, T. (2015b), '"The Smartest Way to Study the Word": Protestant and Catholic Approaches to the Digital Bible', in M. D. Bosch, J. L. Micó and J. M. Carbonell (eds),

Negotiating Religious Visibility in Digital Media, 57–68, Barcelona: Blanquerna Observatory on Media, Religion and Culture.

Hutchings, T. (2017), *Creating Church Online: Ritual, Community and New Media*, New York: Routledge.

Iannaccone, L. (1991), 'The Consequences of Religious Market Structure. Adam Smith and the Economics of Religion', *Rationality and Society*, 3 (2): 156–177.

Iannaccone, L. (1992a), 'Religious Markets and the Economics of Religion', *Social Compass*, 39 (1): 123–131.

Iannaccone, L. (1992b), 'Sacrifice and Stigma: Reducing Free-Riding in Cults, Communes, and Other Collectives', *Journal of Political Economy*, 100 (2): 271–291.

Iannaccone, L. (1994), 'Why Strict Churches Are Strong', *American Journal of Sociology*, 99 (5): 1180–1211.

Iannaccone, L. (1997), 'Rational Choice. Framework for the Scientific Study of Religion', in L. A. Young (ed.), *Rational Choice Theory and Religion: Summary and Assessment*, 25–44, New York: Routledge.

Inglehart, R. (1977), *The Silent Revolution: Changing Values and Political Styles Among Western Publics*, Princeton: Princeton University Press.

Innis, H. A. (1951), *The Bias of Communication*, Toronto: Toronto University Press.

Introvigne, M. (1990), *I Testimoni di Geova*, Milano: A. Mondadori.

Introvigne, M. (2004), 'L'espansione dei Testimoni di Geova in Italia: tra teorie della secolarizzazione e rational choice', *Religioni e Società*, 50: 48–55.

Introvigne, M. (2015), *I Testimoni di Geova. Chi sono, come cambiano*, Siena: Cantagalli.

Introvigne, M. and J. G. Melton, eds (1996), *Pour en finir avec les sectes: Le débat sur le rapport de la commission parlementaire*, Milano: CESNUR.

James, W. (1884), 'What Is an Emotion?', *Mind*, 9 (34): 188–205.

James, W. (1998), *The Varieties of Religious Experience*, Harmondsworth: Penguin.

Jankovic, M. and K. Ludwig, eds (2018), *The Routledge Handbook of Collective Intentionality*, London: Routledge.

Jensen, J. S. (2003), *The Study of Religion in a New Key: Theoretical and Philosophical Soundings in the Comparative and General Study of Religion*, Aarhus: Aarhus University Press.

Jensen, J. S. (2014), *What Is Religion?*, Durham: Acumen.

Jensen, J. S. (2016a), '"Cloning Minds": Religion between Individuals and Collectives', in C. Bochinger and J. Rüpcke (eds), *Dynamics of Religion. Past and Present*, 211–229, Berlin: De Gruyter.

Jensen, J. S. (2016b), 'How Institutions Work in Shared Intentionality and "We-Mode" Social Cognition', *Topoi*, 35 (1): 301–312.

Jensen, J. S. (2017), '"Religion Is the Word, but, What Is the Thing – If There Is One?" On Generalized Interpretations and Epistemic Placeholders in the Study of Religion', *Historia Religionum*, 9: 17–28.

Jerolmack, C. and D. Porpora (2004), 'Religion, Rationality, and Experience: A Response to the New Rational Choice Theory of Religion', *Sociological Theory*, 22 (1): 140–160.

Jödicke, A. (2010), 'Die "Religionsgemeinschaft." Religionspolitik als Stimulus für religionssoziologische und religionswissenschaftliche Begriffsbildung', in M. Baumann and F. Neubert (eds), *Religionspolitik, Öffentlichkeit, Wissenschaft. Studien zur Neuformierung von Religion in der Gegenwart*, 37–58, Zürich: Pano.

Katz, E. and D. Foulkes (1962), 'On the Use of Mass Media as "Escape": Clarification of a Concept', *Public Opinion Quarterly*, 26 (3): 377–388.

Keane, W. (2007), *Christian Moderns: Freedom and Fetish in the Mission Encounter*, Berkeley: University of California Press.

Keele, R. and J. Pelletier (2018), 'Walter Chatton', in E. N. Zalta (ed.), *The Stanford Encyclopedia of Philosophy [Online Edition]*, Stanford: Metaphysics Research Lab, Stanford University.

Kelley, D. M. (1972), *Why Conservative Churches Are Growing: A Study in Sociology of Religion*, New York: Harper & Row.

Kemper, T. D. (2011), *Status, Power and Ritual Interaction. A Relational Reading of Durkheim, Goffman and Collins*, Farnham: Ashgate.

Keppler, A. (2005), 'Medien und soziale Wirklichkeit', in M. Jäckel (ed.), *Mediensoziologie. Grundfragen und Forschungsfelder*, 196–210, Wiesbaden: Springer.

Knoblauch, H. (2009), *Populäre Religion: Auf dem Weg in eine spirituelle Gesellschaft*, Frankfurt am Main: Campus.

Knox, Z. (2011), 'Writing Witness History: The Historiography of the Jehovah's Witnesses and the Watch Tower Bible and Tract Society of Pennsylvania', *Journal of Religious History*, 35 (2): 157–180.

Knox, Z. (2013), 'Jehovah's Witnesses as Un-Americans? Scriptural Injunctions, Civil Liberties, and Patriotism', *Journal of American Studies*, 47 (4): 1081–1108.

Knox, Z. (2018), *Jehovah's Witnesses and the Secular World: From the 1870s to the Present*, London: Palgrave MacMillan.

Krämer, S. (2001), *Sprache, Sprechakt, Kommunikation. Sprachtheoretische Positionen des 20. Jahrhunderts*, Frankfurt am Main: Suhrkamp.

Krüger, O. (2012), *Die mediale Religion*, Bielefeld: Transcript.

Krüger, O. (2018), 'The "Logic" of Mediatization Theory in Religion: A Critical Consideration of a New Paradigm', *Marburg Journal of Religion*, 20 (1): 1–31.

Krüger, O. and A. Rota. (2015), 'Die Verkündigung von Jehovas Königreich in Hörfunk und Internet. Ein Beitrag zur Medienhermeneutik', *Religion – Staat – Gesellschaft*, 16: 75–108.

Krüger, O. and N. B. Weibel, eds (2015), *Die Körper der Religion – Corps en religion*, Zurich: Pano.

Lambert Bendroth, M. (1996), 'Fundamentalism and the Media, 1930–1990', in D. A. Stout and J. M. Buddenbaum (eds), *Religion and Mass Media. Audiences and Adaptations*, 74–84, Thousand Oaks: Sage.

Lawson, R. and R. T. Cragun (2012), 'Comparing the Geographic Distributions and Growth of Mormons, Adventists, and Witnesses', *Journal for the Scientific Study of Religion*, 51 (2): 220–240.

Lehmann, K. and A. Jödicke, eds (2016), *Einheit und Differenz in der Religionswissenschaft. Standortbestimmungen mit Hilfe eines Mehr-Ebenen-Modells von Religion*, Würzburg: Ergon Verlag.

Lewis, D. K. (1969), *Convention: A Philosophical Study*, Cambridge: Harvard University Press.

Lincoln, B. (2003), *Holy Terrors: Thinking About Religion After September 11*, Chicago: The University of Chicago Press.

Luckmann, T. (1967), *The Invisible Religion. The Problem of Religion in Modern Society*, New York: MacMillan.

Lüddeckens, D. and R. Walthert (2010), 'Das Ende der Gemeinschaft? Neue religiöse Bewegungen im Wandel', in D. Lüddeckens and R. Walthert (eds), *Fluide Religion. Neue religiöse Bewegungen im Wandel. Theoretische und empirische Systematisierungen*, 19–53, Bielefeld: Transcript.

Lüddeckens, D. and R. Walthert (2018), 'Religiöse Gemeinschaft', in D. Pollack, V. Krech, O. Müller and M. Hero (eds), *Handbuch Religionssoziologie*, 467–488, Wiesbaden: VS Verlag für Sozialwissenschaften.

Ludwig, K. (2007), 'Foundations of Social Reality in Collective Intentional Behavior', in S. L. Tsohatzidis (ed.), *Intentional Acts and Institutional Facts: Essays on John Searle's Social Ontology*, 49–71, Dordrecht: Springer.

Ludwig, K. (2016), *From Individual to Plural Agency. Collective Action: Volume 1*, Oxford: Oxford University Press.

Luhmann, N. (1996), *Die Realität der Massenmedien*, Opladen: Westdeutscher Verlag.

Lynch, O. M. (1990), 'The Social Construction of Emotion in India', in O. M. Lynch (ed.), *Divine Passion: The Social Construction of Emotion in India*, 3–34, Berkeley: University of California Press.

Lyons, W. (1980), *Emotion*, Cambridge: Cambridge University Press.

MacKenzie, D. and J. Wajcman, eds (1985), *The Social Shaping of Technology: How the Refrigerator Got Its Hum*, Milton Keynes Philadelphia: Open University Press.

MacKenzie, D. and J. Wajcman (1999), 'Introductory Essay: The Social Shaping of Technology', in D. MacKenzie and J. Wajcman (eds), *The Social Shaping of Technology*, 3–27, Buckingham: Open University Press.

Maffesoli, M. (1993), *La contemplation du monde. Figures du style communautaire*, Paris: Grasset.

Maffesoli, M. (1996), *The Time of the Tribes: The Decline of Individualism in Mass Society*, London: Sage.

Malinowski, B. (1934), *Coral Gardens and Their Magic*, London: George Allen & Unwin.

Marett, R. R. (1929), *The Threshold of Religion*, London: Methuen.

Mariña, J. (2004), 'Friedrich Schleiermacher and Rudolf Otto', in J. Corrigan (ed.), *Religion and Emotion. Approaches and Interpretations*, 457–473, Oxford: Oxford University Press.

Marvin, C. (1988), *When Old Technologies Were New. Thinking about Electric Communication in the Late Nineteenth Century*, New York: Oxford University Press.

Marx, K. and F. Engels (1948), *The Communist Manifesto*, New York: International Publishers.

Mathiesen, K. (2002), 'Searle, Collective Intentions, and Individualism', in G. Meggle (ed.), *Social Facts & Collective Intentionality*, 185–204, Frankfurt am Main: Dr. Hänsel Hohenhausen.

McCutcheon, R. T. (1997), *Manufacturing Religion: The Discourse on Sui Generis Religion and the Politics of Nostalgia*, New York: Oxford University Press.

McKinnon, A. M. (2011), 'Ideology and the Market Metaphor in Rational Choice Theory of Religion: A Rhetorical Critique of "Religious Economies"', *Critical Sociology*, 39 (4): 529–543.

McLeod, E. (2010), 'Jehovah's Witnesses and Radio', in C. H. Sterling (ed.), *The Concise Encyclopedia of American Radio*, 385–387, New York: Routledge.

McLuhan, M. (1994), *Understanding Media: The Extensions of Man*, Cambridge: The MIT Press.

McLuhan, M. and Q. Fiore (1967), *The Medium Is the Message*, New York: Bantam Books.

Meggle, G. (2002), 'On Searle's Collective Intentionality. Some Notes', in G. Grewendorf and G. Meggle (eds), *Speech Acts, Mind, and Social Reality. Discussions with John R. Searle*, 259–270, Dordrecht: Springer.

Meijers, A. (2003), 'Can Collective Intentionality be Individualized?' *American Journal of Economics and Sociology*, 62 (1): 167–193.

Meyer, B. (1999), *Translating the Devil: Religion and Modernity Among the Ewe in Ghana*, Trenton: Africa World Press.

Meyer, B. (2004), '"Praise the Lord": Popular Cinema and Pentecostalite Style in Ghana's New Public Sphere', *American Ethnologist*, 31 (1): 92–110.

Meyer, B. (2006a), 'Religious Revelation, Secrecy and the Limits of Visual Representation', *Anthropological Theory*, 6 (4): 431–453.
Meyer, B. (2006b), *Religious Sensations. Why Media, Aesthetics and Power Matter in the Study of Contemporary Religion (Inaugural Lecture)*, Amsterdam: VU University.
Meyer, B. (2008), 'Powerful Pictures: Popular Christian Aesthetics in Southern Ghana', *Journal of the American Academy of Religion*, 76 (1): 82–110.
Meyer, B. (2009), 'From Imagined Communities to Aesthetic Formations: Religious Mediations, Sensational Forms, and Styles of Binding', in B. Meyer (ed.), *Aesthetic Formations: Media, Religion, and the Senses*, 1–28, New York: Palgrave MacMillan.
Meyer, B. (2010a), 'Aesthetics of Persuasion: Global Christianity and Pentecostalism's Sensational Forms', *South Atlantic Quarterly*, 109 (4): 741–763.
Meyer, B. (2010b), '"There Is a Spirit in that Image": Mass Reproduced Jesus Pictures and Protestant-Pentecostal Animation in Ghana', *Comparative Studies in Society and History*, 52 (1): 100–130.
Meyer, B. (2011a), 'Mediating Absence – Effecting Spiritual Presence: Pictures and the Christian Imagination', *Social Research*, 78 (4): 1029–1056.
Meyer, B. (2011b), 'Mediation and Immediacy: Sensational Forms, Semiotic Ideologies and the Question of the Medium', *Social Anthropology*, 19 (1): 23–39.
Meyer, B. (2014), 'Mediation and the Genesis of Presence (Reprint of Inaugural Lecture), with a Response on Comments by Hans Belting, Pamela Klassen, Chris Pinney, Monique Scheer', *Religion and Society: Advances in Research*, 5: 205–254.
Meyer, B. (2015), 'Picturing the Invisible. Visual Culture and the Study of Religion', *Method & Theory in the Study of Religion*, 27 (4–5): 333–360.
Meyer, B. (2016), 'How to Capture the "Wow": R. R. Marett's Notion of Awe and the Study of Religion', *Journal of the Royal Anthropological Institute*, 22 (1): 7–26.
Meyer, B., D. Morgan, C. Paine and B. Plate (2010), 'The Origin and Mission of Material Religion', *Religion*, 40 (3): 207–211.
Meyrowitz, J. (1985), *No Sense of Place. The Impact of Electronic Media on Social Behavior*, Oxford: Oxford University Press.
Mohn, J. (2004), 'Von der Religionsphänomenologie zur Religionsästhetik: Neue Wege systematischer Religionswissenschaft', *Münchener Theologische Zeitung*, 55 (4): 300–309.
Möhring, W. and D. Schlütz (2010), *Die Befragung in der Medien- und Kommunikationswissenschaft. Eine praxisorientierte Einführung*, Wiesbaden: VS Verlag für Sozialwissenschaften.
Monnot, C. (2013), *Croire ensemble: Analyse institutionnelle du paysage religieux suisse*, Zurich: Seismo.
Monnot, C. and J. Stolz, eds (2018a), *Congregations in Europe*, Berlin: Springer.
Monnot, C. and J. Stolz (2018b), 'How Do You Recognize a "Congregation"? Definition and Operationalization Strategies of the Swiss Congregation Census', in C. Monnot and J. Stolz (eds), *Congregations in Europe*, 15–31, Berlin: Springer.
Morgan, D. (1998), *Visual Piety: A History and Theory of Popular Religious Images*, Berkeley: University of California Press.
Mostowlansky, T. and A. Rota. (2016), 'A Matter of Perspective? Disentangling the Emic-Etic Debate in the Scientific Study of Religions', *Method & Theory in the Study of Religion*, 28 (4–5): 317–336.
Naab, T. K. (2013), *Gewohnheiten und Rituale der Fernsehnutzung. Theoretische Konzeption und methodische Perspektiven*, Baden-Baden: Nomos.
Nagel, T. (1986), *The View From Nowhere*, New York: Oxford University Press.

Neumaier, A. (2016), *religion@home? Religionsbezogene Online-Plattformen und ihre Nutzung. Eine Untersuchung zu neuen Formen gegenwärtiger Religiosität*, Würzburg: Ergon Verlag.

Norenzayan, A. (2013), *Big Gods: How Religion Transformed Cooperation and Conflict*, Princeton: Princeton University Press.

Noss, P. (2002), 'Zeugen Jehovas', in M. Klöcker and U. Tworuschka (eds), *Handbuch der Religionen. Kirchen und andere Glaubensgemeinschaften in Deutschland und im deutschsprachigen Raum*, 1–10, Landsberg am Lech: Günter Olzog.

Nussbaum, M. (2001), *Uphevals of Thought. The Intelligence of Emotions*, Cambridge: Cambridge University Press.

Olson, M. (1965), *The Logic of Collective Action. Public Groups and the Theory of Groups*, Cambridge: Harvard University Press.

Ong, W. J. (1958), *Ramus, Method, and the Decay of Dialogue: From the Art of Discourse to the Art of Reason*, Cambridge: Harvard University Press.

Ong, W. J. (1982), *Orality and Literacy. The Technologies of the Word*, London: Routledge.

Orsi, R. (2012), 'Material Children. Making God's Presence Real through Catholic Boys and Girls', in G. Lynch, J. Mitchell and A. Strhan (eds), *Religion, Media and Culture: A Reader*, 147–158, New York: Routledge.

Otto, R. (2004), *Das Heilige. Über das Irrationale in der Idee des Göttlichen und sein Verhältnis zum Rationalen*, München: C. H. Beck.

Penton, M. J. (1976), *Jehovah's Witnesses in Canada. Champions of Freedom of Speech and Worship*, Toronto: MacMillan.

Penton, M. J. (2015), *Apocalypse Delayed. The Story of Jehovah's Witnesses*, Toronto: Toronto University Press.

Plate, B. (2015), 'Looking at Words: The Iconicity of the Page', in J. W. Watts (ed.), *Iconic Books and Texts*, 119–133, Sheffield: Equinox.

Popper, K. R. (1978), 'Three Worlds', The Taner Lecture on Human Values, University of Michigan.

Postman, N. (1985), *Amusing Ourselves to Death: Public Discourse in the Age of Show Business*, New York: Penguin.

Preyer, G. and G. Peter, eds (2017), *Social Ontology and Collective Intentionality. Critical Essays on the Philosophy of Raimo Tuomela with His Responses*, Berlin: Springer.

Price, H. H. (1969), *Belief*, London: Allen & Unwin.

Putnam, R. D. (2000), *Bowling Alone: The Collapse and Revival of American Community*, New York: Simon & Schuster.

Quinton, A. (1976), 'Social Objects', *Proceedings of the Aristotelian Society*, 76: 1–28.

Rakow, K. (2017), 'The Bible in the Digital Age: Negotiating the Limits of the "Bibelness" of Different Bible Media', in M. Opas and A. Haapalainen (eds), *Christianity and the Limits of Materiality*, 101–121, London: Bloomsbury.

Rappaport, R. A. (1979), 'The Obvious Aspects of Ritual', in *Ecology, Meaning, and Religion*, Berkeley: North Atlantic Books.

Rappaport, R. A. (1999), *Ritual and Religion in the Making of Humanity*, Cambridge: Cambridge University Press.

Ratjar, M. (2013), 'Bioethics and Religious Bodies: Refusal of Blood Transfusions in Germany', *Social Science & Medicine*, 98: 271–277.

Ratjar, M. (2016), 'Jehovah's Witness Patients within the German Medical Landscape', *Anthropology & Medicine*, 23 (2): 172–187.

Rawls, A. W. (1996), 'Durkheim's Epistemology: The Neglected Argument', *American Journal of Sociology*, 102 (2): 430–482.

Rawls, A. W. (2001), 'Durkheim's Treatement of Practice. Concrete Practices vs Representations as the Foundation of Reason', *Journal of Classic Sociology*, 1 (1): 34–68.
Rawls, A. W. (2004), *Epistemology and Practice: Durkheim's The Elementary Forms of Religious Life*, New York: Cambridge University Press.
Reddy, W. M. (1997), 'Against Constructionism: The Historical Ethnography of Emotions', *Current Anthropology*, 38 (3): 327–351.
Riis, O. and L. Woodhead (2010), *A Sociology of Religious Emotion*, Oxford: Oxford University Press.
Rink, S. (2002), 'Wandel und Integration', in G. Klinkhammer and T. Frick, *Religion und Recht. Eine interdisziplinäre Diskussion um die Integration von Religionen in demokratischen Gesellschaften*, 151–164, Marburg: Diagonal-Verlag.
Rokeach, M. (1968), *Beliefs, Attitudes and Values: A Theory of Organization and Change*, San Francisco: Jossey-Bass.
Rosaldo, M. Z. (1982), 'The Things We Do with Words: Ilongot Speech Acts and Speech Act Theory in Philosophy', *Language in Society*, 11 (2): 203–237.
Rota, A. (2016), 'Religion as Social Reality. A Take on the Emic-Etic Debate in Light of John Searle's Philosophy of Society', *Method & Theory in the Study of Religion*, 28 (4–5): 421–444.
Rota, A. (2018), 'Innovazione mediatica e rappresentazione di sé. L'esempio dei Testimoni di Geova', *Annali di studi religiosi*, 19: 141–171.
Rota, A. (2019), 'Religion, Media, and Joint Commitment: Jehovah's Witnesses as a 'Plural Subject'', *Online – Heidelberg Journal of Religions on the Internet*, 14: 79–107.
Rota, A. (forthcoming), 'Jehovah online. Magazines in the New Media Landscape of Jehovah's Witnesses', in A.-M. Bassimir and S. Gelfgren (eds), *Keeping the Faith*, Leiden: Brill.
Rota, A. and O. Krüger (2019), 'The Dynamics of Religion, Media, and Community. An Introduction', *Online – Heidelberg Journal of Religions on the Internet*, 14: 1–19.
Russell, B. (1983), *Sour Grapes: Studies in the Subversion of Rationality*, Cambridge: Cambridge University Press.
Sa Martino, L. M. (2013), *The Mediatization of Religion: When Faith Rocks*, London: Routledge.
Salmela, M. (2013), 'The Function of Collective Emotions in Social Groups', in H. B. Schmid and A. Konzelmann Ziv (eds), *Institutions, Emotions, and Group Agents*, 159–176, Berlin: Springer.
Sawyer, R. K. (2002), 'Durkheim's Dilemma: Toward a Sociology of Emergence', *Sociological Theory*, 20 (2): 227–247.
Sbisà, M. (2007), 'How to Read Austin', *Pragmatics*, 17 (3): 461–473.
Schilbrack, K. (2013), 'After We Deconstruct "Religion," Then What? A Case for Critical Realism', *Method & Theory in the Study of Religion*, 25 (1): 107–112.
Schilbrack, K. (2014), *Philosophy and the Study of Religions: A Manifesto*, Chichester: Wiley Blackwell.
Schilbrack, K. (2017), 'A Realist Social Ontology of Religion', *Religion*, 47 (2): 161–178.
Schilbrack, K. (2018), 'What Does the Study of Religion Study?' *Harvard Theological Review*, 111 (3): 451–458.
Schlamelcher, J. (2018), 'Religiöse Organisation', in D. Pollack, V. Krech, O. Müller and M. Hero (eds), *Handbuch Religionssoziologie*, 489–506, Wiesbaden: VS Verlag für Sozialwissenschaften.
Schlieter, J. (2010), 'Paradigma Lost? "Europäische Religionsgeschichte", die Grundlangenkrise der "systematischen Religionswissenschaft" und ein Vorschlag zur Neubestimmung', *ASE-VSH Bulletin*, 36 (1): 42–51.

Schlieter, J. (2017), 'Religiöse Symbole im öffentlichen Raum: Symbolwirkung als kollektive Intentionalität einer Deutungsgemeinschaft', *Zeitschrift für Religionswissenschaft*, 25 (2): 196–232.
Schlieter, J. (2020), 'Four Conjectures on the Future of the Study of Religions: A Plea for Further Differentiation of the Discipline', *Religion*, 50 (1): 121–128.
Schmid, H. B. (2005), 'Wir-Intentionalität: Kritik des ontologischen Individualismus und Rekonstruktion der Gemeinschaft', Habilitationsschrift, Universität Basel.
Schmid, H. B. (2012), 'Shared Intentionality and the Origins of Human Communication', in A. Salice (ed.), *Intentionality: Historical and Systematic Perspectives*, 349–368, München: Philosophia.
Schmid, H. B. and D. P. Schweikard, eds (2009), *Kollektive Intentionalität – Eine Debatte über die Grundlagen des Sozialen*, Frankfurt am Main: Suhrkamp.
Schultze, Q. J. (1990), 'Keeping the Faith: American Evangelicals and the Mass Media', in Q. J. Schultze (ed.), *American Evangelicals and the Mass Media. Perspectives on the Relationship between American Evangelicals and the Mass Media*, 23–46, Grand Rapids: Academie Books.
Schultze, Q. J. (2002), *Habits of the High-Tech Heart*, Grand Rapids: Baker Academic.
Schweikard, D. P. (2011), *Der Mythos des Singulären: Eine Untersuchung der Struktur kollektiven Handelns*, Paderborn: Mentis.
Schweikard, D. P. and H. B. Schmid (2013), 'Collective Intentionality', in E. N. Zalta (ed.), *The Stanford Encyclopedia of Philosophy [Online Edition]*, Stanford: Metaphysics Research Lab, Stanford University.
Schwitzgebel, E. (2015), 'Belief', in E. N. Zalta (ed.), *The Stanford Encyclopedia of Philosophy [Online Edition]*, Stanford: Metaphysics Research Lab, Stanford University.
Searle, J. R. (1964), 'How to Derive "Ought" from "Is"', *The Philosophical Review*, 73 (1): 43–58.
Searle, J. R. (1968), 'Austin on Locutionary and Illocutionary Acts', *The Philosophical Review*, 77 (4): 405–424.
Searle, J. R. (1969), *Speech Acts: An Essay in the Philosophy of Language*, London: Cambridge University Press.
Searle, J. R. (1976), 'A Classification of Illocutionary Acts', *Language in Society*, 5 (1): 1–23.
Searle, J. R. (1979), *Expression and Meaning: Studies in the Theory of Speech Acts*, Cambridge: Cambridge University Press.
Searle, J. R. (1983), *Intentionality. An Essay in the Philosophy of Mind*, Cambridge: Cambridge University Press.
Searle, J. R. (1984), *Minds, Brains, and Science*, Cambridge: Harvard University Press.
Searle, J. R. (1990), 'Collective Intentions and Actions', in P. R. Cohen, J. L. Morgan and M. E. Pollack (eds), *Intentions in Communication*, 401–415, Cambridge: The MIT Press.
Searle, J. R. (1992), *The Rediscovery of the Mind*, Cambridge: The MIT Press.
Searle, J. R. (1996), *The Construction of Social Reality*, London: Penguin.
Searle, J. R. (2001), *Rationality in Action*, Cambridge: The MIT Press.
Searle, J. R. (2002a), 'The Classical Model of Rationality and Its Weaknesses', in G. Grewendorf and G. Meggle (eds), *Speech Acts, Mind, and Social Reality. Discussions with John R. Searle*, 311–325, Dordrecht: Springer.
Searle, J. R. (2002b), 'Collective Intentions and Actions', in *Consciousness and Language*, 90–105, Cambridge: Cambridge University Press.
Searle, J. R. (2004), *Mind: A Brief Introduction*, Oxford: Oxford University Press.

Searle, J. R. (2006), 'Searle versus Durkheim and the Waves of Thought: Reply to Gross', *Anthropological Theory*, 57 (6): 57–69.
Searle, J. R. (2008), 'Fact and Value, "Is" and "Ought," and Reasons for Action', in *Philosophy in a New Century. Selected Essays*, 161–180, Cambridge: Cambridge University Press.
Searle, J. R. (2010), *Making the Social World: The Structure of Human Civilization*, Oxford: Oxford University Press.
Séguy, J. (1966), 'Messianisme et échec social: Les Témoins de Jéhovah', *Archives de sociologie des religions*, 21: 89–99.
Sellars, W. (1963a), 'Empiricism and the Philosophy of Mind', in *Science, Perception and Reality*, 129–194, Atascadero: Ridgeview Publishing Company.
Sellars, W. (1963b), 'Imperatives, Intentions, and the Logic of "Ought"', in H.-N. Castañeda and G. Nakhnikian (eds), *Morality and the Language of Conduct*, 159–214, Detroit: Wayne State University Press.
Sellars, W. (1974), 'On Knowing the Better and Doing the Worse', in *Essays in Philosophy and Its History*, 27–43, Dordrecht: D. Reidel Publishing Company.
Silverstone, R. and L. Haddon (1996), 'Design and the Domestication of Information and Communication Technologies: Technical Change and Everyday Life', in R. Mansell and R. Silverstone (eds), *Communication by Design: The Politics of Information and Communication Technologies*, 44–74, Oxford: Oxford University Press.
Silverstone, R. and E. Hirsch (1994), 'Introduction', in R. Silverstone and E. Hirsch (eds), *Consuming Technologies. Media and Information in Domestic Spaces*, 1–10, London: Routledge.
Silverstone, R., E. Hirsch and D. Morley (1994), 'Information and Communication Technologies and the Moral Economy of the Household', in R. Silverstone and E. Hirsch (eds), *Consuming Technologies. Media and Information in Domestic Spaces*, 13–28, London: Routledge.
Singelenberg, R. (1989), '"It Separated the Wheat from the Chaff": The "1975" Prophecy and Its Impact among Dutch Jehovah's Witnesses', *Sociological Analysis*, 50 (1): 23–40.
Singelenberg, R. (1990), 'The Blood Transfusion Taboo of Jehovah's Witnesses: Origin, Development and Function of a Controversial Doctrine', *Social Science & Medicine*, 31 (4): 515–523.
Skorupski, J. (1976), *Symbol and Theory: A Philosophical Study of Theories of Religion in Social Anthropology*, Cambridge: Cambridge University Press.
Smith, A. (1977), *An Inquiry into the Nature and Causes of the Wealth of Nations*, Chicago: Chicago University Press.
Smith, J. Z. (1978), 'Map Is Not Territory', in *Map Is Not Territory: Studies in the History of Religions*, 289–309, Leiden: E. J. Brill.
Smith, J. Z. (1982a), 'The Bare Facts of Ritual', in *Imagining Religion. From Babylon to Jonestown*, 53–65, Chicago: Chicago University Press.
Smith, J. Z. (1982b), 'The Devil in Mr. Jones', in *Imagining Religion. From Babylon to Jonestown*, 101–120, Chicago: Chicago University Press.
Smith, J. Z. (1982c), 'Introduction', in *Imagining Religion. From Babylon to Jonestown*, xi–xiii, Chicago: Chicago University Press.
Soeffner, H.-G., ed. (2010), *Unsichere Zeiten. Herausforderungen gesellschaftlicher Transformation*, Wiesbaden: VS Verlag für Sozialwissenschaften.
Sosis, R. (2004), 'The Adaptive Value of Religious Ritual', *American Scientist*, 92 (2): 166–172.

Sperber, D. (1997), 'Intuitive and Reflective Beliefs', *Mind & Language*, 12 (1): 67–83.
Stark, R. (1996), 'Why Religious Movements Succeed or Fail: A Revised General Model', *Journal of Contemporary Religion*, 11 (2): 133–146.
Stark, R. (1997), 'Bringing Theory Back In', in L. A. Young (ed.), *Rational Choice Theory and Religion: Summary and Assessment*, 3–23, New York: Routledge.
Stark, R. (1999), 'Secularization, R.I.P.', *Sociology of Religion*, 60 (3): 249–273.
Stark, R. (2004), 'SSSR Presidential Address, 2004: Putting an End to Ancestor Worship', *Journal for the Scientific Study of Religion*, 43 (4): 465–475.
Stark, R. and W. S. Bainbridge (1980), 'Towards a Theory of Religion: Religious Commitment', *Journal for the Scientific Study of Religion*, 19 (2): 114–128.
Stark, R. and W. S. Bainbridge (1985), 'The Nature of Religion', in *The Future of Religion. Secularization, Revival, and Cult Formation*, 1–18, Berkeley: University of California Press.
Stark, R. and W. S. Bainbridge (1987), *A Theory of Religion*, New York: Peter Lang.
Stark, R. and R. Finke (2000), *Acts of Faith: Explaining the Human Side of Religion*, Berkeley: University of California Press.
Stark, R. and L. Iannaccone (1994), 'A Supply-Side Reinterpretation of the "Secularization"of Europe', *Journal for the Scientific Study of Religion*, 33 (3): 230–252.
Stark, R. and L. Iannaccone (1997), 'Why the Jehovah's Witnesses Grow so Rapidly. A Theoretical Application', *Journal of Contemporary Religion*, 12 (2): 133–157.
Stausberg, M. (2009a), *Contemporary Theories of Religion: A Critical Companion*, London: Routledge.
Stausberg, M. (2009b), 'There Is Life in the Old Dog Yet. An Introduction to Contemporary Theories of Religion', in M. Stausberg (ed.), *Contemporary Theories of Religion: A Critical Companion*, 1–21, London: Routledge.
Stausberg, M. (2010), 'Distinctions, Differentiations, Ontology, and Non-Humans in Theories of Religion', *Method & Theory in the Study of Religion*, 22 (4): 354–374.
Stolow, J. (2005), 'Religion and/as Media', *Theory, Culture & Society*, 22 (4): 119–145.
Stolz, J. (2004), 'Religion et structure sociale', in R. J. Campiche and A. Dubach (eds), *Les deux visages de la religion. Fascination et désenchantement*, 51–88, Genève: Labor et Fides.
Stolz, J. (2006), 'Salvation Goods and Religious Markets: Integrating Rational Choice and Weberian Perspectives', *Social Compass*, 53 (1): 13–32.
Stolz, J. (2009), 'Explaining Religiosity: Towards a Unified Theoretical Model', *The British Journal of Sociology*, 60 (2): 345–376.
Stolz, J., J. Könemann, M. Schneuwly Purdie, T. Engelberger and M. Krüggeler (2014), *Religion und Spiritualität in der Ich-Gesellschaft. Vier Gestalten des (Un-)Glaubens*, Zurich: TVZ / NZN.
Stolz, J., J. Könemann, M. Schneuwly Purdie, T. Engelberger and M. Krüggeler (2015), *Religion et spiritualité à l'ère de l'ego*, Genève: Labor et Fides.
Stout, D. A. and J. M. Buddenbaum, eds (1996), *Religion and Mass Media. Audiences and Adaptations*, Thousand Oaks: Sage.
Tambiah, S. J. (1979), *A Performative Approach to Ritual*, London: Oxford University Press.
Tambiah, S. J. (2013), 'Form and Meaning of Magical Acts: A Point of View', in B.-C. Otto and M. Stausberg (eds), *Defining Magic. A Reader*, 178–186, Sheffield: Equinox.
Taylor, C. (2007), *A Secular Age*, Cambridge: Harvard University Press.
Thomas, G. (2016), 'The Mediatization of Religion – As Temptation, Seduction, and Illusion', *Media, Culture & Society*, 38 (1): 37–47.

Tollefsen, D. (2004), 'Collective Intentionality', in J. Fieser and B. Dowden (eds), *Internet Encyclopedia of Philosophy*. Available online: https://iep.utm.edu/coll-int/ (accessed 17 November 2021).

Tollefsen, D. (2018), 'Collective Intentionality and Methodology in the Social Sciences', in M. Jankovic and K. Ludwig (eds), *The Routledge Handbook of Collective Intentionality*, 389–401, London: Routledge.

Tönnies, F. (1912), *Gemeinschaft und Gesellschaft: Grundbegriffe der reinen Soziologie*, 2nd edition, Berlin: K. Curtius.

Tschannen, O. (1991), *Les théories de la sécularisation*, Genève: Droz.

Tsohatzidis, S. L. (2007), *Intentional Acts and Institutional Facts: Essays on John Searle's Social Ontology*, Dordrecht: Springer.

Tuomela, R. (1975), 'Causality and Action', in R. E. Butts and J. Hintikka (eds), *Foundational Problems in the Special Sciences*, Dordrecht: D. Reidel Publishing Company.

Tuomela, R. (1977), *Human Action and Its Explanation: A Study on the Philosophical Foundations of Psychology*, Dordrecht: D. Reidel.

Tuomela, R. (1982), 'Explanation of Action', in G. Fløistad (ed.), *Philosophy of Action*, 15–43, The Hague: Martinus Nijhoff Publishers.

Tuomela, R. (1984), *A Theory of Social Action*, Dordrecht: D. Reidel Publishing Company.

Tuomela, R. (1989), 'Actions by Collectives', *Philosophical Perspectives*, 3: 471–496.

Tuomela, R. (1995), *The Importance of Us: A Philosophical Study of Basic Social Notions*, Stanford: Stanford University Press.

Tuomela, R. (2000a), 'Collective and Joint Intention', *Mind & Society*, 2 (1): 39–69.

Tuomela, R. (2000b), *Cooperation: A Philosophical Study*. Dordrecht: Kluwer Academic Publishers.

Tuomela, R. (2002), *The Philosophy of Social Practices: A Collective Acceptance View*, Cambridge: Cambridge University Press.

Tuomela, R. (2003a), 'Collective Acceptance, Social Institutions, and Social Reality', *American Journal of Economics and Sociology*, 61 (1): 123–165.

Tuomela, R. (2003b), 'The We-Mode and the I-Mode', in F. F. Schmitt (ed.), *Socializing Metaphysics. The Nature of Social Reality*, 93–127, Lanham: Rowman & Littlefield Publishers.

Tuomela, R. (2005), 'We-Intentions Revisited', *Philosophical Studies*, 125: 327–369.

Tuomela, R. (2007), *The Philosophy of Sociality: The Shared Point of View*, Oxford: Oxford University Press.

Tuomela, R. (2013), *Social Ontology: Collective Intentionality and Group Agents*, Oxford: Oxford University Press.

Tuomela, R. (2018), 'Non-Reductive Views of Shared Intention', in M. Jankovic and K. Ludwig (eds), *The Routledge Handbook of Collective Intentionality*, 24–33, London: Routledge.

Tuomela, R. and W. Balzer (1999), 'Collective Acceptance and Collective Social Notions', *Synthese*, 117 (2): 175–205.

Tuomela, R. and K. Miller (1988), 'We-Intentions', *Philosophical Studies*, 53: 367–389.

Uehlinger, C. (2015), 'Approaches to Visual Cultures and Religion. Disciplinary Trajectories, Interdisciplinary Connections, and Some Suggestions for Further Progress', *Method & Theory in the Study of Religion*, 27 (4–5): 384–422.

Van de Port, M. (2010), *Dat wat rest: Over sacralizering en de ongerijmdheden van het bestaan. Inaugural Lecture*, Amsterdam: VU University.

van Peursen, W. (2014), 'Is the Bible Losing Its Covers? Conceptualization and Use of the Bible on the Threshold of the Digital Order', *HIPHIL Novum*, 1 (1): 44–58.

Vargas, M. and G. Yaffe, eds (2014), *Rational and Social Agency. The Philosophy of Michael Bratman*, Oxford: Oxford University Press.
Velleman, J. D. (1997), 'How To Share An Intention', *Philosophy and Phenomenological Research*, 57 (1): 29–50.
Vitullo, A. (2019), 'Multisite Churches – Creating Community from the Offline to the Online', *Online – Heidelberg Journal of Religions on the Internet*, 14: 41–60.
Voas, D. (2010), 'The Trumpet Sounds Retreat. Learning from the Jehovah's Witnesses', in E. Barker (ed.), *The Centrality of Religion in Social Life*, 117–130, Farnham: Ashgate.
Voas, D., A. Crockett and D. V. A. Olson (2002), 'Religious Pluralism and Participation: Why Previous Research Is Wrong', *American Sociological Review*, 67 (2): 212–230.
Waardenburg, J. (1978), *Reflections on the Study of Religion. Including an Essay on the Work of Gerardus van der Leeuw*, The Hague: Mouton.
Waardenburg, J. (1979), 'The Language of Religion, and the Study of Religions as Sign Systems', in L. Honko (ed.), *Science of Religion: Studies in Methodology*, 441–457, The Hague: Mouton.
Waardenburg, J. (1993), *Des dieux qui se rapprochent: introduction systématique à la science des religions*, Genève: Labor et Fides.
Waardenburg, J. (2017), *Classical Approaches to the Study of Religion*, Berlin: De Gruyter.
Wagner, R. (2012), *Godwired: Religion, Ritual and Virtual Reality*, Abingdon: Routledge.
Wah, C. R. (2001), 'An Introduction to Research and Analysis of Jehovah's Witnesses: A View from the Watchtower', *Review of Religious Research*, 43 (2): 161–174.
Walthert, R. (2010), 'Ritual, individuum und religiöse Gemeinschaft. Die International Christian Fellowship Zürich', in D. Lüddeckens and R. Walthert (eds), *Fluide Religion. Neue religiöse Bewegungen im Wandel. Theoreitsche und empirische Systematisierungen*, 243–268, Bielefeld: Transcript.
Walthert, R. (2013), 'Emotion, Ritual, and the Individual: The Production of Community in Evangelicalism', *Journal of Religion in Europe*, 6 (1): 90–119.
Walthert, R. (2017), 'Tradition und Emotion: ein evangelikaler Gottesdienst aus der Perspektive der Theorie der Interaktionsrituale', in H. G. Hödl, J. Pock and T. Schweighofer (eds), *Christliche Rituale im Wandel: Schlaglichter aus theologischer und religionswissenschaftlicher Sicht*, 21–40, Wien: Eskamed Verlag.
Warner, S. R. (1993), 'Work in Progress Toward a New Paradigm for the Sociological Study of Religion in the United States', *American Journal of Sociology*, 98 (5): 1044–1093.
Warner, S. R. and J. G. Winter, eds (1998), *Gathering in Diaspora: Religious Communities and the New Immigration*, Philadelphia: Temple University Press.
Weber, M. (1947), *The Theory of Social and Economic Organization*, trans. T. Parsons, Glencoe: The Free Press.
Weber, M. (1978), *Economy and Society. An Outline of Interpretive Sociology*, trans. G. Roth and C. Wittich, Berkeley: University of California Press.
Wellman, J. K., Jr., K. E. Corcoran and K. Stockly-Meyerdirk, (2014), '"God Is Like a Drug. . .": Explaining Interaction Ritual Chains in American Megachurches', *Sociological Forum*, 29 (3): 650–672.
Wheelock, W. T. (1982), 'The Problem of Ritual Language: From Information to Situation', *Journal of the American Academy of Religion*, 50 (1): 49–71.
Wilke, A. and E.-M. Guggenmos (2008), *Im Netz des Indra: Das Museum of World Religions, sein buddhistisches Dialogkonzept und die neue Disziplin Religionsästhetik*, Zurich: LIT.

Williams, R. and D. Edge (1996), 'The Social Shaping of Technology', *Research Policy*, 25: 865–899.
Wilson, B. (1970), *Religious Sects: A Sociological Study*, London: Weindenfeld and Nicolson.
Wilson, B. (1973), 'Jehovah's Witnesses in Kenya', *Journal of Religion in Africa*, 5 (2): 128–149.
Wind, J. P. and J. W. Lewis (1994), *American Congregations*, 2 vols, Chicago: University of Chicago Press.
Wollschleger, J. (2012), 'Interaction Ritual Chains and Religious Participation', *Sociological Forum*, 27 (4): 896–912.
Wolterstorff, N. (2017), *Acting Liturgically*, Oxford: Oxford University Press.
Yelle, R. A. (2006a), 'Ritual and Religious Language', in R. Asher (ed.), *Encyclopedia of Language & Linguistics*, 633–640, Amsterdam: Elsevier.
Yelle, R. A. (2006b), 'To Perform, or Not to Perform? A Theory of Ritual Performances versus Cognitive Theories of Religious Transmission', *Method & Theory in the Study of Religion*, 18 (4): 372–391.
Zaibert, L. (2003), 'Collective Intentions and Collective Intentionality', *American Journal of Economics and Sociology*, 61 (1): 209–232.
Zimmerman Umble, D. (1992), 'The Amish and the Telephone. Resistance and Reconstruction', in R. Silverstone and E. Hirsch (eds), *Consuming Technologies. Media and Information in Domestic Spaces*, 171–181, London: Routledge.
Zimmerman Umble, D. (1996), *Holding the Line: The Telephone in Old Order Mennonite and Amish Life*, Baltimore: Johns Hopkins University Press.

Index

Page numbers in **bold** refer to figures.

aesthetic experiences, 188, 212, 215–7
aesthetic formations, 13, 192, 195–6
aesthetics of religion, 188, 218
    critical considerations, 189
    Meyer's approach, 189–96
    shared, 190, 191, 195–6
aggregative accounts, 18
agreement, 37–8
altruistic acts, 123
Anderson, Benedict, 191–2
Anna, 145, 148, 208
annual events, Jehovah's Witnesses, 13
anti-reductionist approach, 6
Aristotle, 154
Armon-Jones, C., 154–5
attitudes, 18, 42
Austin, J. L., 32, 77–8, 77–80
authority, 69–70
authority systems, 53–4, 121, 222–3
authorization processes, 191
autonomy, 5
Awake!, 11, 87, 99–100, 138, 203, 204
    circulation, 87–8
    discussion of television, 136–7

Background, presupposition of the, 36–7
Bainbridge, William Sims, 92, 95–6
Bauman, Z., 5
Beal, Timothy, 197
Beck, U., 5
Becker, Gary, 94–5
Beckford, James, 10, 139, 143, 185–6, 221
belief, uniformity of, 221
beliefs, 49
    mutual, 47
belonging, 53
Bentham, J., 94
Bible, The, 87
    aesthetic experience of, 215–7

collective aesthetic experience, 217
collective study, 202
digital media, 197
digital revolution, 189, 214–5
home study, 110–1
media habits, 209–12
and missionary work, 202
personal study, 201–2
publishing, 199–201
reading, 201–12
reading habits, **205**, 206, **207**, 209–12
status, 201, 215–7
translation, 199–200
Bible apps, 197
Bible-handling skills, 187–8
biweekly assemblies, 163–4, **164**
Blanchard, A., 114
Blanchard, Arnaud, 11, 134, 196
Bloch, Maurice, 78–9
Book of Revelation, 100, 187
brain waves, 26
Bratman, Michael, 7, 12, 17, 18, 72, 77
    conceptual reductivism, 21, 21–5, 25–6, 25–8
    critique, 25–8
    Intention, Plans, and Practical Reason, 22
    Modest Sociality and the Distinctiveness of Intention, 21
    Planning Theory of Intention, 22
Bulletin, 109–10
Bulletin Board View, 53–4, 74, 124
Burning Man festival, 5

Campbell, Heidi, 13, 128, 129–36, 134, 142–3, 225
Cartesian dualism, 190
Catholic World Youth Days, 5
causal self-referentiality, 34

Chaves, M., 5
Chryssides, George, 101-2, 105-6, 143
church sociologists, 4
cinematography, use of, 134
class, 19
Classical Model of practical reason, 117
cognitive dimensions, 9
collaboration, 38
collective acceptance, 54, 217
Collective Acceptance Thesis, 52-3, 55
collective action, 13
collective aesthetic experience, 217, 218
collective agents, 1-3
collective belief, 73, 128, 129
collective commitment, 50-1, 76, 81
collective concepts, 69-70
collective consciousness, 6
collective duty, 106-7
collective emotions, 153-86
  building, 179-81
  Collins's approach, 153, 155, 160, 160-2, 184
  conventions as interaction rituals, 163-71
  Durkheim's approach, 153, 155, 156-8, 158-9, 160, 161
  exceptional moments, 164-6
  feedback loop, 161
  Gilbert's approach, 153-4, 155, 173-6, 183
  Hochschild's approach, 171-3, 175-6, 183, 184-5
  participant observation, 166-9
  plural subject theory, 173-6
  preliminary considerations, 169-71
  Rawls's approach, 153, 155, 158-60, 184
  regulating, 181-2
  relevance, 186
  role of, 185
  Walthert's approach, 162-3, 184
collective goals, 50, 120-1
collective intention, 220
collective intentional action, 35-9
  and group formation, 124-5
  theory of action, 44-8
collective intentionality framework, 4-6
collective intentionality, understanding, 18-9
collective intentions
  comparative assessment, 77-8

consequences, 75-7
constitution, 74-5
public availability, 72-4
religious, 226-7
collective life, 19
collective obligations, 67-9
collective realities, 58
collective rights, 2
collective singing, 167
collective success, 107-8
collectively accept, 49
collectivity, 59
Collectivity Condition, the, 49-50
Collins, Randall, 13, 153, 155, 160-2, 164, 169-71, 184, 225
commitment, 27, 37-8, 61-2, 96, 124
  collective, 50-1, 76, 81
  and collective belief, 146-8
  collective obligations, 67-9
  joint, 61, 61-3, 63-4, 64-7, 67-9, 74, 75, 75-6, 81, 122, 129, 146-8, 151, 174-5, 176, 183, 223
  and language, 37-8
  normative expectations, 67-8
  personal, 61, 62, 63-4
  rationality and, 122-4
  social consequences, 63
  and solidarity, 114
  structure of, 62
common cognitive process, 221
common knowledge, 27, 61, 65, 70, 75, 146, 176
communication, 65, 74
communication technologies, 193
communicative behavior, 27
community, 5
  conceptualization of, 142-4, 150-2, 220
  defining, 119
  loss of, 1
  sense of, 74
  understanding, 4
community building, 114
comparative assessment, collective intentions, 77-8
compensators, 95-6
competing positions, 17
conceptual analysis, 59-60
conceptual functionalism, 43

conceptual parsimony, 25
conceptual reductionism, commitment, 27
conceptual reductivism, 20–1
    Bratman's, 21, 21–5, 25–6, 25–8
    limitations, 25–6
conditions of satisfaction, 33, 34, 36
conduct plans, 43–4
Congregation Bible Study, 148–50
Congregation Book Study, 111
congregation studies, 5
congregational structures, 96–7
congregations
    change, 5
    organizational perspective, 5
consciousness, 20
consequences, collective intentions, 75–7
constative statements, 32
constitution, collective intentions, 74–5
constitutive rules, 124–5
continuity thesis, 21
conventions, 153, 155–6
    attendance, 177–8
    biweekly assemblies, 163–4, **164**
    emotional discrepancies, 170
    emotional framing, 182–3
    emotional investment, 166
    emotional moods, 168–9
    emotional regulation, 181–2
    as exceptional moments, 164–6
    excitement, 180–1, 186
    historical accounts, 176–8
    importance of, 164
    as interaction rituals, 163–71
    lack of strong emotions, 185–6
    participant observation, 166–9
    preliminary considerations, 169–71
    preparation, 179–80
    program, 166–7, 168, 180, 182
    in publications, 178
    ritual orchestration, 162–3
    ritual success, 183
    social dimension, 179
COVID-19 pandemic, 224–5
cultural dimensions, 9

Darwin, Charles, 154
data collection, 9
de Vries, Hent, 192–3, 194
decisions and decision making, 61–2

definitional strategies, religious collectivities, 226–7
demand-rights, 76
Derrida, J., 193
Devil, the, 138
Dewey, John, 173
digital media, 197
digital revolution, 188, 202–5, 212, 212–5, 224–5
directed obligation, 76
directed rights, 68
Director for Field Publishers, 110
distinctive constitution, problem of, 26–7
Durkheim, Émile, 4, 13, 20, 59, 72, 153, 155, 156–8, 158–9, 160, 161
duties, 38, 106–7
duty, sense of, 123–4

Edge, D., 131
Ego, Age of the, 1–3
Ekman, Paul, 154
Emma, 103–4, 144–5, 148, 166, 168–9, 209
emotion work, 154, 155, 171–3
emotional energy, 162
emotional investment, 166
emotions
    definition, 154–5, 174
    and obligation, 79–80
    regulating, 181–2
    see also collective emotions
empirical research, 9–12, 26, 222–4
entitlements, 76
e-religion (external), 225–6
Eric, 210
ethnicity, 19
Eva, 103, 165, 210–1
Evangelical Assembly of Vineyard Churches, 11
Examining the Scriptures Daily, 201
exceptional moments, conventions as, 164–6
expectations, 216–7

false friends, 203
feedback loops, 161
feeling rules, 171
feeling-sensations, 173–4
Feinberg, Joel, 68
Felder, E., 137

field ministry. *see* missionary work
Finke, Roger, 92, 123
Finnegan, Ruth, 77–8
first person ontology, 26
for-groupness, 49, 119–20
Foulkes, David, 128
Frank, 141, 165, 213, 215, 215–6, 217
Franz, Fredrick, 87
free riders, 96–7
freedom, 5
Fritz, 104, 144–5, 148, 166, 168–9

Gebhardt, W., 5
Gemeinschaft, 4
German phenomenologists, 7
Gertrud, 141, 211
Gilbert, Margaret, 7, 12, 17, 37–8, 39, 57–70, 72, 77, 80–1, 81, 129, 146–52, 184, 189, 216–7, 218, 220, 223–4
  aim, 59
  central question, 57
  and collective emotions, 153–4, 155, 173–6, 183, 184
  collective obligations, 67–9
  conceptual reductivism, 20–1
  conceptualization of collective intentionality, 60–3, 73–4
  consequences of collective intentionality, 63–4
  constitution of collective intentionality, 64–7
  holistic approach, 58–9
  joint commitment, 223
  methodological considerations, 59, 59–60
  plural subject theory, 57, 73–4, 74–5, 75–6, 173–6, 184
  singularist standpoint, 58
  social ontology, 57–9, 69–70
goals, 50
Goffman, Erving, 160, 171
Golden Age, 99–100, 109, 198
group agency, 6
group belief, 146
group ethos, 50, 51
group formation, and collective intentional action, 124–5
group reasons, 49

group solidarity, 153
group thinking, 6
group will, 53
group-will-formation system, 121, 150

Harré, R., 154
Hart, H. L. A., 68
Harvard Business School, 38
Heath, Anthony, 123
Henschel, Milton G., 87
heroic soldiers, 123
Hindriks, Frank, 75
Hirschkind, Charles, 193
Hochschild, Arlie, 154, 155, 171–3, 175–6, 183, 184
Holden, A., 10, 114, 143
holism, 58
holistic standpoint, 58
Homans, George C., 94
house-to-house ministry. *see* missionary work
human interactions, 4
human nature, 104
Hutchings, Tim, 197, 215

Iannaccone, Laurence R., 10, 92, 96–7, 97
idolatrous practices, 130
I-form, 2
I-intentions, 30–1
imagined communities, 192
I-mode, 48–9, 51, 74, 76
indeterminacy, 75
individual, the, 1
individual feelings, role of, 79
individual freedom, 4
individual intentional action, 29–30, 93
  purposive-causal theory, 43–4
  structure of, 34–6
individual intentionality, 21–2
individual tastes, 149
individualism, 19–20
individualist tendencies, 107
individualization, 5
indoctrination, 114
industrialization, 4
informal witnessing, 101
Informant, 110
Inglehart, Ronald, 1
instability, 24

instrumentalist point of view, 5–6
intention, expression of, 33
intentional action
   the Background, 35, 36–7
   collective, 35–8, 44–8
   individual, 29–30, 34–5, 43–4
   purposive-causal theory, 43–4
intentionality, 6
   individual, 22, 25
   mode of, 21
   shared, 22–5, 26–8
interaction, 65
interaction rituals, 161–2, 163–71, 169–71
International Christian Fellowship, 162, 162–3
Internet, 137–8, 140, 141, 202–4, 205
Introvigne, Massimo, 98
invisible beings, influence of, 138
I-religion (internal), 225–6

James, William, 155
Jankovic, M., 8
Jehovah's Witnesses, 3, 10–2, 12–3, 85–90, 222–4
   aesthetics, 196–7
   annual events, 13
   collective action, 13
   context, 12
   costly activities, 123
   dissonances, 223–4
   foundation, 85–6
   historical background, 85–8
   literature, 10
   media landscape, 13
   media use among, 139–42, **139**
   membership growth, 87–8, 97, 98
   millenarian message, 85
   missionary work. *see* missionary work
   missionary zeal, 87
   organizational structures, 85
   persecution, 86
   question-and-answer discussions, 110–6, **115**
   recruitment, 97
   sources, 90
   use of printed media, 13
   visibility, 153
   see also Watch Tower Society
Jensen, Jeppe, 225–6

joint action, 41, 54
joint attitudes, 49
joint commitment, 57, 58, 61, 61–3, 74, 75, 75–6, 81, 122, 129, 146, 151, 174–5, 176, 183, 223
   and collective belief, 146–8
   conceptual irreducibility, 66–7
   consequences of, 63–4
   creation of, 147
   formation, 64–7
   intrinsic normativity, 68–9
   moral requirements, 69
   permission requirement, 64
   social ontology, 69–70
joint intentions, 51–2, 55
Jörg, 103, 141–2, 205, 211, 214
justificatory explanations, 126
JW Library app, 204–5
jw.org, 188, 202–3, 204, 205, 207

Katz, Elihu, 128
Keane, Webb, 195
Keep Yourselves in God's Love, 149–50
Kelley, Dean M., 96
Kemper, T. D., 170
Knorr, Nathan H., 87, 112, 200
knowledge, 18–9, 22–3, 27
Knox, Zoe, 90
Krüger, Oliver, 130

labor, division of, 95–6
language, 37, 39, 71–2, 74
   and commitment, 37–8
   ritual, 77–80
Lara, 103, 140–1
Latter-day Saints (Mormons), 11, 91
Leonard, 104, 141, 165, 168, 205, 208, 210
Lewis, David, 216
liberties, 68
linguistic anthropologists, 72
liturgical order, 116
liturgical performances, 79–80
Locke, John, 69
Luckmann, Thomas, 4
Ludwig, K., 5, 8
Luhmann, Niklas, 12, 127

MacKenzie, D., 131
McLuhan, Marshall, 129

Maffesoli, Michel, 5, 196
magic, 77–8
Malinowski, B., 77
Marret, Robert R., 194
Martin, David, 185
media and media use, 127–52
    among Jehovah's Witnesses, 139–42, **139**
    appraisal, 142–6
    attitude towards, 127–8
    biblical framing of radio, 135
    Campbell's framework, 128, 129–36
    and collective beliefs, 128, 129
    consumption of inappropriate content, 138–9
    danger of, 136–9, 142
    hermeneutic approach, 128
    idolatrous practices, 130
    individual tastes, 149
    innovation, 134–5
    Internet, 137–8, 140, 141
    methodological problem, 143
    moral economy, 132, 133
    moral order, 133
    officializing discourse, 136–9
    personal attitudes, 144–6
    prescriptive discourse, 135–6
    religious communities, 133
    religious-social shaping of, 129–33
    ritualized, 148–50
    ritualized study, 129
    role of, 129–31, 133–9
    social shaping of, 131–2
    the telephone, 131
    television, 136–7, **136**, 140, 141–2
    validating discourse, 133–5
    video games, 140, 141
    Watch Tower Society, 133–9, **136**
    websites, 134–5, 135–6
media habits, 205–7, **205**, **207**
mediation, 193
    religion as, 190, 212–3
mediatization theory, 130–1
Meeting for Field Service, 122, 125
Meeting Workbook, 110, 112
Meggle, Georg, 39
Meijers, A., 38, 39
Memorial for Christ's Death, 164, 187–8, 225

Memorial Supper, 177
mental states, 43–4
methodology, 80–1, 88–90, *89*
Meyer, Birgit, 13, 188, 189–96, 212–3, 218, 225
Michaela, 103, 165–6, 168
microanalytical approach, 160–2
mind, philosophy of, 26
missionary work, 91–126, 125
    ambivalent attitude toward, 103–4
    attitudes towards, 102–6
    The Bible and, 202
    as collective duty and privilege, 106–7
    collective success, 107
    constitutive rules, 124–5
    costly activities, 91
    engagement, 102–3
    and group formation, 124–5
    hardship, 107
    institutionalization, 99–101
    interviewees, 92
    justifications, 125–6
    Meeting for Field Service, 122, 125
    and membership growth, 97, 98
    motivation, 105
    partners, 104–5
    practical implications, 101–2
    preaching strategies, 207
    rational choice theory, 91–2, 92–9
    rational choice theory analysis, 97–9
    reach, 101
    role of, 98
    Service Meetings, 92, 108–10
    setbacks, 107–8
    social dimension, 104–6
    time commitment, 101–3
    Watch Tower Society framing, 106–10
modest sociality, 25
Monique, 105
moral authority, 156–7
moral economy, 132, 133, 143
moral obligation, 76
moral order, 133
moral requirements, 69
Multilanguage Electronic Publishing System, 198–201
mutual beliefs, 47

nations, 69–70
new religious movements, 4
new style phenomenology, 218
New World Bible Translation Committee, 200
New World Translation of the Greek Scriptures, 200, 204
non-reductivist approaches, 17–8
normative dimension, 25–6
normative expectations, 216–7
Nussbaum, Martha, 174

obligation, 24–5, 79–80
obligation criterion, 63, 68
obligations, 38, 52, 76, 147
    collective, 67–9
Ockham's razor, 25–6, 58
officializing discourse, 136–9
Olga, 103, 209–10
ontological reductivism, 19–20
other, the, 74
otherworldly rewards, 106
Otto, Rudolf, 190
Our Kingdom Ministry, 92, 110, 112, 115, 118, 120, 122, 179, 180, 181, 182, 182–3, 204

parsimony, principle of, 25–6
Paul, 104–5, 165
performative approach, 220
performative language, 71–2
performative statements, 32
permission requirement, 64
personal attitudes, 144–5
personal commitment, 61, 62, 63–4
personal intentions, 17
personal preferences, personal preferences, 217
philosophical approaches, 6–9
plain expectations, 216–7
Planning Theory of Intention, 22
plural subject theory, 57–9, 70, 73–4, 74–5, 75–6, 173–6, 184
plural subjects, 57, 58, 129, 146, 146–50, 151–2
political parties, 19
Popper, Karl, 93
popular culture, 195
pornography, 137–8, 203

post-traditional communities, 5
pragmatism, 26
prayers, 116, 167
preintentional Background, 35, 36–7
prescriptive discourse, 135–6
private attitudes, 18–9
private intentions, 18
privilege, 106–7
public availability, collective intentions, 72–4
public behavior, 145
public phenomena, 26
publishing, 198–201, 212
purposive causation, 43–4
purposive-causal theory, 41
Putnam, Robert, 1

question-and-answer discussions, 110–2, 124, 202, 222–3
    cost–benefit evaluation, 115
    didactic aspect, 113–4
    participant observation, 113–6
    semantics and phrasing, 114–5, **115**
    theoretical reflection, 116–21

radio, biblical framing, 135
Rakow, Katja, 197, 215
Rappaport, Roy, 12, 79–80, 81, 116, 220
rational choice theory, 91–2, 92–9, 123
    criticisms, 93
    foundational ideas, 92–5
    on missionary work, 97–9
    theory of religion, 95–7
rationality, 93, 116–8, 122–4, 220
Rawls, Anne, 13, 153, 155, 158–60, 184
reason, 117
reasons, 48–9
reductivism, 18, 19–21, 25–6
    Bratman's, 21, 21–5, 25–6, 25–8
    limitations, 25–6
Reformation, the, 190
religion
    global resurgence of, 193
    as mediation, 190, 212–3
    Meyer's definition, 192
    study of, 12–3, 224–7
    theory of, 95–7
religious collective intentions, 226–7
religious collectivities

collective intentionality framework, 6–9
  crisis, 4
  definitional strategies, 226–7
  as sociological topic, 4–6
religious collectivity, 3, 219–22
religious communities
  collective rights, 2
  conceptualization of, 142–4, 150–2
  as intentional agents, 1–2
religious media use, 205–7, **205**, **207**
  appraisal, 212–7
  personal preferences, 217
Religious-Social Shaping of Technology, 13
rewards, 95, 106
Richard, 169, 209, 214
rights, 67, 68
ritual, 2–3, 5, 116, 220, 227
  failed interactions, 170
  interaction, 161–2, 163–71, 169–70
  speech acts, 77–80, 81
ritual interaction chains, 160–2
ritual orchestration, 162–3
Russell, Charles T., 85–6, 99, 110, 133–4, 176–7, 198, 199
Rutherford, Joseph F., 86–7, 99–101, 106, 134, 135, 198

Schleiermacher, Friedrich, 190
Schmid, H. B., 6, 8
Schweikard, D. P., 6, 8
Searle, John R., 6–7, 8–9, 11, 12, 17, 26, 29–40, 42, 72, 77, 81, 91, 123, 123–4, 151, 220, 225
  central question, 29–30
  "Collective Intentions and Actions", 29
  and commitment, 37–8
  conceptual reductivism, 20–1
  conceptualization of collective intentionality, 34–6, 35–9, 73, 74, 75
  and justifications, 125–6
  language, 37
  methodological considerations, 31–3
  ontological considerations, 30–1
  presupposition of the Background, 36–7
  social ontology, 39–40

social reality, 29
speech act theory, 31–3, 78, 92
structure of individual intentional action, 34–6
theory of rationality, 75, 116–8
we-intentions, 38–9, 73
Second World War, 4
secularization thesis, 93
Sellars, Wilfrid, 7, 42, 43
semiotic ideologies, 195
sensational forms, 13, 191, 196, 212
Service Meetings, 92, 108–10, 112
shared intention, 63
shared intentionality, 22–5, 72
Silverstone, R., 131–2
Singing, 167, 187
singularism, 58
singularist standpoint, the, 58
Smith, Adam, 94
Smith, Jonathan Z., 10–1, 167
social anthropologists, 78
social cohesion, 158
social control, 125
social convention, 216
social groups, 19
  definition, 57
social media platforms, 140, 140–1
social ontology, 20–1, 39–40, 55, 57–9, 69–70
social phenomena, 39
social reality, 5, 29, 124
social structures, microanalytical approach, 160–2
social ties, loosening of, 1
sociality, 19, 57, 58, 70
  forms of, 3
  human disposition towards, 41–2
socialization, 223
socialized phenomenology, 194
sociological context, 4–6
Sofia, 207, 210
solidarity, and commitment, 114
speech, role of, 116–8
speech act theory, 77–8, 92
speech acts, 31–3, 75, 117–8, 123–4, 124, 220
  ritual, 77–80, 81
Stark, Rodney, 10, 92, 92–4, 95–6, 97, 123, 225

Stolow, Jeremy, 189
Stolz, J., 1
Stranger, the, relationship with, 21
street work, 101
strictness, 96, 97
Studies in the Scriptures (Russell), 86
subjective meaning, 20
success, collective, 107–8
summative accounts, 18–9
symbolic communication, 27

Tambiah, Stanley, 77–8
Taylor, Charles, 1
technological change, dealing with, 213–5
technology, 131–2
    religious-social shaping of, 13, 129–33
telephone, 131
television, 136–7, **136**, 140, 141–2
text
    aesthetic experiences, 212, 215–7
    aesthetics, 196–7
    appraisal, 212–7
    critical considerations, 189
    digital media, 197, 202–5
    digital revolution, 188, 202–5, 213, 213–5
    digitalization, 201, 206
    existing research, 197–8
    material approach to, 187–218
    media habits, 205–7, **205**, 207–12, **207**
    Meyer's approach, 188, 189–96
    publishing work, 198–201
    reading, 201–12
Theocratic Ministry School, 87, 109, 113
third-person perspective, 26
Tönnies, F., 4
Toronto School of Communication, 129–30
transcendent reality, 194–5
translocal communities, 69–70
Tuomela, Raimo, 7, 12, 17, 39, 41–56, 72, 77, 80–1, 91, 92, 119–21, 150, 220, 222–3, 223–4
    Bulletin Board View, 53–4, 74, 124
    central question, 41–2
    Collective Acceptance Thesis, 52–3, 55
    conceptual reductivism, 20–1
    conceptualization of we-intentions, 42, 43–52, 55, 73, 74, 76–7
    joint intentions, 51–2, 55
    methodology, 43
    ontological considerations, 42
    purposive-causal theory, 41, 43–4
    social ontology, 55
    theory of action, 44–8

Uehlinger, Christoph, 218
Umble, Diane Zimmerman, 131
urbanization, 4

Valentin, 103, 208, 209
validating discourse, 133–5
Vergemeinschaftung,, 4
video games, 140, 141
visual piety, 195
Voas, David, 98, 164, 185

Waardenburg, Jacques, 218
Wajcman, J., 131
Walthert, Rafael, 153, 162, 162–3, 184
Watch Tower Society, 10, 12, 13, 86, 87, 88, 91, 113, **136**, 182
    Bible publishing, 199–201
    centralized control, 99
    digital revolution, 202–5, 224–5
    digitalization, 201
    Governing Body, 87, 150, 202
    growth, 100
    media habits, 207–9
    mission, 107
    missionary work framing, 106–10
    missionary work justifications, 125–6
    publications, 11, 85, 92, 223
    publishing work, 198–201, 212–3
    rational choice theory analysis, 97, 98–9
    rationalistic character, 185–6
    role of, 107
    self-representation, 176, 177
    sources, 90
    see also media and media use; missionary work
The Watchtower, 11, 86, 99–100, 109, 177, 203, 204
    biblical framing of radio, 135
    circulation, 87–8
    collective study, 148–50
    discussion of television, 136–7

foundational period, 134
question-and-answer discussions, 111, 115
Watchtower Bible College of Gilead, 87
Watchtower Online Library, 90
Watchtower study meetings, 111–2
we, uses of, 59–60
we-attitudes, 48–9
Weber, Max, 4, 13, 19–20
we-form, 2, 3
we-intentions, 38, 38–9, 73, 74, 76–7, 219
   and attitudes, 42
   ontological considerations, 42
   purposive-causal theory, 43–4
   theory of action, 44–8
   Tuomela's conceptualization, 42, 43–52, 55
we-mode, 48–52, 54, 55, 73, 76–7, 119–20
What Does the Bible Really Teach?, 127
Wheelock, Wade, 78
will, 53
Williams, R., 131
willpower, 145
Wolterstorff, N., 223
World of Warcraft, 141

Yggdrasill, 225

www.ingramcontent.com/pod-product-compliance
Lightning Source LLC
Chambersburg PA
CBHW071813300426
44116CB00009B/1301